JOURNAL · OF MORAL THEOLOGY

VOLUME 6, NUMBER 2

JUNE 2017

NEW WINE, NEW WINESKINS:
PERSPECTIVES OF YOUNG
MORAL THEOLOGIANS

Edited by Conor Hill, Kent Lasnoski,
Matthew Sherman, John Sikorski
and Matthew Whelan

JOURNAL • OF
M • O • R • A • L
THEOLOGY

Journal of Moral Theology is published semiannually, with issues in January and June. Our mission is to publish scholarly articles in the field of Catholic moral theology, as well as theological treatments of related topics in philosophy, economics, political philosophy, and psychology.

Articles published in the *Journal of Moral Theology* undergo at least two double blind peer reviews. Authors are asked to submit articles electronically to jmt@msmary.edu. Submissions should be prepared for blind review. Microsoft Word format preferred. The editors assume that submissions are not being simultaneously considered for publication in another venue.

Journal of Moral Theology is indexed in the ATLA Catholic Periodical and Literature Index® (CPLI®), a product of the American Theological Library Association.
Email: atla@atla.com, www: http://www.atla.com.
ISSN 2166-2851 (print)
ISSN 2166-2118 (online)

Journal of Moral Theology is published by Mount St. Mary's University, 16300 Old Emmitsburg Road, Emmitsburg, MD 21727.

Copyright© 2017 individual authors and Mount St. Mary's University. All rights reserved.

Except for brief quotations in critical publications or reviews, no part of this book may be reproduced in any manner without prior written permission from the publisher. Write: Permissions. Wipf and Stock Publishers, 199 W. 8th Ave., Suite 3, Eugene, OR 97401.

Pickwick Publications, An Imprint of Wipf and Stock Publishers, 199 W. 8th Ave., Suite 3, Eugene, OR 97401. www.wipfandstock.com. ISBN 13: 978-1-5326-3677-6

EDITOR EMERITUS AND UNIVERSITY LIAISON
David M. McCarthy, *Mount St. Mary's University*

EDITOR
Jason King, *Saint Vincent College*

ASSOCIATE EDITOR
William J. Collinge, *Mount St. Mary's University*

MANAGING EDITOR
Kathy Criasia, *Mount St. Mary's University*

EDITORIAL BOARD
Melanie Barrett, *University of St. Mary of the Lake/Mundelein Seminary*
Jana M. Bennett, *University of Dayton*
Mara Brecht, *St. Norbert College*
Jim Caccamo, *St. Joseph's University*
Meghan Clark, *St. John's University*
David Cloutier, *The Catholic University of America*
Christopher Denny, *St. John's University*
John J. Fitzgerald, *St. John's University*
Mari Rapela Heidt, *Waukesha, Wisconsin*
Kelly Johnson, *University of Dayton*
Warren Kinghorn, *Duke University*
Kent Lasnoski, *Quincy University*
John Love, *Mount St. Mary's Seminary*
Ramon Luzarraga, *Benedictine University, Mesa*
M. Therese Lysaught, *Loyola University Chicago*
William C. Mattison III, *University of Notre Dame*
Christopher McMahon, *Saint Vincent College*
Joel Shuman, *Kings College*
Matthew Shadle, *Marymount University*
Msgr. Stuart Swetland, *Donnelly College*
Christopher P. Vogt, *St. John's University*
Brian Volck, *University of Cincinnati College of Medicine*
Paul Wadell, *St. Norbert College*
Greg Zuschlag, *Oblate School of Theology*

Journal of Moral Theology
Volume 6, Number 2
June 2017

Contents

Is New Wine, New Wineskins Still New? Reflecting on Wineskins after Seventeen Years
  Conor Hill, Kent Lasnoski, Matthew Sherman, John Sikorski and Matthew Whelan 1

Before the Eucharist, a Familial Morality Arises
  Matthew Sherman 15

The Works of Mercy: Francis and the Family
  Kevin Schemenauer 32

Mercy Is A Person: Pope Francis and the Christological Turn in Moral Theology
  Alessandro Rovati 48

Morality, Human Nature, and the Sacred Heart of Jesus
  Joshua Evans 70

Living the Mystery: Doctrine, Intellectual Disability, and Christian Imagination
  Medi Ann Volpe 87

Towards a Conjugal Spirituality: Karol Wojtyla's Vision of Marriage Before, During, and After Vatican II
  John Sikorski 103

The Principle of Double Effect within Catholic Moral Theology: A Response to Two Criticisms of the Principle in Relation to Palliative Sedation
  Gina Maria Noia 130

Is Aquinas's Envy Pagan?
  Sheryl Overmyer 149

Resisting the Less Important: Aquinas on Modesty
  John-Mark Miravalle 166

Agere Contra: An "Ignatian Option" for Engagement with American Society and Culture
  Benjamin T. Peters 175

Human or Person? On the Burial of Aborted Children
  Justin Menno 194

Jesus is the Jubilee: A Theological Reflection on the Pontifical
    Council of Justice and Peace's *Toward a Better Distribution of
    Land: The Challenge of Agrarian Reform*
    Matthew Philipp Whelan 204

Laudato Si' on Non-Human Animals
    Anatoly Angelo R. Aseneta… 230

Contributors................ 246

Is New Wine, New Wineskins Still New? Reflecting on Wineskins after Seventeen Years

Conor Hill, Kent J. Lasnoski, Matthew Sherman, John Sikorski, and Matthew Whelan

IN AUGUST OF 2017, THE New Wine New Wineskins (NWNW) symposium will convene for a seventeenth time at Moreau Seminary in Notre Dame, as it has done for most of the years of its existence since its founding by William Mattison III in 2002. As Mattison himself tells the story of its founding, NWNW started, at least in part, as a response to the predicament of Catholic moral theology in the U.S. academy. At that time, there were plenty of conferences where Catholic moral theologians gathered, but none devoted to serious and sustained reflection upon how Catholicism matters for the work of moral theology and all the attendant vocational questions for the moral theologian that this entails.[1] Moreover, according to the "founding generation" of NWNW, among the defining features of Catholic moral theology in the U.S. at that time was its polarization—especially in the decades following the promulgation of Pope Paul VI's 1968 *Humanae Vitae*. In response, NWNW self-consciously sought to be a gathering, not where differences were denied or minimized, but where they could be dealt with constructively through amicable relationships. In Mattison's words, "[W]e wanted to nourish friendships among us moral theologians, trusting that such friendships would not only enrich our scholarly endeavors, but also help us avoid the polarization that had marked our field."[2]

---

[1] As William L. Portier writes in the "Foreword" to the first volume, "Two issues that are at the center of New Wine, New Wineskins [are]: the spiritual formation of theologians and their day-to-day rootedness in the life of the local church." William C. Mattison III, ed. *New Wine New Wineskins: A Next Generation Reflects on Key Issues in Catholic Moral Theology* (Maryland: Rowman and Littlefield, 2005), x.

[2] See Andrew Kim, "New Wine New Wineskins, Reflections from William C. Mattison," *Catholic Moral Theology*, August 25, 2014, catholicmoraltheology.com/new-wine-new-wineskins-reflections-from-william-c-mattison-iii/. For more on the role of friendship in NWNW, see Charles Camosy, "Some Reflections on My Last New Wineskins," September 12, 2014, catholicmoraltheology.com/some-reflections-on-my-last-new-wineskins/.

THE HISTORY OF NEW WINE, NEW WINESKINS

Mattison's account situates NWNW in terms of generations. At the beginning of the twentieth century, the sub-culture Catholics (pre-Vatican II) saw their role in the academy as an insider activity. The vast majority were clergy, asking questions relevant for clergy and often *about* the laity and the world "out there." By the 1940s, lay theologians such as Dietrich von Hildebrand were beginning to shake the paradigm. Folks like Margaret Farley, David Hollenbach, Alasdair MacIntyre, and Stanley Hauerwas[3] were hardly born. Germain Grisez was about 10 years old.

The second generation (transitional Catholics) are characterized as the Vatican II Catholics. They grew up in the subculture Catholicism but were excited to embrace the world that had been opened up by the Second Vatican Council. They experimented with methods from the secular sciences and attempted to put moral theology in dialogue with biology, sociology, and other disciplines. They attempted to practice moral theology in a way that might speak to all. Catholicism, for them, could be taken for granted. They sought to expand beyond the borders of its methods, questions, and assumptions.

Mattison describes the first NWNW generation as post-subculture Catholics. They grew up in the world, decidedly not in a subculture. They knew the world, but they also knew there was something good that they had missed out on. The riches of the Catholic tradition the previous generations had defended and then taken for granted was in great part lost to them through a lack of catechesis and, in some cases, a lack of participation in ecclesial life. Their generation was characterized by a desire to recover what had been lost, not to deny the goods that come from the world, but to put them in dialogue with the full treasury of the Catholic tradition by pointing to what was once taken for granted but was now, they thought, falling out of the picture. They would have this conversation, decidedly and joyfully from within the Church as part of their vocation and their life of discipleship.

What then, has changed about this newest generation of New Wine, seventeen years from the group's founding? The first generation saw the need for a recovery but also knew that there were no "good ol' days" to return to. A natural fruit of their effort has been to set a foundation for a new generation of theological builders who are creatively integrating the task of "doing theology" with their vocations of daily life, teaching, and apostolate. This action of building is

---

[3] Though not a Catholic himself, Hauerwas has formed many Catholic theologians who have come through the Duke doctoral program. These scholars have taken their Hauerwasian influence and spread it through other doctoral programs. Hauerwas, with MacIntyre, is in part responsible for a recovery of virtue ethics within Catholic moral theology.

spurred on, too, by changes in the context. The post-Christian context, what some people consider the death of the "Americanist" Catholic project, has shown this newest New Wine that there may no longer be a natural place for the Catholic to "fit in." Aspects of the world, which the pre-Vatican II theologians theologized apart from, the transitional Catholics welcomed, and the post-subculture Catholics grew up in, are becoming increasingly inhospitable to Catholicism. The newest generation of New Wine is not running from this world in fear but is rather building alternative, equally real worlds within it, through intentional communities, schools, parish programs, etc. Others of the newest New Wine, however, might challenge the very notion that there ever was a "natural place" for the Catholic, arguing instead that the world has always been inhospitable—now in this way, now in that way. Both of these positions equally demonstrate a stance toward the world dramatically differing from that of previous generations.

A second distinction of the newest New Wine is a change in where theologizing happens. The introduction of blogs, the explosion of Facebook, and myriad social media means that, more often than not, an idea has been the subject of countless debates before it is ever published in a printed, peer-reviewed journal. While the latter remains the gold-standard of scholarship in the field, electronic forms of publication have sped up the conversation. This increased rate of conversation is not everywhere a boon. There is more redundancy, less care to detail, and often more vitriol than one finds in academic journals. These media cannot replace the careful, well-researched and documented work that takes place in the slower conversations of academic, peer-reviewed journals.

While not intended, Mattison worried that NWNW would be received as a judgment against senior colleagues and mentors. Even though a central part of the annual Symposium is a senior scholar who spends about six hours with the participants, the name of the group seems to communicate something along these lines. As the straightforward application of Jesus's saying suggests, the building pressure of the new wine—the questions and concerns of a new generation of young Catholic moral theologians—simply could no longer be contained by the worn skins of their forebears. New wineskins, new frameworks for the practice of moral theology, were necessary (Matt 9:14-17, Mark 2:21-22, Luke 5:33-39).[4]

Has NWNW achieved the ends for which it was founded? Has the existence of the group made a mark? That NWNW has made an impact on individual moral theologians is abundantly clear. There is no shortage of participants who would attest to the significance of the

---

[4] See Portier, *New Wine New Wineskins*, ix.

NWNW symposium in their own development as moral theologians.[5] However, the nature and extent of NWNW's impact on Catholic moral theology in the U.S. is much more complex and difficult to assess. Since its founding, for instance, NWNW has published two edited volumes, *New Wine New Wineskins: A Next Generation Reflects on Key Issues in Catholic Moral Theology* in 2005 and then *Leaving and Coming Home: New Wineskins for Catholic Sexual Ethics* five years later in 2010.[6] Both of these volumes have been well received. The present special edition of the *Journal of Moral Theology*, which collects a number papers that have been presented at NWNW conferences over the previous five years, as well as some new submissions, can be thought of as a third such volume.[7]

If we limited ourselves to contributors of the first two volumes, former participants in NWNW hold academic posts at colleges and universities throughout the U.S. There are several at large, doctorate-granting theology programs. William Mattison and Margaret Pfeil are both at Notre Dame. David Cloutier is at Catholic University of America. Charlie Camosy is at Fordham University. Jana Bennett and Kelly Johnson are at the University of Dayton. Darlene Fozard Weaver is at Duquesne. Julie Hanlon Rubio is at St. Louis University. Christopher Steck, S.J., is at Georgetown University. M. Therese Lysaught is at Loyola University Chicago. At research and teaching institutions are Jason King at St. Vincent College, David Matzko McCarthy at Mount St. Mary's University, Christopher Vogt at St. John's University, and Kari-Shane Davis Zimmerman at College of Saint Benedict/St. John's University.

Former participants in NWNW have impacted moral theology in the U.S. in other ways as well. They have impressive publishing records, with books in leading presses and articles in top journals. They have an important presence—and even occupy leadership positions—in the major academic conferences of the field, including the Academy of Catholic Theology, Catholic Theology Society of America, College Theology Society, and Society of Christian Ethics. David Matzko McCarthy founded and edited this journal, and Jason King succeeded as editor. They founded, run, and regularly contribute

---

[5] See, for instance, Kim, "New Wine New Wineskins" and Camosy, "Some Reflections on My Last New Wineskins."

[6] David Cloutier, ed. *Leaving and Coming Home: New Wineskins for Catholic Sexual Ethics* (Oregon: Cascade Books, 2010).

[7] The influence of NWNW can also be felt in the edited volume, *Gathered for the Journey: Moral Theology in Catholic Perspective* (Michigan: William B. Eerdmans Publishing Company, 2007), to which many former participants in NWNW were contributors.

to websites like catholicmoraltheology.com, online venues that were not a reality at the inception of NWNW.[8]

WHAT'S NEW WITH NEW WINE, NEW WINESKINS
How NWNW Works

Employment patterns have shifted among the New Wine, New Wineskins community. For instance, the original members of New Wineskins included those who took full time, junior positions at large Catholic universities. The present generation of New Wineskins has largely found employment at small colleges in the Catholic tradition. Many New Wineskins participants have spent a portion of their career as part-time, adjunct, or visiting faculty. Such an employment pattern is typical for the current generation of academics, wherein more than three-quarters of current teachers in higher education are contingent faculty.[9] For NWNW members, these workforce statistics might also be a product of an increased number of schools producing moral theology graduates. New Wineskins now has representatives from twice as many doctoral programs as there were at the group's founding.

For those NWNW members who have full-time higher education employment, these positions have often been achieved only via a period of contingent employment. For other NWNW members, full-time employment has been found in allied professions, such as parish or diocesan ministry or Catholic secondary education. Furthermore, a number of the current NWNW constituency have found full-time vocational work by combining these avenues of employment, namely, by working for a parish or high school while also teaching college-level courses.

This NWNW generation has thus taken a new approach to grappling with the challenges brought about by changing family dynamics, institutional structures, economic forces, and other trends

---

[8] The spirit of NWNW, for instance, is clearly evident in the site's "mission statement" in the emphasis upon theology as a vocation, the ecclesial rootedness of the moral theologian, and finally in the attempt to deal with theological difference and polarization through friendship. The statement reads: "We are a group of North American Catholic moral theologians who come together in friendship to engage each other in theological discussion, to aid one another in our common search for wisdom, and to help one another live lives of discipleship, all in service to the reign of God. We understand our role as scholars and teachers to be a vocation rooted in the Church and so we seek to place the fruits of our training at the service of the Church, as well as the academy and the world. We recognize that we as a group will have disagreements, but want to avoid the standard 'liberal /conservative' divide that often characterizes contemporary conversation, as well as the bitterly divisive tone of so much ethical discussion (particularly on the internet). We therefore endeavor to converse with each other and others in a spirit of respect, charity, and humility."

[9] Gerald J. Beyer, "Labor Unions, Adjuncts, and the Mission and Identity of Catholic Universities," *Horizons* 42, no. 1 (2015): 10.

that millennials face. Still further, this generation of NWNW members often finds itself facing unsteady income from semester to semester, and, even with steady employment, such income may be limited and without benefits. In fact, for many in the current NWNW generation, it is not uncommon to live at or below the federal poverty line for some years beyond graduate residency.[10] For those with full-time employment, it is often at small to medium-sized Catholic colleges and universities. Such employment is not always tenure-track, with non-tenured employment lines becoming an increasing trend in higher education. Also, those with full-time higher education employment work for institutions that often have heavy loads and limited resources.

While all of this might sound dire, we do not want to suggest that there is no grace in this changed climate for moral theology. While many New Wineskins participants face work and resource limitations, they nevertheless keep working. As discussed previously, New Wineskins members continue to publish, they continue to teach in colleges and universities across the country, and they have begun to share their professional talents where the work of morals is most real: in the parish and in the neighborhood. They do all of this for admittedly limited compensation because, just as it was at the founding of New Wine, New Wineskins, many young Catholic moral theologians are driven by a sense of vocation. Increasingly, this sense of vocation is taking NWNW members to be invested in the local—in local colleges, in local churches, and in their homes.

Where NWNW Works

Currently, New Wineskins participants work in roughly three arenas: in parishes, in secondary education, and in small-to-medium sized colleges and universities. For those in the parish, they often assume positions in religious education or as pastoral associates. Such positions are a natural fit for moral theologians for several reasons: (1) they are rooted in human formation and the observation of human nature; (2) they often involve service-oriented work and leadership by example; and (3) they allow the minister to make the parish a seat of holistic education in a virtuous Christian life. Parish work is a seedbed for the work of charity, and charity, of course, is the heart of morals. Especially since moral theology emerged from the quotidian (and confessional) struggles of religious communities, clergy, and laity, the pastoral work of NWNW participants marks a kind of return of moral theology to its roots.

Other NWNW members are immersed in the work of secondary education, working in administration and/or teaching theology or allied subjects in the humanities. Secondary education is as much

---

[10] Beyer, "Labor Unions, Adjuncts, and the Mission and Identity of Catholic Universities," 9.

about forming teenagers as it is about educating them. It involves building relationships, helping young people to make sound life choices, and laying an essential foundation for how to learn, how to reason, and how to engage the Catholic tradition as an adult. Secondary education is thus a pericope of the good life and the work of morals.

The majority of NWNW members continue to work in higher education. Those who do often work at institutions focused on undergraduate teaching, with a student population of about 2500 undergraduates or fewer. Many of these institutions were founded by Catholic religious orders, and many of these schools are focused on urban or regional recruitment. Often, these schools actively recruit first-generation college students, students with financial need, and students who intend to live and work within the region of the college itself. Also, a number of the higher education institutions where New Wineskins members work are mission-focused schools. Several members work on faculties preparing students for seminary and lay ministry. Moreover, a number of New Wineskins members work at schools with programs that combine theological education, spiritual formation, and professional preparation for Church-based work. These students not only go on to be lay ministers but also professionals in healthcare, the nonprofit sector, and the Catholic business community. Thus, NWNW members exemplify a trend in Catholic higher education for school branding, recruitment, and education that is focused upon Catholic identity and evangelization. There are now more than thirty Catholic undergraduate institutions in the United States—several of which employ NWNW members—that offer programs integrating theological education with a ministerial internship. The most intensive of these programs also combine theological education with worship, retreat, and service-based experiences.[11]

At the same time, the newest NWNW generation has seen the explosion of classical liberal arts programs, combining great-books curricula with various other educational elements. The founding of Wyoming Catholic College, the success of the Augustine Institute in Denver, and the expansion of Thomas Aquinas College to a second campus (East Coast) serve as three examples at the higher-education level, while Chesterton Academies and others participating in the Institute of Catholic Liberal Education are examples at the secondary and primary levels.

---

[11] For these statistics, I want to thank Mark Erdosy, Executive Director of the San Damiano Scholars Program at Marian University in Indianapolis. For more information on these missional trends in higher education, please also see Mark Erdosy's article, "Catholic Colleges and Universities Step up to Educate a New Generation of Lay Ecclesial Ministers," *Momentum* 41, no. 1 (2010): 64-69.

How NWNW Lives

As seen above, the current generation of New Wineskins members often embark upon non-traditional career paths, which combine ministerial and pastoral immersion with the work of moral theology. Even when they take jobs in higher education, New Wineskins members often work for institutions that are less focused on traditional liberal arts education as they are dedicated to justice, intentional community, ministerial formation, or some combination of all of these. Responding to both necessity and desire, there is a way in which NWNW members are increasingly accepting their *lifestyle* as the nexus of their moral vocation more so than their work at any one institution.[12]

This commitment to holistic (integrated) life choices has led New Wineskins members to seek both employment and intentional non-employment based upon two major priorities: (1) family well-being and (2) participation in the life of the Church. Several New Wineskins members have intentionally chosen to raise their families as their primary vocation, out of a moral commitment to the good life, especially for their children. Other NWNW members have chosen to take new jobs, or have refused to take new job offers, based on a choice to immerse their families in healthy, stable, and faithful communities. This choice for community can take NWNW members away from posh urban centers and high-paced academic settings. Likewise, many NWNW members express their commitment to integrated living through their educational and parish choices. First of all, a number of NWNW families are enthusiastic supporters of the homeschooling movement. They take pride in the ability to build up their families as a domestic Church, where the home is, in reality and not just in theory, the center of faith formation, education, and community commitment. This choice allows home-schooling families to saturate their children's education with Catholic values and a sense of a living faith commitment—often shared with other area families that home-school.

Secondly, other NWNW families who have not chosen homeschooling make their career choices with the primary intention of being immersed in a parish environment, through enrollment at the parish school, a close connection to religious education, or involvement in parish life. The motivation for parish schooling and belonging is identical to that of homeschooling: for many New

---

[12] These vocational choices among NWNW members are consistent with trends among millennial Catholics. For a perspective on Catholic millennials, see Maureen H. O'Connell, "No More Time for Nostalgia: Millennial Morality and a Catholic Tradition Mash-up," in *Handing on the Faith: College Theology Society Annual Volume 59*, ed. Matthew Sutton and William L. Portier (New York: Orbis Books, 2014), 75-86.

Wineskins participants, having a family with a living faith is a primary moral commitment.

Therefore, across current New Wine, New Wineskins work patterns, institutional affiliations, and family choices, it would seem that *how* NWNW members live is more important than *where* NWNW members live, and where they work is highly connected to the kind of faithful life that their work enables. In their life choices, both personal and professional, the current NWNW participants seem to seek out Catholic identity, visible commitments to justice and virtue, and a clear sense of Church belonging.

MORAL THEOLOGY AS EXPERIENCED BY NEW WINE, NEW WINESKINS

The emerging issues in moral theology for the newest generation of New Wine track well onto the shape of the cultural context, their employment, and lifestyle situations. Articles on social media abound. Studies in marriage and sexuality continue to be undertaken but with attention to the relevant concerns of the day to day. Much work centers around the study of Catholicism in the post-Christian (let-alone post sub-culture) setting. The questions of moral theology are no longer simply how can Catholics in polarized camps come together, but how can Catholics live authentically in the world at all?

The unavoidable questions of refugees and reproductive technology are being taken up by New Wineskins theologians, but Pope Emeritus Benedict's encyclicals and especially the pontificate of Pope Francis have largely determined the questions at stake for New Wineskins scholars. Pope Francis's call for "a new morality" arising from the merciful embrace of Christ, as well as the concerns raised by and in *Amoris Laetitia* and *Laudato Si'*, have eclipsed many other important questions in the field.

Perhaps a best answer to the question of what is new in the moral theology of the Newest Wine can be answered by a summary of the articles in this edition of the *Journal of Moral Thelogy*. We will see here articles responding to "current questions" raised by Pope Francis, articles considering the perennial questions of virtue, and essays on the contextual question of how to live and do theology in a post-Christian world. The key difference of New Wine, however, is their method in answering these questions, which comes from an attempt to situate their approach and to find their goal in a marriage of spirituality and doctrine, of practice and theory, of orthodoxy and creativity.

The edition begins with articles responding directly to Pope Francis's call for and daring identification of a "new morality." Matthew Sherman's "Before the Eucharist, a Familial Morality Arises," takes up Pope Francis's bold assertion that "the privilege[d] locus of the encounter [with God] is the caress of the mercy of Jesus

Christ on my sin," that, "in front of this merciful embrace...a new morality arises."[13] Sherman points to Francis's exhortations on the Eucharist as signs that, for Francis, this "caress of the mercy of Jesus Christ" will be first and foremost liturgical, where we "participate in the mystery of the Redemption."[14] It follows, then, that the "new morality" that arises will be eucharistic. Sherman then uses this central claim as the basis for an ethic of the family that unites differing approaches (from Virgil Michel, O.S.B., to John Paul II, to Florence Caffrey Bourg and Julie Hanlon Rubio, and finally Pope Francis) around a common sacramental backbone drawing the family into service with the world and for the world. Sherman's work is characteristic of New Wineskins; centered liturgically, practice-oriented, and done with the attempt to gather a variety of theological voices for the purpose of better articulating and developing the Catholic moral tradition.

A second essay responding directly to Pope Francis comes from Alessandro Rovati, "Mercy is a Person: Pope Francis and the Christological Turn in Moral Theology." His main concern is to show "how Pope Francis's description of Christian morality is rooted in the renewed Christological turn inaugurated by the Second Vatican Council that invites theologians to discover again that Christian morality surges from the surprising discovery that, to say it with Francis, 'the Gospel responds to our deepest needs, since we were created for what the Gospel offers us: friendship with Jesus and love of our brothers and sisters' (*Evangelii Gaudium*, no. 265). Christian morality should not be described primarily as following rules but as following a person, Jesus, 'the face of the Father's mercy' (*Misericordiae Vultus*, no. 1)." As Sherman's before it, Rovati's article shows the character of New Wineskins: an attempt to do moral theology explicitly as a vocation from within the Church and for the Church in response to her expressed needs—here, as a response to the Pope's beckoning.

Kevin Schemenauer, in his "The Works of Mercy: Francis and the Family," looks to the Pope's work as a spring for understanding the daily round of the domestic church as a paradigmatic setting for the works of mercy. Taking his heuristic from James Keenan's influential *The Works of Mercy: The Heart of Catholicism*, Schemenauer notes that, although people mention the family as fundamental for the works of mercy, the scholarship lacks a sustained account of how this is the case. Through a study of the Gospels and Francis's *Amoris Laetitia*, *Misericordiae vultus*, as well as his homilies and interviews, Schemenauer fills the gap in the theology of the works of mercy,

---

[13] Jorge Cardinal Bergoglio "The Encounter with Christ," www.catholiceducation.org/en/religion-and-philosophy/spiritual-life/the-encounter-with-christ.html.
[14] Jorge Cardinal Bergoglio, "The Encounter with Christ."

firmly establishing that the daily life of the family offers an authentic opportunity for mercy and her works.

A second group of articles focuses on a return to the sources to answer questions on the connection between spirituality, morality, and doctrine. Joshua Evans, in his essay, "Morality, Human Nature, and the Sacred Heart of Jesus" again demonstrates the common approach of the newest generation of the New Wineskins. He begins with and orders his work toward pastoral and spiritual questions that lie at the heart of historic theological concerns. He begins and continues from the perspective of the theologian *as a Catholic, Christian disciple.* Evans puzzles over the necessity that we imitate Jesus, whose combination of divinity and humanity would seem to make him inimitable, especially in the fact that he never sinned. To respond, Evans "appeals to two unexpected sources: Augustine of Hippo and twentieth-century papal encyclicals on the Sacred Heart of Jesus." His contention is that this approach makes "sense of the concept of sin and the concept of salvation and provides a more robust case for the necessity of Christ's true humanity." We see here another characteristic of a New Wineskins approach: a return to patristic sources for more than historical moral theological interest but as a source of wisdom on questions still being considered by the Christian disciple and theologian today.

Medi Ann Volpe's article, "Living the Mystery: Doctrine, Intellectual Disability, and Christian Imagination," is a fitting companion to Joshua Evans's on the Sacred Heart. Both demonstrate the New Wineskins point of departure (the intersection of doctrine and spirituality, dogma and moral development). Volpe's splendid essay begins with a question that arose in the ivory tower about rationality, the Arian controversy, and Christian discipleship, but took on a pressing, new aspect upon her daughter's birth with Down Syndrome: does a failure to grasp complex Christian doctrines like the Trinity prevent someone from being a true Christian? Taking her direction from St. Gregory of Nyssa's catechetical instructions, especially regarding the nature and effects of baptism, Volpe upholds the importance of orthodox doctrine but argues that "the aim of catechesis was not informative but transformative." She draws upon the apophatic and ascetical tradition to argue for the importance of intellectual humility, reminding us theologians that "the possibility of our thoughts leading us astray suggests that the intellectual dimension of our discipleship bears considerable weight." She concludes her essay with a beautiful reflection on the frailty of Christ in the crib and on the cross, to make clear by the end of the essay that "Cognitive impairment does not hinder anyone from approaching God, because God is the one doing the approaching!"

John Sikorski, too, makes his own return to the sources in his article "Toward a Conjugal Spirituality: Karol Wojtyła's Vision of Marriage Before, During, and After Vatican II." He takes a question many might have thought was "done" (John Paul II on marriage and family) and rigorously researches, uncovers, and explains neglected and, in most cases, untranslated sources. He shows how Wojtyła's contributions to Vatican II, as well as his papal encyclicals and catechesis on marriage and sexuality, developed from his pastoral interactions with married and single people in social settings (e.g., camping), as well as from his more formal pastoral setting as a priest and bishop. It was in these settings that Wojtyła developed a vision of the vocation of marriage which is "shaped by the practice of the virtues," and one in which, through the practice of the "counsels of poverty, chastity, and obedience, a couple is able to live their marriage as a gift and a task entrusted to them.

Gina Maria Noia represents well an approach to medical ethics from the newest generation of moral theologians with her essay, "The Principle of Double Effect within Catholic Moral Theology: A Response to Two Criticisms of the Principle in Relation to Palliative Sedation." Hoping to be of service to the Church and in response to critiques of the principle of double effect, Noia offer four values for this principle. "The principle of double effect can: (1) be used as one way to articulate more fully why the Church teaches what it teaches, (2) aid individual discernment in particular situations, (3) assist theological debate, not despite, but because of the redescription problem, and (4) serve as a vehicle of case-based reasoning." Finally, Noia exemplifies a trend among the newest scholars—conceding the possibility that the outsider may find Catholic doctrine incomprehensible or uncompelling while offering answers to critics from a position decidedly within the Church and the Church's whole body of definitions and assumptions.

In the first of the essays on virtue ethics, Sheryl Overmyer traces envy through Scripture and the Fathers only to find in Aquinas a strange formulation to grapple with. She demonstrates Aquinas's first account of envy as being "pagan," that is, articulated without reference to Christian diction, and then she shows how Aquinas seems to shift toward a "Christian envy" when considering it as the contrary to charity. Overmyer is not engaged in a purely exegetical enterprise but is studying it to enlighten the context of moral theologians living a vocation of Christian discipleship within the Church.

Returning to virtue ethics for a fuller understanding of Christian discipleship and theological reflection is also seen in the second article on virtues. In "Resisting the Less Important: Aquinas on Modesty," John-Mark Miravalle seeks a richer understanding of the virtue of modesty in Aquinas, one that goes beyond the important, though at times narrow, recovery of modesty within Catholicism. Miravalle relates Aquinas's virtues of modesty and magnanimity in order to "yield a portrait of a person grounded in truth and defended from superficial influence." Such superficiality is a result of the pervasive cultural vanity, most present in modern communications technology with its endless ability to entice with the new experiences that are temptations to the traditional vice of *curiositas*. Against this cultural *curiositas* and vanity, Miravalle proposes a restoration of modesty which, following Aquinas, must be understood in relation to magnanimity and humility, virtues which can build authentic friendships and ground relationships in the truth, instead of in the shallow realities of modern social life.

Ben Peters's article, "*Agere Contra*: An 'Ignatian Option' for Engagement with American Society and Culture," worthily enters the melee of recent theological and political disputes on the question of the "American Project." Peters seeks to supplement this engagement and the so-called "Benedict option"[15] with an "Ignatian Option." This essay, too, could only have been written by a scholar growing up as this generation has, in a post-Christian society intentionally considering identity options and seemingly unconcerned with being an accepted power-broker at the cultural or political level. Whereas Catholic theologians of the past few generations had to justify Catholic presence in the world, the newest generation of moral theologians must consider how to encounter and relate to a world that seems to have little interest in them and, in places, a growing distaste for them.

Following upon the Ignatian option are three articles that treat live, theo-political issues. Justin Menno's article opens a section that reprises the theme of engaging moral theological questions from within the context of Catholic discipleship and engagement with a post-Christian world. His essay, "Human or Person? On the Burial of Aborted Children," carefully and critically assesses a groundbreaking piece of legislation and the judicial order that has temporarily blocked it. He provides a Thomistic lens that further clarifies the issue in question: what is the importance of the terms "personhood" or "humanity" when it comes to burial? In "Jesus is the Jubilee: A Theological Reflection on the Pontifical Council of Justice and Peace's *Toward a Better Distribution of Land: The Challenge of Agrarian Reform*," Matthew Philipp Whelan offers a constructively critical reading of the Pontifical Council's document on land reform in light of its own theological principles and how they might be obscured. Whelan weaves the biblical view together with principles of Catholic social teaching to offer a discussion of property rights that challenges the current practices of property and dominion at the level

---

[15] Rod Dreher, *The Benedict Option: A Strategy for Christians in a Post-Christian Nation* (New York: Sentinel, 2017). This book has generated a storm of conversation, in part facilitated by *First Things*.

of both discipleship and politics. Finally, in "*Laudato Si'* and Non-Human Animals," Anatoly Angelo R. Aseneta represents the interest (growing for some time now) in ecological ethics. Focused on extending the insights of *Laudato Si'* on human use of non-human animals is of a piece with Matthew Whelan's article on the proper understanding of dominion.

On behalf of New Wine New Wineskins: Young Catholic Moral Theologians, we invite you to sit down and enjoy the energy, creativeity, and complexity of Catholic Moral Theology's New Wine. Many thanks to Jason King for encouraging younger scholars and making possible this special edition of the *Journal of Moral Theology*.

Before the Eucharist, a Familial Morality Arises

Matthew Sherman

AS POPE FRANCIS HAS articulated in a number of his writings, to realize fully who we are as moral creatures is to sit at the feet of the Incarnation, the perfect synthesis of God's mercy and human creation. As Pope Francis explained years ago, as Cardinal Bergoglio of Argentina,

> I dare to say that the privilege[d] locus of the encounter is the caress of the mercy of Jesus Christ on my sin.
>
> In front of this merciful embrace…we feel a real desire to respond, to change, to correspond; a new morality arises….
>
> Jesus is encountered, just as two thousand years ago, in a human presence, the Church, the company of those whom he assimilates to himself, his Body, the sign and sacrament of his Presence.[1]

It should be no surprise, then, that Pope Francis chose to devote several of his public addresses to the importance of encountering Christ in the Eucharist. As the Pope explained in a February 2015 General Audience, "The Eucharist is the summit of God's saving action: the Lord Jesus, by becoming bread broken for us, pours upon us all of His mercy and His love, so as to renew our hearts, our lives, and our way of relating with Him and with the brethren."[2] In a February 2014 homily, Pope Francis called the Eucharistic celebration a theophany, wherein "God approaches and is with us, and we participate in the mystery of the Redemption."[3] To participate in the Mass is to allow ourselves to be available to God's mystery most fully and, in that mystery, to encounter the merciful embrace of Christ Himself.

---

[1] Jorge Cardinal Bergoglio, "The Encounter with Christ," www.catholiceducation.org/en/religion-and-philosophy/spiritual-life/the-encounter-with-christ.html.
[2] Francis, General Audience, February 5, 2014, www.adoremus.org/0414PopeFrancis.html.
[3] Francis, Homily at *Casa Santa Marta*, February 10, 2014, www.adoremus.org/0414PopeFrancis.html.

To encounter the Eucharistic Christ is to recognize that we must respond to this redemptive love in our own lives. This is why the Eucharistic celebration is only realized when we see others as a reflection of the face of Christ. Pope Francis notes that these "others" include the elderly, children, the rich and the poor, the immediate neighbor and the stranger, families and those who are alone.[4] In order to encounter Christ's merciful embrace in the Eucharist, we must embrace others as Christ's very Body. Far from lending itself to privatized or atomistic practices, the Eucharist always draws us into the corporate life of Christ.

The work of morally responding to Christ, and to the Eucharist, is the task of all Christians. In what follows, I focus on Pope Francis's hopes of rooting ethics, and family ethics, in a Christic and Eucharistic encounter. I illustrate that this is not a new development but rather the latest such articulation in a century of sacramental-moral reflections. While differing ecclesiologies have informed family ethics throughout the last one hundred years, it is instructive that these distinctive lenses on the family's theological identity can each be understood as having a common sacramental backbone, which draws the family into service within and for the world.

To demonstrate this thesis, I draw upon several sources spanning the past century. Firstly, this essay looks at the liturgical movement, specifically the work of Virgil Michel, O.S.B., who uses a Mystical Body of Christ ecclesiology to argue that the liturgy is both nourishment for family unity and a source of social transformation. Secondly, this essay examines John Paul II's *Christifideles Laici*, which draws upon a People of God ecclesiology to argue that the family is formed through sacramental grace in order to be a domestic covenant of self-gift. Thirdly, this essay explores the more recent theologies of Florence Caffrey Bourg, who stresses an ecclesiology of sacramental virtue, and Julie Hanlon Rubio, who stresses an ecclesiology of hospitality and forgiveness. Taken together, Bourg and Rubio argue that the family is a domestic church, a unit of Eucharistic welcome efficaciously acting in the world. Fourthly, I return to Pope Francis through a particular examination of his encyclicals. *Lumen Fidei* and *Laudato Si'* exemplify Pope Francis's use of an ecclesiology of unity, which shapes the family's vocation of solidarity and stewardship in the Church and in the world. Fifthly and finally, I demonstrate that Pope Francis's sense of familial unity is consonant with his Eucharistic reflections in *Amoris Laetitia,* his Apostolic Exhortation on the family, as well as the wider familial and sacramental reflections of the past century. An ecclesiology of unity supports not only the family's mission of teaching and enacting

---

[4] Francis, General Audience, February 12, 2014, www.adoremus.org/0414 PopeFrancis.html.

solidarity but also a Eucharistic theology of encounter and response, whereby the sacramental gift we receive demands an ever-widening community with, custodianship for, and forgiveness among God's creation.

VIRGIL MICHEL: RESPONDING WITH THE LITURGICAL LIFE

Pope Francis calls our attention to the communal nature of the Eucharist. As the embodiment of Christ's love, the Eucharist calls us out of ourselves and into the embrace of our neighbors. This use of the Eucharist's personal call yet communal import is analogous to what the liturgical movement wanted to achieve through its call to enact the liturgical life. On the American side, the liturgical movement was forged in the early twentieth century, in the period during and between the World Wars. As long-standing imperial powers faded and as genocidal dictators vied for power in their place, many sought theological models which privileged the power of Christ over human tyranny and which privileged relationship over impersonal and political institutions alone. In this climate, the liturgical movement looked to the Church as the Mystical Body of Christ, a sacramental font of grace making Christ available to all believers. While the institution of the Church was real, the emphasis here was on the role of the clergy in bringing about Christ's sacramental proximity to all Christians. This way, the sacraments could be a source of graced social equality and unity over and against the tyranny and atomism seen in society.

Therefore, about eighty years before Pope Francis, Benedictine Fr. Virgil Michel asserted that the Christian family could be a means of combatting society's excessive emphasis on autonomy. As Michel explains in a 1936 lecture, "Over against the extreme individualism Christianity stresses the kinship of all men as fellows in the mystical body of Christ in which all men are brethren of Christ and common children of our common Father in heaven."[5] Like Pope Francis, Michel believes that the missional call of Christian love is best witnessed through an encounter with Christ himself. Christian morals are a response to the activity of Christ upon us. In a 1928 lecture to Catholic women of the Central Verein organization, Michel refers to the "moulding powers of the one true Sacrifice eternal of the Altar."[6] By encountering and receiving the Eucharistic Christ, a Christian becomes "another Christ, burning with His own zeal to spread His

---

[5] Virgil Michel, "The Unchristian Character of Modern Life," given during the 1936 Winter Lecture Series on Christian Home and Family Life in the Modern World, at the Diocesan Teachers College, St. Paul, MN. St. John's Abbey Archives, folder Z 32:1: Conferences, Lecture notes.
[6] Virgil Michel, "The Liturgy and Catholic Women," *Orate Fratres* 3, no. 9 (1929): 275.

kingdom in the hearts of men."⁷ To encounter Christ in the liturgy, Michel advances, is to become the kind of person who "will everywhere radiate the life of Christ."⁸ The Mystical Body theology Michel uses here is a means of explaining the unifying power of Christ's embrace. Just as we are each conformed to Christ's embrace, so we must embrace others with Christ's love.

Michel's conception of the liturgically-informed life has great import for the family at large because Christian witness can have its greatest effect in the family, and it is through the family that a communal example of Christian living can radiate into the world. In a number of articles, which appeared in *Orate Fratres* in the 1930s, Michel argues that the liturgy should serve as a source of the family's identity and everyday living. Michel explains that the marriage liturgy itself is a source and template for Christian life. The sacrament of marriage is one of "mutual giving over of each one to the other." This mutual offering is done at the foot of the altar, which is, in turn, "merged" with the self-offering of Christ in the Mass. "Thus," says Michel, "the Christian family takes its rise out of the central liturgical life of the Church, as is most fitting and proper for it as a miniature of the mystical body of Christ."⁹

Michel offers a vision of family life that finds its origin and grounding in the Mass itself. The family can be identified by its mutual self-giving of spouses, a giving which is also an offering to God. Moreover, the communion of the spouses is strengthened by Christ's offering of Eucharistic communion. This communion empowers the spouses, and their children, to be a unit of the Mystical Body. Their place in the Mystical Body is not only found in church, though. As Michel notes, in receiving the "sacrificial action" of Eucharistic communion, family members are given nourishment so that they might gratefully worship God both in the liturgy and in daily life:

> If Communion is spiritual nourishment for living the divine life, then the only true way of showing our gratitude is to go out and live the divine life—live it from the very moment of reception on, first in our prayers as far as possible according to circumstances, and then throughout the day.¹⁰

Paralleling Pope Francis's ethic of Christic response, Michel advances that to encounter Christ in the liturgy is to become a family transformed through likeness to Christ and through a spirit of

---

⁷ Michel, "The Liturgy and Catholic Women," 275.
⁸ Michel, "The Liturgy and Catholic Women," 276.
⁹ Virgil Michel, "The Family and the Liturgy," *Orate Fratres* 11, no. 9 (1937): 393.
¹⁰ Virgil Michel, "Communion at Mass," *Orate Fratres* 4, no. 8 (1930): 366-367.

gratitude. As noted above, such a family "will everywhere radiate the life of Christ." The family has great import because, in it, the sacramental and socially unitive power of Christ is fully alive. In the Mystical Body, the family is an essential unit of grace and social transformation.

JOHN PAUL II: RESPONDING TO THE EUCHARISTIC COVENANT

Like Virgil Michel, John Paul II articulated a theology of family life that was centered upon a sacramental call to service in the world. Yet, influenced by Vatican II, Pope John Paul seized upon a different ecclesiological model—that of the Church as the People of God, the visible continuation of God's covenant with Israel and a visible source of Christ's love in the world. In a period now distanced from the World Wars and influenced by the Cold War, the Church and John Paul II looked to more visible models of God's power. In contrast to the seemingly more ethereal model of the Mystical Body of Christ, the visible and covenantal model of the People of God served as a way of asserting Christ's visible order in a world racked by the disorder of violent and atheistic political blocks. In addition, the People of God model preserved the personal call of the covenant over and against the depersonalization of radical Marxism.

As a source for a covenantal theology of family, John Paul's *Christifideles Laici* is surely a lesser-known document than his *Familiaris Consortio*, but the former develops a theology of Eucharist in tandem with a theology of discipleship. In *Christifideles Laici*, John Paul II works with a nearly identical anthropology to that of *Familiaris Consortio*. Humans are created to be social, both in identity and in mission: "The human person has an inherent social dimension which calls a person from the innermost depths of self to *communion* with others and to the *giving* of self to others" (*Christifideles Laici*, no. 40). This sense of vocation resonates with Pope Francis's identification of Christ's love and the embrace of the neighbor.

For John Paul II, living fully human lives therefore involves "responsible parenthood, the right to participation in public and political life, the right to freedom of conscience and the practice of religion" (*Christifideles Laici*, no. 5). Such participation in the life of the world, *Christifideles Laici* notes, is necessary for the full realization of what it means to be "People of the New Covenant" (no. 22). The members of the Church are in the image of a relational and life-giving God by being "creators of a new, more humane culture" (no. 5). The family's role in society, then, is to be "the *primary place of 'humanization'* for the person and society" (no. 40). To humanize society is the family's surest means of living out its covenantal vocation, and, like Virgil Michel, John Paul explains that vocation always arises from the sacraments, an outgrowth of the baptismal call to priesthood, prophecy, and kingship.[11]

John Paul explains that Christian baptism forms the faithful into the covenanted People of God by incorporating them into Jesus Christ (*Christifideles Laici*, no. 14). The Eucharist is the fullest celebration of what it means to be united as Christ's Body, by receiving and becoming that Body most fully. Drawing upon Vatican II's *Sacrosanctum Concilium*, John Paul asserts that laypersons are called to the "active participation in the Liturgy," whereby the faithful are reminded that "Jesus offered himself on the cross and continues to be offered in the celebration of the Eucharist for the glory of God and the salvation of humanity" (*Christifideles Laici*, nos. 2, 14). Becoming united in Christ by virtue of his self-gift, the faithful take on his priestly mission by "the offering they make of themselves and their daily activities" (no. 14). Such a sense of Christic and Eucharistic mission, John Paul argues, is the apex of Christian charity, and is in line the Second Vatican Council's *Apostolicam Actuositatem*, which he quotes as follows: "In the very early days, the Church added the *agape* to the Eucharistic Supper, and thus showed herself to be wholly united around Christ by the bond of charity" (*Christifideles Laici*, no. 41; *Apostolicam Actuositatem*, no. 8). The work of creating charitable communion, then, entails "mercy to the poor and the sick" and "works of charity and mutual aid intended to relieve human needs of every kind" (*Christifideles Laici*, no. 8). This self-offering participation in the Church and in society is the family's way of embodying the New Covenant and the Eucharistic gifts of union and self-offering that Christ has left for the Church.

To encounter the Eucharist is also to encounter the Incarnation, and here John Paul notes the important connection between Jesus Christ and the family by quoting *Gaudium et Spes*: "The Word made flesh willed to share in human fellowship" and, in so doing, "He sanctified those human ties, especially family ones, from which social relationships arise..." (*Christifideles Laici*, no. 15; *Gaudium et Spes*, no. 32). Indeed, Jesus "chose to lead the life of an ordinary craftsman of his own time and place" (*Christifideles Laici*, no. 15; *Gaudium et Spes*, no. 32). By encountering the Incarnate Christ in the Eucharist, families encounter someone who lived a life much like their own, and whose life is indivisibly united to their daily work in the world as God's People. Closely united to the quotidian and Eucharistic Christ, the faithful can live out their prophetic mission as they "allow the newness and the power of the gospel to shine out every day in their

---

[11] Casting John Paul's familial reflection in terms of covenant is by no means a new concept. Richard M. Hoan and John M. Levoir, for instance, have a 1985 work entitled *Covenant of Love: Pope John Paul II on Sexuality, Marriage, and Family in the Modern World* (New York: Doubleday, 1985).

family and social life" (*Christifideles Laici*, no. 14). In order to go about the work of social transformation, though, John Paul notes that laypersons must overcome the "kingdom of sin" within themselves; therefore, the laity shares in the kingly work of Christ (no. 14). Drawing upon Scripture and *Lumen Gentium*, John Paul urges the lay faithful to allow their interior conquering of the kingdom of sin to enable an inward and outward building of the Kingdom of God. Laypersons "make a gift of themselves so as to serve, in justice and in charity, Jesus who is himself present in all his brothers and sisters, above all in the very least" (*Christifideles Laici*, no. 14; *Lumen Gentium*, no. 31). In the secular world, laypersons simultaneously find an arena for service as well as an arena to hear God's call (*Christifideles Laici*, no. 18).

Nourished by baptismal and Eucharistic self-offering, Christian families are called to be the People of God, an incarnate unit of covenantal concern for the neighbor. Responding to Christ, who Himself lived an earthly and relational life, families are called to imitate his "communion with others" through "mercy to the poor," "mutual aid," and through their evangelical approach to "social life." John Paul II's understanding of covenanted and missional family life shares the Eucharistic emphasis seen in Virgil Michel before him and Pope Francis after him. Moreover, like Michel and Pope Francis, John Paul calls upon a sacramentally-rooted family to gaze inward at Christ only to be sent outward to the world.

CONTEMPORARY ACADEMIC THEOLOGY: THE FAMILY'S RESPONSE TO EUCHARISTIC COMMUNION

At present, we live in a post-modern and post-Cold War era marked by diffuse power centers, yet also the strong political pull of radical and violent socio-religious ideologies. These phenomena often belie the great wealth disparities and cultural differences that exist in our globalized world. As in the early twentieth century, many contemporary Catholics are wary of group-think and power politics and are looking for the priority of Christ's charity over the injustices of human powers. As in the Cold War era, contemporary Catholics are nevertheless interested in models of Church that retain the Church's role as a tangible, communal alternative to the radical, violent, and exclusive communities, which so often dominate the world stage.

Two such Catholics, who voice this concern for alternative formation and community, are Florence Caffrey Bourg and Julie Hanlon Rubio. While theirs are well-known treatments of family, I specifically wish to draw out the Eucharistic reflections within these authors' larger thought on family life. In so doing, we will see an emphasis, consonant with Pope Francis's hopes, on responding to the Eucharistic encounter by seeking communion with others. I argue that

Bourg stresses an ecclesiology of sacramental virtue, wherein the Eucharist is a source of sacramentally-patterned character within family life. Similarly, I argue that Rubio stresses the role of the Eucharistic meal in forming families as units of hospitality and forgiveness.

In her 2004 book, *Where Two or Three Are Gathered: Christian Families as Domestic Churches*, Flossie Bourg argues that, while the family may not have a sacramental identity that is coterminous with the institutional Church, the family does serve to make the Church and its charity more present in the world.[12] Like Virgil Michel and John Paul II, Bourg sees the family's work of charity in society as flowing from sacramental participation, beginning with Baptism and culminating in Eucharistic worship. Drawing upon Karl Rahner's conception of the "liturgy of the world," Bourg argues that the domestic church serves as a bridge between the institutional Church and the messy needs of daily life. Baptism is a moment of joining couples more deeply into the life of God, a God who would offer his very life to his people. It is a moment of being inscribed with a kenotic willingness to give of oneself not only to one's spouse but also to children and to the world at large.[13] Baptismal commitment therefore becomes the foundation of the family's practice of Eucharistic self-offering to one another. Citing Frank O'Loughlin, William Roberts, and Patricia McDonough, Bourg explains that these authors see paschal realities expressed in familial experiences, such as breaking oneself for another or in giving of one's body for the nourishment of a loved one.[14]

Indeed, Bourg herself presents a potent example of how she realized Eucharistic self-offering in daily life. Unable to attend Holy Thursday liturgy, she found herself instead tending to her young son who had vomited all over himself. As Bourg washed off his feet, she realized that she had stumbled into a sacramentally significant moment embedded within her family relationships.[15] As Bourg discusses, such a Eucharistic willingness to offer oneself to another can be translated into family-wide commitments to the sacredness of human life, to the alleviation of poverty, and to just models of hospitality and consumption.[16] Thus, the family is a primary arena for virtuous living, and especially for living with Christian charity, which "identifies love of God with love of neighbor."[17] Fostered by the

---

[12] Florence Caffrey Bourg, *Where Two or Three Are Gathered: Christian Families as Domestic Churches* (Indiana: University of Notre Dame Press, 2004), 35.
[13] Bourg, *Where Two or Three Are Gathered*, 78-79.
[14] Bourg, *Where Two or Three Are Gathered*, 67.
[15] Bourg, *Where Two or Three Are Gathered*, 133-134.
[16] Bourg, *Where Two or Three Are Gathered*, 145, 149.
[17] Bourg, *Where Two or Three Are Gathered*, 154.

sacraments, these other-concerned and socially-concerned virtues allow the family to "[manifest] Christ's presence in a particular locale."[18] The family, as a local and sacramental unit of charitable living, is therefore a domestic church.

As a domestic church, the family shares in the wider Church's mission of training people to respond to the world with God's charity, by imparting the emotional and intellectual sensitivity required for a truly loving response to the Church's sacramental life.[19] Consonant with Pope Francis's ethic of Eucharistic response, Bourg argues that the domestic church trains its members to respond to Christ's love by becoming formed in virtues of self-donation and care for the vulnerable.

Like Bourg, Julie Rubio's 2010 book *Family Ethics: Practices for Christians* also affirms that the Eucharist is at the core of Christian life and that it is the template by which families can model the Church's unifying mission in the world. Whereas Bourg focuses on the character-formation of the sacramental encounter, Rubio stresses the role of the sacraments as a source of communal hospitality and reconciliation. Just as the Eucharist is a communion that sends forth, marriage is a full communion only when it "flows outward."[20] The marriage rite itself is most properly set in the context of the Eucharist precisely because both are efficacious celebrations of the unifying presence of Christ.[21] Rubio writes that the "Eucharist fulfills the fundamental human need for communion with God and others."[22]

Citing Monika Hellwig and David Hollenbach, Rubio asserts that Jesus himself asked his followers to remember him in the Eucharist, and they were to remember that their mission was inextricable from union both with Christ and with their neighbors. As Rubio describes, "Jesus honored the dignity of people in his community who were considered ritually and morally unclean, and called his followers to do likewise."[23] Family unity, moreover, must find itself through a community of forgiveness and hospitality. These two practices are at the heart of Rubio's sense of the Body of Christ, the family, and family mission. Drawing on Joann Heaney-Hunter, Rubio observes that family members experience sinful tendencies, strained relationships with one another, and the need for renewal and forgiveness.

Patterned after Christ's willingness to eat and drink with sinners, the family table can be, physically and metaphorically, a site for

---

[18] Bourg, *Where Two or Three Are Gathered*, 158.
[19] Bourg, *Where Two or Three Are Gathered*, 146.
[20] Julie Hanlon Rubio, *Family Ethics: Practices for Christians* (Washington, D.C.: Georgetown University Press, 2010), 29.
[21] Rubio, *Family Ethics*, 22.
[22] Rubio, *Family Ethics*, 132.
[23] Rubio, *Family Ethics*, 141.

communion and reconciliation.²⁴ Just as the bread is broken, so it is also the means of communion.²⁵ Furthermore, by being committed to the feeding of one another, the Body of Christ cannot overlook sharing food with the hungry and "helping a stranger."²⁶ Christian family identity must, therefore, be founded upon the practice of Jesus's inclusive table fellowship. Without a conscious sense of having a table of hospitality and reconciliation, families lose touch with their communal identity and potential for service in the world.²⁷ By being committed to Eucharistic growth and healing, the family can realize that it is only fully charitable if it extends Christ's love beyond itself, by preparing meals for others, welcoming the hungry, or even simply engaging in just food purchases and eco-friendly consumption.²⁸ Resonant with the theologies of both Pope Francis and Florence Caffrey Bourg, Rubio claims that, responding to and patterned after the Eucharist, families are united to the Church in its work of unity, for its members and for the broken relationships of society at large.

POPE FRANCIS'S ENCYCLICALS: THE FAMILY'S PARTICIPATION IN THE WORK OF UNITY

Reacting to the oft-violent divisions of power and material wealth that mark the contemporary situation, Pope Francis expresses an ecclesiology of unity. He affirms that, responding to the merciful embrace of Christ, families are called likewise to embrace the world with Christ's unifying grace. As Pope Francis explained in his 2015 Corpus Christi homily,

> Christ, present among us under the sign of bread and wine, demands that the power of love overcomes every fracture and, at the same time, becomes communion with the poor, support for the weak and fraternal concern for those who struggle to bear the weight of daily life and are in danger of losing their faith.²⁹

While Francis's recent Apostolic Exhortation on the family, *Amoris Laetitia*, will be explored in the final section of this essay, it is important to note that *Amoris Laetitia* follows from Pope Francis's other teachings on family vocation. In particular, both of Pope Francis's encyclicals, *Lumen Fidei* and *Laudato Si'*, demonstrate that the family's call is to learn faith and care for the neighbor through the

---

²⁴ Rubio, *Family Ethics*, 79.
²⁵ Rubio, *Family Ethics*, 79.
²⁶ Rubio, *Family Ethics*, 132-133, 138.
²⁷ Rubio, *Family Ethics*, 134, 143.
²⁸ Rubio, *Family Ethics*, 143-155.
²⁹ Francis, Homily on *Corpus Christi*, June 4, 2015, www.catholicherald.co.uk/news/2015/06/05/the-eucharist-unites-us-in-a-marvellous-communion-with-god-says-francis/.

education and practice of home life; however, the unity that the family learns in the personal encounters of the home must necessarily extend outward to embrace all of God's children and creation writ large.[30] While this section of the essay highlights Pope Francis's employment of unity as a hermeneutic for family mission more generally, the subsequent section explores how Pope Francis's *Amoris Laetitia* uses the Eucharist to inform and anchor the Christian concern to reconcile sinners and outcasts alike. Through the work of unity, strengthened in faith and worship, the family can be a joyful sacrament of Christ to the world.

Lumen Fidei situates faith within a communal context, and it is as a communal reality that faith is readily linked to family life. As the encyclical remarks, "It is impossible to believe on our own....By its very nature, faith is open to the 'We' of the Church; it always takes place within her communion" (no. 39). Here, Pope Francis draws upon the structure of the baptismal rite. He calls it a "rebirth" in faith, yet one that is brought about by the agents of our first birth, our parents (no. 43). As Pope Francis notes, infant baptism necessitates that we enter the Church together with our earthly parents and godparents, who profess the faith on our behalf. "Since faith is a reality lived within the community of the Church, part of a common 'We', children can be supported by others, their parents and godparents, and welcomed into their faith, which is the faith of the Church..." (no. 43). To become a part of the Church is to become not an "I" before God but rather a "we" in Christ. Baptism extends the "we" of family to the "we" of Church life, the "new family" of faith (*Lumen Fidei*, no. 39).[31]

Lumen Fidei proceeds to relate the communal character of both the family and the People of God to the stories of Noah and Abraham. The People of God emerged from Noah's care for his family on the ark, and Abraham's care for his family in his tents. Yet, both ministered to their families and forged God's People through an act of faith (no. 50). Pope Francis explains, "Then comes Abraham, of whom it is said that by faith he dwelt in tents, as he looked forward to the city with firm foundations (cf. Heb 11:9-10). With faith comes a new reliability, a new firmness, which God alone can give" (no. 50). Through faith, we can care for our families, and, through the art of caring for another in faith, we can shed "light" on "every human relationship" (no. 52).

Indeed, family is the "first setting" in which faith enlightens the "human city" (*Lumen Fidei*, no. 52). Faith first enters the family

---

[30] For heightening my awareness of the family's movement from particular to universal participation in God's plan, I wish to thank my former student Mark Babbey. His 2015 research paper on charism and marriage highlighted this important vocational trajectory.

[31] Also see Tertullian, *De Baptismo*, 20, 5.

through the fidelity of spouses to one another. Such fidelity is a love "for ever" that is only possible because marriage situates itself not in the atomistic life of the couple but in the wide plan of God's love (no. 52). This faith enables the couple to share in the love of the Creator through the generation of children (no. 52). The family is not merely a biological unit, to be raised up in faith by baptism; the family is, rather, a unit of steadfast and intergenerational love.

According to *Lumen Fidei*, faith shapes the very genesis and structure of the family, yet it is also the mission of the family. It is in the family that children first learn trust and love from their parents, which is an essential groundwork for faith life: "This is why it is so important that within their families, parents encourage shared expressions of faith which can help children gradually to mature in their own faith" (no. 52). Through the personal and everyday ties of family, faith is gradually known and thus becomes a "light capable of illumining all our relationships in society" (no. 52).

As it was for Abraham, the care and trust gained in our "family tents" sows the seeds of being a unified people in and for the world. Just as marriage enables a kind of human solidarity only possible in the permanence and wideness of God's plan, so family life can enable a kind of societal solidarity only possible when all relationships—familial, communal, civic—are seen as part of "the oneness, which attains its fullness in Jesus, so that all may be one" (*Lumen Fidei*, no. 54). Through the family, we learn to see that "the face of God shines on me through the faces of my brothers and sisters" (no. 54). While this is quite literally true as children grow to understand how to care for those close to them, good families help us to realize that what we owe to those close to us is also what we owe to those who are part of our human family in society at large. This same sense of the widening of God's care and covenant is what Abraham experienced. His "nation" continued to grow, for God had promised that from him would come "a great people on whom the divine blessing rests (cf. Gen 12:1-3)" (no. 54).

Through the family, we realize the possibility of a "universal brotherhood," a community in which true unity can be present (*Lumen Fidei*, no. 54). As Pope Francis notes, this community of equal belonging is not based on modern liberalism, but rather, the human family is based on "a common Father" who enables us "to see that every man and women represents a blessing for me" (no. 54). Society can be one of "brothers and sisters," not because human community is without conflict but because a truly human society discerns a familial bond "in the Fatherhood of God" (no. 54). Unity, learned in family life, is not about perfection or the absence of disagreement but about acknowledging a solidarity that grounds and surpasses the human family. The ties of family life are bound by a personal God, and, through this personal encounter, all of humanity can begin to recognize its common ties.

Laudato Si' continues Pope Francis's resolve to locate our obligations to the whole human family *via* our particular experiences of family life. Drawing on Catholic social teaching, Pope Francis identifies the family as one of the "intermediate groups" that enables social and environmental welfare (*Laudato Si'*, no. 157). It is in the family that stewardship for others and for the earth can be taught. Families, at their best, teach responsible consumption, "to ask without demanding," and "care for all creatures" (no. 213). Furthermore, the family has the potential to teach children, at an early age, "to control aggressivity and greed" as well as "to ask forgiveness when we have caused harm" (no. 213). Yet, if the family has a chief place in forming a virtuous character, it can also inculcate those vices which abuse human community and the earth. For instance, parents can model the kind of "wasteful consumption" that can impair their own children's opportunity to find and use resources for their own families (no. 162). In all, Pope Francis challenges families to see themselves as a subsidiary unit of education. Through what they model to their children and through the practices that shape their lives, parents can not only instill virtues of stewardship and solidarity in their children, but they can also impact "future generations" and "today's poor" (no. 162). This kind of familial vocation and education highlights the family's role in promoting both "intergenerational solidarity" and "intragenerational solidarity" (no. 162).

Through the interpersonal practices and pedagogy of family life, we not only come to a better realization of faith as *from God, for us*, and *for others*, but we also come to a better understanding of care for the earth as part of how we live out our faith. The earth, too, is *from God, for us*, and *for others*. This parallel between God's design for creation and God's purpose in creation is why Pope Francis draws upon the bishops of Paraguay: "Every campesino has a natural right to possess a reasonable allotment of land where he can establish his home, work for subsistence of his family and secure life" (*Laudato Si'*, no. 94). All members of the human family have a right to land because they have a duty to honor what God has given. Yet, because this is a universally given right to the goods of the earth, the entire human family has an obligation to ensure that the earth belongs to all of God's children. The preservation of the earth is indispensably related to the prosperity of our brothers and sisters and the unity of the human race. A full realization of God's will demands that we extend community not only to the whole human family but also to the creation that sustains both our immediate families and the families of our brothers and sisters across the globe. As Pope Francis remarks,

> The urgent challenge to protect our common home includes a concern to bring the whole human family together to seek a sustainable and integral development, for we know that things can change. The Creator does not abandon us; he never forsakes his loving plan or repents of having created us. Humanity still has the ability to work together in building our common home (*Laudato Si'*, no. 13).

As seen in both *Lumen Fidei* and *Laudato Si'*, family is God's gift to His People, and it affords an opportunity to grow into our mission in this world through relations of interpersonal care. The solidarity of God's People in and with creation is the inevitable outcome of authentic family life and growth. In fact, *Laudato Si'* asserts that through the responsibility learned in family life and enacted both at home and in the world at large, Christians have an opportunity to share in the solidarity and stewardship modeled by the Holy Family itself. Mary, too, learned to care for the human family at large, through her particular task of raising the child Jesus and accompanying him all the way to the Cross:

> Mary, the Mother who cared for Jesus, now cares with maternal affection and pain for this wounded world. Just as her pierced heart mourned the death of Jesus, so now she grieves for the sufferings of the crucified poor and for the creatures of this world laid waste by human power (no. 241).

Authentic familial care thus requires the incorporation of the broken and the wounded; Mary's care for her suffering Son extends to care for all of suffering creation. Yet, the lessons that Mary learned though family life do not merely culminate in a witness to suffering but rather extend to Mary's labors to perfect a broken world through the power of God's life: "Completely transfigured, she now lives with Jesus, and all creatures sing of her fairness" (no. 241).

Mary is, then, a template for the vocation of the Christian family. Like Mary, we are called to journey, through the care and learning of family life to a life of compassion for all of creation. Through this ever-wider growth, we labor in the hope of a God who offers us transfigured life, and our transformation of a barren world is a small sign that God's promise of renewed life is not in vain. This journey, from our childhood home, to care for our common home, to our heavenly fulfillment, is truly God's plan for the Christian family and its vocation of unification with and among creation.

Mary is not, however, the only model for this growth from our particular homes to our wider concern for the human family and the world. Joseph, too, models this vocation as "custodian of the universal Church" (*Laudato Si'*, no. 242). Joseph begins his journey through his care for and protection of Mary and Jesus, "delivering them from the violence of the unjust by bringing them to Egypt" (no. 242). Joseph is a "just man" from the start of his vocation with the Holy Family (no. 242). As our parents ought to model to us moral character, protection and care, so Joseph models this kind of stewardship for all of the Church and for the world at large: "He too can teach us how to show care; he can inspire us to work with generosity and tenderness in protecting this world which God has entrusted to us" (no. 242). Alongside Mary, Joseph is a model of the vocational journey that all Christians are called to embrace —from familial care for its vulnerable children to ecclesial and global custodianship for a vulnerable world. As such, the vocation of the family, as a unit of Church, would seem to be the virtuous education of an ever-widening unity, understood as custodial concern for our nearest, for our more distant and hurting neighbors, and for all of creation. In both *Lumen Fidei* and *Laudato Si'*, Pope Francis endorses an ecclesiology of unity to explain Christian faith and mission.

UNITY AS A EUCHARISTIC GIFT AND TASK FOR THE FAMILY

As Pope Francis describes it, faith leads to an ever-wider concern for God's care for creation. Our prayerful learning at home always redounds to unitive work among our neighbors and in the world. As the union of faith and self-gift, it follows that the Eucharist is true nourishment for the unifying work of the family. For Francis, the family's unity does not arise simply from nature or habit, but rather, family unity arises from sacramental grace: "The food of the Eucharist offers the spouses the strength and incentive needed to live the marriage covenant each day as a 'domestic church'" (*Amoris Laetitia*, no. 318). The family is charged with "expressing and strengthening this paschal faith" through its "communal journey of prayer" (no. 318). Echoing Pope Francis's encyclicals, *Amoris Laetitia* explains that, sacramentally formed in unity, family life is an outward-growing vocation of community. Here, Pope Francis asserts that the Eucharist is itself the greatest revelation of how God's love moves us from our local and limited experiences of community to a widening care for those on the margins. Drawing upon 1 Corinthians 11, Pope Francis explains,

> The celebration of the Eucharist thus becomes a constant summons for everyone "to examine himself or herself" (v. 28), to open the doors of the family to greater fellowship with the underprivileged, and in this way to receive the sacrament of that eucharistic love which makes us one body (*Amoris Laetitia*, no. 186).

For Pope Francis, the Eucharist is both a template of family concern for the marginalized and the very source of this concern. The Eucharist causes us to discern what it means to be incorporated as the

Body of Christ, and use that discernment to seek to incorporate others. Pope Francis is clear to note that the unifying nature of Christ's Body does not only extend to the materially "underprivileged" but also to those with need for reconciliation (*Amoris Laetitia*, no. 186). After all, Pope Francis reminds us, all those who receive the Eucharist are in need of healing; the Eucharist is "not a prize for the perfect, but a powerful medicine and nourishment for the weak" (*Amoris Laetitia*, note 351; *Evangelii Gaudium*, no. 47). Likewise, we sinners who receive the Eucharist must be careful to seek out and reconcile with our fellow sinners. As *Amoris Laetitia* explains, the "Church's message on marriage and family" must echo Jesus who "never failed to show compassion and closeness to the frailty of individuals like the Samaritan woman or the woman caught in adultery" (*Amoris Laetitia*, no. 38).

Pope Francis also shows a concern for a special arena of human struggle, namely, "family breakdown" (*Amoris Laetitia*, no. 242). *Amoris Laetitia* is careful to mention that, under appropriate canonical, spiritual, and moral circumstances, the Eucharist can provide family members "the nourishment they need to sustain them in their present state of life," which may include the need to forgive abandonment, to sustain fidelity in martial separation, and to care for children affected by separation (no. 242). Pope Francis further notes that those who are both materially marginalized and marginalized by marital separation are "doubly vulnerable to abandonment and possible harm" (no. 242). Such persons are greatly in need of the Church's presence to "accompany" them on their journey (no. 242). The Eucharist may well be a part of this journey, if not for those who are separated then certainly for those who minister to them. For those most in danger of family division and loss, the unity of sacramental grace is truly relevant.

In all, Pope Francis reminds families that sacramental grace both nourishes and gathers them in order to promote the greater unity of God's family. According to *Amoris Laetitia*, no. 318,

> Jesus knocks on the door of families, to share with them the Eucharistic supper (cf. Rev 3:20). There, spouses can always seal anew the paschal covenant which united them and which ought to reflect the covenant which God sealed with mankind in the cross. The Eucharist is the sacrament of the new covenant, where Christ's redemptive work is carried out (cf. Lk 22:20).

The Eucharist is the very source of the paschal covenant, which creates the marriage bond and which assists the family in becoming "ever more fully a temple in which the Spirit dwells" (no. 29). From the temple of family life springs a covenantal concern to overcome all "scandalous distinctions" present in our communities, whether among the spiritually "weak" or materially "underprivileged" (no. 186; note 351). The family is formed in sacrament, oriented toward the neighbor and the world, and sustained in its paschal mission of inclusion, forgiveness, and healing. Aptly drawing upon Pope Benedict XVI's *Deus Caritas Est*, Francis therefore affirms, "We must not forget that 'the "mysticism" of the sacrament has a social character'" (*Amoris Laetitia*, no. 186; *Deus Caritas Est*, no. 14).

CONCLUSION:
BEFORE THE EUCHARIST, A MORAL FAMILY EMERGES

Pope Francis's *Amoris Laetitia*, along with *Lumen Fidei* and *Laudato Si'*, offers a theology of familial unity, within sacramental marriage but also on account of the Eucharistic and paschal communion of God's Church. As such, Pope Francis shares in the corporate and covenantal themes which inform the ecclesiological and moral reflections elucidated over the past century. Before the Eucharist, the family is formed for service to its members and for service to the world. As Virgil Michel reminds us, it is through the Eucharist that we receive graced incorporation into the Mystical Body of Christ, in which families become part of the Eucharistic offering. Because of this sacramental incorporation into Christ, John Paul II affirms that families can be a unit of priestly self-gift, called to continue the covenanting action of the Eucharist. Patterned after the Eucharist, Bourg and Rubio assert that family mission is always other-concerned and outward-growing, through the work of forming character and forging hospitable community. In a tone complementary to a century of sacramental-moral reflections on the family's role in the Church, Pope Francis reminds us that the Eucharist is the sum and source of the embrace of Christ. Before Christ, the family's identity and mission is given greater light: "The Eucharist opens our eyes to the larger picture and gives us renewed sensitivity to the rights of others. And so the day of rest, centered on the Eucharist, sheds its light on the whole week, and motivates us to greater concern for nature and the poor" (*Laudato Si'*, no. 237).[32]

---

[32] Special thanks to Katharine Harmon for her help in refining this essay.

The Works of Mercy: Francis and the Family

Kevin Schemenauer

BEFORE POPE FRANCIS initiated a year of mercy, James Keenan had completed *two* editions of his influential book *The Works of Mercy: The Heart of Catholicism*. The focus of the second edition, Keenan notes, is to address a question posed by his editor: "Isn't mercy a part of ordinary life?"[1] To address this question, Keenan adds a chapter on family life in which he writes, "If mercy is entering the chaos of another, then parents of young children are the merciful ones par excellence. Parents are the merciful guardians of their very vulnerable children."[2]

Keenan should be commended not only for highlighting both the works of mercy and the family's fundamental character for mercy but also because his work invites further questions on the significance and implications of the family for mercy. Can mundane family interactions, like preparing a snack for a child, be works of mercy? Or are such actions better understood as acts of justice? If so, what counts as mercy? Should works of mercy be limited to public and dramatic actions, as common usage often implies, or almsgiving, as it was in the early church?[3]

To investigate these questions, I draw on the writings and speeches of Pope Francis. Those who are only somewhat familiar with his papal ministry will quickly see his relevance for our questions. He initiated a year of mercy, during which he issued an apostolic exhortation on the family. He also insists that faith is not merely an abstract commitment but something that must be lived in the everyday. Engaging and building on Pope Francis's work, I propose that not only can everyday family interactions be a work of mercy but that the family is foundational for understanding and being formed in mercy.

I will develop this claim in six steps. First, I briefly describe the nature of mercy. Second, I explain some of the personal, political, and theological influences that incline Pope Francis to be attentive to the everyday. Third, I highlight how Francis's presentation of mercy

---

[1] James Keenan, *The Works of Mercy: The Heart of Catholicism* (Maryland: Sheed and Ward, 2008), xvii.
[2] Keenan, *The Works of Mercy*, 140. Keenan's statement here is more than an if-then hypothetical. Entering into the chaos of another is his working definition of mercy (Keenan, *The Works of Mercy*, 9).
[3] Keenan, *The Works of Mercy*, 10.

through the language of the family is rooted in the biblical witness and the formative character of the family. Fourth, I draw out passages from Pope Francis to argue that mercy is needed in the family because family members stand before each other in vulnerability and weakness. Fifth, I connect everyday family interactions with two corporal works of mercy: feeding the hungry and caring for the sick. Finally, I reflect on the nature of a work of mercy and argue that everyday family interactions can be a work of mercy insofar as God's mercy is manifested through the one serving.

MERCY

In *Misericordiae Vultus*, the Bull of Indiction initiating a year of mercy, Pope Francis does not offer a definition of mercy but points the reader to God. Francis proposes that mercy "reveals the very mystery of the Most Holy Trinity" (no. 2). Mercy is a basic attribute of God, and God's mercy is a mystery. Francis proposes that one begins to explore this mystery by seeing in Jesus Christ the *misericordiae vultus*: "the face of the Father's mercy" (*Misericordiae Vultus*, no. 1). Christ reveals the mercy that comes from God. Mercy is "the ultimate and supreme act by which God comes to meet us... the bridge that connects God and man, opening our hearts to the hope of being loved forever despite our sinfulness" (*Misericordiae Vultus*, no. 2). Francis highlights that everyone is in need of God's mercy. He emphasizes that our salvation depends on it (*Misericordiae Vultus*, no. 2).

In turn, the recipients of God's mercy are called to be instruments of that same mercy to the world. Francis repeats and highlights that "we are called to show mercy because mercy has first been shown to us" (*Misericordiae Vultus*, no. 9).[4] As instruments, individuals are merely passive. This apostolate of God's mercy "requires dedication and sacrifice" (*Misericordiae Vultus*, no. 2). In addition to seeing good in others and avoiding negative judgment, Francis writes, "Jesus asks us also to *forgive* and to *give*" (*Misericordiae Vultus*, no. 14). Knowing that God is the source of mercy allows one to extend mercy to those who are weak, needy, or hardened sinners without being overwhelmed by the weight of the world. Francis writes,

> From the heart of the Trinity, from the depths of the mystery of God, the great river of mercy wells up and overflows unceasingly. It is a spring that will never run dry, no matter how many people draw from it. Every time someone is in need, he or she can approach it, because the mercy of God never ends. The profundity of the mystery surrounding it is as inexhaustible as the richness which springs up from it (*Misericordiae Vultus*, no. 25).

---

[4] See also nos. 13, 14, and 25.

In summary, mercy is an attribute of God and a meeting place between humanity and God. Everyone is in need of God's mercy, which is extended in particular to those who are in need, weak, and entrenched in sin. Those who receive God's mercy are in turn called to draw on the great river of mercy that flows from God and to share this mercy with others.

THE POPE OF THE EVERYDAY

One might say that Pope Francis grew up as an everyday person. He was raised in a lower, middle class, Italian immigrant family. He had close relationships with his parents, siblings, and grandparents. He had many friends and did not miss a game of his favorite soccer team, San Lorenzo.[5] Pope Francis's upbringing as an everyday person found political support in Argentina. Following the financial crisis of the Great Depression and a United States embargo during World War Two, Argentina's political landscape saw a shift from a liberal political and economic system seeking to modernize Argentina to a nationalist movement. This movement, led by Colonel Juan Domingo Perón, sought to reclaim Argentinian heritage and offered concrete benefits to the poor.[6] A significant part of Perón's appeal was his ability to speak for the ordinary values of the people.[7] Since this nationalist movement reclaimed, among other things, the Catholic heritage of Argentina, many Catholics, including Jorge Bergoglio, were sympathetic to its cause. Austen Ivereigh writes in his excellent biography of Pope Francis entitled *The Great Reformer*, "Peronism transformed the Argentine political landscape and dominated the adolescence of the future pope."[8]

Jorge Bergoglio's sympathies for the everyday also found theological support in the Second Vatican Council and the Latin American bishops' Medellín statement. Pope Francis's Jesuit formation extended over the time before, during, and after the Second Vatican Council. The Council's emphasis on the People of God would have particular resonance with his rich childhood experiences of Catholic culture. In a 2010 inquiry, then Cardinal Bergoglio said, "At the Second Vatican Council the Church was redefined as the People of God and this idea really took off at the Second Conference of the Latin-American bishops in Medellín."[9] In the Argentinian application

---

[5] Austen Ivereigh, *The Great Reformer: Francis and the Making of a Radical Pope* (New York: Henry Holt, 2014), 9-17.
[6] Ivereigh, *The Great Reformer*, 22f.
[7] Ivereigh notes that Perón had the sympathies of ordinary Catholics even after he had reacted violently in a dispute with the Church over who had the authority to appoint bishops. See Ivereigh, *The Great Reformer*, 28-30.
[8] Ivereigh, *The Great Reformer*, 23.
[9] Ivereigh, *The Great Reformer*, 95.

of Medellín, found in the San Miguel declaration, Father Lucio Gera endorsed the theme of liberation and care for the poor embodied in the Medellín statement while rejecting Marxism as foreign to Christianity and the spirit of the Argentinian people. Ivereigh writes,

> The San Miguel declaration saw the people as active agents of their own history; startingly [sic], it asserted that "the activity of the Church should not only be oriented toward the people but also primarily derive *from* the people." The vision of San Miguel was of a Church with a clear option for the poor, but understood as a radical identification with the ordinary people as subjects of their own history.[10]

In other words, as Gera would later clarify, the people are not a passive mass needing to be made aware but agents of history: "they have their project; we don't give it to them."[11]

The Argentinian "theology of the people" articulated by Gera and others gives particular attention to the poor, not to the exclusion of others but as a privileged group within the broader category of the people of God. The idea is not to impose ideology on the people but to cultivate the faith of the people found in their everyday lives and popular pieties. One does not have to listen to Pope Francis or read his writings very long to see the influence of his childhood, Vatican II's emphasis on the People of God, and the San Miguel declaration. The importance of the everyday and the need to live concretely one's faith permeate his ministry, preaching, and writings. In *Amoris Laetitia*, no. 201, Pope Francis writes,

> "This effort calls for missionary conversion by everyone in the Church, that is, one that is not content to proclaim a merely theoretical message without connection to people's real problems." Pastoral care for families "needs to make it clear that the Gospel of the family responds to the deepest expectations of the human person: a response to each one's dignity and fulfillment in reciprocity, communion and fruitfulness. This consists not merely in presenting a set of rules, but in proposing values that are clearly needed today, even in the most secularized of countries."

PRESENTING MERCY THROUGH THE LANGUAGE OF THE FAMILY

Pope Francis's presentation of mercy through the language of the family is rooted in the biblical witness and the foundational social character of the family. In *Misericordiae Vultus*, Francis highlights the necessity of Scripture for understanding and living mercy: "to be capable of mercy, therefore, we must first of all dispose ourselves to

---

[10] Ivereigh, *The Great Reformer*, 95-96.
[11] Ivereigh, *The Great Reformer*, 112.

listen to the Word of God" (no. 13).[12] I highlight how Francis presents mercy through the language of the family, focusing in particular on three scripture passages that figure prominently in *Misericordiae Vultus*: Luke 6:36, Matthew 25:31-45, and Luke 15:11-32. Since I focus on these passages, my emphasis will be on the familial language of father, son, and brothers.[13]

In *Misericordiae Vultus*, Francis quotes Luke 6:36, "Be merciful just as your Father is merciful."[14] This passage underscores the movement of mercy from God to the faithful and then in turn from the faithful to others. To be merciful as the Father, one must know the Father's mercy and share that mercy with others. In typical form, Pope Francis highlights that the mercy that comes from God is expressed not merely as an abstract principle but "concretely demonstrated in his many actions throughout the history of salvation" (*Misericordiae Vultus*, no. 6). Francis reflects on how these concrete actions are retold and celebrated in Psalms 103, 146, and 147.[15] Significant for the theme of mercy and the family, Pope Francis connects this concrete expression of mercy to parental loving care:

> The mercy of God is not an abstract idea, but a concrete reality with which he reveals his love as of that of a father or a mother, moved to the very depths out of love for their child. It is hardly an exaggeration to say that this is a "visceral" love. It gushes forth from the depths naturally, full of tenderness and compassion, indulgence and mercy. (*Misericordiae Vultus*, no. 6)

The name of the Father speaks of the relationship of the Divine Persons and but also of the relationship between God and the faithful. In Christ, we become the adopted sons and daughters of the merciful and loving Father. Both the Gospel of Luke and Pope Francis speak

---

[12] See also *Amoris Laetitia*, no. 227, where Pope Francis writes, repeating the works of the 2014 *Relatio Synodi*, "The word of God is the source of life and spirituality for the family. All pastoral work on behalf of the family must allow people to be interiorly fashioned and formed as members of the domestic church through the Church's prayerful reading of sacred Scripture. The word of God is not only good news in a person's private life but also a criterion of judgement and a light in discerning the various challenges that married couples and families encounter."

[13] Pope Francis also employs the language of motherhood and spouse. For references to the maternal solicitude of the Church, see *Misericordiae Vultus*, nos. 4 and 22 as well as *Amoris Laetitia*, no. 49. For discussion of Mary as the mother of mercy, see *Misericordiae Vultus*, no. 24. For discussion of the need for the Church to live in mercy as the spouse of Christ, see *Misericordiae Vultus*, nos. 4, 12, and 22.

[14] A few paragraphs later, in no. 14, Pope Francis writes, "*Merciful like the Father*, therefore, is the 'motto' of this Holy Year."

[15] Psalm 146 speaks of how God "upholds the widow and the fatherless." Quoted in *Misericordiae Vultus*, no. 6.

not of the Father, but your Father. God's mercy is revealed and expressed concretely as a loving parent.[16]

In Matthew 25, the scriptural font for the works of mercy, Christ speaks the haunting words, "whatever you did for one of these least brothers of mine, you did for me" (Mt. 25:40). Commenting on this pericope, Francis writes, "We cannot escape the Lord's words to us, and they will serve as the criteria upon which we will be judged: whether we have fed the hungry and given drink to the thirsty, welcomed the stranger and clothed the naked, or spent time with the sick and those in prison (cf. Mt. 25:31-45)" (*Misericordiae Vultus*, no. 15). This character of judgment is not arbitrary but wrapped into the very nature of mercy. If one rejects the flow of God's mercy through one's hearts to others then one has closed one's heart to the mercy of God, which is necessary for citizenship in the Kingdom of God. In a papal audience focused on the works of mercy, Francis reflects, "Those who have experienced in their own lives the Father's mercy cannot remain indifferent before the needs of their brothers."[17] Similarly, Francis writes:

> Mercy is not only an action of the Father, it becomes a criterion for ascertaining who his true children are. In short, we are called to show mercy because mercy has first been shown to us. Pardoning offences becomes the clearest expression of merciful love, and for us Christians it is an imperative from which we cannot excuse ourselves (*Misericordiae Vultus,* no. 9).

Mercy comes to us from the Father, but it should not stop with us. If God's mercy is active in one's heart and mind then one's life will reflect that mercy. The presence or absence of God's mercy in one's life becomes a criterion of faith.

In his ministry, Pope Francis frequently recalls the parable of the prodigal son, which he refers to as the parable of the merciful father or the parable of the father and two sons. In *Misericordiae Vultus*, Francis highlights how the father in the parable "runs out to meet his son despite the fact that he has squandered away his inheritance" (no. 17). Following the tradition of the San Miguel declaration, Francis sees the prodigal son's poverty as deserving privileged focus but not to the exclusion of others. He continues: "Let us never tire of also going out to the other son who stands outside, incapable of rejoicing, in order to explain to him that his judgement is severe and unjust and meaningless in light of the father's boundless mercy" (*Misericordiae*

---

[16] See *Misericordiae Vultus,* nos. 9 and 12 where Francis speaks of mercy with the language of fatherhood.
[17] Pope Francis, "Address on the Works of Mercy," 30 June 2016, http://w2.vatican.va/content/francesco/en/audiences/2016/documents/papa-francesco_20160630_udienza-giubilare.html.

Vultus, no. 17). Like Luke 6, Luke 15 invites us to contemplate the mercy of the Father. Francis explains that, in the parable of the father and the two sons, "Jesus reveals the nature of God as that of a Father who never gives up until he has forgiven the wrong and overcome rejection with compassion and mercy" (*Misericordiae Vultus,* no. 9).[18] While Luke 6 generally challenges one to extend the Father's mercy to others, Matthew 25 highlights the need to care for the least brothers of Christ. Luke 15 seems to go even a step farther. The least brother clearly has not been an honest and sincere individual who has done his part. He has greedily grasped for his father's wealth (essentially wishing his father dead), intemperately squandered his possessions, and brought a great deal of shame to the family. The parable of the father and the two sons then invites the reader to extend and even to rejoice in the extension of mercy to those who have repented of the harm they have done, even when that harm has been done to one's self and those one loves.[19]

These three passages from scripture highlight key features of mercy. Everyone is in need of the Father's mercy and the flow of mercy extends from the Father and then through the one who receives mercy to others. Mercy must be extended in particular to the poor and to those who have lived in grave sin. In each passage, mercy is presented with the language of the family. God is a merciful parent. Those in need of mercy are one's brothers and sisters. One must rejoice in the extension of mercy even to a repentant sibling who has hurt one deeply.

By employing the language of the family, Pope Francis, following the example of Sacred Scripture, presents mercy in a manner that is both accessible and challenging. This familial language is familiar. Most people can relate to these family dynamics even if one's own family did not embody merciful love. The language of the family also is a challenge. The familial language invites one to see the weakness

---

[18] Francis continues in no. 9, "We know these parables well, three in particular: the lost sheep, the lost coin, and the father with two sons (cf. *Lk* 15:1-32)."

[19] Since mercy is a caring for the vulnerable, the extension of God's mercy implies that one must protect the vulnerable from those who continue to cause serious harm. In *Amoris Laetitia,* no. 241, Pope Francis writes, "In some cases, respect for one's own dignity and the good of the children requires not giving in to excessive demands or preventing a grave injustice, violence or chronic ill-treatment. In such cases, 'separation becomes inevitable. At times it even becomes morally necessary, precisely when it is a matter of removing the more vulnerable spouse or young children from serious injury due to abuse and violence, from humiliation and exploitation, and from disregard and indifference.'" In such circumstances, Pope Francis praises a merciful love that continues even through separation. In *Amoris Laetitia,* no. 119, he writes, "I am sometimes amazed to see men or women who have had to separate from their spouse for their own protection, yet, because of their enduring conjugal love, still try to help them, even by enlisting others, in their moments of illness, suffering or trial. Here too we see a love that never gives up."

and vulnerability of one's family members. To put the issue more strongly, since Christ presents mercy in the language of the family, living mercy in the family becomes a requirement not only of personal faith but also for the credibility of the Gospel. If one does not live mercy as a father or a mother, or as a brother or sister, then the Gospel presentation of mercy will become more difficult for others to understand.

The importance of living mercy in the family is made all the more important due to the foundational character of the family. Catholic social teaching highlights that individuals first learn about the faith and develop habits of thinking, feeling, and acting in their early experiences in the family.[20] Interactions within the family, especially for children, are foundational. If the Christian community is to be a community of mercy, it is because that same community was first made up of families of mercy.[21] Mercy is not merely serving in an occasional food line or clothing drive but a habitual and infused virtue that comes from God. God's habitual grace must be exercised repeatedly so that God's grace can permeate and transform one's heart, mind, and will. In turn, by recognizing how one serves a vulnerable infant or a sick spouse, one is formed and then more able to see the vulnerability and dignity of others outside of the family. Since mercy is a virtue, service beyond the family then becomes an important test for the authenticity of one's service and formation in the family.

Christian faith requires the works of mercy in everyday family life because the credibility of the gospel and our personal faith require it. The formational character of the family also demands familial mercy. If we are to become a Christian community of mercy, this will happen largely because we were first families of mercy.

WEAKNESS AND VULNERABILITY IN THE FAMILY

Beyond safeguarding the credibility of the Gospel and one's personal faith, as well as recognizing the formative role of the family, I posit that the most important reason for mercy in the family is the need of family members who stand before one another every day in their vulnerability and weakness, crying for the face of the Father's mercy. In *Amoris Laetitia*, Francis writes about "that 'gaze' which

---

[20] In *Amoris Laetitia*, no. 259, Pope Francis echoes this tradition when he writes, "Parents always influence the moral development of their children, for better or for worse. It follows that they should take up this essential role and carry it out consciously, enthusiastically, reasonably and appropriately." See also no. 263, where Francis writes, "A person's affective and ethical development is ultimately grounded in a particular experience, namely, that his or her parents can be trusted." See also nos. 264-266.

[21] In *Amoris Laetitia*, no. 87, Pope Francis writes, "The Church is a family of families, constantly enriched by the lives of all those domestic churches."

contemplates other persons as ends in themselves, even if they are infirm, elderly or physically unattractive" (*Amoris Laetitia*, no. 128). He continues, "A look of appreciation has enormous importance, and to begrudge it is usually hurtful. How many things do spouses and children sometimes do in order to be noticed!" (*Amoris Laetitia*, no. 128). In one's household, one has opportunities for extending mercy to family members available to no one else. God asks the faithful to be instruments of His mercy to their family members so that they, the faithful and the family members, can experience the joy of that mercy.

Extending mercy in the family requires that one recognizes weakness and vulnerability in the family. Francis, in his concern for the everyday, repeatedly cautions against presenting an ideal of family life without recognition of human weakness and struggle. One of the great strengths of *Amoris Laetitia* is Pope Francis's attentiveness to the struggles of family life.

> It is not helpful to dream of an idyllic and perfect love needing no stimulus to grow. A celestial notion of earthly love forgets that the best is yet to come, that fine wine matures with age. As the Bishops of Chile have pointed out, "the perfect families proposed by deceptive consumerist propaganda do not exist. In those families, no one grows old, there is no sickness, sorrow or death . . . . Consumerist propaganda presents a fantasy that has nothing to do with the reality which must daily be faced by the heads of families." It is much healthier to be realistic about our limits, defects and imperfections, and to respond to the call to grow together, to bring love to maturity and to strengthen the union, come what may (no. 135).[22]

Families need to be reminded that they are called to image Christ's love for the Church and the communion of the Trinity. They also need guidance in their everyday struggles as they encounter one another's weaknesses and vulnerability. Every individual is in need of God's mercy. Family members are by no means the exception.

To see the works of mercy in everyday family life, one first needs to identify those who are particularly vulnerable in the family. In *Misericordiae Vultus*, Pope Francis highlights the poverty of children. In his commentary on Matthew chapter 25, he focuses on the need to care for "children deprived of the necessary means to free them from the bonds of poverty. . . . in each of these 'little ones,' Christ himself is present. His flesh becomes visible in the flesh of the tortured, the crushed, the scourged, the malnourished, and the exiled" (no. 15). This focus on the unique vulnerability of children is a recurring theme in

---

[22] The reference within the quotation comes from the Chilean Bishops' Conference, *La vida y la familia: regalos de Dios para cada uno de nosotros* (21 July 2014). For similar statements, see *Amoris Laetitia*, nos. 201, 221, 231-58, 269-73, 320, and 325; and *Misericordiae Vultus*, nos. 6, 7, 9, and 25.

Francis's ministry and writings. He writes, for example, in *Laudato Si'*:

> Since everything is interrelated, concern for the protection of nature is also incompatible with the justification of abortion. How can we genuinely teach the importance of concern for other vulnerable beings, however troublesome or inconvenient they may be, if we fail to protect a human embryo, even when its presence is uncomfortable and creates difficulties? (no. 120).[23]

Pope Francis also regularly emphasizes the poverty and vulnerability of the mentally disabled and the elderly. In *Amoris Laetitia*, he observes, "The elderly who are vulnerable and dependent are at times unfairly exploited simply for economic advantage. Many families show us that it is possible to approach the last stages of life by emphasizing the importance of a person's sense of fulfilment and participation in the Lord's paschal mystery" (no. 48).[24]

The works of mercy provide a fruitful framework for thinking about everyday service to another's weakness and vulnerability. Certainly, one of the central themes in Pope Francis's ministry during the year of mercy has been to live out and encourage others to live out the works of mercy. He writes in *Misericordiae Vultus*:

> It is my burning desire that, during this Jubilee, the Christian people may reflect on the *corporal and spiritual works of mercy*. It will be a way to reawaken our conscience, too often grown dull in the face of poverty. And let us enter more deeply into the heart of the Gospel where the poor have a special experience of God's mercy. Jesus introduces us to these works of mercy in his preaching so that we can know whether or not we are living as his disciples (no. 15).

In order to highlight the character of the everyday, I focus on two corporal works of mercy that occur fairly regularly in family life: feeding the hungry and caring for the sick.[25]

FEEDING THE HUNGRY AND CARING FOR THE SICK

Every human being needs food and water. These basic material goods stand at the foundation of various moral concerns. Food should be properly distributed to decrease world hunger. Food and water

---

[23] See also *Amoris Laetitiae*, nos. 45-46, 49, 51 and 241, where Francis decries the sexual exploitation of youth and the threats posed to children by migration, poverty, drug use, and divorce.
[24] See also nos. 47, 82, 128, 191-93, and 197.
[25] In his discussion on the family, Francis also provides ample discussion of two spiritual works of mercy – forgiving sins and bearing wrongs patiently. For these themes, see especially *Amoris Laetitia*, nos. 86-92, 98, 105-113, 118, 133, 162-63, 261, 266-73, and 295.

should, in principle, be provided for dying patients. Children are in particular need of food. Unlike adults who can thrive on two or three meals a day, children often need snacks in between meals to prevent breakdowns. Newborn infants need to be fed every few hours. Despite this unique need for food, children disproportionately go without adequate food and water. One reason for this is that children, as Pope Francis frequently reminds us, are weak and vulnerable. They are not in a position to make their needs heard.

In *Amoris Laetitia*, Pope Francis presents God as a Father who tenderly feeds His children. Francis references the prophet Hosea, who in remembrance of the manna in the desert, writes, "'When Israel was a child, I loved him… I took them up in my arms… I led them with cords of compassion, with the bands of love, and I became to them as one who eases the yoke on their jaws, and I bent down to them and fed them' (Hos 11:1, 3-4)" (no. 28). God's children were hungry every day and He fed them.

Francis also references Psalm 131: "'I have calmed and quieted my soul, like a child quieted at its mother's breast' (Ps 131:2)" (*Amoris Laetitia,* no. 28). God tenderly and intimately cares for the faithful like a mother breastfeeding a child. Perhaps inspired by this passage, Pope Francis occasionally reflects on the merciful character of breastfeeding. In a January 2015 homily, Pope Francis states:

> You, mothers, give *milk* to your children — even now, if they are crying with hunger, feed them, don't worry. Let us thank the Lord for the gift of milk, and let us pray for those mothers — there are so many, unfortunately — who are unable to breast-feed their children. Let us pray and let us try to help these mothers.[26]

Newborn children are weak and vulnerable. Pope Francis is concerned that their hunger will be ignored because of public pressures to avoid breastfeeding. He proposes that to breastfeed a newborn child is an example of feeding the hungry.

In a 2015 interview with *La Stampa*, Pope Francis connects the public pressure to avoid breastfeeding a child in public with other public structures that fail to distribute food to the hungry of the world. Responding to a question about child hunger, Francis states:

> At the Wednesday General Audience the other day there was a young mother behind one of the barriers with a baby that was just a few months old. The child was crying its eyes out as I came past. The mother was caressing it. I said to her: madam, I think the child's hungry. "Yes, it's probably time…" she replied. "Please give it something to eat!" I said. She was shy and didn't want to breastfeed

---

[26] Pope Francis, "Homily on the Feast of the Baptism of the Lord," 11 January 2015.

in public, while the Pope was passing. I wish to say the same to humanity: give people something to eat! That woman had milk to give to her child; we have enough food in the world to feed everyone. If we work with humanitarian organisations and are able to agree all together not to waste food, sending it instead to those who need it, we could do so much to help solve the problem of hunger in the world. I would like to repeat to humanity what I said to that mother: give food to those who are hungry![27]

Infants need to be fed even when parents would like to be sleeping. Toddlers can prevent their caregivers from sitting down to enjoy a meal with requests for food and assistance. If feeding the hungry is a work of mercy, one can indeed say with James Keenan that "parents of young children are the merciful ones par excellence."[28]

One can make similar observations about growing adolescent children who eat twice their share leaving little to nothing for their parents and for feeding those who are mentally handicapped or the elderly. This task of feeding the hungry is made all the more difficult when food is not available or when those who are hungry do not wish to eat: they do not like the food, or they lack a desire to eat, or they are distracted by something else. Often times, feeding the hungry requires resources, creativity and planning.

Pope Francis also connects caring for the sick to family life. While many praise doctors and nurses, often overlooked is the similar but hidden care that individuals provide for their family members. Pope Francis speaks to familial care for the sick in a Wednesday audience he delivered on June 10th, 2015. He affirms that illness is part of human existence and highlights that we often experience illness in the home. He proposes, "The family we can say has always been the nearest 'hospital'. Still today, in so many parts of the world, a hospital is for the privileged few and is often far away. It is the mother, the father, brothers, sisters, and grandparents who guarantee care and help one to heal."[29]

Francis notes the heart wrenching trials of witnessing the illness of one's child: "So often for a father or a mother, it is more difficult to bear a son or daughter's pain than one's own."[30] He praises those who

---

[27] "Interview with Pope Francis," December 2013, *La Stampa*, www.lastampa.it/2013/12/14/esteri/vatican-insider/en/never-be-afraid-of-tenderness-5BqUfVx9r7W1CJIMuHqNeI/pagina.html.

[28] Keenan, *The Works of Mercy*, 140.

[29] Pope Francis, *On the Family*, trans. *L'Osservatore Romano* (California: Ignatius Press, 2015), 84. See also Pope Francis, "Message for the 24th World Day of the Sick – 2016," w2.vatican.va/content/francesco/en/messages/sick/documents/papafrancesco_20150915_giornata-malato.html where Pope Francis speaks of "a mother at the bedside of her sick child, or a child caring for an elderly parent, or a grandchild concerned for a grandparent."

[30] Pope Francis, *On the Family*, 84.

care for their sick children or their grandparents: "These are heroic deeds, the heroism of families! That hidden heroism carried out with tenderness and courage when someone at home is sick."[31] Francis also highlights daily care for those with special physical or mental needs. Quoting the 2015 *Relatio Synodis*, Francis writes in *Amoris Laetitia*:

> Families who lovingly accept the difficult trial of a child with special needs are greatly to be admired. They render the Church and society an invaluable witness of faithfulness to the gift of life. In these situations, the family can discover, together with the Christian community, new approaches, new ways of acting, a different way of understanding and identifying with others, by welcoming and caring for the mystery of the frailty of human life (no. 47).[32]

Since illness is a part of human existence, Francis argues that children should be formed to care for the sick: "How important it is to teach children, starting from childhood, about solidarity in times of illness. An education which protects against sensitivity for human illness withers the heart. It allows young people to be 'anaesthetized' against the suffering of others, incapable of facing suffering and of living the experience of limitation."[33]

Reflecting on care for the sick in the family, Francis echoes Christ's response concerning the blind man's illness: "He is so in order that the works of God may be made manifest in him."[34] Extending Pope Francis's reflections, one might say that Christ's words are an invitation to reflect on the mystery of our loved one's weakness, vulnerability, and suffering. Perhaps, they are so in order that the merciful works of God might be made manifest through us.

WORKS OF MERCY

Francis connects everyday family activities with those actions the Christian tradition refers to as the works of mercy. While individuals may not usually connect the works of mercy to these ordinary tasks, most people experience or recognize that family members feed one another and take care of one another in their sickness. Recognizing that individuals do such things for their family members, one might still ask: do these everyday family interactions really constitute a work of mercy?

Feeding others certainly is a good action that develops virtuous habits. Nonetheless, insofar as the works of mercy are human actions,

---

[31] Pope Francis, *On the Family*, 86. Francis also speaks about care for the elderly in *Amoris Laetitia*, no. 48.
[32] See also nos. 82 and 195.
[33] Pope Francis, *On the Family*, 86. Pope Francis quotes this section again in *Amoris Laetitia*, no. 277.
[34] Pope Francis, *On the Family*, 85.

they necessarily involve the knowledge and intention fitting for such action. One does not perform a work of mercy who feeds another in spite and anger or who does so unknowingly. Neither does one perform an act of mercy who is motivated by selfish reasons (e.g. not wanting to deal with ornery children). An act of mercy must knowingly and willingly serve the weakness or vulnerability of another.

Beyond the proper knowledge and intention, however, one might ask the further question: does not justice demand that parents feed their children or that adult children care for their elderly parents? If these actions are an obligation of justice, do they not fall short of mercy? In response, one could identify some unique circumstances that seem to go beyond justice. For example, one could argue that a child who endures heroic sacrifices in order to keep an elderly parent at home rather than in a capable elderly care facility goes beyond the mere demands of justice, but what about those everyday actions that are due to another? In fact, stepping back from the family focus, one sees that family obligations do not introduce but only heighten the general responsibility that one has to provide for the weak and vulnerable. As Saint Gregory the Great writes, "When we attend to the needs of those in want, we give them what is theirs, not ours. More than performing works of mercy, we are paying a debt of justice" (*Compendium of the Social Doctrine of the Church*, no. 184).[35] As creatures, who have received all things including life, one has a responsibility to share with others, especially those in need. How then can one act in mercy to those in need?

In the end, only God has the ability to act in mercy. As the Creator and Redeemer, God offers to the needy something that goes beyond obligation. His mercy is truly free and undeserved. Left to one's own capacity, one cannot perform a work of mercy while feeding a child a snack or getting medicine for one's elderly parents. To act in mercy, one must be invited to mercy by God. However, in the theological virtue of charity, that is, a life that operates in God's Love, one can participate in the mercy of God – one can be merciful as the Father is merciful. This participation is possible only through the grace of God, which enables one to be, as Pope Francis indicates, an instrument of God's mercy to others (*Misericordiae Vultus*, no. 14). The one performing a work of mercy, then, must intend not only to help another but also must welcome and invite God's mercy to work in and through one's action. In God's mercy, and only in God's mercy, can individuals do what Francis invites us to do – to live mercy in our everyday lives. Even in mundane, familiar interactions, justice and the works of mercy can meet in the charity of God.

---

[35] The *Compendium* reference cites Saint Gregory the Great, *Regula Pastoralis*, 3, 21: PL 77, 87.

Here, a word of caution is necessary. One should not turn this invitation to mercy into an impossible and overwhelming demand. Surely in hectic, routine, thankless service to one's children, parents, spouses, or siblings, one will not always feel God's grace or have the time and attitude to contemplate the presence of God's mercy. God's invitation to be an instrument of His mercy is not an impossible expectation that one should place on the mountain of utopian parental expectations. Rather, the works of mercy – those actions which make up so much of one's everyday family life – provide an opportunity, when one has the space, time, and attitude to see it, to step back and do what one must do as a Christian – invite God's mercy to work through one's life to touch those one encounters. God's mercy reminds one that everyone needs mercy, including the one who fails or forgets to serve as an instrument of God's mercy in the everyday, mundane aspects of family life.

Conclusion

Can one perform a work of mercy in one's everyday service to one's family? Pope Francis has much to offer on this question. His life experiences and his theological and political background leave Pope Francis particularly attentive to everyday life. His presentation of mercy in the language of the family, however, has foundations deeper and more stable than cultural or historical tendencies, namely the witness of Scripture. The faithful must live mercy in their everyday lives because the credibility of their faith demands it. They also must do so to provide a witness for the biblical language of mercy. Beyond questions of credibility and witness, the foundational social character of the family requires that individuals experience mercy and become formed in mercy in the family. Still more significant, individuals must live mercy in their everyday family lives because humans are vulnerable and impoverished and family members often are the only ones positioned to show them the face of God's mercy.

Among the works of mercy, Pope Francis uniquely connects everyday family life to two corporal works of mercy: feeding the hungry and caring for the sick. The external action itself is not sufficient for a work of mercy. Since justice often demands feeding one's child and caring for one's elderly parents, the one performing a work of mercy must further know the vulnerability and weakness of the other and intend to care for the other in their vulnerability and weakness. Moreover, acts of mercy ultimately belong to the domain of God, who alone can care for others as undeserved gift, but individuals can perform an act of mercy by participating in God's mercy, by inviting and cooperating with God as He works in and through one to share His mercy with another. While the idea of participating in the mercy of God sounds audacious, the possibility does not put yet another impossible expectation on the mountain of parenting ideals. Rather, works of mercy in everyday life present a reminder of the Good News that God invites us to live in His Love and Mercy. 🅼

Mercy Is a Person: Pope Francis and the Christological Turn in Moral Theology

Alessandro Rovati

> Before all else, the Gospel invites us to respond to the God of love who saves us, to see God in others and to go forth from ourselves to seek the good of others. […] If this invitation does not radiate forcefully and attractively, the edifice of the Church's moral teaching risks becoming a house of cards, and this is our greatest risk. It would mean that it is not the Gospel which is being preached, but certain doctrinal or moral points based on specific ideological options. The message will run the risk of losing its freshness and will cease to have 'the fragrance of the Gospel' (*Evangelii Gaudium*, no. 39).

THESE WORDS FROM THE APOSTOLIC Exhortation *Evangelii Gaudium* represent one of the main concerns of Francis's pontificate, namely, the desire to call the Church back to the heart of the Gospel message so that her preaching may not be distorted or reduced to some of its secondary aspects.[1] Francis put it strongly in the famous interview he released to his Jesuit brother Antonio Spadaro, "The Church's pastoral ministry cannot be obsessed with the transmission of a disjointed multitude of doctrines to be imposed insistently. Proclamation in a missionary style focuses on the essentials, on the necessary things: this is also what fascinates and attracts more, what makes the heart burn. … The proposal of the gospel must be more simple, profound, radiant. It is from this proposition that the moral consequences then flow."[2]

Francis's witness and invitation challenge moral theologians to reflect about the ways in which their work too might contribute to the renewal of the Church's missionary presence in the world. I want to

---

[1] This emphasis has been present from the beginning of Francis's Petrine ministry. In fact, in his very first homily he described walking, building, and confessing Jesus Christ crucified as his main concern for the pontificate and nothing else. See "Homily at the 'Missa Pro Ecclesia' with the Cardinal Electors," March 14, 2013. In her biography, Elisabetta Piqué reports that Bergoglio expressed similar sentiments even during the General Congregations that preceded the Conclave, something that clearly was very well received by the cardinals in the audience. See Elisabetta Piqué, *Pope Francis: Life and Revolution* (Illinois: Loyola Press, 2013), 186.

[2] Antonio Spadaro, *A Big Heart Open to God: A Conversation with Pope Francis* (New York: Harper One, 2013), 34-35.

suggest that this entails at least three things for the way we understand, study, and teach Christian morality. First, Francis emphasizes that the foundation of Christian morality is the relationship with the Lord and not one's own capacity for coherence and perfection. Again and again, the Pope has insisted on the primacy of grace, the "beacon which constantly illuminates our reflections" (*Evangelii Gaudium*, no. 112).[3] While human beings are called to participate with generosity in God's plan for humanity, the life of discipleship is not a matter of individual heroism (no. 12). In fact, the Church and all the faithful need first and foremost to make themselves available to the Lord, for "the first word, the true initiative, the true activity comes from God" (no. 112).[4] Second, Francis shows us that Christian morality is the response to God's gratuitous initiative and not faithfulness to some abstract principles, for it is the encounter with God's love that liberates people from narrowness and self-absorption (no. 8), transfiguring their lives and leading them onto a path that has distinctive moral implications (no. 177). Third, Pope Francis indicates that Christian morality is not a matter for isolated individuals but rather a response to Christ's initiative that always implies embarking on a communal journey. "God had found a way to unite Himself to every human being in every age," explains Francis, but "He has chosen to call them together as a people and not as isolated individuals. …This people which God has chosen and called is the Church" (no. 113).[5] According to Francis, these three elements are the foundation of Christian morality and should thus shape the work of moral theology.

Commenting on the legacy of the Second Vatican Council, Cardinal Ratzinger identified one of its most significant features with the desire to "return to a substantially biblical and Christological

---

[3] Francis insisted on the transformative power of the grace even as a bishop. For example, see Jorge M. Bergoglio, *Nuestra Fe Es Revolutionaria* (Buenos Aires: Planeta, 2013), 155-177.

[4] Francis is here making his own an expression of Benedict XVI. See his "Meditation During the First General Congregation of the XIII Ordinary General Assembly of the Synod of Bishops," October 8, 2012. Unless otherwise indicated, all the quotes from Papal meditations, meetings, general audiences, addresses, homilies, and letters come from the online version that can be found on the official Vatican website, w2.vatican.va/content/francesco/en.html.

[5] Francis expanded this thought in one of his weekly catecheses. "Certainly faith is a personal act: 'I believe,' I personally respond to God who makes himself known and wants to enter into friendship with me (cf. *Lumen Fidei*, no. 39). But […] we do not become Christians in a laboratory, we do not become Christians alone and by our own effort. […] Faith is a gift from God given to us in the Church and through the Church." Francis, "General Audience," September 18, 2013.

ethics, inspired by the encounter with Christ."[6] From the beginning of his pontificate, Pope Francis has followed in the footsteps of his predecessors by articulating a moral vision that is rooted in the Gospel and in a deep relationship with the living Christ.[7] It is no coincidence that Francis has recalled on many occasions the opening words of Benedict XVI's Encyclical Letter *Deus Caritas Est*: "Being Christian is not the result of an ethical choice or a lofty idea, but the encounter with an event, a person, which gives life a new horizon and a decisive direction" (no. 1).[8]

Before delving into his Christocentric vision, it is important to notice that Francis's call for a return to the essential is void of any dissent with or diminishing of the Catholic moral tradition, and, in fact, the Pope has time and again forcefully defended the Church's teachings in the public square.[9] His insistence on the need to go back to the origin of Christian morality cannot be mistaken either with the dismissal of the wisdom that the Church has accumulated over her long history or with an opposition to particular Church's teachings.[10] Rather, it should be understood as a going back to its source, so that the faithful might rediscover the joy that comes from following Christ

---

[6] Joseph Ratzinger, "The Renewal of Moral Theology: Perspectives of Vatican II and Veritatis Splendor," *Communio: International Catholic Review* 32, no. 2 (2005): 358-359.

[7] For a description of Benedict XVI's Christological focus, see Emery De Gaal, *The Theology of Pope Benedict XVI: The Christocentric Shift* (New York: Palgrave Macmillan, 2010). The judgment about John Paul II's moral teachings is more contested, but the importance of his description of Christian morality as "following Jesus Christ" (*Veritatis Splendor*, no. 119) is not denied even by his most outspoken critics.

[8] Pope Francis has disclosed his fondness for this passage in his Apostolic Exhortation *Evangelii Gaudium*. In it he describes Benedict XVI's insight as something that "take[s] us to the very heart of the Gospel." *Evangelii Gaudium*, no. 7. For another example of Francis's use of this passage, see his "Address to the Bishops of the Episcopal Conference of the Ivory Coast on Their 'Ad Limina' Visit," September 18, 2014. Also, "Address to the Bishops of the Episcopal Conference of Senegal-Mauritania-Cape Verde-Guinea Bissau on Their 'Ad Limina' Visit," November 10, 2014.

[9] Pope Francis's 2015 visit to the United States, for example, stands as a remarkable witness of his commitment to the full breadth of the Church's moral teachings and his passionate advocacy for them. See Francis, "Meeting with the Bishops of the United States of America," September 23, 2015. Francis, "Address to the Joint Session of the United States Congress," September 24, 2015. Francis, "Meeting with the Members of the General Assembly of the United Nations," September 25, 2015.

[10] For example, in the aforementioned interview, Pope Francis's followed his criticism of an exaggerated insistence on the Church's position about abortion, gay marriage, and contraception by describing himself as a "son of the Church" who follows teachings that are clear and that, accordingly, do not need to be talked about all the time. See Spadaro, *A Big Heart Open to God*, 34.

and his commandments.[11] In this sense, Francis's approach to Christian morality represents both a correction of certain legalistic attitudes that reduce faith to the application of rules of conduct[12] and a bold reaffirmation of the Church's moral proposal that stressing the attractiveness of the Christian life makes the rejection of certain evils more understandable.[13] In this way, explains Francis, the faithful will stand amidst the world as "joyful messengers of challenging proposals, guardians of the goodness and beauty which shines forth in a life of fidelity to the Gospel" (*Evangelii Gaudium*, no. 168). Discipleship entails a new life whose true spring is the "yes" that we say to God's infinite preference for us. Thus, even the "nos" pronounced by the Church are a result of this more fundamental "yes." As Francis put it in one of his daily homilies in St. Martha's Chapel, "Jesus asks all of us to remain in his love. So it is precisely from this love that the observance of his commandments is born. …It is this love that 'leads us to fidelity to the Lord… Because I love the Lord, I will not do this' or that."[14] Life changes when a person is touched and

---

[11] When asked whether he could be considered a revolutionary, Francis answered that "for me, the great revolution is going to the roots, recognizing them and seeing what those roots have to say to us today. There is no contradiction between [being a] revolutionary and going to the roots. Moreover, I think that the way to make true changes is identity. You can never take a step in life if it's not from behind, without knowing where I come from, what last name I have, what cultural or religious last name I have." Henrique Cymerman, "Interview with Pope Francis," *La Vanguardia*, June 12, 2014, www.lavanguardia.com/internacional/20140612/54408951579/entrevista-papa-francisco.html#ixzz34VC9wXkh. That is why Francis eschews ideological labels that always reduce people; he is not interested in being conservative or progressive, as he just wants to be "faithful to the Church, yet always open to dialogue." Austen Ivereigh, *The Great Reformer: Francis and the Making of a Radical Pope* (New York: Picador, 2014), 262.

[12] Francis has warned the faithful on many occasions from the temptation of becoming like the scholars of the law whose formal adherence to rules ends up being harmful and hypocritical. For example, see his *The Name of God Is Mercy: A Conversation with Andrea Tornielli* (New York: Random House, 2016), 60-73.

[13] The Pope has often reflected on the need to resist both the Pelagian temptation and the gnostic one. See Francis, "Meeting with the Participants in the Fifth Convention of the Italian Church," November 10, 2015. For a beautiful example of how Francis's pontificate escapes the common ideological divisions within the Church, one can look at the way he discerned the different temptations that Christians face when looking at the ethical consequences of their faith. See "Address for the Conclusion of the 14th Ordinary General Assembly of the Synod of Bishops," October 24, 2015. The Pope's harshest critique of the "adulterated forms of Christianity" that make an ideology rather than Christ the faith's protagonist can be found in *Evangelii Gaudium*, nos. 93-97. Studying Francis's life, it is interesting to notice how his unchanging commitment to remain faithful to the Lord's witness gained him enemies and criticisms from both the so-called "liberals" and "conservatives."

[14] Francis, "Morning Meditation in the Chapel of the Domus Sanctae Marthae," May 2, 2013. Unless otherwise indicated, the text of Pope Francis's morning homilies is

moved by God's loving initiative that invites us on a path of conversion. Accordingly, the Church's moral teachings are first and foremost an attempt to articulate the kind of life that ensues from the calling to become disciples.[15] If we take away the awe of the encounter with the Father's mercy, what is left is the formal adherence to rules and mental schemes that are void of joy, and we end up "being Christians without Christ."[16] Instead, the Lord is the center, and faith "always begins with the encounter with Jesus and always continues in life with the little daily encounters with Jesus."[17]

In what follows, I show how Pope Francis's description of Christian morality is rooted in the renewed Christological turn inaugurated by the Second Vatican Council[18] that invites theologians to discover again that Christian morality surges from the surprising discovery that, to say it with Francis, "the Gospel responds to our deepest needs, since we were created for what the Gospel offers us: friendship with Jesus and love of our brothers and sisters" (*Evangelii Gaudium*, no. 265).[19] Christian morality should not be described primarily as following rules, but as following a person, Jesus, "the face

---

taken from *Encountering Truth: Meeting God in the Everyday*, ed. Antonio Spadaro (New York: Image, 2015).

[15] "When there is God ... our very being is transformed; our way of thinking and acting is made new, it becomes Jesus' own, God's own, way of thinking and acting. Dear friends, faith is revolutionary and today I ask you: are you open to entering into this revolutionary wave of faith?" Francis, "Welcoming Ceremony for the Young People at the XXVIII World Youth Day," July 25, 2013. This transformation invests not only the way we lead our personal lives, but also how we contribute to society with our engagement and witness. For Francis's meditation on the relationship between the beatitudes and citizenship, see Jorge M. Bergoglio, *La Patria Es Un Don, La Nación Una Tarea: Refundar Con Esperanza Nuestros Vínculos Sociales* (Buenos Aires: Editorial Claretiana, 2013), 97-110.

[16] Francis, "Morning Meditation in the Chapel of the Domus Sanctae Marthae," June 27, 2013.

[17] Francis, "Morning Meditation in the Chapel of the Domus Sanctae Marthae," April 18, 2013.

[18] While there is consensus about the Christological turn that happened during the Second Vatican Council, the opinions regarding the consequences of such turn for the discipline of moral theology in general and specific moral issues in particular are differing. The goal of the article is to provide an articulate account of Pope Francis's theological proposal regarding Christian morality. The question regarding the relationship between Francis's magisterium and the different strands of post-conciliar theology, instead, remains open for further inquiry. For a list of a very diverse group of authoritative scholars' assessment of the legacy of Vatican II that highlights both the continuities and the stark differences between competing interpretations of the council, see note 27 below.

[19] Of course, the Jesuit formation of the Pope has also played a decisive role in articulating his vision and commitments. For a series of meditations that show the Christocentric nature of Ignatian spirituality, see Jorge M. Bergoglio, *In Him Alone Is Our Hope* (New York: Magnificat, 2013). On Francis's Jesuit background, see also Ivereigh, *The Great Reformer*, 51-55 and Jorge M. Bergoglio, *Meditaciones Para Religiosos* (Buenos Aires: Mensajero, 1982).

of the Father's mercy" (*Misericordiae Vultus*, no. 1). In fact, without God's gratuitous initiative the call to conversion and sainthood intrinsic to moral theology would be void, and it would amount to an unreachable ideal (*Lumen Gentium*, nos. 39-42).

THE CHRISTOLOGICAL TURN IN THE SECOND VATICAN COUNCIL

There is no better way to appreciate the shift that the Second Vatican Council represented for moral theology than to look briefly at its situation before the council. Many great scholars have helped us describe this shift,[20] but, for the purpose of the present article, I want to focus on the work of Benedict XVI. Not only was he one of the protagonists of the council, he has also given a substantive contribution in guiding and shaping its reception, both before and after becoming Pope. I have chosen to comment on some texts of then-cardinal Ratzinger also because a certain ideological appropriation and critique of his theology[21] has made us blind to the profound continuity between him and Pope Francis.[22]

---

[20] To mention only a few in no particular order, see: Paulinus Ikechukwu Odozor, *Moral Theology in an Age of Renewal: A Study of the Catholic Tradition since Vatican II* (Indiana: University of Notre Dame Press, 2003); Charles E. Curran, *Catholic Moral Theology in the United States: A History* (Washington, DC: Georgetown University Press, 2008); James F. Keenan, *A History of Catholic Moral Theology in the Twentieth Century: From Confessing Sins to Liberating Consciences* (New York: Continuum, 2010); Servais Pinckaers, *The Sources of Christian Ethics* (Washington, DC: The Catholic University of America Press, 1995). This journal has also weighed in on the issue, see "Formative Figures of Contemporary American Catholic Moral Theology," *Journal of Moral Theology* 1, no. 1 (2012) and "Christology," *Journal of Moral Theology* 2, no. 1 (2013).

[21] I am especially thinking about the way Benedict XVI's nuanced call for a "hermeneutic of reform" has many times been reduced to a hermeneutic of continuity both by his (supposed) supporters and his detractors, thus recasting the German Pope as a figure who pushed back against the renewal brought about by the Second Vatican Council. Ratzinger's positive assessment of the event of the council and the renewal it engendered can be found in his *Theological Highlights of Vatican II* (New Jersey: Paulist Press, 1966). For Benedict XVI's reflections on the importance of developing a proper hermeneutic of the council, see his "Address to the Roman Curia," December 22, 2005.

[22] Pope Francis has always been vocal about his reverence for and devotion to Benedict XVI, showing with both words and gestures a profound unity with his predecessor. The powerful bond between the two Popes was most evidently on display during the celebrations for the 65th anniversary of Benedict XVI's priestly ordination. There, Francis praised the Pope Emeritus for his lifelong witness that the Lord's presence is the most decisive thing and thanked him for the way he emanates "a tranquility, a peace, a strength, a trust, a maturity, a faith, a dedication and a fidelity that helps me so much and that gives such strength to me and to the entire Church." Francis, "Address During the 65th Anniversary of the Priestly Ordination of Pope Emeritus Benedict XVI," June 28, 2016. Benedict XVI, in turn, greeted Francis with these powerful words: "Your goodness, evident from the moment of your election, has continually impressed me, and greatly sustains my interior life. The Vatican

Reflecting on the renewal of moral theology started with Vatican II, Ratzinger identified the malaise of the previous manualist tradition in its rationalism and naturalism. "The atmosphere of the Scriptures was totally lacking," explains Ratzinger, "as was the reference to Christ, in whom human beings find the truth and the way in person, and therefore also find open the door to life, reconciliation with God, and communion with him."[23] While biblical citations appeared here and there, the general tone of moral theology was set by the philosophical commitments of the age and the practical requirements of penitential casuistry. The result was a moral theology that, in the words of Cardinal Ratzinger, "no longer allowed people to see the great message of liberation and freedom given to us in the encounter with Christ. Rather, it stressed above all the negative aspect of so many prohibitions, so many 'nos.'"[24]

Given this state of affairs, many felt the need to revitalize and reform the discipline of moral theology,[25] and Ratzinger argues that one of the Second Vatican Council's intentions was to return to "an ethics conceived not as a series of precepts but as the event of an encounter, of a love that then also knows how to create corresponding actions. If this event happens — a living encounter with a living person who is Christ — and this encounter stirs up love, it is from love that everything else flows."[26] The council fathers sought to pursue such a radical reform by creating an interdependent movement between *ressourcement* and *aggiornamento*. A lot has been written about them,[27] but I think that Robert Imbelli has been able to capture

---

Gardens, even for all their beauty, are not my true home: my true home is your goodness. There, I feel safe." Benedict XVI, "Address During the 65th Anniversary of the Priestly Ordination of Pope Emeritus Benedict XVI," June 28, 2016. A beautiful account of the unity between Francis and Benedict that gives justice also to the differences between the two can be found in Ivereigh, *The Great Reformer*, 88-89. See also P. A. McGavin, "Responding to the Moral Theology Inheritance of Benedict XVI in the Era of Francis I," *Pacifica* 27, no. 3 (2014): 271-293.

[23] Ratzinger, "The Renewal of Moral Theology," 358.

[24] Ratzinger, "The Renewal of Moral Theology," 358. A similar assessment of the manualist tradition can be found also in Darlene Fozard Weaver, "Vatican II and Moral Theology," in *After Vatican II: Trajectories and Hermeneutics*, eds. James L. Heft and John W. O'Malley (Michigan: William B. Eerdmans Publishing Company, 2012): 23-42. James F. Keenan, "Vatican II and Theological Ethics," *Theological Studies* 74, no. 1 (2013): 162-188. Diego Alonso-Lasheras, "Moral Theology at the Dawn of Vatican II: A Brief Presentation of Arregui-Zalba's *Compendio De Teología Moral*," *Asian Horizons* 9, no. 1 (2015): 7-19.

[25] James F. Keenan gives an account of the movement that led to the renewal of moral theology during Vatican II in his "Bernard Haring's Influence on American Catholic Moral Theology," *Journal of Moral Theology* 1, no. 1 (2012): 23-42.

[26] Ratzinger, "The Renewal of Moral Theology," 359.

[27] The literature on this topic is vast. Among others, see John W. O'Malley, *What Happened at Vatican II* (Massachusetts: Harvard University Press, 2008). Matthew L. Lamb and Matthew Levering, eds., *Vatican II: Renewal within Tradition* (New

their nature in an especially fitting way. *Ressourcement* can be described as the rediscovery of "the wellsprings of the faith, in particular the Scriptures themselves and the reception of and reflection upon [them] by the early bishops and theologians of the church."[28] *Aggiornamento*, instead, continues Imbelli, consisted in bringing "the Good News of Jesus Christ proclaimed by the tradition into the world of today, addressing the aspirations and concerns of contemporary men and women in language that speaks to them in a way both intelligible and pastorally inviting."[29]

This is not the place to delve into the history of the reception of the council or to investigate in detail the way these movements of rediscovery and renewal have been related to each other and implemented. Suffice it to say that the creative tension that can be found throughout the council documents has not always been properly understood and faithfully followed. An honest look at post-conciliar theology must come to terms with the partial and partisan[30] readings of the council that have profoundly harmed the Church. To say it once again with Imbelli, "Without the complement of *aggiornamento*, *ressourcement* risks becoming mere antiquarianism: a museum tour through ancient artifacts. Without *ressourcement*, *aggiornamento* can easily slip into a cultural accommodation that lacks substance: salt losing its savor."[31] This is why, after sixty years, the need to study and meditate on the council documents has not come to an end. We are confronted with the task of going beyond past divisions and tracing the interconnections that can help us discern the fundamental principles that guide the council's vision,[32] for in it we can find "a sure

---

York: Oxford University Press, 2008). Massimo Faggioli and Andrea Vicini, eds., *The Legacy of Vatican II* (New Jersey: Paulist Press, 2015). Nigel Zimmermann, ed., *The Great Grace: Receiving Vatican II Today* (London: Bloomsbury T&T Clark, 2015). James L. Heft and John W. O'Malley, eds., *After Vatican II: Trajectories and Hermeneutics* (Michigan: William B. Eerdmans Publishing Company, 2012). Agostino Marchetto, *The Second Vatican Council Ecumenical Council: A Counterpoint for the History of the Council* (Illinois: University of Scranton Press, 2010).

[28] Robert P. Imbelli, *Rekindling the Christic Imagination: Theological Meditations for the New Evangelization* (Minnesota: Liturgical Press, 2014), xiii.

[29] Imbelli, *Rekindling the Christic Imagination*, xiii-xvi.

[30] A short history of the Second Vatican Council's reception that accounts for the very extreme polarization that characterized the post-conciliar Church can be found in Massimo Faggioli, *Vatican II: The Battle for Meaning* (New Jersey: Paulist Press, 2012).

[31] Imbelli, *Rekindling the Christic Imagination*, xv.

[32] Readers of this journal are probably familiar with New Wine, New Wineskins, a group of young theologians who gather yearly to "reflect on their work in the discipline of Catholic moral theology as a vocation in service to the Church and the academy." William C. Mattison, III, ed., *New Wine, New Wineskins: A Next Generation Reflects on Key Issues in Catholic Moral Theology* (Maryland: Rowman

compass" (*Novo Millennio Inuente*, no. 57) – to use an expression of Saint John Paul II – that can guide us in these challenging times.

Following Imbelli, I argue that "though the council issued no formal document on Christology, all its teaching is Christologically saturated. Thus, the deepest *ressourcement* the council engaged in was [...] a return to the unique Source who is Jesus Christ."[33] The Trinitarian and Christocentric message of the council emerges in all its evidence if we read the different documents – especially the four constitutions – as a whole, focusing on an inter-textual analysis that does not isolate the different issues addressed by the council fathers. To appreciate the relevance of the Christocentric message of the council for moral theology in general and for Francis's pontificate in particular, it is important to briefly outline the council's Christological vision.

It is well known that the first part of *Gaudium et Spes* developed a theological anthropology that describes Christ as the "the key, the center, and the purpose of the whole of human history" (no. 10) who "fully reveals human beings to themselves and makes their supreme calling clear" (no. 22). These statements are not isolated; in fact, the distinctive theological basis of *Gaudium et Spes* can and should be placed alongside the Christological focus of the other documents of the council because in them, explains Antonio Lopez, Christ, "the light of nations" (*Lumen Gentium*, no. 1), is described both as "the ground and form of the Church herself" and as the "origin and content of the Church's liturgy."[34] The proclamation at the beginning of *Dei Verbum* that "through Christ, the Word made flesh, human beings might in the Holy Spirit have access to the Father and come to share in the divine nature (see Eph. 2:18; 2 Peter 1:4)" (no. 2) sets the tone for a proper hermeneutic of the council as in all the documents the Church's commitment to and involvement with the world is stated in a radically Christocentric fashion. This is so because revelation "leads us to a deeper understanding of the laws of social life which the Creator has written into human beings' moral and spiritual nature" (*Gaudium et Spes*, no. 23). Consequently, Christians go forth announcing the

---

& Littlefield, 2005), xiii. I have been honored to be part of this group since I graduated in 2015, and I have been thrilled to witness firsthand the good work of many theologians whose scholarship "appreciates the insights driving both sides of past debates yet manages to avoid their impasses. Rather than approach these methodological controversies with a 'you're for us or you're against us' mentality, there is an attempt to make sense of the concerns underlying both sides of the argument, coupled with a willingness to be critical of both sides as well." Mattison, *New Wine, New Wineskins*, 17.

[33] Imbelli, *Rekindling the Christic Imagination*, 79.

[34] Antonio Lopez, "Vatican II's Catholicity: A Christological Perspective on Truth, History, and the Human Person," *Communio: International Catholic Review* 39, no. 1-2 (2012): 83.

Gospel confident that only God "meets the deepest longings of the human heart" (no. 41). In fact, "human beings will always yearn to know, at least in an obscure way, what is the meaning of their lives, of their activities, of their deaths. [...] But only God [...] provides the most adequate answer to the questions [...] through what he has revealed in Christ His Son, Who became man. Whoever follows after Christ, the perfect human being, becomes herself more of a human being" (no. 41).

Despite the competing interpretations of the Second Vatican Council, many scholars with diverse backgrounds have emphasized the renewed Christological turn that it inaugurated, a fact that seems to reinforce Imbelli's sense that "the way forward to a comprehensive reception of the council lies in the direction that *Dei Verbum* has affirmed: the way that recognizes in Jesus, crucified and risen, the Word of God in person."[35] Coming to terms with such a turn is certainly one of the most pressing tasks of contemporary moral theology, and Pope Francis's pontificate represents a new, powerful invitation for us moral theologians to better appreciate and embody the council's Christological focus.[36]

POPE FRANCIS'S CHRISTOLOGICAL MORALITY

One way to identifying Pope Francis's understanding of Christian morality is to pay attention to his meditations on the twenty-first chapter of the Gospel of John, certainly one of the pivotal texts to understand the Christian moral proposal. "When, after the Resurrection, Jesus asks Peter: 'Do you love me?' and Peter responds: 'Yes;'" says Francis, "this yes was not the result of a power of will, it did not come only by decision of the man Simon: it came even before

---

[35] Imbelli, *Rekindling the Christic Imagination*, xvii. Imbelli's claims about the Christological thrust of the council are not isolated, as other scholars have developed a similar reading. For example, see Lopez, "Vatican II's Catholicity." Richard R. Gaillardetz, "Vatican II and the Humility of the Church," in *The Legacy of Vatican II*, ed. Massimo Faggioli and Andrea Vicini (New Jersey: Paulist Press, 2015), 87-128. William L. Portier, "What Kind of a World of Grace? Henri Cardinal De Lubac and the Council's Christological Center," *Communio: International Catholic Review* 39, no. 1-2 (2012): 136-151. Tracey Rowland, "From Correlationism to Trinitarian Christocentrism: Receiving the Council in the Church in Australia," in *The Great Grace: Receiving Vatican II Today*, ed. Nigel Zimmermann (London: Bloomsbury T&T Clark, 2015), 57-74.
[36] During the celebrations for the 50th anniversary of Second Vatican Council, Francis has warned the Church not to transform it into a monument that does not disturb us. Instead, the Pope invited us to ask ourselves "if we have done everything which the Holy Spirit told us to do in the Council, in the continuity of the Church's growth." Francis, "Morning Meditation in the Chapel of the Domus Sanctae Marthae," April 16, 2013.

from Grace, it was that '*primerear*,' that preceding of Grace."[37] The Pope continues, "Jesus Christ is always first, He *primareas* us, Jesus Christ always precedes us; and when we arrive, He has already been waiting."[38] That is why Francis insists that "the will to respond and to change, which can give rise to a different life, comes thanks to this merciful embrace. Christian morality is not a titanic voluntary effort of one who decides to be coherent and who manages to do so, a sort of isolated challenge before the world. No. This is not Christian morality, it is something else."[39] Instead, explains the Pope, "Christian morality is a response, it is the heartfelt response before the surprising, unforeseeable – even 'unfair' according to human criteria – mercy of One who knows me, knows my betrayals and loves me just the same, appreciates me, embraces me, calls me anew, has expectations of me."[40] In summary, "Christian morality is not a never falling down, but an always getting up, thanks to his hand which catches us."[41]

I have quoted at length Francis's own words to describe his Christological understanding of morality. In doing so, one element that has emerged is the Pope's emphasis on the reality of mercy.[42] "The privileged place of encounter," says Francis, "is the caress of Jesus's mercy regarding my sin."[43] This insistence on mercy is directly related to Francis's Christological focus because, as the Pope has helped us understand during the Holy Year of Mercy, mercy is not merely gentleness, compassion, generosity, and understanding. While it certainly entails all of these things, mercy is first and foremost a description of God's nature. Mercy is not an abstract ideal because "mercy," explains the Pope, "has become living and visible in Jesus of Nazareth" (*Misericordiae Vultus*, no. 1). Mercy is a person. To encounter mercy, we need to encounter a person, Jesus of Nazareth. We would not know what mercy is, if it were not for the encounter with the forgiving and compassionate glance with which God came to meet us in Jesus Christ. In fact, to quote again from Francis, "With our eyes fixed on Jesus and his merciful gaze, we experience the love of the Most Holy Trinity" (no. 8). We can confidently repeat John's confession that "God is love" (1 John 4:8), for this love has been made

---

[37] Francis, "Address to the Movement of Communion and Liberation," March 7, 2015.
[38] Francis, "Address to the Movement."
[39] Francis, "Address to the Movement."
[40] Francis, "Address to the Movement."
[41] Francis, "Address to the Movement."
[42] Another beautiful statement of Francis's Christocentric spirituality and its consequences for the various aspects of the Church's ministry can be found in *The Church of Mercy: A Vision for the Church* (Illinois: Loyola Press, 2014), 1-20. As it is the case with all aspects of Francis's pontificate, even his emphasis on mercy started well before his election. See Jorge M. Bergoglio, *Reflexiones Spirituales Sobre La Vida Apostolica* (Bilbao, Spain: Mensajero, 1987), 50-51.
[43] Francis, "Address to the Movement."

"visible and tangible in Jesus's entire life" (no. 8). Mercy, the Pope says, is "God's identity card."[44] That is why Francis insists that we turn our gaze to the tender love God has for us by "focusing our attention on the essential contents of the Gospel: Jesus, Mercy made flesh."[45] Accordingly, Francis emphasized many times that celebrating the Jubilee of Mercy meant first and foremost "placing once again the specific nature of the Christian faith, namely Jesus Christ, the merciful God, at the center of our personal life and that of our communities."[46]

Everything in Jesus's life speaks of mercy, which is why a Christocentric view of morality cannot but put at its center the reality of mercy.[47] By paying attention to Jesus's words and deeds, we can come to know the difference between our human logic and the logic of God who "welcomes, embraces, and transfigures evil into good, transforming and redeeming my sin, transmuting condemnation into salvation."[48] While we are tempted to make ours the complaints of the older brother of the parable of the Prodigal Son against his father's mercy (Luke 15:29-30), Christ shows us that God desires to save those who are lost, for "there will be more joy in heaven over one sinner who repents than over ninety-nine righteous people who have no need of repentance" (Luke 15:7). No human sin can limit God's mercy. God never tires to forgive; it is we human beings who at times get tired of asking for forgiveness.[49] Instead the Lord, like a father who awaits his children at the doorway, is patient and always waits for us "so that he can enact his forgiveness and his charity within us."[50] God is not an apathetic God who stands in his distant throne. Instead, he "let himself be moved by human wretchedness, by our need, by our suffering"[51] and sought to get involved with human beings, suffering with and for us to make evident his visceral love.[52]

---

[44] Francis, *The Name of God Is Mercy*, 9. On Jesus Christ as the revealer of the Father, see Jorge M. Bergoglio, *Reflexiones En Esperanza* (Madrid: Romana Editorial, 2013), 88-95.
[45] Francis, "General Audience," December 9, 2015.
[46] Francis, "General Audience."
[47] Just to mention the episodes quoted the most by Pope Francis, see Lk 15: 1-32, Lk 10:25-37, Jn 8:1-11. For an insightful meditation on the gospel of mercy, see Raniero Cantalamessa, *The Gaze of Mercy: A Commentary on Divine and Human Mercy* (Maryland: The Word Among Us Press, 2015).
[48] Francis, *The Name of God Is Mercy*, 66.
[49] This is a recurring thought in Francis's homilies and addresses. For one instantiation of the claim, see *Evangelii Gaudium*, no. 3.
[50] Francis, *The Name of God Is Mercy*, 34.
[51] Francis, *The Name of God Is Mercy*, 92.
[52] Saint Bernard of Clairvaux famously said that "impassibilis est Deus, sed non incompassibilis" – "God is incapable of suffering, but He is not incapable of sharing another's suffering." Saint Bernard of Clairvaux, *Commentary on the Song of Songs*,

The mercy of God is always available to us, but, clarifies Francis, "in order to be filled with his gift of infinite mercy, we need to recognize our need, our emptiness, our wretchedness. We cannot be arrogant."[53] Like the prodigal son, we too need to come to our senses (Luke 15:17) because without recognizing ourselves as sinners we will not be able to receive God's mercy; as Augustine said beautifully, "The one who created us without us does not want to redeem us without us."[54] God takes our freedom so seriously that he does not force us to accept his love. He patiently waits for our response, never giving up and always renewing his merciful initiative toward us. Jesus came to redeem those who are sick and in need of healing (Mark 2:17), for the righteous think themselves self-sufficient and are not open to God's embrace. Accordingly, we need to "take a small step toward God, or at least express the desire to take it. […] All we need to do is to take our condition seriously. We need to remember and remind ourselves where we come from, what we are, our nothingness."[55]

God goes to great lengths to enter the human heart, finding the smallest opening to grant us his saving grace. "Thinking back on my own life and my experiences to September 21, 1953 when God came to me and filled me with wonder," says Francis, "I have always said that the Lord precedes us, he anticipates us."[56] On that day, the 17 year-old Jorge Maria Bergoglio felt compelled to enter his parish church as he was passing in front of it. Upon entering, he perceived the need to go to confession and that moment marked his life. "I do not know what happened, but I came out different, changed. I returned home with the certainty of having to consecrate myself to the Lord."[57] By encouraging all the faithful to open their hearts to the mercy of God, Francis does not follow an abstract pastoral program. In fact, he has experienced first-hand that "only one who has been touched and caressed by the tenderness of his mercy really knows the Lord"[58] and that only "when you feel his merciful embrace, when you let yourself

---

26, 5. Meditating on this mystery of God suffering with his people, Benedict XVI added: "Human beings are worth so much to God that he himself became man in order to *suffer with* them." *Spe Salvi*, no. 39.

[53] Francis, *The Name of God Is Mercy*, 43.

[54] "Qui ergo fecit te sine te, non te iustificat sine te" (Augustine, Sermon 169 c. 11 n. 13), quoted in Walter Kasper, *Mercy: The Essence of the Gospel and the Key to Christian Life* (New Jersey: Paulist Press, 2013), 75.

[55] Francis, *The Name of God Is Mercy*, 58.

[56] Antonio Rizzolo, "Interview with Pope Francis," *Credere: La Rivista Ufficiale del Giubileo*, December 6, 2015, 11.

[57] Rizzolo, "Interview with Pope Francis." A further description of the circumstances that led to his priestly vocation provided by Francis himself can be found in Francesca Ambrogetti and Sergio Rubin, *Pope Francis: His Life in His Own Words. Conversations with Jorge Maria Bergoglio* (New York: G. P. Putnam's Sons, 2010), 34-48.

[58] Francis, *The Name of God Is Mercy*, 34.

be embraced, when you are moved – that's when life can change, because that's when we try to respond to the immense and unexpected gift of grace."[59]

THE CHURCH OF MERCY

Francis describes mercy as the "Lord's most powerful message,"[60] and he has come to understand it as Jesus's most defining teaching.[61] At the same time, as the Pope's autobiographical testimony makes clear, in order to have such a radical effect on people and accomplish such a real and life-giving transformation, mercy cannot remain just a lofty idea. Granted that mercy constitutes the most distinctive trait of Jesus's ministry, how does it remain visible and tangible today? What is the concrete reality through which God reveals his love to the men and women of the twenty-first century?

It is the Church – Francis tells us – whose primary task "is to introduce everyone to the great mystery of God's mercy."[62] The Church exists, continues the Pope, "to bring about an encounter with the visceral love of God's mercy" (*Misericordiae Vultus*, no. 25). The Church is where we can experience the joyful amazement of encountering Christ and the sweetness of his forgiveness.[63] In fact, God in his love commissioned the apostles and all their successors to be instruments of the Father's mercy (cf. John 20:19-23), so that we might encounter it concretely and not just as an abstract idea. "The Church is 'God's house,'" explains Francis, "the place of his presence, where we can find and encounter the Lord."[64] Accordingly, following in the footsteps of Jesus, the Church, too, pours out mercy over all those who recognize themselves as sinners, and thus she is always on the move, going outside to "look for people where they live, where

---

[59] Francis, *The Name of God Is Mercy*, 34-35.
[60] "Homily for the Holy Mass in the Parish of Saint Anna in the Vatican," March 17, 2013.
[61] Francis, *The Name of God Is Mercy*, 5.
[62] Francis, "Homily for the Holy Mass in the Parish of Saint Anna in the Vatican."
[63] Livio Melina nicely articulates how John Paul II's *Veritatis Splendor* emphasized the connection between a Christocentric morality and the ecclesial nature of the faith in his *The Epiphany of Love: Toward a Theological Understanding of Action* (Michigan: William B. Eerdmans Publishing Company, 2010), 102-123.
[64] Francis, "General Audience," June 26, 2013. Francis also observes that "still today some say: 'Christ yes, the Church no. [...] But it is the Church herself which brings Christ to us and which brings us to God. The Church is the great family of God's children. Of course, she also has human aspects; [...] but what is beautiful is that when we realize we are sinners we encounter the mercy of God who always forgives." Francis, "General Audience," May 29, 2013.

they suffer, and where they hope,"[65] so as to be like a field hospital, capable of providing immediate care to those who are wounded.[66] As the words and deeds of Jesus in the Gospel, in the same way even the Church's "language and her gestures must transmit mercy, so as to touch the hearts of all people and inspire them once more to find the road to the Father" (*Misericordiae Vultus*, no. 12).[67]

Mercy is the foundation of the life of the Church, and the Church's credibility is seen in how she shows merciful and compassionate love. "Wherever the Church is present," insists Francis, "the mercy of the Father must be evident" (*Misericordiae Vultus*, no. 12), which is why Francis chose as the motto for the Holy Year of Mercy Jesus's commandment to "be merciful, even as your Father is merciful" (Luke 6:36). As disciples, we are sent forth into the world to live in the logic of love and selflessness so that, filled by Christ's presence, we might become bearers of mercy for all our fellow human beings. This missionary zeal, argues the Pope, is essentially connected with the recognition of the mercy that God has for us. "The more conscious we are of our wretchedness and our sins," says Francis, "the more we experience the love and infinite mercy of God among us, and the more capable we are of looking upon the many wounded we meet along the way with acceptance and mercy."[68] We can be witnesses of mercy for the world because the Lord has looked upon us with mercy.[69]

One should not characterize Francis's insistence that the Church regains her missionary impetus as an invitation to mere activism. All the contrary, for the Pope the works of mercy "are a consequence, a response to that merciful love that saves us."[70] Becoming merciful like the Father is merciful does not entail transforming the Church into a well-organized NGO that has a lot of programs and initiatives but forgets the essential, namely, the presence of the Lord in its midst.

---

[65] Francis, *The Name of God Is Mercy*, 52. Francis never tires to emphasize the need for the Church to go forth, exiting its comfort zone to reach the peripheries that are in need of the light of the Gospel. On this, see *Evangelii Gaudium*, nos. 20-24.
[66] Antonio Spadaro, *A Big Heart Open to God*, 30-31.
[67] The Pope emphasized this point also when meeting with the United States Bishops during his 2015 Apostolic Journey: "The brother or sister we wish to reach and redeem, with the power and closeness of love, counts more than their positions, distant as they may be from what we hold as true and certain. Harsh and divisive language does not befit the tongue of a pastor, it has no place in his heart; although it may momentarily seem to win the day, only the enduring allure of goodness and love remains truly convincing." Francis, "Meeting with the Bishops of the United States of America." Francis is truly a man of dialogue that does not only speak about building a culture of encounter but actually contributes to creating it. For example, see his interreligious conversations with Rabbi Abraham Skorka collected in Jorge M. Bergoglio and Abraham Skorka, *On Heaven and Earth* (New York: Image, 2010).
[68] Francis, *The Name of God Is Mercy*, 67.
[69] Antonio Spadaro, *A Big Heart Open to God*, 7-8.
[70] Francis, "Morning Meditation in the Chapel of the Domus Sanctae Marthae," October 14, 2013.

Instead, we are called to participate in the dynamism of God's love, so that the more we are centered in Christ, the more we will be led to go out to announce him. As Francis explained before becoming Pope, "Paradoxically, for us to be centered in Christ requires that we decenter. Where there is true life in Christ, in fact, there is exiting in the name of Christ. This is what it really means to begin again in Christ! It is to recognize ourselves called by him to stay with him, but also to realize that we are disciples to experience the grace of being sent, to exit in order to bring the announcement, to go and encounter the other."[71] Still, we would not be able to announce him, if God was not present with us, for without him we cannot do anything (cf. John 15:5). Our gracious Lord, though, "becomes one of us and journeys with us," says Francis, "remains with us, remains in his Church, remains in the Eucharist, remains in his word, remains in the poor, remains with us journeying."[72] Human beings are wretches that commit plenty of sins, but, under the filth of our limits, there are the "embers of desire for God" and "the embers of God's image in us" that need someone to fan them into flame. "This is what the gaze of Jesus did," and "all of us [who are part of the Church] in our lives have felt this gaze, and not just one time: many times."[73]

AMORIS LAETITIA

All these aspects of Pope Francis's witness are rooted in his desire to give space to the essential, that is, the "treasure of the living Christ"[74] and the "living the wonder of having being saved."[75] By way of example,[76] I want to consider briefly the Apostolic Exhortation *Amoris Laetitia*, for I consider it a telling way Francis's theological commitments and spirituality inform the way he meditates upon moral issues. While the discussion about this document has been mostly focused on the parts concerning the pastoral care of the baptized who are divorced and remarried, for the purpose of this article, it would be good to take a step back from the heated polemics and appreciate the

---

[71] Jorge M. Bergoglio, *Salgan a Buscar Corazones: Mensajes a Los Catequistas* (Buenos Aires: Editorial Claretiana, 2013).

[72] Francis, "Morning Meditation in the Chapel of the Domus Sanctae Marthae," June 7, 2013.

[73] "Morning Meditation in the Chapel of the Domus Sanctae Marthae," September 21, 2013.

[74] Ambrogetti and Rubin, *Pope Francis*, 105.

[75] Ambrogetti and Rubin, *Pope Francis*, 122.

[76] For a discussion of the Christological nature of Francis's social teachings, see my "Everything Is a Caress of God," *Catholic Moral Theology*, www.catholicmoraltheology.com/everything-is-a-caress-of-god/. Also, see the Pope's interview published in Andrea Tornielli and Giacomo Galeazzi, *This Economy Kills: Pope Francis on Capitalism and Social Justice* (Minnesota: Liturgical Press, 2015), 147-153.

depth and breadth of Francis's proposal.[77] Above all, I want to focus on an invitation that emerges time and again in Francis's *Amoris Laetitia*, namely, to put Christ at the center of our living and thinking.

"Only in contemplating Christ," writes the Pope, "does a person come to know the deepest truth about human relationships" (*Amoris Laetitia*, no. 77). Engaging *Gaudium et Spes*, Francis insists that the Church and Christian families need to immerse themselves once again in the mystery of the Incarnate Word because in that mystery light is shed on the human condition (*Gaudium et Spes*, no. 22). Families should be centered in Christ so that he might unify and illumine their entire lives (*Amoris Laetitia*, no. 317). Spouses are called to contemplate their loved ones "with the eyes of God" (no. 323), seeing beyond the others' limitations and "contemplating and appreciating their innate beauty and sacredness" (no. 127), thus learning to "seek their good" (no. 127) and not the pursuit of one's own selfish projects and interests. In turn, the Church as a whole is also called to turn her gaze to the living Christ (no. 59) because "the example of Jesus is a paradigm for the Church" (no. 64). The Church's way is the way of Jesus (no. 296), which is why the Church strives to make "her own the attitude of the Lord Jesus, who offers his boundless love to each person without exception" (no. 250). Much has been said about the pastoral nature of Francis's exhortation, but we should not forget that, for the Pope, pastoral care is nothing else than seeing things with the eyes of Christ, imitating him who "goes out to everyone without exception" (no. 309). This is why any attempt to pit doctrinal and pastoral considerations against each other ought to be rejected, for, as Francis beautifully said, "Christian doctrine is called Jesus Christ."[78]

Realizing the importance of the Christ-centered gaze that Francis embodies is fundamental if we want to truly appreciate and understand his reflections about the pastoral care of those who live in so-called "irregular" situations, a care that, as the document makes clear, includes but is not limited to the issue of admission to the sacraments. The Pope's insistence that they need to be helped in finding their "proper way of participating in the ecclesial community" (no. 297) cannot be separated from his desire for the Church and all the faithful to better embody Christ's loving gaze in their lives. Francis, in fact, sincerely believes that "Jesus wants a Church attentive to the goodness which the Holy Spirit sows in the midst of human weakness, a Mother who, while clearly expressing her objective teaching, 'always does what good she can, even if in the process, her shoes get soiled by the

---

[77] For an analysis of the Exhortation that engages in the patient and careful reading that the Pope called for (*Amoris Laetitia*, no. 7), see Francesco Coccopalmerio, *Commentary on Chapter Eight of Amoris Laetitia* (New Jersey: Paulist Press, 2017).
[78] Francis, "Meeting with the Participants in the Fifth Convention of the Italian Church."

mud of the street'" (no. 308). Following in the footsteps of Jesus, the Church never tires of proclaiming the demands of the Kingdom, while at the same time looking to people and their weakness with love and tenderness, "accompanying their steps in truth, patience and mercy" (no. 60). These are powerful words, and it would be foolish to think that they are addressed only to the divorced and remarried. Everyone, Francis makes clear, is in need of God's mercy, and the Pope's announcement that God's logic is to touch his children with an unmerited, unconditional, and gratuitous mercy represents the Good News that brings hope and joy to each one of us (no. 297).

By emphasizing the need to be rooted in the Word of God, in fact, Francis is not inviting us to be distracted by abstract ideas or celestial pictures that ignore the actual condition of families. Just the opposite, Francis insists on the need to focus on concrete realities because "the call and the demands of the Spirit resound in the events of history" (no. 31). Paying attention to our present situation entails realizing that we live in a time where cultural and economical factors militate against permanent decisions and family life. Because of economical struggles that make the future uncertain (no. 40), of the "culture of the ephemeral" that reduces everything to what can be possessed and quickly discarded (no. 39), and of the legal deconstructions of the family (no. 53), we are confronted with a reality where marriage is often treated "as an old-fashioned and outdated option" (no. 53). This means that "neither today's society nor that to which we are progressing allow an uncritical survival of older forms and models" (no. 32).

In such context, we face the urgent need of rediscovering and proposing anew the beauty of marriage (no. 205) as "a dynamic path to personal development and fulfillment" (no. 37) where love can endure and grow (no. 131), and where spouses can "help one another become, respectively, more a man and more a woman" (no. 221). This means shifting from lament to witness, from the defensive denouncing of a decadent world to "being proactive in proposing ways of finding true happiness" (no. 38). Instead of being discouraged and "trapped into wasting our energy in doleful laments" (no. 57), the Pope invites us to look at the current challenges as a "summons to revive our hope and to make it the source of prophetic visions, transformative actions and creative forms of charity" (no. 57). We are called to a renewed missionary impetus that with creativity goes "out to where people are" (no. 230), not limiting ourselves to being like the beacon of a lighthouse for those who are seeking help, but becoming like a "torch carried among the people to enlighten those who have lost their way or who are in the midst of a storm" (no. 291).

To adopt a missionary style, Francis stresses that it is necessary to concentrate on the essentials, on what is "most beautiful, most excellent, most appealing and at the same time most necessary" (no. 58). The kerygma – "the beauty of the saving love of God made manifest in Jesus Christ who died and rose from the dead" (*Evangelii Gaudium*, no. 36)[79] – needs to be put at the center of our evangelizing activity (no. 58) so that people might discover that the Gospel "responds to the deepest expectations of the human person" (no. 201). Nothing is more important to this renewed missionary evangelization than the joy-filled witness of families (no. 200) that by reflecting the beauty of the Gospel in their lives arouse the desire for God in those they meet (no. 184). Faith is a gift, but "its care is entrusted to us" (no. 287). By genuinely trusting God, seeking him, and sensing our need for him, we offer our creative commitment to cooperate with the Lord's plan for those he gives us and, in this way, speak to others of Jesus. With a beautiful expression, Francis invites us to let "our lives become wonderfully complicated" (no. 308) because of our willingness to get involved with people's lives to help them grow "in appreciation of the demands of the Gospel" (no. 38).

In a passage that shows Francis's impressive capacity to discern the signs of the time, the Pope warns us that "today, it is less and less effective to demand something that calls for effort and sacrifice, without clearly pointing to the benefits which it can bring" (no. 265). This means that the proclamation of objective truths is not enough to convert people's hearts. For our witness to impact the lives of others, we need to realize that "a good ethical education includes showing a person that it is in his own interest to do what is right" (no. 265), so we need to help others "arrive at the point where the good that the intellect grasps can take root in us as a profound affective inclination, as a thirst for the good that outweighs other attractions and helps us to realize that what we consider objectively good is also good 'for us' here and now" (no. 265). Without this step, the Church's teachings end up being perceived as a burden rather than a source of joy.

For the same reason, the Church is also "called to form consciences, not to replace them" (no. 37) because, for a person to grow in maturity and certainty, she needs to learn the capacity to use freedom wisely and responsibly so that she may "come to possess the wherewithal needed to fend for [herself] and to act intelligently and prudently whenever [she] meet[s] with difficulties" (no. 261). As families do with their children, the Church too needs to educate people by cultivating their freedom so that each one may "act out of conscious

---

[79] On the primacy of the *kerygma*, see also Ambrogetti and Rubin, *Pope Francis*, 103-105.

and free choice, as moved and drawn in a personal way from within" (no. 267).[80]

Moral education, though, does not happen all of a sudden. As we can easily see in the lives of children, education is a journey made of small steps (no. 271). This is true not only for children but everybody. No one, in fact, "drops down from heaven perfectly formed" (no. 325), and everybody needs "constantly to grow and mature in the ability to love" (no. 325). What we need is a journey, which is why Francis encourages us to "stop demanding of our interpersonal relationships a perfection, a purity of intentions and a consistency which we will only encounter in the Kingdom to come" (no. 325). Rather than being scandalized by our weaknesses and limitations, we should be aware that a person always "knows, loves and accomplishes moral good by different stages of growth" (no. 295), thus trusting that "the Lord's presence dwells in real and concrete families, with all their daily troubles and struggles, joys and hopes" (no. 315).

Conclusion

Amoris Laetitia stands as a powerful example of how, following in the footsteps of the Second Vatican Council, Pope Francis is helping us deepen our understanding of Christian morality as primarily attending to and following the life of Jesus, whose very way of being, to say it with Imbelli, "manifests the true humanity God desires."[81] Theological reflections about morality need to start from the gratuitous initiative that God took in coming to meet us in Jesus Christ, and the primacy of this grace that introduced a new way of being and living in the world needs to be cherished and rediscovered ever anew, without being relegated to a mere presupposition. Accordingly, when it comes to the work of moral theology, the renewed Christological focus advocated by Pope Francis entails the need to give priority to the Scriptural witness, especially the Gospels, thus overcoming the modern opposition between truth and history. As Lopez argues, "the universal truth that Christ re-presents and his historical singular existence [...] are inseparable,"[82] which means that the universal call of Christian morality happens only through the particularity of God's self-revelation in Jesus Christ. It is because of the importance of Jesus's testimony that Francis encourages theologians to better

---

[80] The need to educate people's freedom to foster their maturity has been a constant concern of Francis, even before being elected Pope. For example, see the messages he wrote to teachers while he was bishop of Buenos Aires that are collected in *Education for Choosing Life: Proposals for Difficult Times* (California: Ignatius Press, 2014), 83-117.
[81] Imbelli, *Rekindling the Christic Imagination*, 7.
[82] Lopez, "Vatican II's Catholicity," 88.

incorporate mercy within moral theology for, as he says, "Although it is quite true that concern must be shown for the integrity of the Church's moral teaching, special care should always be shown to emphasize and encourage the highest and most central values of the Gospel, particularly the primacy of charity as a response to the completely gratuitous offer of God's love" (*Amoris Laetitia*, no. 311).

The discussion regarding the implications of Francis's emphasis on the fact that Christian morality represents a response to God's unforeseeable initiative for moral theology would be lengthy. Certainly, though, one way moral theologians can respond to the Pope's vision is to place discipleship at the center of their reflections, thus integrating the discussion of casuistry and moral norms with thick accounts of moral formation and the virtues. "Theology and holiness are inseparable,"[83] insists Pope Francis, because we learn in order to live and not to develop abstract systems. Of course moral theologians have to master a specific tradition of theological thinking that has its own technical language to address particular issues, but they should also be people "capable of building humanity around [them], passing on the divine Christian truth in a truly human dimension."[84] We ought avoid the temptation of becoming "bureaucrats of the sacred,"[85] striving instead to announce the Gospel in a way that "meets the needs of the people to whom it should be proclaimed in an understandable and meaningful way."[86]

Furthermore, it is important never to forget the ecclesiological context of theology and the moral life. One cannot be a disciple alone; instead, as *Lumen Gentium* states, God saves human beings by bringing them "together as one people, a people which acknowledges Him in truth and serves Him in holiness" (no. 9). Salvation consists in being made part of a story that God started without us, but that nonetheless has reached us and is proposed to us through the new polity that God created, namely, the Church. This is why moral theology needs to pay greater attention to and find its inspiration in the practices that constitute the moral formation of the faithful within the Church, the liturgy and the sacraments above all.

Finally, moral theology needs also to go beyond theologically neutral accounts of human nature and natural law, for, as Francis beautifully explained, an authentic anthropology starts from the centrality of Jesus.[87] Christian humanism, in fact, is "the humanism of

---

[83] Francis, "Letter to the Grand Chancellor of the 'Pontificia Universidad Catolica Argentina,'" March 3, 2015.
[84] Francis, "Letter to the Grand Chancellor."
[85] Francis, "Letter to the Grand Chancellor."
[86] Francis, "Letter to the Grand Chancellor."
[87] Francis, "Meeting with the Participants in the Fifth Convention of the Italian Church."

the 'mind of Christ Jesus' (Philemon 2:5)."[88] There are many signs that the Enlightenment project of affirming Christian values while separating them from Christ has failed. Now it is the time to follow Francis's call to take up a "shared commitment [...] which brings us back to the essential and which is solidly focused on the essential; that is, on Jesus Christ. To get diverted by many secondary or superfluous things does not help; what helps is to focus on the fundamental reality, which is the encounter with Christ, with his mercy and with his love, and to love our brothers and sisters as he has loved us."[89] By taking up this invitation, moral theologians can not only renew and advance their discipline, but also, and most importantly, give their contribution to great Church's mission of bringing salvation and healing to the world. Ⓜ

---

[88] Francis, "Meeting with the Participants in the Fifth Convention of the Italian Church."
[89] Francis, "Address to Participants in the Plenary of the Pontifical Council for Promoting the New Evangelization," October 14, 2013. I am grateful to Kent Lasnoski, Matthew Whelan, Mark Fisher, Stanley Hauerwas, Ramón Luzárraga, James F. Keenan, Alan Schreck, Grattan Brown, Jane Russell, Rachelle Ramirez, and all the members of New Wine New Wineskins for their comments on earlier versions of this article.

Morality, Human Nature, and the Sacred Heart of Jesus

Joshua Evans

CHRISTIANS HAVE LONG BEEN putting the following pointed question to Jesus: "Why are we commanded to imitate you? Were we born of the Holy Spirit and of the Virgin Mary?" (*c. Iul. imp.* IV.87).[1] Jesus is the Son of God, fully human and fully divine. At our worst moments, we might act like we are gods, but, deep down, we know we are frail, finite, mortal beings. Forgiving our enemies is the closest we get to performing miracles. Jesus is like us, but he is better than us, and his being "better" seems to have a lot to do with his divine nature. How, then, can we be expected to imitate him? Furthermore, if Christ's virtue is a function of his divine nature, then how is Jesus truly human? If he is human and divine and we are merely human, it seems that we cannot be like him and he cannot be like us.

This problem—we are expected to imitate a person who is at the same time human and divine—is not only one for spiritual groups and pastoral conversations. Theologian Gerald O'Collins helpfully sums up the problem classical Christology—two natures, one person—poses for moral theology: "How could we reconcile an absolute, intrinsic impeccability with Christ's complete humanity—in particular, with his genuine human freedom? If Jesus could not have sinned under any circumstances whatsoever, was he truly free? Furthermore…[i]f, absolutely speaking, Jesus could not have disobeyed the divine will, how could he then have identified with the human condition?"[2] Jesus's invitation to "come, follow me" seems to be a kind of cruel mockery of our impotent ability to imitate him fully, much like Superman challenging us to a race.

There are essentially two theological solutions to this problem entailed by classical Christology. One solution is to suggest that the moral life Jesus exemplifies and invites us into is not different in kind

---

[1] Unless otherwise stated, for any of Augustine's works cited herein, I will use the following English translation: "Unfinished Work in Answer to Julian," in *Answer to the Pelagians III: The Works of Saint Augustine: A Translation for the 21st Century* I/25, trans. by Roland J. Teske (New York: New City Press, 1999).

[2] Gerald O'Collins, *Christology: A Biblical, Historical, and Systematic Study of Jesus*, Second Edition (New York: Oxford, 2009), 269.

from what is possible for human nature as such. That is, both the moral teachings of Christianity and the person of Jesus are not so foreign to the human nature we inhabit. As a result, we are able to imitate Jesus because his being born of the Holy Spirit does not mean that his moral capabilities are different in kind from human nature as such. This solution is offered in both ancient and contemporary Christian thought, and it is widely respected. Within this solution there are two distinct but complementary kinds of approaches.

The first is a certain version of the natural law approach to morality. Fr. John Piderit, for instance, begins with what seems like an uncontroversial claim: "The pursuit of excellence is somewhere in our human genes."[3] This pursuit of excellence does not necessarily require any unique insight or ability possessed by Jesus: "Natural law does assume that a person believes in God, but it does not rely on belief in the divinity of Christ. God is the creator and God places us in the world in a framework by which we can know what God wants us to do. However, the natural law conviction is that by our human nature, we know what it is that we are supposed to strive for and what we are supposed to avoid."[4] Catholic virtue is something we are capable of achieving just by being human. Another example of this perspective comes from Lawler, Boyle and May's popular book *Catholic Sexual Ethics: A Summary, Explanation, & Defense.* According to these authors, while desire can go awry, "[s]exual desire and emotional affectivity are part of the raw stuff out of which authentic human love can be shaped, but this material needs to be shaped intelligently if it is to become integrally and fully a component of love." They apply this account of chastity to Christ:

> Jesus, the complete human, provides a striking model of chastity. He is a sexual being, a virile yet affectionate male. His life was full of close and affectionate friendships with men and women alike. Yet Jesus was a celibate, a virgin because of the demands of his personal vocation as redeemer of the world. His example teaches us that the chaste person is the one who has his or her priorities right, who intelligently loves the goods of human nature and integrates his or her affective life into the vocation by which each one of us is called by God to pursue these goods.[5]

---

[3] John Piderit, S.J., *Sexual Morality: A Natural Law Approach to Intimate Relationships* (New York: Oxford, 2011), 8.
[4] Piderit, *Sexual Morality*, 45.
[5] Ronald Lawler, Joseph Boyle Jr., and William E. May, *Catholic Sexual Ethics: A Summary, Explanation, & Defense*, Second Edition (Indiana: Our Sunday Visitor Press, 1998): 124-25.

While this kind of natural law approach might not make significant Christological claims, it does seem to answer the questions that opened this essay by saying that we are able to imitate Jesus because he too is human just like us. Implicitly, it seems that his divine nature does not impact his ability to live out the moral life. We might say that on this view Jesus is the Most Virtuous Man in the philosophical sense: the man who lives the virtues to their fullest human extent.

A complementary approach also suggests that Jesus is not so different from us, and to do so this approach "humanizes" Jesus in a way that seems to avoid the chasm between Jesus and us that is at the heart of classical Christology. This approach is not so much about the content of morality as it is about interpreting Jesus as a familiar exemplar. Fr. Thomas Weinandy has given a very fascinating account of this interpretation of Jesus.[6] Weinandy's core claim is "Only if Jesus assumed a humanity at one with the fallen race of Adam could his death and resurrection heal and save that humanity."[7] That is, Jesus must have adopted fallen human nature in all its senses (except for the propensity to sin) if he is to be the savior and moral exemplar of humanity: "To be *homoousious* [of the same substance] with us demands more than an ahistorical sameness of species, but a communion with us as we are in reality—brothers and sisters defiled by the sin of Adam."[8] This Christology becomes clearly relevant to moral theology in Weinandy's account of the temptations of Jesus toward sin. Jesus, though he lacked concupiscence, must have had even worse temptations than the rest of us because he was never undivided in his desires: temptations "confronted him with a sharpness and force we do not experience."[9] It was Jesus's very human experience of temptations that made him a true savior: "Only [because] the Son inherited an enfeebled humanity does his sinless life possess any soteriological value."[10] On Weinandy's view, it was the deeply human life of Jesus that enabled him to become the savior and moral exemplar for the rest of us. As with the version of the natural law approach above, Weinandy also avoids the objection that Jesus is not our moral exemplar because of his human and divine natures. Rather, it is Jesus's inhabiting of the fullness of fallen humanity that makes him our moral exemplar. He becomes just like us, and, because of that, we can be like him.

These two kinds of approaches are long-standing and widely respected, and I will show below that these approaches are anticipated

---

[6] Thomas Weinandy, *In the Likeness of Sinful Flesh: An Essay on the Humanity of Christ* (Edinburgh: T & T Clark, 1993).
[7] Weinandy, *In the Likeness of Sinful Flesh*, 28.
[8] Weinandy, *In the Likeness of Sinful Flesh*, 35.
[9] Weinandy, *In the Likeness of Sinful Flesh*, 99.
[10] Weinandy, *In the Likeness of Sinful Flesh*, 38.

in the thought of an important ancient theologian. This essay argues, however, that there is a better approach to understanding the relationship between Christ's human and divine natures and the moral life to which we are called. The outlines of this alternative approach are rooted in the patristic tradition, and the details of this approach are given expression in a unique way in recent papal writings on the Sacred Heart of Jesus. If the essential question is how we mere humans can imitate someone who is both human and divine, the approach defended in this essay suggests that the question is based on false premises. I argue that Augustine of Hippo shows us why it is good news for us that the human nature of Jesus is impacted by its confluence with his divine nature, and then I argue that recent popes—I focus primarily on Pius XI and Pius XII—apply this assumption to their interpretations of Jesus as moral exemplar in their writings on the Sacred Heart of Jesus. Perhaps the turn to the Sacred Heart is unexpected; it is not, however, unfitting. The Sacred Heart of Jesus is not merely a devotional image but also a symbol expressing the deepest core of the person of Jesus.[11] The popes give us good reason to think that the confluence of divinity and humanity in the one person of Jesus is crucial for our understanding of a moral life in imitation of Jesus.

AUGUSTINE AND THE TRANSFORMATION OF HUMAN NATURE

Augustine is relevant to this essay for two reasons, both related. First, he very clearly connects his Christology to his claims about both moral theology and soteriology, and, in that way, he gives us an example of what might be called "Christological morality." His Christology shapes and is shaped by his other commitments regarding the nature of creation, the effects of grace, and the purpose of redemption. Second, much of what he has to say comes within his engagement with a long-time theological opponent, Julian of Eclanum, and Julian's ideas in many ways anticipate the same solutions offered by the approaches that we saw at the beginning of this essay. What Augustine has to say in response to Julian can also be extended as a response to those more recent approaches. Augustine clears away the objections, and then the popes help to fill in the details regarding why classical Christology is good news for moral theology.

Writing in the Mediterranean world in the early fifth century, Julian was the most consequential theologian of what has been called Pelagianism. As a good Pelagian, Julian believed in the integrity of creation and rejected any concept of the fall: "All elements in

---

[11] Karl Rahner, S.J., "Devotion to the Sacred Heart," *Theological Investigations,* Volume 3, trans. Karl Kruger and Boniface Kruger (New York: Crossroads, 1982), 321-52.

absolutely all creatures which are found to be natural were made in the very best way so that any supposed improvement in them is found to be stupid and sacrilegious" (*c. Iul. imp.* V.15). Julian explains the seemingly problematic elements of creation by saying, essentially, that they are not actually problematic: "From God's wisdom [human beings] received in their bodies beautiful parts and shameful parts so that they might learn in themselves both modesty and confidence" (*c. Iul. imp.* V.15). If nature as it currently exists is in the pristine condition God intends for it, then it would be logically impossible for Jesus to have a human nature that was both different and better than ours. For Julian, our human nature sets the standard for what it means to be human. As a result, Christ's relation to moral theology is exclusively as moral exemplar and teacher, much like the philosopher's virtuous man. We are able to imitate Jesus because, like us, he is human, and there could be no way to possess a human nature better than what we possess because all of creation is integrally perfect in the way God intends it.

Because of the Pelagian commitment to the integrity of creation, Pelagians necessarily reject the claim that God must enable human beings to achieve their full flourishing through the infusion of grace. No extra help is needed. Indeed, extra help would be a detriment to human freedom and human flourishing. The same must be true of Jesus. He cannot both be truly human and have had extra help in living a virtuous life. To say as much would be to "separate the nature of Christ from the community of human beings" (*c. Iul. imp.* IV.50 [429]). Rather, according to Julian, "We are emphatically taught by clear testimony that the righteousness of the man he assumed came, not from the difference of his nature, but from his voluntary action" (*c. Iul. imp.* IV.84 [449]).

If it were otherwise—if Jesus was uniquely enabled to live out virtue because of the confluence of human and divine in his one person—then he would not be a fitting example for us: "Whom would he have presented to human beings for their imitation, if the nature of a strange flesh set him apart and if the difference of his substance undermined the severity of his teaching" (*c. Iul. imp.* IV.86 [451]). From Julian's perspective, Augustine's Christology is loathsome: "As someone more fortunate by birth, not by virtue, [Jesus] would have lost not only trophies won by his actions, but would have also been pressed with charges of fraud if he said to mortals: Strive for the patience of him who feels nothing, and come through true crosses to the virtues of a false body that suffers nothing.... Certainly nothing more irreligious, nothing more wicked can be thought up than these lies" (*c. Iul. imp.* IV.49-50). Not only would Jesus be an impossible exemplar to imitate, but he would not even be worthy of imitation. On the other hand, if Jesus is just like us in that his connection to the divine did not affect his humanity in a unique way then we are able to imitate him and he is worthy of our respect and admiration. He lives human nature better than us, but we are able to live it as he lives it.

Augustine has a few pointed questions that seem to undermine Julian's tidy connections between Christology and moral theology. The essential question for Augustine is this: "Did...that assumption of a human nature which made God and man one person contribute nothing to that man toward the excellence of the righteousness you say he had from voluntary action?" (*c. Iul. imp.* IV.84 [450]) Augustine's answer is, of course, that Christ's "excellence of righteousness" did come somehow from the confluence of divine and human in his one person. Augustine offers three penetrating criticisms of Julian's Christology that suggest Augustine is right to defend this claim.

First, in response to Julian's claim that Christ's virtue is exclusively a matter of human willpower, Augustine wonders whether Julian gains Christ's moral exemplarity at the extreme cost of implicitly advocating an Adoptionist Christology:

> Does the defense of free choice so drive you headlong against the grace of God that you say that even the mediator himself merited by his will to be the only Son of God?....For, according to you, the man was not assumed by the Word of God so that he was born of the Virgin, but having been born of the Virgin, he afterward made progress by the power of his own will and brought it about that he was assumed by the Word of God. That is, he did not have a will of such goodness and greatness because of that union, but arrived at that union by a will of such goodness and greatness. And the Word was not made flesh in the womb of the Virgin, but afterward by the merit of the man and his human and voluntary virtue. (*c. Iul. imp.* IV.84 [450])

In other words, Julian's assumption that Christ's virtue cannot be a consequence of being the Son of God seems to suggest that being supremely virtuous caused him to become the Son of God. A corresponding problem for Julian is that Christ loses his distinctiveness as Son and Savior: "It also follows for you [Julian] that, as you believe that he was assumed by the Word of God because he willed to be, so you believe that many could have been assumed in that way, if they too had likewise willed it, or could be assumed if they would will it." Christ's distinctiveness is only one of degree, not of kind, and the moral exemplarity of Christ is an implicit judgment on the rest of us: Jesus "turns out to be the only [Christ] because of the laziness of the human will, though there could have been more, if human beings had willed it" (*c. Iul. imp.* IV.84).

In a second kind of response, Augustine also pushes back against Julian's account of virtue and its relation to sin and temptation. On Julian's terms, if virtue is found in conquering desires, then Julian seems to hold that people are "more praiseworthy in their virtue to the extent that they resist more strongly a greater good than if they fought against a lesser one" (*c. Iul. imp.* IV.53 [431]). Thus it would make sense, on Julian's terms, that "Christ ought to have been most filled with desires in his flesh, just as he was the greatest of all human beings in his virtue" (*c. Iul. imp.* IV.49). To be the most virtuous man, he must have undergone the most extreme temptations. This is perfectly logical if one assumes that virtue is premised on the possibility of vice. Augustine completely rejects that premise in his third criticism of Julian's views.

Augustine's third criticism is at the intersection of soteriology and eschatology. If human nature as it exists now is in the pristine condition God intended for it then what was the point of Christ's death and resurrection? The point would not seem to be a transformation of human nature from fallen to eventually perfected in heaven. In fact, Julian's claims about the pristine state of human nature now and the necessity of the possibility of sin for human virtue seem to entail that there can be no transformation into something better in heaven. Augustine draws out the logical conclusion of Julian's premises: "You say that human nature 'could not have been capable of its own good, unless it were also capable of evil.' Why, then, after piously living this life will it be capable of good alone and not of evil, removed, that is, not only from all will or necessity, but even from the possibility of sinning? Or will we perhaps have to fear that we might sin even when we will be equal to the holy angels?" (*c. Iul. imp.* V.58 [582]) Julian's claim that the possibility of sin is essential to human nature seems to mean that Christ does not overcome sin once for all, but instead the fight against sin is projected even into heaven. Or, if Julian wants to say that there is no possibility of sin in heaven, he must say that human nature does not exist in heaven, because human nature cannot exist without the possibility of sin. Human beings who cannot sin—such as the saints in heaven—are not really human beings on Julian's account. On Julian's terms, heaven entails the annihilation of human nature.

From Augustine's perspective, the entire point of calling Christ our moral exemplar is that Christ reveals to us a better way to be human. He overcomes the limitations inherent to "fallen" human nature and elevates us through grace to become like him. Augustine writes, "It has, rather, become clear that the nature of human beings, in comparison to that integrity, rectitude, and good health in which it was originally created, now has all these things to a lesser degree. Christ came to restore this nature to integrity, to correct it, and to heal it, for he had integrity without any corruption, rectitude without any depravity, good health without any desire for sin" (*c. Iul. imp.* IV.59 [437]). One of the fundamental differences between Jesus and us is that Jesus did not suffer from the effects of original sin: "Christ, then, who most perfectly fulfilled the law, desired nothing that was forbidden, because he certainly did not have the discord between the flesh and the spirit which was turned into the nature of human beings by the transgression of the first human being, for he was born of the Spirit and the Virgin, not through the concupiscence of the flesh." Augustine immediately applies this Christological claim to moral theology: "With this example of perfection set before us, each imitator ought to aim at this: to strive and to long not to have at all the desires of the flesh which the apostle [Paul] forbids us to carry out. For in that way we can by daily progress lessen those desires which we will not have at all when salvation is complete" (*c. Iul. imp.* IV.57 [435]). Christ's perfection is not a cause of our despair. His perfection is the reason to have hope for ourselves, because he anticipates what we hope to become.

What Augustine means by "when salvation is complete" is quite straightforward: we are not fully saved until we rise from the dead and enter fully into God's glory. Augustine fills this claim out by reflecting on a passage from 1 Corinthians:

> *And so, just as we have borne the image of the earthly man, so let us bear the image of the heavenly man.* The former is repeated as a fact; the latter is given as a command. The former is, of course, already present; the latter is in the future. And so, we have borne the former image because of the condition of being born and because of the contagion of sin, but we bear this latter image because of the grace of being reborn. But we meanwhile bear it in hope; we shall bear it in reality as a reward when we shall rise and reign in blessedness and righteousness (*c. Iul. imp.* VI.31 [696]).

The salvation that Christ brings is lived out now through our imitation of him but is only fully realized when the last evil has been overcome.

What the contrast between Augustine and Julian shows us is that Christ's distinctive virtue is good news for us because it anticipates the life to which Christ calls us. Julian's account of Christ's merely human virtue is compelling only if we think that the best we can hope for is to capitalize on the intrinsic capacities of human nature as we experience it now. For Augustine, on the other hand, the divinely human virtue of Jesus highlights the way in which grace perfects nature and takes nature where it cannot go on its own. The *telos* of Augustine's account of morality is not merely the virtue of the philosophers but a sharing in the perfection of human nature lived out by Jesus: "Christ was said to be the heavenly man even according to the flesh, not because he took his flesh from heaven, but because he raised it too up into heaven" (*c. Iul. imp.* VI.40 [714]). Christ's experience of a humanity that completely lacks sin and struggle and, after the resurrection, even the possibility of death, is what we hope for: "By forgiving our debts and by not bringing us into temptation, he brings us to the final victory by which the death even of the body will be swallowed up so that those who boast do not trust in their own virtue, but boast in the Lord" (*c. Iul. imp.* VI.41 [720]). Christ's divinely human virtue is bad news only if we are attached to the limited, fallen human nature we now inhabit.

CHRISTOLOGY OF THE SACRED HEART

If we turn to recent papal encyclicals on the Sacred Heart of Jesus, we can see a robust application of the kind of transformative Christological moral theology advocated by Augustine. For Augustine and the popes, true salvation is the integration of our own lives according to the life of God, the bringing of all aspects of our identity into harmony so that by our very lives we honor and worship God. What we see in Christ's Sacred Heart is the model for integration. Christ's heart is infused with divine love, so that Christ sees all things and loves all things in a way consonant with a human life fully permeated by God's life.

As the *Catechism of the Catholic Church* says in its section on the Incarnation, quoting Pius XII, the Sacred Heart of Jesus "'is quite rightly considered the chief sign and symbol of that ... love with which the divine Redeemer continually loves the eternal Father and all human beings without exception" (no. 478). The *Catechism* could have also referred to Pius XI, who suggests that the Sacred Heart contains "the sum of all religion and therefore the pattern of more perfect life" (*Miserentissimus Redemptor*, no. 3). It could also have gone a bit further back, to Leo XIII, who consecrated the entire world to the Sacred Heart, proclaiming, "In that Sacred Heart all our hopes should be placed, and from it the salvation of men is to be confidently sought" (*Annum Sacrum*, no. 12). Of course, we also have the writings and homilies of John XXIII, Paul VI, John Paul II, Benedict XVI, and Francis to mine for insights.[12] The rich history of papal reflection on

---

[12] For instance, see Pope Benedict XVI, "Letter of His Holiness Benedict XVI on Occasion of the Fiftieth Anniversary of the Encyclical '*Haurietis Aquas*,'" May 15, 2006, w2.vatican.va/content/benedict-xvi/en/letters/2006/documents/hf_ben-xvi_let_20060515_50-haurietis-aquas.html: "When we practice this devotion, not only do we recognize God's love with gratitude but we continue to open ourselves to this love so that our lives are ever more closely patterned upon it." Other representative papal writings on the Sacred Heart include Paul VI's apostolic letter *Investigabiles Divitias Christi*, February 6, 1965, w2.vatican.va/content/paul-vi/la/apost_letters/documents/hf_p-vi_apl_19650206_investigabiles-divitias.html; John Paul II, "Letter of John Paul II on the 100th Anniversary of the Consecration of the Human Race to the Divine Heart of Jesus," June 11, 1999, w2.vatican.va/content/john-paul-ii/en/letters/1999/documents/hf_jp-ii_let_19990611_consagrazione-sacro-cuore.html; John Paul II's encyclical *Dives in Misericordia*, November 30, 1980, w2.vatican.va/content/john-paul-ii/en/encyclicals/documents/hf_jp-ii_enc_30111980_dives-in-misericordia.html. For two useful secondary texts, see Timothy O'Donnell, *The Heart*

the Sacred Heart unfailingly suggests that the Sacred Heart is a privileged and distinctively important Christian reality to which theology should turn.

For the Popes, reflection on the Sacred Heart does not remain merely at the level of recognition that in the heart of Jesus God shows his love for us. Rather, reflection on the Sacred Heart also teaches us how to properly respond to the love God has for us. In other words, the Sacred Heart is immediately relevant for moral theology. For example, for a period in the mid-twentieth century, the Sacred Heart of Jesus was an important point of reference for Catholic Social Teaching, a connection modeled on Pius XI's social encyclical of the Sacred Heart, *Caritate Christi Compulsi*.[13] More importantly for our purposes here, the popes draw out fundamental principles regarding what the Sacred Heart has to teach us about being truly human in the way that the Son of God is truly human.

Below I draw from the papal encyclicals two essential points for moral theology inspired by the Sacred Heart. The first is that theological reflection on the Sacred Heart highlights in a unique way that human nature is in need of healing. In contrast to those theologies that attempt to humanize Jesus to be more like us, a moral theology informed by reflection on the Sacred Heart emphasizes that it is precisely in gazing on the pure, Sacred Heart of Jesus that we see how desperately we need a savior. By looking at Christ, we recognize that we are ill and we realize with more certainty why the Church must be, in the words of Pope Francis, a "field hospital."[14] Second and relatedly, the popes point out that the healing process for our wounded nature can only be understood by looking at a fully healthy human nature: as Pius XI puts it, Christ's heart contains "the pattern of more perfect life" (*Miserentissimus Redemptor*, no. 3). Christ shares in our nature precisely in order to heal and save it, and that healing and saving is already on display in the way Christ lives a distinctive life of virtue.

Pope Pius XI, who was pope between the two great wars (1922-1939), emphasizes more than any recent pope that the Christian call to perfection corresponds fundamentally to the Christian claim that

---

of the Redeemer (California: Ignatius Press, 1994) and Prosper Gueranger, "Feast of the Sacred Heart of Jesus," in *The Liturgical Year: Time After Pentecost* (London: Burns & Oates, 1901).

[13] See Carl Moell, "America and the Sacred Heart," *America: The Jesuit Review*, May 26, 1956, americamagazine.org/issue/100/america-and-sacred-heart, which summarizes *America* magazine's period of important articles on the Sacred Heart and social ethics.

[14] Antonio Spadaro, "A Big Heart Open to God: An Interview with Pope Francis," *America: The Jesuit Review*, September 30, 2013, americamagazine.org/pope-interview.

human beings are fallen. According to Pius XI, both the recognition of our fallen nature and the call to perfection have been drowned out in recent times by the noise of a kind of neo-Pelagian naturalism very reminiscent of the thought of Julian of Eclanum. This new naturalism has infiltrated modern society and ethics: "The wise men of this age of ours … following the ancient error of Pelagius, ascribe to human nature a certain native virtue by which of its own force it can go onward to higher things" (*Miserentissimus Redemptor*, no. 8). The "pernicious error" of neo-Pelagianism is the presumption that "the instinctive tendencies of the will are, all of them, good, and hence are neither to be feared or checked" (*Ad Salutem Humani*, no. 36).[15] For the neo-Pelagians, there would not seem to be a need for a new model of perfection since that need would be based on the false assumption that something is wrong with humanity. Neo-Pelagians suggest both that we are not wounded and that we do not need healing. Or, one might say, healing for neo-Pelagians is found precisely in embracing "the instinctive tendencies of the will."

For Pius XI, reflection on the Sacred Heart necessarily requires the admission of our own imperfection, rooted in our complicity in Adam's sin.[16] Through seeing the Sacred Heart we are reminded that we are sinners redeemed. Returning love to God is of course the "first and foremost thing in" devotion to the Sacred Heart, but our return of love is intimately connected to what Pius calls reparation or expiation: a love flowing from the admission of our sinfulness.[17] In other words, the point of devotion to the Sacred Heart is that we "might have a more vehement hatred of sin, and make a more ardent return of love for His love" (*Miserentissimus Redemptor*, no. 11).[18] As an alternative to the emergent neo-Pelagianism, Pius advises us to "crucify our flesh with its vices and concupiscences," in order that "the life of Jesus may be

---

[15] This encyclical is published as *Encyclical Letter of Pope Pius XI on "Saint Augustine,"* trans. Vatican Press (Washington, DC: National Catholic Welfare Conference, 1930).

[16] See *Miserentissimus Redemptor*, no. 8: "Moreover, this duty of expiation is laid upon the whole race of men since, as we are taught by the Christian faith, after Adam's miserable fall, infected by hereditary stain, subject to concupiscences and most wretchedly depraved, it would have been thrust down into eternal destruction."

[17] See *Miserentissimus Redemptor*, nos. 6–7: "For since we are all sinners and laden with many faults, our God must be honored by us not only by that worship wherewith we adore His infinite Majesty with due homage, or acknowledge His supreme dominion by praying, or praise His boundless bounty by thanksgiving; but besides this we must need make satisfaction to God the just avenger, 'for our numberless sins and offenses and negligences.'"

[18] For Pius, this hatred of sin is emphasized above through a kind of fire-and-brimstone exhortation that closes out the document. Pius reminds us sinners to fear that we "shall bewail" ourselves when we "see Him whom they pierced 'coming in the clouds of heaven'" (no. 21).

manifested in our mortal flesh" (*Miserentissimus Redemptor*, no. 9).[19] The contrast between the Sacred Heart and our hearts unfailingly shows us that our human nature is in need of healing.

It is tempting to see a kind of fear-mongering in Pius XI's warnings about neo-Pelagianism. Is it really so bad to think that our "instinctive tendencies" are good? Might one not say that seeing in human nature "a certain native virtue by which of its own force it can go onward to higher things" is a great compliment to God's creation (*Miserentissimus Redemptor*, no. 8)? Pius shows in a second encyclical on the Sacred Heart why an overly-trusting attitude toward human nature *is* so bad for human life. In *Caritate Christi Compulsi* (1932), Pius XI suggests that the consequences of neo-Pelagian attitudes to human nature can clearly be seen in the wreckage left in the wake of the great financial crisis of the time. Trusting in the natural virtue of human desires leads to substantial problems. In 1932, it was not an overstatement for Pius to point out that "the desire of money is the root of all evils" (no. 3). According to Pius it is a short distance from neo-Pelagian ethics to the world's financial destitution: avaricious desire, in its early stages, breeds "mutual suspicion" and fosters a "self-love which orders and subordinates all things to its own advantage," the consequence of which is an "unequal division of 'possessions'" (no. 3). By forgetting God and focusing only on human nature, we fail to distinguish between the "legitimate appetites of nature" and our "unbridled lusts" (no. 6). This forgetting of God "removes all checks from the most powerful lusts of man," causing us to omit "the idea of an original sin and of a first rebellion of man against God" (no. 23). The result of this neo-Pelagianism is a widespread "cupidity," a "sordid seeking for each one's own benefit," and the "insatiable greed for earthly goods" (nos. 3, 18). This unholy greed is "the chief reason why we see now, to our great sorrow, that mankind is brought to its present critical condition" (no. 3). Disordered desires and the pernicious errors of neo-Pelagianism are relevant to more than just the topics dealt with in *Casti Connubii*, the famous encyclical on marriage released under Pius XI. Lust is not confined to the bedroom, and fallen human nature is always with us.

For Pius, there is no question that humanity needs a savior who can break us out of the bonds of our "natural" desires and tendency toward sin. The "spirit of loving reparation" to the Sacred Heart, then, remains essential to human life, since it helps "the noble-hearted Christian subdue the base passions that tend to make him violate the moral order" (*Caritate Christi Compulsi*, nos. 25, 30). Reparation expressed through penance "is a weapon that strikes right at the root of all evil,

---

[19] I have substituted the RSV translation for the quotation from 2 Cor.

that is, at the lust of material wealth and the wanton pleasures of life" (no. 25). Reflection on the Sacred Heart of Jesus cannot fail to call us to this reparation, because the contrast between Christ's true humanity and our own limited human nature is so stark and our need for transformation so apparent.

If Pius XI places special emphasis on the ways the Sacred Heart turns us to see our own sinfulness, Pius XII builds upon Pius XI by showing how the human nature of Christ distilled in the concept of the Sacred Heart illuminates our sinfulness and points toward true virtue. Pius XII quotes Pius XI to establish that the Sacred Heart "more easily leads our minds to know Christ the Lord intimately and more effectively turns our hearts to love Him more ardently and to imitate him more perfectly" (*Haurietis Aquas*, no. 15). This love of Christ for us, according to Pius XII, is intimately connected to our own sinfulness. Quoting Hosea, Pius XII reminds us that God says to us, "I will draw them with the cords of Adam, with the bonds of love ... I will heal their wounds, I will love them" (*Haurietis Aquas*, no. 26).[20] Pius reminds us that the love of God is a healing love that seeks to overcome our brokenness and call us to a higher life than we can live on our own.

While approaches like Julian of Eclanum's claim to take the "true humanity" of Jesus seriously, the popes see their own Sacred Heart Christology as equally serious about Christ's human nature. Christians, says Pius, "must clearly understand the reasons why the Church gives the highest form of worship to the Heart of the divine Redeemer." First, "we recognize that His Heart, the noblest part of human nature, is hypostatically united to the Person of the divine Word." Secondly, "His Heart, more than all the other members of His body, is the natural sign and symbol of His boundless love for the human race" (*Haurietis Aquas*, nos. 21–22). In other words, the Sacred Heart is distinctively an image of the Incarnation because it is both human and sacred.

The love symbolized in the image of the Sacred Heart has three essential aspects, according to Pius XII. The first two are obvious: the love between the Father and Son, and the love of God for humanity (*Haurietis Aquas*, nos. 36–37). For our interests here, however, it is the third aspect of that love that matters most: the human love of Christ. As Pius says, "We must note well that His love was not entirely the spiritual love proper to God inasmuch as 'God is a spirit'" (no. 38).

---

[20] Here Pius is quoting Hosea 11:4–14:5. The text of Hosea used by him is of course from the Vulgate and so differs from modern translations. One is reminded here of Francis' exhortation to "heal the wounds," in Spadaro, "A Big Heart Open to God," www.americamagazine.org/pope-interview. See also Pope Francis, "Morning Meditation in the Chapel of the *Domus Sanctae Marthae*," February 5, 2015, m.vatican.va/content/francesco/en/cotidie/2015/documents/papa-francesco-cotidie_20150205_i-will-cure-you.html.

Rather, "The love which breathes from the Gospel, from the letters of the Apostles and the pages of the Apocalypse, all of which portray the love of the Heart of Jesus Christ, expresses not only divine love but also human sentiments of love. All who profess themselves Catholics accept this without question" (no. 38). The love symbolized by the Sacred Heart includes, in a special way, the human love of Jesus.

Pius has no doubt that the human love of the Sacred Heart is premised on Christ's true humanity.[21] Only someone truly human can love in a truly human way, and to deny Christ's true humanity is to be, in the words of John (quoted by Pius), "a seducer and the antichrist" (*Haurietis Aquas*, no. 39). Furthermore, according to Pius, if Christ's human nature is to be truly human, it must be truly embodied and emotional: "[S]ince there can be no doubt that Jesus Christ received a true body and had all the affections proper to the same, among which love surpassed all the rest, it is likewise beyond doubt that He was endowed with a physical heart like ours; for without this noblest part of the body the ordinary emotions of human life are impossible" (no. 41).

In turning to the emotions, Pius highlights a distinctive contribution of theological reflection on the Sacred Heart. As we have seen, for some accounts of Christian morality, it is Christ's emotions and temptations that show us in a unique way that Christ truly adopted our humanity. For Pius however, what is most relevant about Christ's emotions is their perfection, not merely their presence. It is precisely the interplay between Christ's divine and human natures that allows Christ to live a perfect emotional life free from internal temptation and sin.

> the Heart of Jesus Christ, hypostatically united to the divine Person of the Word, certainly beat with love and with the other emotions but these, joined to a human will full of divine charity and to the infinite love itself which the Son shares with the Father and the Holy Spirit, were in such complete unity and agreement that never among these three loves was there any contradiction or disharmony (*Haurietis Aquas*, no. 41).

Pius quotes Augustine to establish the crucial theological principle for a Christological moral theology: "Like a choir singing in harmony with the note that has been sounded, so should His Body learn from

---

[21] "Nothing, then, was wanting to the human nature which the Word of God united to Himself. Consequently, He assumed it in no diminished way, in no different sense in what concerns the spiritual and the corporeal: that is, it was endowed with intellect and will and the other internal and external faculties of perception, and likewise with the desires and all the natural impulses of the senses" (*Haurietis Aquas*, no. 40).

its Head" (no. 50).[22] To suggest that Christ cannot be the choir director unless he too sings a bit off key is to miss the point of having a choir director. His role as model and savior is rooted not in his struggle but in his exemplarity.

For both Augustine and the popes, Christian salvation is not merely a forensic claim about the significance of Christ's death on the cross and its mitigation of our guilt before God. Christian salvation is about the integration of our nature according to the love of God, and the model for that integration is Christ as both human and divine. The Sacred Heart, the encapsulation of a human nature infused by divine love, shows us that we are saved only through a transformation of our fallen nature into the very nature Christ reveals to us by being Emmanuel, "God with us." The Sacred Heart of Jesus shows that the human nature assumed by the Word is an earthly anticipation of the same human nature we will all possess when the Spirit that raised Christ from the dead fully infuses our human nature too (Rom. 8:11).

Conclusion

Pope Francis stands in the same long line of emphasizing the transformation of our human nature through theological reflection on the Sacred Heart of Jesus. Francis has a unique capacity for helping us see what is lost when we overlook or downplay the distinctiveness of the Christian call to perfection. He writes in his Lenten message for 2015: "In the Incarnation, in the earthly life, death, and resurrection of the Son of God, the gate between God and man, between heaven and earth, opens once for all." The encounter with Jesus is not a challenge to our humanity, as the questions that opened this essay seemed to assume, but is instead based on a need for a change in our humanity. For Francis, the encounter with Jesus points the way toward our need for a "formation of the heart." Francis invites us to pray to Jesus, in the words of the Litany of the Sacred Heart, "*Fac cor nostrum secunduum cor tuum.*"[23] That is, "make our hearts according to your heart." The need to have our hearts formed into the heart of Jesus is built into the logic of the Gospel. To think otherwise, to see Jesus merely as the best of what we are already capable of, is to settle for an ersatz version of salvation.

In a later homily, Francis highlights what happens when we prefer old wine to new: "if your heart is closed to the newness of the Holy Spirit, you will never reach the full truth.... your Christian life will be a half-and-half life, a patched up life, mended with new things but on a structure that is not open to the Lord's voice: a closed heart, because

---

[22] Here Pius is quoting Augustine, *Enarr. in Ps.* LXXXVII, 3.

[23] Francis, "Message of His Holiness Pope Francis for Lent 2015," October 4, 2014, w2.vatican.va/content/francesco/en/messages/lent/documents/papa-francesco_20141004_messaggio-quaresima2015.html.

you are not capable of changing the wineskins." The Pope exhorts us to pray that "the Lord give us the grace of an open heart, of a heart open to the voice of the Holy Spirit, which can discern what must not change because it is fundamental from what has to change in order to be able to receive the newness of the Holy Spirit."[24] While some would see in Francis's words merely an ecclesio-political shot across the bow of those of a certain rightward theological disposition and stale pastoral habits, what Francis is getting at is something much more fundamental. His emphasis on the newness of the Gospel is fundamentally an anthropological commitment about the need for a fundamental transformation of human life through God's help.

Francis emphasizes the "revolutionary" character of Christian morality, a revolution that is so new and surprising because in Jesus we encounter and respond to a kind of "unjust" mercy.[25] This mercy seems unjust to us precisely because it is so undeserved, since, in encountering Jesus, we see just how broken we are. Or, as the Pope puts it, "The privileged place of the encounter with Jesus Christ is my sin."[26] In suggesting that Jesus brings about a "revolution" in morality, Francis is expanding on a principle articulated in the Second Vatican Council's document *Gaudium et Spes*. According to the Council Fathers, "Christ, the new [*novissimus*; ever-new] Adam, by the revelation of the mystery of the Father and His love, fully reveals man to man himself and makes his supreme calling clear" (no. 22). It is Christ's true humanity that reveals us to ourselves and makes our supreme calling clear. The Word has assumed human flesh and "worked with human hands...thought with a human mind, acted by human choice, and loved with a human heart." Because of this true humanity, "He blazed a trail, and if we follow it, life and death are made holy and take on new meaning" (no. 22). Christ "is Himself the perfect man" who "restores [to us] the divine likeness which had been disfigured from the first sin onward" (no. 22). In gazing at Christ's human nature, we confirm our suspicions that we are not flourishing, and we thereby begin to catch a glimpse of the full flourishing of human nature found in "'the redemption of the body,'" a redemption in which our entire nature is enlivened by the Spirit and "the whole person is renewed from within" (no. 22). Christian morality is premised on a merciful healing of our sinfulness, and this healing is what

---

[24] Pope Francis, "Morning Meditation in the Chapel of the Domus Sanctae Marthae: New Wineskins," January 18, 2016, w2.vatican.va/content/francesco/en/cotidie/2016/documents/papa-francesco-cotidie_20160118_new-wineskins.html
[25] Silvina Premat, "The Attraction of the Cardinal," *Traces: Litterae Communionis*, July 2001, archivio.traces-cl.com/Giu2001/argent.htm.
[26] Pope Francis, "Address of His Holiness Pope Francis to the Communion and Liberation Movement," March 7, 2015, w2.vatican.va/content/francesco/en/speeches/2015/march/documents/papa-francesco_20150307_comunione-liberazione.html.

makes it necessary that Jesus "*primereas* us." That is, Jesus goes ahead of us and calls us forward.[27] Jesus "is like the almond blossom: the one that blooms first, and announces the arrival of spring."[28] What is new and revolutionary about this morality is that Jesus both models it for us and makes it possible for our hearts to be made into his heart. Ⓜ

---

[27] Francis, "Address."
[28] Francis, "Address."

Living the Mystery: Doctrine, Intellectual Disability, and Christian Imagination

Medi Ann Volpe

THIS ESSAY CONSIDERS THE ROLE of doctrine in spiritual and moral growth by examining the way it connects teaching, mystery and imagination. Contemplating the mystery of our salvation, I suggest, fosters humility, reminding us that what we *see* (physically or with the mind's eye) is not all that *is*. For the "rationally capacious,"[1] Christian teaching guides the constant giving-over of imagination and attention to the work of remembering Jesus faithfully.[2] Not every person requires this same blessing from doctrine, however. The question about how doctrine functions, specifically with respect to those who cannot grasp its technical or abstract principles, frames the discussion. The core of the analysis concerns the function of doctrine, yet my conclusion is fundamentally practical: doctrine builds up the body of Christ.

A question I was asked when I was a teaching assistant at Duke provides a good point of departure. The student (a bright MDiv student, who has since earned a PhD and embarked on his own academic career) wanted to know what the real problem was with Arianism. On his view, the Christian life consisted in an orientation to the world summed up (usually) in the idea of "following Jesus." To follow Jesus implied, in its turn, a set of practices corresponding to a

---

[1] For discussion of the "rationally capacious" and the image of God, see Peter Andrew Comensoli, "Recognising Persons: The Profoundly Impaired and Theological Anthropology" (Ph.D. thesis, University of Edinburgh, 2011), 264-267.
[2] The amount of space-clearing and place-holding required is different for each of us, depending on how much extraneous or erroneous stuff we have accumulated in our minds, and the work of clearing that space is different, depending on how skillful we are at wielding the necessary tools. But this is quite complicated: it may be that because of our upbringing, we've accumulated a good deal of nonsense where our ideas of God ought to be, but because of the limitations of our intellectual faculties, we are not able to wield the necessary tools with enough skill. I want to be clear from the outset that words like 'anathema' or 'heresy' are inappropriate in such cases. Childish understandings of God that linger because of intellectual incapacity are not blameworthy. I know it is not nice to say, in an era in which every child is taught to nurture the same expectations, but it is true. Not every person will have the same needs or abilities intellectually. The real problem is not that there is this discrepancy, but that we have mistakenly come to value intelligence and intellectual achievement above the virtues intelligence ought to serve.

social ethic tied closely to the Gospels and often perceived as relatively independent from dogmatic concerns.[3] The Arian heresy did not appear to affect any of the practices integral to Christian life. Could you not carry on the path of discipleship without bothering with the technical intricacies of a doctrine we find difficult to articulate and impossible to grasp fully? Later, when my daughter was born with Down Syndrome, the question took on a new aspect: does a failure to grasp Christian doctrines like the Trinity prevent someone from being a true Christian?

Although I did not realize it at the time, the question opened up a persistent fissure in relating doctrine and ethics, one that the rule function of doctrine has been unable to bridge.[4] I knew instinctively that it mattered profoundly: somehow our salvation was at stake in these technical intricacies. I had begun to see that our understanding of who Jesus is, and the nature of our salvation in Christ, would be undermined completely without the doctrine of the Trinity. The First Council of Nicaea in 325 did not anathematize Arius' belief "that there was a time that he [the Son of God] was not" as a matter of semantics.[5] But are these technical descriptions of the second person of the Trinity really so very important for us *all* to get right? After all, the vast majority of Christians are not theologians, and the Arian controversy bears little relationship to their experience of God or their imitation of Christ. Is it not possible to "confess with your mouth Jesus as Lord, and believe in your heart that God raised him from the dead" (Romans 10:9) and so be saved without grasping such esoteric distinctions in Trinitarian theology?

The short answer is yes: we can certainly put our faith in Jesus without having any knowledge whatsoever of the Arian controversy, or grasping fully the import of the language of the creeds. But it does not follow from that reality of Christian discipleship that doctrines, even the most technical and esoteric points of doctrine, do not matter for Christian practice. The Arian controversy was not about technical language, nor was it merely a struggle for power within the young Church.[6] The debate was about how best to describe and contemplate

---

[3] Such a perception might develop, for example, by reading an essay like Stanley Hauerwas's "Jesus: The Story of the Kingdom," *A Community of Character: Toward a Constructive Christian Social Ethic* (Indiana: University of Notre Dame Press, 1981), 36-52, in isolation from the rest of his work and his sources.

[4] I make this argument in my *Rethinking Christian Identity: Doctrine and Discipleship* (Oxford, UK: Wiley, 2013), especially 12-20.

[5] For discussion of the anathemas, see JND Kelly, *Early Christian Creeds*, 3rd edition (New York: Continuum, 1972), 211.

[6] See Rowan Williams, *Arius: Heresy and Tradition*, Second Edition (Michigan: Eerdmans, 2002), 233-245; Robert C. Gregg and Dennis Groh, *Early Arianism: A View of Salvation*; and Lewis Ayres, *Nicaea and its Legacy: An Approach to Fourth-Century Trinitarian Theology* (Oxford: Oxford University Press, 2004), 15-20.

the God who saves us, to whom the Scriptures bear witness. Over the course of the fourth century, the young Church came to see that salvation in Christ depends upon Jesus being God the Incarnate Word. The Church articulated ever more clearly the doctrine of the Trinity in the ongoing effort to make sense of God in light of the coming of Jesus Christ. Every Christian doctrine is in some measure involved in the task of setting forth the Church's faith in the God who came to save us in the person of Christ.[7]

My exploration of the territory begins in the catechetical instruction of Gregory of Nyssa, a fourth century bishop. Although the question I ask is not Gregory's question, he can nonetheless guide our thinking about the place of doctrine in Christian life. Gregory's instruction centers on how the doctrine of the Trinity should be taught and suggests its key function in the life of a new believer. The second half of the essay focuses on this aspect of doctrine and argues that mystery not only teaches us how to regard God but also to regard as sacred God's image in every human being. Truly to take this belief to heart and practice it in everyday life is part of the reformation of our patterns of attention as we seek to imitate Christ and to grow in the Christian virtues of faith, hope, and love.

CATECHESIS: LEARNING TO GRASP THE MYSTERY

The Holy Spirit is the primary agent in the creation and sustenance of Christian discipleship. Church doctrine and our profession of faith are examples of responses to God's saving work. Catechesis draws us into the mystery of God, teaching us to hold in tension the truth of what we believe (for example, that God is Trinity) with our inability fully to comprehend that truth (since we cannot grasp how God is three and God is one). As the Spirit bestows faith, hope, and love on Christians, doctrine shapes the imagination to receive these gifts. The more fertile and expansive our imaginations, the more tending they require to ensure healthy growth.

My first step in disclosing the relationship between doctrine and Christian discipleship is to return to the controversial and theologically fruitful period of the early Church. After the Council of Constantinople (381), the creed we now call 'Nicene' was promulgated. Gregory of Nyssa was one of the (six) bishops commended to the Church at large as interpreters of the creed.[8] If a

---

[7] For a clear and convincing account of the "affective salience" of Melanchthon's account of forensic justification, which resonates with my argument here, see Simeon Zahl, "On the Affective Salience of Doctrine," *Modern Theology* 31, no. 3 (2015): 428-444.
[8] See "Biography," in *The Brill Dictionary of Gregory of Nyssa*, eds. L. F. Mateo Seco and G. Maspero (Leiden, Netherlands: Brill, 2010).

bishop wanted to know what the creed, or a portion of it, meant, he could confidently consult Gregory of Nyssa. To that end, Gregory wrote a treatise sometimes called *The Great Catechism*[9] to those who were preparing catechumens for baptism.

Gregory grounds his catechetical instruction in the doctrine of the Trinity. The faith into which catechumens will be baptized is faith in the Trinity, so the first part of his guidance for catechists consists in a clear and apologetic account of the Christian God. In specific conversation with those who would oppose his account of God, Gregory sets out the key points of the doctrine. The logic of the very idea of God, he reasons, points to the oneness of God. But the Hebrew Scriptures suggest that the one God is not a monolith. Using Psalm 33:6 as his key text, Gregory shows that the "Word of the Lord" and "the Breath of his mouth" by which the heavens were made point us to distinctions within the Godhead.[10]

Gregory goes on to provide a detailed account of the doctrine of the Trinity that has two key aims. The first of these is, as I have indicated, apologetic. God is Trinity: the Scriptures and our reasoned reflection upon them should draw us to that conclusion. Because God is Trinity, we can say that the Word is God, and it is because Jesus is the Incarnate Word that he can save us. The second aim is epistemological. Even as Gregory examines the evidence and draws carefully-reasoned conclusions, he insists that the doctrine of the Trinity only traces the outline of an impenetrable mystery. "In effect," Gregory writes,

> a studied examination of the depths of this mystery does, in a veiled way, give [one] a fair, inward apprehension of our teaching on the knowledge of God. [One] cannot, of course, express the depth of the mystery in words, how the same thing is subject to a number and yet escapes it; how it is observed to have distinctions and is yet grasped as a unity; how it admits distinction of Persons and yet is not divided in essence.[11]

The confidence *that* God is Trinity should not be confused with any inkling of *how* God is Trinity. We do not comprehend God; we only make sense of God through our interpretation of the Scriptures. Gregory might well have agreed with Karl Barth's famous dictum that

---

[9] Gregory of Nyssa, "An Address on Religious Instruction," in *Christology of the Later Fathers*, ed. and trans., Cyril Richardson (Pennsylvania: The Westminster Press, 1954), 268-325.

[10] Gregory, "An Address," 274-275. In the section immediately prior to section three (270-274), Gregory has argued that God must have *logos* and that *logos* cannot be uttered without *pneuma*.

[11] Gregory, "An Address," 273-74.

the revelation of God in Christ hides as much as it reveals.[12] Jesus reveals truly, but we see in a glass darkly. The epistemological point here is that we *cannot come to know exactly how God is God*. Our perception is limited by the fact that we are creatures. The uncreated God remains beyond the grasp of our knowledge.

I hasten to add, however, that God's transcendence does not distance God from creation. Rather, for Gregory, the distinction in essence between God and creatures is absolute because "[o]therwise we could not conceive of the power that governs the universe as equally pervading all things."[13] God's difference from creation allows God to be present to all creation immediately and fully.[14] Christian faith thus involves holding in tension a firm belief *that* God was in Christ, reconciling the world to himself, with the humble admission that we cannot understand *how*. It is a mystery.

According to Gregory, the candidate for baptism should have a solid grasp of the "mystery of the faith." Learning that Christian faith involves embracing a mystery is an essential part of catechesis. Gregory does not set out, in the remainder of the *Great Catechism*, specific propositions to which the catechumen should give assent, nor does he offer specific guidelines as to the manner of instruction. He does say forthrightly where the rubber (or in this case perhaps the wood of the chariot-wheel) meets the road: in the profession of faith at baptism.

In the first place, Gregory sets up the discussion of baptism by explaining what he believes is at stake. The instruction of catechumens teaches them to recognize "by whom [they are] born, and what kind of creature[s they become]" at baptism. That is, they are born again into Christ and take on his nature; being baptized into Christ makes them partakers of the divine nature, which alone has the power to save them. Gregory supposes that there is a choice being made at baptism:

> What happens in ... baptism depends on the disposition of the heart of [the one] who approaches it. If [s/he] confesses that the holy Trinity is uncreated [s/he] enters on the life which is unchanging. But if, on a false supposition, [s/he] sees a created nature in the Trinity and then

---

[12] Karl Barth, *Church Dogmatics* II/1, (Edinburgh, Scotland: T&T Clark, 1957), 199 & 343

[13] Gregory, "An Address," 305. The absolute distinction plays a starring role in Gregory's theological epistemology as well as in his doctrine of God. See Volpe, *Rethinking Christian Identity*, 193-194.

[14] This is the characteristic of divine being that grounds the claim that God is present to every creature as the cause of its existence. See ST I, q. 44, a., 1; with reference to the Incarnation, see ST III, q. 2, a. 10, ad. 2.

is baptized into *that*, [s/he] is born once more to a life which is subject to change."[15]

Leaving aside the question about the nature of baptism and what Gregory means by "the life which is unchanging," I wish to draw attention to the onus of faith and understanding apparently placed on the catechumen. It seems as if Gregory is saying that the intellectual grasp of the doctrine of the Trinity is as important for baptism as the confession of faith in the Trinity. Without this understanding to accompany faith, the baptism seems not to "take"; it is not an effective Christian baptism. Failure to "believe that the nature of the holy Trinity is uncreated"—the Father, the Son, and the Holy Spirit sharing in the uncreated nature—leads to a wrong turn in the life of faith. At first, this description of baptism and of the dire consequences of a misplaced faith seems harsh. To require such a precise and technical grasp of the proper terminology seems rather exclusive. Does it mean that people with learning difficulties cannot be saved?

The short answer here is no. Gregory approaches the problem with misunderstanding the nature of God with catechumens in mind; catechumens would have been reasonably intelligent people who would have been able to grasp the distinction Gregory describes in the passage quoted above. We must remember also that Gregory is addressing himself to catechists, not to the catechumens themselves. He insists that the *teaching* on Christian doctrine be perspicacious. The real burden does not rest on the shoulders of the one being baptized but on the one who has taught her.

Moreover, the aim of catechesis was not informative but transformative. Baptism marked the turn off a path leading to death, signalling repentance unto life.[16] Thus, the crucial intellectual point here is not semantics but virtue: Gregory explains that "a person who brings himself under the yoke of anything created unwittingly puts his hope of salvation in that and not in God."[17] Intelligent catechumens needed to have their hope directed precisely to the Saviour who is fully God: "For only the one who had originally given [them] life was both able and fitted to restore it when it was lost."[18] Gregory demands a high level of precision and humility from teachers of the faith, but he does so for the sake of the spiritual growth of catechumens. The mystery does not preclude a certain hope but grounds it properly.

---

[15] Gregory, "An Address," 322 (italics in original).
[16] We ought to note well that Gregory is speaking to us, readers and writers of theology: be clear and precise in your teaching, because it *matters*. Getting the terms right is not crucial in the way that the proper pronunciation of *wingardium leviosa* (along with the 'swish and flick') is essential for the efficacy of the spell. Getting the terms right is important for discipleship.
[17] Gregory, "An Address," 322
[18] Gregory, "An Address," 286.

This brings us back to Arius, and the question about the Trinity and Christian faith and practice. If Gregory had been in the room with me when I was asked, he might have helped me by reminding me that the doctrine of the Trinity teaches me who Jesus is. Without the doctrine of the Trinity, we would lose some of our best Christological hymns. To give just one example, we could no longer sing, "Amazing love, how can it be / that thou, my God, shouldst die for me?" Arguments about the Trinity, from Arius to Karl Barth, are never about semantics but about salvation. Our life in Christ is lived by the Spirit, in relationship to the Father. The way we conceive of the Trinity bears directly on the character of our faith and practice.

I hope that this answer would have satisfied the student who asked about the problem with the Arian heresy, but he might have followed up by asking about the place of doctrine in the Christian life. As I have indicated, Gregory addresses himself to catechists and assumes that the candidates for baptism will be intelligent adults. He says nothing of children, or of the mentally ill or infirm. What he says seems to imply that there is some minimum knowledge requirement. I have argued that this is not a requirement for salvation but a discipline for Christian hope. This leaves us with a crucial question: how can we say at one and the same time that the doctrine of the Trinity matters so profoundly if, in some cases, it doesn't seem to matter at all? Gregory does not ask this question, but what he says about baptism invites us to consider it.

DOCTRINE AND INTELLECTUAL HUMILITY

The answer, I think, can be found in the words of St Paul: "For though we live in the world we are not carrying on a worldly war, for the weapons of our warfare are not worldly but have divine power to destroy strongholds. We destroy arguments and every proud obstacle to the knowledge of God, and take every thought captive to obey Christ" (2 Corinthians 10: 3-5). This passage is a complex one, in the midst of a complicated epistle. St Paul is concerned about various things that seem to be undermining the faith of the disciples at Corinth.[19] St Paul writes, a little further on, "I am afraid that as the serpent deceived Eve by his cunning, your thoughts will be led astray from a sincere and pure devotion to Christ" (2 Corinthians 11: 3). I argue that doctrine has a crucial role to play in the work of destroying strongholds, of taking every thought captive to obey Christ, and in the preservation of "sincere and pure devotion to Christ." Before we can address the question about the cases in which doctrine seems not to

---

[19] I cannot adjudicate the question whether 2 Corinthians is a "composite epistle," but merely observe that the letter does not present a consistent argument or develop an organized and coherent set of themes.

matter at all, we need to take a closer look at how doctrine plays its role in the lives of the people Gregory had in mind.

Gregory would have recommended two "weapons" in the struggle to obey Christ: ascetic practice and the contemplation of Christian doctrine.[20] Gregory's theological epistemology offers a very good example of the work doctrine does in the service of discipleship. Intelligent catechumens were bound to develop their own ideas about God; Gregory insists on an epistemological reserve that prevents those ideas from running amok. However catechumens might like to think about God, there are certain boundary-lines that human cognition can never cross.

The possibility of our thoughts leading us astray suggests that the intellectual dimension of our discipleship bears considerable weight. We might associate "sincere and pure devotion" primarily with the heart, as a matter of affection rather than reason, but Paul connects such devotion with "thoughts." Hence, his insistence on "taking every *thought* captive." As we endeavor to remember Jesus faithfully[21] and remain true to his gospel in our daily lives, we grow in faith partly by striving to love God with our minds as well as our hearts. "Thought" also has a long history (in the Bible) of being inseparable from the movement of the heart. In Genesis, we find that "the Lord saw that the wickedness of man was great in the earth, and that every imagination of the thoughts of his heart was only evil continually" (Genesis 6:5). To take every *thought* captive to Christ involves the whole person: reason, imagination, and desire.[22] Moreover, the way we think about God is not the same as the way we think about gravity or addition; it is more like the way we think about love. How we conceive of love shapes our actual loving. So also our conception of God guides our perceptions of and engagement not just with God but with all creation.

We need to realize as well that the intellect also faces the temptation to *libido dominandi*. Our minds strive for satisfaction and control, for an explanation that settles our questions and resolves every paradox. What deception did Paul fear, precisely? We cannot be absolutely certain, but the Arian controversy several generations later centered on an eclipse of the mystery, explaining Jesus's status in a way that would make the doctrine of the Trinity make sense. Gregory

---

[20] Ascetic practice helps by reminding Christians that bodily longings not only prompt us to take care of physical needs but can also remind us of our soul's need for God. Much more might be said about the place of ascetic practice in the Christian life, but my focus here is on the other 'weapon': doctrine. See Volpe, *Rethinking Christian Identity*, chapters 4 and 5. The whole of the fourth chapter is devoted to asceticism and the formation of the soul for Christian practice.

[21] I owe this phrase, to which I return again and again in teaching systematic theology, to my teacher Mary McClintock Fulkerson.

[22] See, for example, Richard Kearny, *The Wake of Imagination: Toward a Postmodern Culture* (New York: Routledge, 1988).

of Nyssa insisted upon an epistemological reserve, which always draws us back to the mystery. We hold in tension what we believe with what is apparent to sensory perception and our ordinary experience. In our experience, there is nothing that is both one and three, nothing that is fully divine and fully human. The mystery of God thus challenges reason and imagination. God incarnate is a stumbling block for the intellect; the oneness of God, the Father, Son and Holy Spirit, defies comprehension. For this reason, Rowan Williams's reading of Vladimir Lossky yielded the insight that "the doctrine of the Trinity is a crucifixion of the intellect."[23] Doctrine helps us to know what we can and ought to say about God and how we should express our faith in God and, at the same time, keeps us cognizant of our limitations. God is beyond all we can ask or imagine.

Thus, doctrine is a tool for us, to rein in the "imagination of our heart" when it has gone, or is at risk of going, astray. Less agile imaginations incur less risk. This does not imply that someone with a profound intellectual disability cannot know God. I mean, instead, that such an intellectual disability generally prevents one presuming to know God by reason of her own intelligence or capacity for abstraction. Cognitive impairment does not hinder anyone from approaching God, because God is the one doing the approaching![24] People who understand less well remind us that we are always dependent on God to reveal God to us: we are all equally incapable of reaching up to heaven, even with our minds, to grasp the nature of the divine. Knowledge of God comes from God; we who are talented with words and ideas and imagination share with one another our conceptions of God, trying to explain to each other what it is we are talking about when we say "God." Still, our words and ideas and concepts and pictures all fail us. Not that we shouldn't try. We must, actually, speak of what we have heard and seen and experienced, but we must remember that all that we can conceive or imagine cannot hold God.

---

[23] Benjamin Myers, *Christ the Stranger: The Theology of Rowan Williams* (New York: Continuum, 2012), 17. Myers uses the phrase in describing Williams's engagement with the thought of Vladimir Lossky. See also Rowan Williams, "Lossky, the *Via Negativa*, and the Foundations of Theology" in *Wrestling with Angels*, ed. Mike Higton (Michigan: Eerdmans, 2007), 1-24.

[24] See John Swinton, "Known by God," in *The Paradox of Disability: Responses to Jean Vanier and L'Arche Communities from Theology and the Sciences* (Michigan: Eerdmans, 2010), and *Dementia: Living in the Memories of God* (Michigan: Eerdmans, 2012), especially chapters 5-10. Swinton gives a very good account of the way we are held by God, who secures us eternally against the disintegration of our being.

IMAGINATION AND DISCIPLESHIP

In what follows, I give an account of the relationship between our imaginative grasp of the mystery of God and our Christian discipleship by way of two key illustrations. In the first place, I want to ask: how do we imagine God? How does doctrine teach us to imagine God? My starting place is a text that will be familiar to readers: the Nicene (Nicene-Constantinopolitan) creed. "I believe in God, the Father Almighty, maker of heaven and earth." As a proposition, it tells us something about God; we affirm that we are in a particular relationship to God, and we recognize God as the Creator. Christian teaching is in the business of *explaining* to us what it is we articulate when we repeat the creed. Because we might imagine, if we took these words in isolation, that God was like an earthly father, who might be kind or stern or even cruel; we might imagine that God made heaven and earth as a sort of experiment or as a toy. Doctrine connects this phrase, which identifies the Creator, to those that follow, especially those that describe his coming in Christ Jesus, who suffered "for our sake." This alters our interpretation of the Almighty Creator. There is more to be said about God than this concept can communicate on its own.

Christian teaching also puts the Creed in the context of broader theological reflection. There is such a thing as our 'doctrine of God.' We find out something more about God when we look at the creed together with Genesis 1 and in light of what theologians (like Gregory of Nyssa and Augustine) have said about God. When we say that God created the heavens and the earth, we are saying that God brought into being everything that is, from nothing—*ex nihilo*. As Christian theologians, we explain further, that this understanding of God as creator implies that there is no violence involved in God's creation.[25] God does not have to overcome anything or anyone in order to bring the world into existence.

The picture of God that begins to emerge, as we put the Almighty Creator in context, is tender, compassionate, and magnanimous. If we read further into Scripture and tradition we would further enrich our picture of God. God is fully sufficient love; God does not create human beings because God needs our love. God's love for us is perfectly free (as Karl Barth said, God is the One who loves in

---

[25] One theologian who takes up this theme and makes it central to the whole of theology is John Milbank. The ontology of peace is one of the pillars of Milbank's theological project. See Volpe, *Rethinking Christian Identity*, 113-117; I hope to return to the argument for the fruitfulness of the ontology of peace and the concept of active reception for theological reflection on Christian discipleship in future work. Milbank does not invent the doctrine of creation *ex nihilo*, of course: he draws heavily on Augustine, but the exegetical reasoning that delivers the doctrine of creation can be found throughout early Christianity.

freedom[26]), and our response of love is likewise free: we love simply because God first loved us.

From even this rudimentary account of the Christian God, a picture of God as steadfast and generous love emerges. Such an understanding of God colors our experience of God and the world, and even ourselves. We interpret events differently, finding God at work where healing and peace are happening. We expect certain things from God in our own lives: healing and peace, and also conviction of our sin, forgiveness, direction, and wisdom. We *see* things differently. Doctrine provides a vision of reality. Tutored in Christian doctrine, we see strength in weakness and honor in humility; we see the cross as the symbol not of defeat but of victory. An imagination that has been nourished and chastened by the Church's teaching about God perceives the world differently.[27]

My second illustration shows how this teaching changes the way we make sense of what is happening around us.[28] On visits to the disciples in Lystra, Iconium, and Antioch (described in Acts 14), Paul and Barnabas "[strengthened] the souls of the disciples, exhorting them to continue in the faith, and saying that through many tribulations we must enter the kingdom of God" (Acts 14:22). Since Christians in those cities endured vigorous persecution, the news that tribulations signposted the way to the kingdom would have reassured believers that they were still on the path of discipleship. Like the encouragement Paul and Barnabas gave, Christian teaching is not a stern schoolmaster, standing over us, waiting to rap our knuckles with a ruler if we slip up. It is rather, as I suggested earlier, a gift, meant to aid us on our journey. Doctrine helps by guiding our imagination and giving us ways to make sense of our experience. If there is a sense in which doctrine "saves," it is only by pointing toward the One in whom we are saved. God gives the gift of doctrine to those who require it; God does not demand understanding of doctrine from those who do not need its discipline.

---

[26] This is a topic Barth discusses at length in the *Church Dogmatics* II/1, 300. God's freedom may look different from Barth's point of view, but divine freedom from necessity is a constant, and an idea Barth derived at least in part from his reading of Anselm. See Barth, *Anselm*: Fides quaerens intellectum: *Anselm's Proof of the Existence of God in the Context of his Theological Scheme* (London: Pickwick Press, 1960).
[27] Kathryn Greene-McCreight provides an excellent example of a doctrine-shaped imagination at work in her *Darkness is My Only Companion: A Christian Response to Mental Illness,* Second Edition (Michigan: Brazos, 2015). Chronicling and reflecting on her experience of mental illness, Greene-McCreight shows us the soul's path of discipleship as it passes through mental illness.
[28] I use Acts 14 and Luke 5 to make a similar point in Volpe, *Rethinking Christian Identity*, chapter 6.

I have argued that insofar as we *do* imagine God, we need our minds and hearts, our memories and our intellect, to be trained for the exercise of contemplation. The *insofar as* is important: doctrine is a gift for the lively and energetic mind, and a rule for those who are clever with words and ideas.[29] The breadth of our knowledge and the capacity of our imaginations can be put to the service of the gospel.

The ability to discern the mystery of God also involves a responsibility to recognize and to guard that mystery in every human being. Being formed for the vision of God—both to see God in the world and to behold God in heaven for eternity—must involve a deeper appreciation for God's own image, found in each and every human being. Those who can grasp the principle of our creation in God's image are to regard as brothers and sisters those who cannot grasp it. When our imaginations are impaired, our need for doctrine to help us "take every thought captive" decreases accordingly. In that situation doctrine has a different function. Then, doctrine teaches our companions how to regard us, how to hold us, how to make sense of our lives when we cannot make sense of them for ourselves.

BODY-BUILDING: INTELLECTUAL DISABILITY, DOCTRINE, AND CHRISTIAN VIRTUE

At the beginning of the paper, I suggested that the work of the doctrine-trained imagination was to remember Jesus faithfully. So far, I have talked mostly about the place of doctrine in the minds and hearts of individual Christians with reasonably capacious imaginations. In this, the final section of the paper, I argue that we go most seriously awry when we suppose that the business of perceiving what the Father is doing is something for which such individuals are primarily responsible. Thus, I shift the focus of the discussion in two ways. First, I say a bit about the Church as the faithful remember-er of Jesus. Second, I ask about the teaching function of the weaker members of the body—those with the least capacious imaginations. This can include people at both ends of life as well as those with cognitive impairments who are at various places in between.

If we think about doctrine primarily in terms of its function in individual lives, we get a skewed picture. Doctrine safeguards the knowledge of God for the whole Church, not just for *me*. The task of remembering Jesus faithfully has been entrusted not to individual Christians but to the body of Christ. The faith that saves is not the belief of individuals but the faith of the Church. The Church is constantly involved in meditation on the Scriptures in the light of past interpretation and in the face of new questions to which Jesus is the

---

[29] See Comensoli, "Recognizing Persons," 264-267; and John Berkman, "Are the Severely Mentally Disabled Icons of Heavenly Life? Aquinas on Impairment," *Studies in Christian Ethics* 26, no. 1 (2013): 83-96.

answer, and new situations in which the Spirit's power is desperately needed. Together, we look to Holy Scripture and to those men and women who have opened the Scriptures to us through the ages, guiding us on the path of discipleship and leading us to a deeper knowledge of God. Theologians and all teachers of the faith bear the *Church's* memory. This should inspire both relief and dread! With the help of the Holy Spirit, those entrusted with the task of handing on the faith, must carry it so that it is intact, supple and resilient. The intellect must be brought to bear fully in the attempt to articulate Christian teaching in a way that keeps the mystery of faith.

Gregory of Nyssa would insist that we see clearly the place of such men and women within the body of Christ. He in no way idealizes or idolizes those people who are involved in the work of expressing the Church's teaching. For Gregory, the mouth (which is the part of the body he associates with teachers of the faith) is just another part of the body. When "the servants and interpreters of the Word"[30] faithfully articulate "good teachings" they benefit the whole body of Christ. Another set of Christians supersedes them: the "champions of the faith" whose lives testify to the gospel.[31] Those who help the Church to remember Jesus faithfully serve those "champions"—not the other way around. Being a champion of the faith consists primarily in an exercise of obedience to Jesus: remembering him faithfully and yielding to the transforming work of his Spirit so that our lives proclaim his gospel.

In order to consider, finally, the function of doctrine in the lives of those who cannot grasp its nuances, we must consider our theological anthropology in the light of what I have argued thus far. The doctrine of God I set out in the previous section implies a particular understanding of human beings as creatures of the God who is generous and compassionate love. As such, the doctrine of God guides our consideration of our fellow human creatures. God the Creator is the source of life, hope and redemption. As the psalmist reminds us, "It is He who made us, and not we ourselves" (Psalm 100:3). A faithful understanding of what it is to be human begins with the affirmation that our primary relationship, the one that marks us as human beings, is our participation in God, the One in whom "we live and move and have our being" (Acts 17:28). Being human means being a creature of

---

[30] Gregory of Nyssa, *Homilies on the Song of Songs*, trans. Richard A. Norris, Jr., (Georgia: Society of Biblical Literature, 2012), 451; quoted in Volpe, *Rethinking Christian Identity*, 215.
[31] See his *Life of Macrina* (GNO VIII) and *On the Soul and the Resurrection* (PG 46), both translated by Anna M. Silvas in *Macrina the Younger, Philosopher of God* (Turnhout, Belgium: Brepols, 2008).

God, first and foremost. The image of God identifies human beings among God's creatures, because *that's how God created human beings*: in His image.

So far, we have merely reiterated the basics of Christian theological anthropology. As the source of our existence and identity, God makes us who and what we are. We affirm that the gift of being in God's image is a gift freely given by God. Yet, quite often, we nevertheless attempt to identify with precision just what it is about human beings that constitutes the "image" and forget that it is not something we have to prove we are by the force of intellect or will.[32] The point of theological reflection on our being created in the image of God must ultimately be, as with the Trinity, a contemplation of the mystery, not an attempt to solve a puzzle.

Not only is the doctrine of the Trinity a crucifixion of the intellect, but our doctrine of humanity is as well. We cannot understand how God is God, and a similar mystery is at the heart of what it means to be human. As with the sketch of Trinitarian doctrine we drew from Gregory's catechetical instruction, so also with our theological anthropology. In the latter case, "A studied examination of the depths of the mystery does, in a veiled way, give one a fair, inward apprehension of Christian teaching on the knowledge of human being. One cannot, of course, express the depth of the mystery in words, how the same thing is at once finite and yet participates in the infinite, how it is observed to have difficulty with moral behavior or intellectual concepts, and yet is enlivened by the breath of God, how it remains a physical body, yet reflects the image of the immortal, immaterial One."[33] The core of Christian theological anthropology is not an explanation of how human beings are the image of God, but the irreducible mystery *that* human beings are the image of God. Before that mystery, we must be equally careful about our imaginative craftiness. Here again, we must hold in tension what we know about human beings with what appears to us: the broken body of the person with a cognitive impairment nonetheless bears the image of God.

---

[32] Rowan Williams captures this notion from another angle in his "The Suspicion of Suspicion: Wittgenstein and Bonhoeffer," in *Grammar of the Heart: New Essays in Moral Theology and Philosophy*, ed. Richard H. Bell (California: Harper & Row, 1988). See also Volpe, *Rethinking Christian Identity*, 52-56; Volpe, "'Taking time' and 'Making sense': Rowan Williams and the Habits of Theological Imagination," *International Journal of Systematic Theology* 15, no. 3 (2013), 345-360; and Medi Ann Volpe and Jennifer Moberly, "'Let your light so shine': Rowan Williams and Dietrich Bonhoeffer," in *Engaging Bonhoeffer: The Impact and Influence of Bonhoeffer's Life and Thought*, ed. Matthew Kirkpatrick (Minnesota: Fortress Press, 2016).

[33] This is my adaptation of Gregory's summary of the teaching on the doctrine of the Trinity; see Gregory, "An Address," 273-74.

In the face of this mystery, we can ask a different question. Our temptation might be, if we were trying to solve a puzzle, ask *how* the person with a severe cognitive impairment *can be* in God's image, if freedom and rationality were the basis for our understanding the *imago Dei*. If we hold fast to the mystery of human being in the image of God, however, and begin *there*, our question becomes, "in what way does the person with a severe cognitive impairment reflect God's image?"

While addressing that question thoroughly is the topic for another essay,[34] I do want to suggest that being mindful of our own frailty is a necessary component of our discipleship and the *sine qua non* of spiritual growth. As for St. John the Baptist, so also for each of us, "I must decrease; he must increase." During the weeks between Christmas and Candlemas, the Church puts the fragility of human life and the humility of Jesus on constant display: our worship is framed by the crib and the cross. We should see Jesus in those whose vulnerability is like that of the newborn babe and whose fragility is like that of the crucified Lord. Drawing the imagination back again and again to the image of humility and brokenness has two benefits (at least). First, we are bound together in Christ, who was broken for us, as we remember that the broken bodies among us help us to remember Jesus faithfully. Second, the increase of humility that should be fostered by such reflection entails a decrease of all in us that crowds out the tender and compassionate love of God.

How would I now respond to the question about the shortcomings of Arianism? On the basis of what I have argued here, I would say that the doctrine of the Trinity helps us to remember Jesus faithfully and truly and guides our understanding of God's salvation through his incarnation, death, resurrection and ascension into heaven. At the same time, it indicates the irreducible mystery that attends all of salvation history. So, it is important for all of us involved in theological and catechetical work to fix our minds on it and allow it to penetrate our hearts and shape our imaginations. We, like that doctrine, will be fingerposts, living signs of the Gospel, and so should work to point as clearly and unambiguously as possible to the truth. Returning to 2 Corinthians, we are reminded that

> we do not preach ourselves but Christ Jesus as Lord, and ourselves as your bond-servants for Jesus' sake. For God, who said, 'Light shall shine out of darkness,' is the One who has shone in our hearts to give the light of the knowledge of the glory of God in the face of Christ.

---

[34] Berkman's "Are the Severely Mentally Disabled Icons of Heavenly Life?" takes up a related question and suggests that people with severe intellectual disabilities reflect a key aspect of our relationship with God.

> But we have this treasure in earthen vessels, that the surpassing greatness of the power may be of God and not from ourselves. (2 Corinthians 4: 5-7)

For those of us inclined to forget that we have this treasure in earthen vessels, contemplation of Christian doctrine involves a crucifixion of the intellect, to turn us again and again back to the source of the light.[35]

We may not be subject to the persecution that beset the churches Paul and Barnabas visited. Yet we need help in learning to pay attention to Jesus and "take every thought captive" to the obedience that was his. The difference that the obedient imagination makes is immense—something that David Foster Wallace reminds us as well as any theologian or spiritual writer of our day.[36] In his 2005 commencement address at Kenyon College, Wallace was talking about attention—but you might well think of 'attention' here as the imagination of the thoughts of our hearts. He says,

> If you really learn how to pay attention, then you will know there are other options. It will actually be within your power to experience a crowded, hot, slow, consumer-hell type situation as not only meaningful, but sacred, on fire with the same force that made the stars.[37]

David Foster Wallace stops short of identifying "the force that made the stars," but we do not have to stop there. We have read Colossians 1 and the prologue to John's gospel. We know (or ought to know) the pertinent verse of "The Servant King": "hands that flung stars into space / to cruel nails surrendered." This Jesus is our God: the force that made the stars. Finding him in the vexations of daily life and in the faces of our fellow human beings—with and without intellectual disabilities—*is* taking every thought captive to Christ. And *that* is what doctrine is for.

---

[35] A note of clarification, in response to a question about this from Kathryn Greene-McCreight: the crucifixion of the intellect is not a sacrifice, in the sense that we give it up entirely. The intellect is crucified by the irreducible mystery of the faith, in order to belong fully to God and to be raised with Christ. The *via negativa*, from which this idea derives, is not an abandonment of doing theology. It suggests a theologically-rich silence filled with awe in God's presence.

[36] See my Volpe, "The Virtue of Tenderness: David Foster Wallace and the Practice of Love," *Church Life* 3, no. 4 (2015): 109-116.

[37] The YouTube video can be found at www.youtube.com/watch?v=8CrOL-ydFMI; the transcript is at web.ics.purdue.edu/~drkelly/DFWKenyonAddress2005.pdf.

Towards a Conjugal Spirituality: Karol Wojtyła's Vision of Marriage Before, During, and After Vatican II

John Sikorski

THE TRAJECTORY AND DEVELOPMENT of Pope John Paul II's (Karol Wojtyła's) thought on marriage and the family, though a fairly obscure topic for American moral theologians, serves as an important hermeneutic key to understanding his subsequent papal corpus. With an eye toward clarifying that obscurity, this article recovers and explores some underappreciated (and untranslated) resources from his early years as a pastor in Kraków, his interventions at the Second Vatican Council, and his subsequent implementation of the Council in his diocese to bring to light key aspects of his early thought regarding marriage and the family. In part one of this article, I re-trace the development of *Gaudium et Spes* with a specific focus on Wojtyła's role in shaping the central concerns during the drafting of this crucial document. Indeed, Wojtyła played a larger role than is typically thought, and he established himself as an authoritative voice in the Council's direction during the last two sessions. Focus then shifts to his written intervention *in sessio* about marriage, which demonstrates some of his most important pastoral concerns regarding marriage as a specific vocation. Part two turns to several untranslated essays by Wojtyła to show his insistence on the importance of developing an authentic "conjugal spirituality" as one of the most important tasks in the Church today. In light of his work at the Council, Wojtyła returned to Kraków with a clear vision of continuity with the work he had begun and developed new diocesan initiatives to implement the Council, especially helping married couples understand their call to holiness according to their specific state in life. I conclude by gesturing toward important further research that needs to be done, both in order to appreciate, and effectively appropriate, the thought of a figure as influential as John Paul II, and in order to reflect with greater depth on the specifically unique character of the married vocation as a path to holiness in the Church.

WOJTYŁA AND *GAUDIUM ET SPES*

The following presents several translations of Bishop Karol Wojtyła's interventions during the Second Vatican Council with regard to marriage, which show that his impact upon the conciliar teachings was the fruit of his own pastoral experience and which emphasize that his conciliar contributions constitute an indispensable prism through which to view his papal corpus.[1] However, it is first necessary to point to several difficulties when engaging in a discussion of thought in this area.

Critiques and Omissions

Pope Saint John Paul II's theology of marriage and the family and his vision of sexual ethics have received critiques from many sectors.[2] In addition to criticism of papal teachings, many accounts of the Second Vatican Council overlook Bishop Wojtyła's role in debates concerning the sacramentality of marriage, conjugal life, and its

---

[1] During the first two periods of the Council (fall of 1962 and 1963), Bishop Karol Wojtyła was "vicar capitular" of the Archdiocese of Kraków and was elevated to Metropolitan Archbishop of Kraków in December of 1963, thus attending the last two conciliar periods as an archbishop (the youngest from Poland).

[2] While it lies beyond the scope of this article to summarize such critiques, the journalist Robert Blair Kaiser offers an account that summarizes many common criticisms. See Robert Blair Kaiser, *The Politics of Sex and Religion* (Missouri: Leaven Press, 1985). In a discussion of John Paul II's positions on gender roles, contraception, and the teaching authority of the Church, Kaiser argues that the pope's views exhibit the "limitations of his own culture and his own nation" (10), characterized by a citation of "cultural norms, especially old rules on sexual behavior, as if they were direct revelations of God" (227). His teachings are indicative of an "absolutist" (231) vision of the papacy that does not heed the experience of faithful Catholics but seeks rather to impose norms "written...by a tiny group of celibate clerics who were more eager to preserve what they perceived as traditional doctrine than inclined to plumb the depths of God's intentions for humankind" (239). Rather than listening to the sense of the faithful of the universal church, the pope has a slant of "a cleric, a celibate and a Pole with old world (if not pre-Christian) ideas about the 'roles' of husbands and wives" (242). While perhaps not all critics of John Paul II would hold his nationality against him, many critics of John Paul II have suggested that his theology of marriage misses the mark, since it does not comport with daily experiences of married Catholic lay people. Kaiser identifies John Paul II as being historically insensitive, personally authoritarian, and out of tune with the "signs of the times" in relation to the contemporary Church, as a result of his formation in an antiquated and simplistically pious cultural tradition. Most recently, strong critiques emerged during a closed-door meeting of fifty theologians and bishops in the time leading up to the 2015 Synod of Bishops, in which some theologians and bishops suggested rejecting John Paul II's idea of a "theology of the body" in favor of a "theology of love." As will be seen, to oppose these two ideas is to radically misunderstand John Paul II's vision of Christian marriage. See Chris Deardurff, "The Secret Meeting," *Inside the Vatican*, June 1, 2015, www.insidethevatican.com/news/the-secret-meeting. For a recent criticism of John Paul's position on sex differences, see Megan K. DeFranza, *Sex Differences in Christian Theology: Male, Female, and Intersex in the Image of God* (Michigan: William B. Eerdmans, 2015).

related moral norms. Theodore Mackin, S.J., offers an insightful account of the revision of Catholic marriage law in the light of the Second Vatican Council's debate concerning the section on marriage in *Gaudium et Spes*.³ Although he notices the rising influence of personalist language in this discussion in the final draft, Mackin omits a discussion of Wojtyła's role in that language. Likewise, Michael Walsh presents an intellectual biography of Wojtyła's thought, rightly acknowledging the dynamic role of theologians such as Yves Congar, O.P., and Henri de Lubac, S.J., at the Council, but he overlooks any discussion of Wojtyła's role at the Council, which these theologians themselves greatly praised.⁴ George Huntston Williams does provide a discussion of Wojtyła's role at the Council, especially in the drafting of *Gaudium et Spes* but omits from his account Wojtyła's crucial intervention *in sessio* about marriage and chastity (which I analyze in what follows).⁵

Given these omissions, one might conclude that the conciliar discussions were foreign to Wojtyła, given the lack of analysis of his role in the drafting of this constitution, and common critiques of his conjugal ethics. On the contrary, through his role in drafting *Gaudium et Spes*, and his intervention *in sessio* on the Council floor, Wojtyła re-oriented the debates of the Council itself, and his subsequent papal magisterium must be seen in light of his pre-conciliar ministry and his conciliar work.

Bishop Wojtyła and the Ante-preparatory Commission

While the origins of *Gaudium et Spes* attract ample treatment in historical scholarship, it was by the end of the deliberations that Wojtyła emerged as a respected leader among the worldwide

---

³ See Theodore Mackin, S.J., *Divorce and Remarriage* (New Jersey: Paulist Press, 1984), 453-504.
⁴ Michael Walsh, "From Karol Wojtyła to John Paul II," in *The Vision of John Paul II: Assessing His Thought and Influence,* ed. Gerard Mannion (Minnesota: The Liturgical Press, 2008), 10-28. See also Paul McPartlan, "John Paul II and Vatican II," in *The Vision of John Paul II: Assessing His Thought and Influence,* ed. Gerard Mannion (Minnesota: The Liturgical Press, 2008), 45. De Lubac's comments can be found in Henri de Lubac, SJ, *At the Service of the Church* (California: Ignatius Press, 1993), 171. For Congar's comments, see *History of Vatican II.* Vol. 4, ed. Joseph Komonchak (New York: Orbis, 2003), 537.
⁵ George Huntston Williams, *The Mind of John Paul II* (New York: The Seabury Press, 1981), 164-185. In an *entire chapter* devoted to Wojtyła's conciliar work, Williams omits one of the most important interventions which Bishop Wojtyła made. This can either be due to a selective choice of texts for reasons of pragmatic organization of his chapter, or due to a judgment of the relative unimportance of Wojtyła's intervention in this area, or a simple oversight. In what follows below, I hope to show how this short intervention actually encapsulates Wojtyła's vision of marriage and the Church's pastoral care for couples, and must not be ignored.

episcopate. According to León-Josef Cardinal Suenens, whose relationship and friendship with Wojtyła was strengthened during the work of the Council, Wojtyła's theological contributions were driven by his pastoral sense and universal vision of the Church, and its needs in the modern world. "He thinks right in the way that those in authority must; he feels with all humanity, because you can only bring God to that humanity if you feel with it from the inside."[6] His "feeling with" humanity was based on his strong Christocentric personalism, the conviction that only Christ fully reveals the human person to himself and that only in the light of Christ does the fullness of the human vocation become clear.[7] He believed in the "priority of Christ for the Christian, the priority of the true Christian values, of allowing Christ to be in you, with all the human consequences, and with all the spiritual consequences."[8]

Suenens argued that a robust Christocentric personalism is the key to John Paul II's theological vision, a claim that would later become evident in John Paul II's first encyclical, *Redemptor Hominis*. A central consequence of this personalistic vision, which respects each person as a locus of the encounter with Christ, is not an authoritarian and doctrinaire imposition of teachings upon the faithful but an insistence on the value of the experience of each person, created in the image and likeness of God, redeemed by Christ, and joined within the Church to all the baptized, who possess, in communion and complementarity, many diverse vocations and their charisms.[9] Wojtyła presented this theological vision consistently at the Council, and it gained force from his personality, as he was recognized as a man of "deep spirituality, prayer, and contemplation," and whose abilities as an intellectual, professor, and scholar were matched by his experience as a shepherd and a teacher.[10]

---

[6] Leon-Josef Cardinal Suenens, "The Pope and the Person," in *The Pastoral Vision of John Paul II*, ed. Joan Bland, SND de N (Illinois: Franciscan Herald Press, 1982), 3-21.
[7] As *Gaudium et Spes* would express it in its final draft; see *Gaudium et Spes*, 22.
[8] Suenens, "The Pope and the Person," 10.
[9] See Suenens, "The Pope and the Person," 10-15.
[10] See Bishop Alfred Abramowicz, "Who is Karol Wojtyła," in *The Pastoral Vision of John Paul II*, ed. Joan Bland, SND de N (Illinois: Franciscan Herald Press, 1982), 21-31. Abramowicz concludes that while Wojtyła was certainly a man of extraordinary abilities and talent, he was also the product of his Catholic culture, which was marked by sincere intellectualism, dialogue with the modern world, and possessed a highly educated intellectual class which constantly sought to engage with the world, in an effort to most persuasively articulate the position of the Church vis-à-vis the problems and dilemmas of modernity. It was not therefore an "unenlightened" or pietistic Church, and anyone who thinks this "is ignorant of Catholicism in Poland. Fervent and devout the people are, but the greatest moral and social problems in Catholic Poland are and have been for the past twenty-five years" issues of poverty, deprivation of human rights, injustices, oppressions, poor housing, and secular pressure on family life.

The central importance of Wojtyła's personalist thought and the insistence on drawing from personal experiences to articulate the Church's doctrine emerged as early as 1959. In his response to Domenico Cardinal Tardini, who had asked for suggestions from the world's bishops about the council's deliberative scope, Wojtyła broke from the usual method of providing a short list of doctrinal or legal questions that ought to be discussed. In contrast to even his fellow Polish bishops, Wojtyła submitted a lengthy philosophical discussion (which has not been translated into English) of nine points, all focusing on practical themes articulated in light of the human person's calling to participate intimately in the heart of the Trinitarian God, who is the answer to the human person's deepest yearnings.[11] The beginning of his submission is particularly important, providing the "anthropological framework" for the remainder, including the section on married persons.

> The question of Christian personalism seems necessary and appropriate in order to sketch out doctrine. Human personhood, after all, is expressed in a particular way in the relation of the human person to a personal God—this is the very pinnacle of all religion, especially a religion based on supernatural Revelation. Participation in the Divine nature and the inner life of the Trinity by grace, thanks to which we can expect perfect union in the beatific vision—all of these things can only be found among persons.
>
> Christian personalism therefore establishes the foundation of all the ethical doctrine that the Church always teaches, basing itself on the Gospel. The human person as a subject [*suppositum*] acting freely and relying upon his conscience in his acts, in a sense, "closes" morality. Indeed, in the acts of the person one needs to pay attention to the relation between the acting person and other things and persons. This is why Catholic moral doctrine indicates certain rules regarding the use of things, without abusing them, as well as rules pertaining to the

---

[11] See, for example, the submission of Stefan Cardinal Wyszyński, dated September 15th, 1959, in which the primate of Poland divides his response into sections devoted to questions regarding religious life, juridical and penal acts, liturgical matters, and social questions. See *Acta Synodalia Sacrosancti Concilii Oecumenici Vatican II: Series I (Antepraeparatoria), Volumen I: Consilia et vota Episcoporum ac Praelatorum—Pars II: Europa*. (Vatican City: Typis Polyglottis Vaticanis, 1975), 673-686. Hereafter *AS*. Wojtyła's submission can be found on 741-748. The nine points he proposes relate to 1) The fundamental re-articulation of doctrine in a personalist manner; 2) The relation between the Church and those referred to as "schismatics or heretics"; 3) The supernatural calling of the laity; 4) The discipline and formation of clergy; 5) Clerical celibacy; 6) The renewal of formation in seminaries; 7) Renewed emphasis on the evangelical counsels for both clergy and laity; 8) Greater lay participation in the liturgy; 9) A reform of canon law, especially with regard to marriage.

love of persons. The commandment to love assumes, and yet also supersedes, all that mutual and social justice requires.

Having considered all these things, the difference between Christian personalism and all other kinds of personalism becomes clear, as any other kind can carry with it traces of individualism, or even an economic materialism. The fact that the problem of the human person and his "situation" in the world is intensively studied in today's world is an important fact. This study leads some to an excess of "humanistic faith"; others, perhaps more often, are led to despair in human existence. For this reason, not only the faithful, but even the unbelieving await the future words of the Council in this regard.[12]

In this submission, provided three years before the beginning of the Council (the same year Wojtyła published *Love and Responsibility*), at least three central themes emerge.[13] First, he desires to re-articulate the fundamentals of Catholic doctrine in light of the human person's call to participate in the life of the Trinitarian God, who is the ultimate end of human life and in whom is found beatitude.[14] Secondly, such a discussion necessitates a treatment of the moral life: in what kind of actions ought the human person to engage, in order to reach his final goal of partaking in the intimacy of the communion of persons of the Trinity? What is the relationship between inner-worldly action and the final goal of beatitude? Wojtyła argues that moral theology should avoid a legalistic mindset focusing on obligations of justice, the effects of sin, and the accrual of merit but rather ought to place emphasis on the actions of the person as expressions of a freely acting subject who,

---

[12] See *AS*, 741-742. These submissions have yet to be translated into English. Unless otherwise noted, any citations of the *Acta Synodalia* are my translation.

[13] *Love and Responsibility*, published by Bishop Wojtyła in 1959, is a philosophical and personalist analysis of the human person and the phenomenon of human love and also includes a treatment of sexual ethics. The reflections in the book were the fruit of Wojtyła's ministry among young people, particularly married couples, and Wojtyła himself notes that conversations with married persons about their experiences were a large influence for the argument in the book (as I will demonstrate in part two). Of particular note was his close friend and interlocutor the Servant of God Jerzy Ciesielski, an engineer with whom Wojtyła spent many hours conversing about married life and conversations with whom "formed one of the sources of inspiration" for *Love and Responsibility*. See Karol Wojtyła, "Słowo o Jerzym Ciesielskim," in *Aby Chrystus sie Nami Poslugiwał*, ed. Józefa Hennelowa (Kraków, Poland: Znak, 2009), 111. The English critical edition of *Love and Responsibility* is Karol Wojtyła, *Love and Responsibility*, trans. Grzegorz Ignatik (Massachusetts: Pauline Books and Media, 2013).

[14] It is possible to see here, therefore, the influence of Wojtyła's early acquaintance with and influence by the mystical tradition, especially through the work of St. John of Cross (the subject of his first dissertation), and the lay mystic Servant of God Jan Tyranowski. For a discussion of this period of Wojtyła's life and thought, see Williams, *The Mind of John Paul II*, 77-81, 93-103. Also see George Weigel, *Witness to Hope* (New York: Harper Perennial, 2001), 58-62, 82-87.

through his moral actions, becomes more capable of responding to the call to participate in divine life. Wojtyła seeks to rehabilitate charity as the central virtue in the Christian life, which, as the form of the virtues, provides the only and adequate response toward others, who exist as persons to be loved, and not objects to be used.[15] Finally, such a "personalism" must be thoroughly Christian, and not Kantian, and guard against any kind of "personalism" that seeks to place emphasis on the centrality of the person apart from the truth about his good, a term that often appears throughout Wojtyła's writings.[16] Thus, any forms of "personalism" denying transcendence, or exalting the individual over-against relationships to others, are false forms of humanism that cannot lead to integral human fulfillment. Only in light of the ultimate calling to divine communion can one develop a proper personalism.[17]

Wojtyła therefore proposes that the Council ought to discuss the human person and her vocation in light of the mystical calling to love, the only adequate anthropology by which to safeguard against using others in interpersonal relationships and against social injustice.[18] Furthermore, he emphasizes that the Council make this calling clear to the laity in particular.

> The laity, who do not appear many times in the *Code of Canon Law*, appear to be presently occupying an ever greater role in the activity of Christ's Church. The vernacular refers to the activity of these laity as "*mouvement de laicat*." Perhaps it would be fitting to doctrinally delineate the proper character and the supernatural foundation of their activity. Then the vocation of the laity in the Church (or: diverse

---

[15] Again evident here is the argument from Wojtyła's earlier work, *Love and Responsibility*, in which he argues for this "personalistic norm," see Karol Wojtyła, *Love and Responsibility*, trans. H.T. Willetts (California: Ignatius Press, 1993), 41.

[16] See Adrian Reimers, *The Truth about the Good: Moral Norms in the Thought of John Paul II* (Florida: Sapientia Press, 2011).

[17] Wojtyła had already made this argument earlier in his habilitation thesis, in which he argued that the personalism of Max Scheler, while an important and even necessary component of ethics, cannot ultimately ground Christian ethics, since it is devoid of reference to metaphysics and the truth about the good for the human person.

[18] By "mystical" I do not mean "otherworldly," but rather I use the term as it has been understood by the mystical tradition out of which Wojtyła works, in which the mystic is the one who, already here on earth, experiences the fruits of the union with God which will come to full fruition in the beatific vision. Wojtyła here follows his first dissertation advisor, the famed Thomist Fr. Reginald Garrigou LaGrange, OP, who had taken this position contrary to other theologians of the so-called Roman School of the early twentieth century, who argued that the unitive way was reserved for only a few people who were endowed with special graces. Wojtyła and Garrigou-LaGrange argue that the unitive way is available to all human persons who respond to and cooperate with the grace of God, which moves them to increasing friendship with God.

vocations) would be more evident…The edification of the Body of Christ without the mutual labor of the laity with the clergy cannot be brought into being.[19]

Even prior to the Council, therefore, Wojtyła insisted that the universal Church take into account the experience of lay persons. For their part, the laity, who often organized through movements such as Catholic Action, could serve as a hermeneutic by which to articulate doctrine. At the same time, pastors should clearly articulate doctrine to help the laity more effectively guide their apostolate in the world.[20] It was with these pastoral and theological commitments that Wojtyła arrived in Rome to participate in the general sessions of the Second Vatican Council, as one of only twenty-five Polish bishops (out of a total of sixty) who were given passports by the Polish communist government to attend.[21]

Drafting Gaudium et Spes

By his own account, Wojtyła did not participate vocally in many of the early sessions of the council: "*The Council was a unique occasion for listening to others, but also for creative thinking.* Naturally, the older and more expert bishops contributed the most to the development of the Council's thought. At first, since I was young, I learned more than I contributed. Gradually, however, I came to participate in a more mature and creative manner."[22] By the time of the third session (fall of 1964), Wojtyła had been elevated to Archbishop of Kraków and soon emerged as a regular contributor to the conciliar deliberations on the floor of St. Peter's Basilica. It was during this period that he began to emerge as a crucial figure in the drafting of what came to be known as *Gaudium et Spes*, and established close relationships with Gabriel Cardinal Garrone, Henri de Lubac, S.J., Yves Congar, O.P., and Fr. Joseph Ratzinger. During this period, Wojtyła increasingly articulated the need for a personalist vision for the documents of the Council, and especially for *Gaudium et Spes*, a task that de Lubac encouraged, "Yes, yes, yes, that's the way forward."[23]

Wojtyła came to be recognized as an authority and central influence upon this document as a result of both his work on the drafting committee and of his spoken interventions. In particular, he

---

[19] Again, the translation is mine. See *AS*, I, *Antepraeparatoria*, 743-744.
[20] In 1947, a young Fr. Karol Wojtyła traveled to France, where he became familiar with Catholic Action and the worker-priest movement.
[21] See Williams, *The Mind of John Paul II*, 125.
[22] John Paul II, *Crossing the Threshold of Hope,* trans. Jenny McPhee and Martha McPhee (New York: Alfred A. Knopf, 1994), 158.
[23] See John Paul II, *Rise, Let us Be on Our Way*, trans. Walter Ziemba (New York: Warner Books, 2004), 165.

played a central role during the discussion of the document by the general sessions in October and November of 1964, during the "intersession" in the spring of 1965, and again during the fourth general period in November of 1965. The document had originally been proposed as "Schema XVII" by Leo Cardinal Suenens, and was entrusted to a "Mixed Commission" of members from the Doctrinal Commission and the Commission for the Lay Apostolate in the spring of 1963, with Msgr. Pietro Pavan as the secretary.[24] This Roman commission produced a largely "sociological" text, with which the Council's Central Commission was dissatisfied, especially after the publication of Pope John XXIII's *Pacem in Terris*. The drafting and revision of the text was then entrusted to Cardinal Suenens, who appointed Msgr. Gerard Philips to oversee the drafting of a new document, which was completed in October of 1963. This so-called "Malines Schema" exhibited a more "theological approach" but was criticized for its lack of a social analysis.

The imbalanced sociological and theological perspectives of the first Rome draft and the "Malines schema" led to the appointment of Fr. Bernard Häring, C.S.S.R., by the general subcommission entrusted with this document under the direction of Bishop Emilio Guano, whose task would be to combine the insights of the previous two documents. However, the draft produced by this subcommission resulted in a completely new document which treated the Church as a "servant of humanity," from which followed four chapters: the anthropological foundations; the relationship between the Church's mission and the world; the active involvement of Christians in the world; and specific problems and urgent tasks. This schema was presented to and edited by the general subcommission, which met in Zürich in February of 1964, and which consisted of seventeen members, including two lay persons. This draft elicited much criticism from several members of the subcommission who belonged to the Holy Office, including a direct attack on Häring's discussion of marriage, but was eventually approved and sent to the Central Commission.

Having gone through many drafts and revisions in committee, "Schema XVII" was now renamed "Schema XIII" by the Central Commission, and was distributed to bishops around the world in July

---

[24] For a history of the drafting of *Gaudium et Spes*, I am drawing from the following sources: Joseph Komonchak and Giuseppe Alberigo, ed., *History of Vatican II*, Vol. 3 (New York: Orbis, 2000), 402-419; Joseph Komonchak and Giuseppe Alberigo, ed., *History of Vatican II*, Vol. 5 (New York: Orbis, 2006), 520-537; Jan Grootaers, *Actes et Acteurs à Vatican II* (Leuven: Leuven University Press, 1998), 105-132; Bernard Häring, "La mia participazione al concilio Vaticano II," *Cristianismo nella storia* 15, no. 1 (1994): 161-181.

of 1964. During the summer, Bishop Guano suggested forming two subcommissions, one theological and one which would focus on "the signs of the times," to revise and edit the document in light of the questions that bishops would raise in the upcoming third period of the Council. Among those invited to the second subcommission was Archbishop Wojtyła. While the subcommissions had been drafting documents in Rome, Malines, and Zürich, Wojtyła had been working with the Polish bishops on an alternative draft of "Schema XVII," which was to have a significant effect on the final result of deliberations.

In June of 1964, Archbishop Wojtyła of Kraków and Archbishop Kominek of Wrocław, in the name of the Polish bishops, composed two alternative schemata on the relationship between the Church and the modern world, and sent them to Cardinal Suenens, informing him of their intention to provide these, not as replacements, but as suggested improvements on certain elements of the schema being discussed.[25] Drawing largely from Paul VI's new encyclical *Ecclesiam Suam* and from *Pacem in Terris*, one schema argued that the "Presence of the Church depends not only on the will of God but also the will of human beings who freely manifest their agreement with the divine will."[26] This schema, composed in Kraków under Wojtyła's leadership, was sent to Fr. Häring during the summer of 1964. Wojtyła presented the same schema to the general session of the Council on October 21, 1964.[27] According to his notes from the subcommission's meeting, Häring deemed this schema inadequate and in need of re-articulation, especially when it argued, "The People of God draws its strength from the institutional Church."[28] Häring noted that Wojtyła's role in the "collaboration on the final schema was as a whole constructive, never aggressive and rude. A large number of his suggestions were heeded."[29]

Nevertheless, Häring remained generally unsympathetic to Wojtyła's suggestions for the officially-drafted text, but the majority of the subcommision's members were impressed and recognized the need to establish a new editorial committee. Häring was revoked as editor-in-chief in November of 1964, and Congar noted that this decision had long been deliberated, as Häring had been too inflexible

---

[25] See Grootaers, *Actes et Acteurs à Vatican II*, 110-111.
[26] See Komonchak and Alberigo, *History of Vatican II*, Vol. 3, 414. Evident in this statement is a striking similarity to the argument made by Wojtyła in his submission of 1959, in which he also emphasizes the relationship between freedom and the truth about the person and his end, and a non-competitive account of divine and human agency.
[27] See Joseph Komonchak and Giuseppe Alberigo, ed., *History of Vatican II*, Vol. 4 (New York: Orbis, 2004), 521.
[28] See Häring, "La mia participazione al concilio Vaticano II," 179.
[29] Häring, "La mia participazione al concilio Vaticano II," 179.

in defending his own views and insufficiently open to compromises.[30] At the same time, a new theological subcommission was established, to which Wojtyła was appointed, and a new editorial committee chaired by Bishop Pierre Haubtmann was chosen. Haubtmann asked all of those involved in the work of the "Schema XIII" subcommission to send him notes and revisions, which he would compile into a redrafted version of the document, to be discussed in Ariccia, a suburb of Rome, in the spring of 1965.

Wojtyła arrived at the Ariccia meeting with a "second Polish schema," drafted in light of the previous criticisms on January 29th, 1965, which he presented to more than one hundred members of the various subcommittees of the subcommission. He was critical of the official draft for being "too optimistic" and insufficiently taking into account the concrete and attractive, but ultimately false answers, offered by communist and capitalist societies as a response to the modern person's questions. Among other presentations, he collaborated with Fr. Jean Daniélou, S.J., in presenting a discussion of Christian anthropology and the Church's service to the vocation of each human person. It was necessary to answer the questions of the modern world with a specifically Christian humanism and in light of the vocation of the human person to participate in the intimate life of God.[31]

Häring was generally impressed by Wojtyła's participation and noted that Wojtyła spoke on ecclesiology, atheism, humanism, and on marriage and chastity. He noted, however, a few elements that he disliked about Wojtyła's draft, including a discussion of:

> periodic continence connected with the ethical dignity of the person. He [Wojtyła] did not want a discourse on the dignity of the person in itself, but on the dignity founded on virtue. He spoke on how the order of nature can be understood by both believers and unbelievers, and that it was necessary to guard energetically against concupiscence and "carnal love."[32]

Häring's critiques notwithstanding, the Dominican Master General, Aniceto Fernandez Alonso, O.P., affirmed that Wojtyła's draft and his critiques were much better than any previous drafts of Schema XIII,

---

[30] See Komonchak and Alberigo, *History of Vatican II*, Vol. 4, 520.
[31] Komonchak and Alberigo, *History of Vatican II*, vol. 4, 284. Bishop Gerard Philips, the secretary of the meeting, notes that the origin of the officially-approved "Chapter Four" of the final version of *Gaudium et Spes* emerged from this meeting under the authorship of Yves Congar, O.P., and K. Wojtyła. See Grootaers, *Actes et Acteurs à Vatican II*, 119.
[32] See Häring, "La mia participazione al concilio Vaticano II," 180.

and "most fathers welcomed it as a 'basis for discussion.'"[33] They remained divided, however, since it was not prepared "officially" under the specific order of the Mixed Commission. Nevertheless, they decided to correct Haubtmann's official version in light of Wojtyła's schema and his criticisms.[34]

According to the accounts of these participants in the Ariccia meeting during the third intersession, which would produce the final draft of Schema XIII, it is clear that, by this time, Wojtyła was widely recognized as an authoritative theologian, leader, and bishop who brought his pastoral experience from the Church behind the Iron Curtain to bear on the teachings of the universal Church. Jan Grootaers summarizes that Wojtyła was able to disrupt the general tendency of the Council, which had been to articulate the "order for the day" in primarily "western" terms. His pastoral and theological experience from the "East" gave him authority to pronounce on many questions offered by contemporary philosophy, such as Marxist humanism. His contacts in Poland with a broad range of Catholic intellectuals and adult laity provided insight into the experience of the faithful who daily experienced a violation of the most basic human rights. His feelings of responsibility for an exceptionally difficult pastoral situation and a regime that limited religious freedom and opinion impelled him to articulate a position that could promote human freedom in genuine dialogue. His amicable relations with other bishops, both within the Polish episcopate and internationally, established him as an increasingly significant conciliar father.[35] The final intersession provided an opportunity for Wojtyła to "make himself known and appreciated,"[36] and even Häring reflected that Wojtyła's work on *Gaudium et Spes* confirmed for many his ability to lead and that without this commitment to the drafting of this document, "John Paul II would not have been elected."[37] In his journal, Yves Congar, O.P., noted, "Wojtyła made a remarkable impression. His personality dominates. Some kind of animation is present in this person, a magnetic power, prophetic strength, full of peace, and impossible to resist."[38]

The Written Intervention on Marriage

While Wojtyła emerged during the Arricia phase of the drafting of *Gaudium et Spes* as an able leader and recognized pastor, who largely

---

[33] Komonchak and Alberigo, *History of Vatican II*, vol. 4, 525.
[34] Komonchak and Alberigo, *History of Vatican II*, vol. 4, 525.
[35] See Grootaers, *Actes et Acteurs à Vatican II*, 130. We have already mentioned that both de Lubac and Congar recognized the extraordinary weight of his participation in the latter period of the Council, and particularly at the Ariccia meeting.
[36] Komonchak and Alberigo, *History of Vatican II*, vol. 4, 639.
[37] Häring, "La mia participazione al concilio Vaticano II ," 181.
[38] Yves Congar, O.P., Unpublished *Diary*, as quoted in Weigel, *Witness to Hope*, 168.

influenced the final drafting of the document, he also contributed increasingly to the debates *in sessio* [on the floor] before the worldwide episcopate. Wojtyła became widely respected for his oral contributions regarding religious freedom, the problem of atheism, and the role of the laity.[39] However, there is no significant treatment to this day (to my knowledge) of Wojtyła's vision of marriage and the family during the Council. Häring noted Wojtyła's treatment of these issues in his discussions of Schema XIII at the Ariccia meeting, and there are suggestions of the argument which Wojtyła would pursue in his written preparatory submission to Cardinal Tardini, in which he emphasized the need for a robust Christian personalism and the important role of the lay vocation. These themes are seen again in an oral intervention about atheism on September 28th, 1965. "All pastoral solicitude presupposes the human person as both a subject and as an object [of pastoral care]. For all pastoral attentiveness, every apostolate, whether priestly or of laymen, proceeds to the end that the human person, out of his own integral calling, might know and, in act, express the truth in every relationship: with himself, with other persons, with the world."[40] It was within this intellectual trajectory that Wojtyła submitted his fairly critical intervention on marriage during the fourth session:

> 1. The chapter "On Marriage and the Family" does not appear altogether adequate from a pastoral perspective. None of the difficult questions which married persons ask of us, who are their pastors, appear in it, nor does it attempt to respond to them. *The issue is not the content of doctrine, but the manner of speaking*, which in this matter ought to take on the manner of a dialogue. A dialogue certainly consists in providing answers to questions, not only for the purpose of making clear a norm, or a teaching, but also to present the reason, or argument, on which the norm is based. Thus the manner of speaking here is essential, since questions pertaining to marriage are not only of a moral nature, but also touch upon the human person in his most concrete existence and most personal vocation. It is therefore necessary to *begin a dialogue not with "marriage" in the abstract, but with all those who are married,* whose pastoral care belongs to us; marriages in the Church, and the world, since marriage as a sacrament of the Church presupposes marriage as a sacrament of nature.
>
> 2. There are many opinions and suggestions regarding the moral dilemmas of marriage during the time of this Council. In these opinions, there can exist a particular danger, namely, that the solutions

---

[39] See Weigel, *Witness to Hope,* 166-169; Williams, *The Mind of John Paul II,* 174-180.
[40] *AS,* 4:II, 12. The translation is Williams's, as cited in *The Mind of John Paul II,* 178.

to these most personal and natural problems are offered in a rather artificial manner. The question concerns the use of marriage, *where the union of the persons, the husband and wife, is truly achieved in a personal way, when each of them has respect for the order of nature in the other.* For this personal union and respect for the order of nature to be real, true virtue is needed. This virtue is charity, which combines within itself continence and due tenderness. Never can knowledge of the rules of natural fertility or the aspects of sexual life form by themselves a morally perfect exercise of marriage without mutual practice of the virtues. This awareness gives rise to the possibility of the use of marriage in a prudent and conscientious manner, which also most greatly corresponds to the dignity of the human person. It is important to note the voice of reason, of which His Eminence Cardinal Suenens spoke, since knowledge makes virtue easier, on the condition that this knowledge is incorporated into the virtue.

3. We are taking part in this Council as pastors of souls. We ought to speak about marriages both inside and outside of the Church in a pastoral manner and language. As pastors, we are aware of various difficulties, which are characteristic of married life, just as St. Paul was already aware of them (cf. 1 Cor.). We should therefore proclaim the full meaning of married life and its sacred character that results from the grace of the sacrament. We should also proclaim the solidarity which, among the people of God, in the human family, unites us to all who are living in the married state. *The responsibility which falls to them, is a fundamental responsibility* for the life and dignity of the human person, since marriage and the family create the environment/milieu *in which the human person is loved.* It is a school of love and charity. The Council must make clear precisely this love and charity, and not only doctrine. In a spirit of pastoral love let us also clearly name those natural and supernatural virtues, which govern men and women in marriage. We have the responsibility to explain, *in what manner the good use of marriage* corresponds to the good use of intellect, will, and the heart, and in what manner it corresponds to the *good* use of sacramental grace. Increasingly, our brothers and sisters in marriage are confronted with a certain despair as a result of their specific moral questions, the result of which is a weakening of their faith, at least in practice. The effect of the chapter on "Marriage and the Family" should build up faith and hope.[41]

Wojtyła thus divides his treatment of marriage, chastity, and the family in this conciliar intervention into three short themes. First, he severely criticizes any approach to marriage which does not take seriously into account the experience(s) of those who live the "most personal vocation" of marriage. It is not enough for the Church in the modern world to simply re-affirm traditional doctrine without showing how the doctrine both corresponds to, and is the fruit of, the

---

[41] See *AS*, 4:III, 242-243. The translation is mine.

truth about the good of the human person's vocation to love.[42] A true dialogue cannot take place if the Church either imposes its norms in a rigid manner or the married couple is unwilling to examine the manner in which they might be living according to, or failing to keep, the "rule" of authentic love. In order to fully and adequately understand conjugal love, the Church must be willing to enter into the daily challenges, struggles, and sufferings that married couples can face and must also be aware of the difficulty in living out the vocation to sacramental marriage.

Secondly, Wojtyła recognizes the difficulty entailed in the married vocation and, specifically, in the responsible parenthood to which spouses are called through the natural ordering of their love. True interpersonal love, and its expression through the conjugal act, can only occur when the act corresponds to, and is in keeping with, the order of nature. There can be no true interpersonal union when either of the spouses rejects the totality of the other's gift. This moral norm, however, requires that couples live out responsible parenthood, which might require marital continence. Such continence, however, cannot be seen as simply a burden but, like all virtues, as a habit that requires practice over time and so shapes the character of spousal love. The virtue is not only a part of temperance, however, but must be governed by charity, which properly orders and fosters the tenderness that ought to be a natural part of marital love. The Church ought therefore to develop a way of articulating the traditional doctrine that focuses less on the language of "ends or purposes" but places emphasis on charity and tenderness, without juxtaposing these against the order of nature.[43]

Finally, this vision, while recognizing the real difficulties entailed within it, can be truly sustained through the grace of the sacrament, which forms married couples into witnesses to the Gospel through their vocation to love. "Marriage and the family therefore constitute for them the proper sphere in which the human person is loved. It is a school of love and charity. It is necessary that such love and charity—not only doctrine—be made clear on the part of the Council." He encourages the pastors of the Church to promote marriage and family life in a manner that does not adopt a "gradualness of the law," but which encourages couples to live according to the virtues of faith,

---

[42] In our own day, we see an echo of this idea in Pope Francis's *Amoris Laetitia*, no. 59: "Our teaching on marriage and the family cannot fail to be inspired and transformed by this message of love and tenderness; otherwise, it becomes nothing more than the defense of a dry and lifeless doctrine."

[43] Again Francis, *Amoris Laetitia*, no. 28: "Against this backdrop of love so central to the Christian experience of marriage and the family, another virtue stands out, one often overlooked in our world of frenetic and superficial relationships. It is tenderness."

hope, and charity, in the desire that the living of the virtues makes obedience to the law less difficult.[44]

Those familiar with *Love and Responsibility* will recognize the striking similarities between Wojtyła's conciliar intervention and the main themes of the book, which he had published five years prior.[45] Married love is spoken of in terms of charity. Wojtyła argues that only the kind of love that respects the order of nature can also truly respect the dignity of the other person and thus lead to an authentic interpersonal union. "Betrothed love"—the highest form of love in *Love and Responsibility*—requires the practice of virtue, and the integration of the sexual urge into the full meaning of interpersonal love.

The immediate effect of Wojtyła's written intervention upon the final form of the section on marriage in *Gaudium et Spes* remains unclear. However, it is clear that many of the Council fathers were not pleased with the form presented for a vote, which received the most *non placet* votes of any section of *Gaudium et Spes*.[46] Although the text did receive the necessary votes for approval by the Council on November 16th, 1965, the final text was nevertheless further modified through a direct intervention by Paul VI. Paul included four *modi*, which emphasized more strongly the Church's need to propose chastity as an essential component for growth in married love, certainly a theme that resembles the main trajectories of Wojtyła's written intervention and early thought.[47] The themes of virtue, marital chastity, and the grace to live out the sacrament, proposed by Wojtyła to the council fathers during the fourth session, would remain central to Wojtyła in his own work as archbishop and emerge in their most developed form during his subsequent pontificate.

DRAWING UPON THE KRAKÓW EXPERIENCES

In contrast to the often haphazard or rash ways in which many of the fruits of the Council were implemented in western Europe, the Council took longer to implement in Poland. Not least among the reasons was the continued repression of the Church under a communist regime, but a further reason was the desire to prudently apply its insights in a deeply traditional Catholic country by carefully studying the texts and understanding their claims. To this end, upon returning to his archdiocese after the conclusion of the Council,

---

[44] In *Amoris Laetitia*, no. 206, Pope Francis articulates a similar vision: "The importance of the virtues needs to be included. Among these, chastity proves invaluable for the genuine growth of love between persons."

[45] See especially Wojtyła, *Love and Responsibility*, 73-140, on various kinds of "love" and their relationship to instinct and freedom.

[46] Komonchak and Alberigo, *History of Vatican II*, Vol. 5, 404.

[47] For an account of the "last minute" modifications of the text, see Komonchak and Alberigo, *History of Vatican II*, Vol. 5, 408-419.

Wojtyła engaged immediately in a campaign to explore and apply the conciliar teachings in a comprehensive manner and was elected as vice-president of the conference of the Polish episcopate in 1969. As a way of furthering the insights of the Council on the tenth anniversary of its opening, he published *Sources of Renewal (U Podstaw Odnowy)* in 1972 and became one of the only Council fathers to write a systematic work analyzing the main themes of the Council's documents. Wojtyła proposes that his book is a *vademecum* for the study of the texts, in order to form attitudes and more deeply adopt the Council's teachings.[48] The vision of marriage and the family articulated in the work continues the thoughts he offered to the Council fathers.

While the Council is now a thing of the past, he argues it is "spiritually still in being," and it is his task as a bishop, indebted to the Holy Spirit for the Council's work, to "introduce and initiate into the reality of the Council itself."[49] Wojtyła provides a rich discussion of *Gaudium et Spes*, which he identifies as teaching "in particular how the redemption of man by Christ brings out the value of the human community in the multiform activities of man in the world."[50] Marriage and family life must therefore be understood in relation to the redemption of humanity by Christ, and several key themes emerge in Wojtyła's assessment of the conciliar treatment of marriage.

First, marriage and family life is a fundamentally important vocation that must be governed by charity. Wojtyła introduces the importance of the evangelical counsels of poverty, chastity, and obedience to answer how charity grows and what specific demands it makes upon married couples. "The evangelical counsels, even more than the commandments, should serve and promote charity. Charity is the essence of holiness in a Christian, and his progress towards sanctity is measured by the increase of his charity."[51] Marriage, governed by charity and strengthened by the evangelical counsels, is an "intimately personal vocation," which "must be realized in communion with other men."[52] Drawing upon the insights of *Gaudium et Spes*, no. 24, he argues that marriage is a real participation in and image of the divine *communio personarum*.[53] This is why the Council

---

[48] Karol Wojtyła, *Sources of Renewal*, trans. P.S. Falla (California: Harper and Row, 1980), iii-v.
[49] Wojtyła, *Sources of Renewal*, 11.
[50] Wojtyła, *Sources of Renewal*, 81.
[51] Wojtyła, *Sources of Renewal*, 194.
[52] Wojtyła, *Sources of Renewal*, 117.
[53] See *Gaudium et Spes*, no. 24, "Indeed, the Lord Jesus, when He prayed to the Father, 'that all may be one...as we are one' (John 17:21-22) opened up vistas closed to human reason, for He implied a certain likeness between the union of the divine Persons, and the unity of God's sons in truth and charity. This likeness reveals that

fathers placed a discussion of marriage at the beginning of the chapter on the Christian's responsibility in the modern world. "It is worth re-reading the whole of this Chapter of the pastoral Constitution, which, in light of its introductory note on marriage and the family in the modern world, emphasizes the sanctity of marriage and the family, their place in the divine plan of salvation, and the true meaning of married love in relation to procreation."[54]

Secondly, marriage is not only an earthly image of the divine *communio personarum*, but it is also a means by which the couple "bears witness to Christ" and His love and by which husband and wife are for their family and their children "cooperators of grace and witnesses of faith."[55] Their union therefore takes on a prophetic character and "proclaims aloud both the present power of the Kingdom of God and the hope of the blessed life."[56] In addition to witnessing to the love of Christ and teaching the Church and the world this love and its practical effects on society, a couple also builds up the Church and the world by fostering Christian living in their home, which is an "outstanding school for the lay apostolate."[57] For this reason, the Council itself, Wojtyła notes, draws on the "lively tradition of the primitive Church and on the rich experience of the Church in our own day," in which it is clear that the family constitutes the "first, fundamental community of lay Christians."[58] Again, we see here Wojtyła's emphasis on the importance of the lay vocation, which he had already expressed in his response sent to the conciliar antepreparatory commission.

Pastoral Experience and the Vision of Marriage

It is often claimed that John Paul II's "contacts with women were limited by the exclusively male context of the Curia and his personal staff."[59] While this might be true for many priests formed in the 1940's, such an assessment cannot apply to Wojtyła. From an early point in his priestly ministry, he was often surrounded by both female and male university students and young professionals, with whom he developed a special relationship, especially during his assignment as

---

man, who is the only creature on earth which God willed for itself, cannot fully find himself except through a sincere gift of himself."

[54] Wojtyła, *Sources of Renewal*, 117.
[55] Wojtyła, *Sources of Renewal*, 212.
[56] Wojtyła, *Sources of Renewal*, 248. Wojtyła is quoting *Lumen Gentium*, no. 35.
[57] Wojtyła, *Sources of Renewal*, 393. He is again quoting *Lumen Gentium*, no. 35.
[58] Wojtyła, *Sources of Renewal*, 392.
[59] See Susan Rakoczy, I.H.M., "Mixed Messages: John Paul II's Writings on Women," in *The Pastoral Vision of John Paul II*, ed. Joan Bland, SND de N (Illinois: Franciscan Herald Press, 1982), 177.

parochial vicar at St. Florian's Church in Kraków.[60] An informal group of students began to form around Wojtyła, which eventually took upon itself the name "*Środowisko*," ("milieu" or "environment") and whose members called their chaplain *wujek*, or "uncle," as it was illegal for any priest under the regime to carry out ministries outside of a church.[61] In 1953, the first of many outdoor excursions was organized, accompanied by Wojtyła, who would serve as a chaplain and a spiritual director. These excursions would become a yearly event, in which recreation was combined with a focus on communal prayer and the liturgy. Wojtyła's interactions with this group, composed of engineers, physicists, philosophers, and young adults from diverse fields of study allowed him to gain invaluable insight into the daily lives of lay persons, as well as an opportunity to "test ideas" through retreats. Among themes he articulated was the unity of life in relation to the truth, the universal call to holiness leading to concrete action, the humanity of Christ, and the beauty of human love.[62]

By his own account, this pastoral experience helped Wojtyła understand and perceive the need to articulate the beauty of human love in God's plan:

> It is this vocation to love that naturally allows us to draw close to the young. As a priest I realized this very early. I felt almost an inner call in this direction. It is necessary to prepare young people for marriage, it is necessary to *teach them love*. Love is not something that is learned, and yet there is nothing more important to learn! *As a young priest I learned to love human love*. This has been one of the most fundamental themes of my priesthood…If one loves human love, there naturally arises the need to commit oneself to the service of "fair love," because love is fair, it is beautiful.[63]

One of the most important lay persons whom Wojtyła met through the excursions of the *Środowisko* was (now Venerable) Jerzy Ciesielski, a young and accomplished engineer from Kraków and outdoor enthusiast who felt a deep call to the vocation of marriage. In addition to being a founding member and organizer of the *Środowisko*, Jerzy also became a model of spirituality for the group. He would make use of these trips to experience moments of solitude and personal prayer, from which he was reinvigorated to meet the demands of the academic, professional life in an urban setting.

---

[60] A simple Internet search reveals many photos of Bishop Wojtyła in civilian clothing surrounded by smiling young men and women, often on excursions in the mountains.
[61] Weigel, *Witness to Hope*, 102-112.
[62] Weigel, *Witness to Hope*, 108.
[63] John Paul II, *Crossing the Threshold of Hope*, 158.

In the context of these vigorous outings, Wojtyła and Ciesielski developed a deep friendship, common vocational understanding, and deep appreciation of God's beauty reflected in the natural world. "Everyone recognized, and accepted, the special bond between *Wujek* and Jurek Ciesielski."[64] They discussed many issues: the call to holiness in response to love; the married vocation; the priesthood; unity of life in the midst of professional and cultural challenges. This bond of friendship carried far beyond the mountains and kayaks and revealed the true complementarity of the vocation to marriage and the priesthood. In 1957, they co-wrote an article for *Homo Dei*, a Polish priests' magazine. Ciesielski wrote of the priest as one who ought to help "modern Catholics" look at their questions from a "different perspective" and to look at "all things in the Spirit of the Gospel."[65] For his part, Wojtyła recalled, "[The questions of] marriage and the family always occupied him . . . Discussions with Jerzy about this topic were for me a source of inspiration. My study *Love and Responsibility* arose among other things, as a result of these conversations."[66] On an August 1958 kayaking trip (just a few months prior to the submission of his written response to Cardinal Tardini), Wojtyła brought along a manuscript entitled *Love and Responsibility* and distributed fragments of it to the students to have a discussion about its themes and to solicit feedback.[67] It is thus safe to say, both from John Paul II's own accounts, and from those of the *Środowisko*, that Wojtyła's conversations with Ciesielski and other young Catholics helped him gain priceless insights into the nature of human love.[68]

Emerging Vision of the Sacramentality and Spirituality of Marriage

In addition to *Love and Responsibility*, Wojtyła wrote several short essays on the meaning of marriage and sacramental grace during the period of his ministry to the young lay Catholics. In an essay from Christmas 1957, entitled "Reflections on Matrimony," he distinguishes between two senses of "sacrament."[69] He argues that

---

[64] John Paul II, *Crossing the Threshold of Hope*, 103.
[65] John Paul II, *Crossing the Threshold of Hope*, 104.
[66] Karol Wojtyła, "A Reflection about Jerzy Ciesielski," in *Aby Chrystus się nami posługiwał.* (Kraków, Poland: Wydawnictwo Znak, 2009), 107-114. The translation does not yet exist in English, and the one here is my own.
[67] See Jarosław Kupczak, *Destined for Liberty* (Washington, D.C.: Catholic University of America Press, 2000), 44.
[68] One might ponder whether Ciesielski and Wojtyła therefore may have had an indirect influence on *Humanae Vitae*, as according to Paul Johnson, Paul VI was reading a copy of the book while overseeing the final draft of the encyclical. See Paul Johnson, *Pope John Paul II and the Catholic Restoration* (New York: St. Martin Press, 1981), 32-33, as cited in Kupczak, *Destined for Liberty*, 44.
[69] See Karol Wojtyła, "Myśli o Małżeństwie," in *Aby Chrystus się nami posługiwał*, 442. The translation is mine.

marriage is a "sacrament" in a natural sense, as it is "a fertile communion of persons, which gives life, and inasmuch as it is the foundation of the family...is a reality that carries in itself the *sign* of God—Creator and Giver of life."[70] Thus, the order of nature is already seen to be a sacramental reality, one in which nature and its ends already constitute a locus of encounter with God as creator. Marriage is of its nature a reflection of God's mysterious working in creation. Of course, marriage is also a sacrament in the supernatural sense because the natural union between a man and a woman has been elevated by Christ to become the earthly representation of a divine reality. "The energies of...grace are hidden in the nature of the persons who are reciprocally united in matrimony...As regards the life of the couple...they *are near* to God as the loving communion of persons, man and woman, founded on the mystery of the Incarnation—the mystery of grace that penetrates and is poured out on the natural."[71]

Two important themes emerge. First, Wojtyła is clear that natural human married love is already a sign of God in the world, insofar as God is the creator of all life.[72] Second, conjugal love that is also sacramental (between baptized persons) is a real means of grace for the couple, who form in the sacrament an image of the mystery of the Triune God, in Whom Father, Son, and Holy Spirit dwell eternally in a communion of reciprocal self-giving love.[73] As Wojtyła strikingly attests, one's coming to terms with the reality of sacramental marriage is "capable of lifting up and illuminating, but also of upsetting and frightening, especially if it is confronted with the well-known weakness of human beings who become participants in that extraordinary nearness to God."[74]

Hence, couples are always placed at the center of two discordant forces: the loftiness of the vocation and the weakness due to sin. They are called to transform their weakness and fear into love by love. Both as a result of their natural human love and as a result of their nearness to God by virtue of the sacrament, they are obliged to grow in the covenant of love which they share. They are called to *become who they are* by means of sacramental grace. It is up to the couple to "draw out from the sacramental powers all that they contain and to make

---

[70] Wojtyła, "Myśli o Małżeństwie," 446.
[71] Wojtyła, "Myśli o Małżeństwie," 447.
[72] He will argue later as pope, in the "theology of the body," that marriage in the order of nature is already a "primordial sacrament." See John Paul II, *Man and Woman He Created Them*, Michael Waldstein, trans. (Massachusetts: Pauline Books and Media, 2006), 19:3-4; 28:2.
[73] Recall the similarities between this language and that of the preparatory submission, written just two years later.
[74] Wojtyła, "Myśli o Małżeństwie," 449.

them enter into their personal life."[75] The two persons, bound together by virtue of the matrimonial graces, "are the direct instruments of God's acting and, in a certain manner, also the conductors of the current of life which is in Him and of which they become participators through the sacrament."[76]

Wojtyła is therefore clear that marriage is an objective reality that exists by virtue of the freely consented choice made out of "betrothed" love. The wedding day becomes the beginning of an intimate partnership of love and life that is entrusted to them as an ethical obligation. This partnership will face many trials, tribulations, struggles, and challenges, both as a result of human weakness, and external pressures, and Wojtyła makes clear that it is "by no means an exaggerated affirmation" to suggest that the problem of conjugal life necessitates a certain "heroism."[77] Arguing in the same manner as he would eight years later in the conciliar debates and the Ariccia meeting, Wojtyła recognizes that the call to heroism in marriage finds its source from the deep reserves of authentic virtue and love, flowing most especially from the suffering of Christ on the cross.

One cannot therefore understand Wojtyła's notion of conjugal life in marriage without pointing to Christ's cross. Married people face many daily challenges, some resulting from the culture and some by virtue of conjugal life itself, such as economic pressures, challenges in educating and disciplining children, difficulties living God's plan in the sphere of sexual intimacy, loss of communication, conflict with extended families, and illness. However, these are the "crosses" that married people encounter and by which they are victorious in becoming more perfectly who they are called to be.[78]

The Christocentric dimension of marriage is not one of simple representation or symbolic witness. Husband and wife are also, by virtue of their baptism and through the sacramental grace of marriage by which they are made "near" to God, called to imitate and participate in the virtues of Christ Himself, to "put on Christ" (Gal. 3:27).[79] While God's plan for marriage may be difficult to accept and realize, the Church understands this but remains faithful to the words of the Lord

---

[75] Wojtyła, "Myśli o Małżeństwie," 449.
[76] Wojtyła, "Myśli o Małżeństwie," 449.
[77] Wojtyła, "Myśli o Małżeństwie," 453.
[78] Over twenty years later, John Paul II will argue in *Familiaris Consortio*, no. 13, that spouses' "belonging to each other is the real representation, by means of the sacramental sign, of the very relationship of Christ with the Church. Spouses are therefore the *permanent reminder to the Church* of what happened on the Cross; they are for one another and for the children witnesses to the salvation in which the sacrament makes them *sharers*."
[79] For this reason, John Paul II will reflect on the many aspects of Christ's life in both the *Letter to Families* and *Familiaris Consortio*—the Incarnation, the hidden life in Nazareth, the teaching ministry, and the Paschal Mystery, etc.

in her teachings.⁸⁰ Despite hardships, husband and wife are called witness to the real grace given in the sacramental encounter with Christ, and it is their ethical task to form a "culture of the person" within marriage, in which authentic love is fostered and cultivated and is accomplished by the freely given grace of God.

The "Rule" of Love

The grace of marriage invites a response from the spouses. Both individually and as a couple, they must answer the call to become more perfectly conformed to Christ by means of the married vocation. This call to participate in God's love, however, places quite a demand on human love weakened by sin. The most authentic human love enjoins a certain responsibility, requiring guidance and maturing. But what kind of "rule" can command love?⁸¹ In his essay, "Love and the Moral Foundations of Marriage," Bishop Wojtyła meditates on Christ's injunction, "Be perfect as your heavenly Father is perfect" (Mt. 5:48). He juxtaposes marriage and the so-called "state of perfection" (a traditional term referring to religious or consecrated life), which is marked by vows of the evangelical counsels of poverty, chastity, and obedience. Without rejecting the Church's traditional teaching on a superiority of the consecrated life, he nevertheless points to various exaggerations of this notion. A religious's belonging to the "state of perfection" does not imply a moral superiority to a married couple. Similarly, although marriage is not a "state of perfection," this is no reason to downplay the call to perfection in the conjugal state. "It appears that the teaching on [the universal call to] perfection may have been slightly obscured by the teaching on the *state* of perfection," Wojtyła argues, "and consequently there was born a certain minimalism, almost programmed, in relation to the life of the married couple."⁸² He discusses the negative impact of the manual tradition's

---

⁸⁰ Cf. Pope Francis, *Amoris Laetitia*, no. 307. "To show understanding in the face of exceptional situations never implies dimming the light of the fuller ideal, or proposing less than what Jesus offers to the human being."

⁸¹ Recall, again, that in his submission to the antepreparatory session, Wojtyła speaks of the relationship between charity and its "rules."

⁸² See Karol Wojtyła, "Miłość jest moralnym fundamentem małżeństwa," in *Teksty poznańskie,* ed. M. Jędraszewski (Poznań, Poland: Ks. Św. Wojciecha , 1986), 49-61. He will return to this theme in *Man and Woman He Created Them*, 78:2-3, "Marriage and celibacy do not divide the Christian community into "two camps" [as if there were] those who are 'perfect' because of continence and those who are 'imperfect' or 'less perfect' because of the reality of married life;" and later, "The perfection of Christian life is measured, rather, by the measure of love. It follows that a person who does not live in the 'state of perfection' or in a religious institute, but in the 'world,' can *de facto* reach a higher degree of perfection—the measure of which is love—than a person who lives in the 'state of perfection' with a lesser degree of love…Such a

focus on those acts prohibited in marriage, rather than on the ethos of holiness underlying the conjugal ethic. In contrast, Wojtyła proclaims: "The sacramental grace of matrimony is not a theory."[83] If at various times in the history of the Church the call to perfection within marriage has not been sufficiently appreciated, it is necessary to call to mind that marriage is a "reality of God, as one of the terrains on which not only the human being with his concupiscence and fallen nature, but also the *Lord and His grace*, play a role."[84] The "dramatic moment" that determines the entire structure of a couple's conjugal life is their acceptance or rejection of the strenuous effort which the call to perfection will require. The sacramental grace of matrimony is precisely what sustains that effort.

This effort to perfect themselves, in response to and guided by marital grace, requires *ascesis*, for both the individual spouses and their life as a couple. Wojtyła insists that the ascetical life is absolutely indispensable to the sanctification of a marriage. Husband and wife must devote themselves to "a progressive education in self-control of the will, of sentiments, of emotions, which must be developed from the simplest gestures, in which it is relatively easy to put the inner decision into practice."[85] More specifically, a husband and wife must contemplate and apply in their communal lives the spirit of the evangelical counsels: poverty, chastity, and obedience. The evangelical counsels, though not vowed by the married couple, must nevertheless provide the foundation for an authentic conjugal spirituality.

Wojtyła's insistence on the evangelical counsels as a means by which to sustain conjugal charity and a conjugal spirituality is seen in his book *Sources of Renewal* and in his conciliar interventions. He sought to lay further the foundations for the development of such a spirituality in 1968, shortly after the publication of *Humanae Vitae*, when he wrote a "Rule for *Humanae Vitae* Groups of Married Couples."[86] This short rule of six points advocates the formation of groups of married couples who can assist one another in fidelity to the life of grace and confront together the challenges to marriage and

---

perfection is possible and accessible to every human being, whether in a 'religious institute' or in the 'world.'"

[83] Karol Wojtyła, "Miłość jest moralnym fundamentem małżeństwa," in *Bellezza e spiritualità dell'amore coniugale*, eds. S. Grygiel, L. Grygiel, and P. Kwiatkowski (Siena, Italy: Edizione Cantagalli, 2009), 59.

[84] Wojtyła, "Miłość jest moralnym fundamentem małżeństwa," 55.

[85] He develops these thoughts as John Paul II in *Man and Woman He Created Them*, 128:1. The theology of the body, though delivered during the years of his pontificate, was written prior to his ascent to the papacy and stands in continuity with his previous thoughts on marriage, as is clearly evident here.

[86] For this recently re-discovered "rule," see S. Grygiel, L. Grygiel, P. Kwiatkowski, *Bellezza e spiritualità dell'amore coniugale* (Siena, Italy: Edizione Cantagalli, 2009).

family in the modern world through formation, discussion and fellowship. Wojtyła addressed the *Rule* to couples (and not to husband or wife individually) and argues that it is "not enough to simply observe the letter of the Church's laws pertaining to conjugal life." To truly live the Christian married vocation requires a proper spirituality—the interior life—which is only achieved by constant effort. "Such a spirituality does not exist in a ready-made form, such as the spirituality of various religious orders, but it ought to be constantly worked out." To counter a consumerist culture, a married couple lives the evangelical counsel of poverty; they live the counsel of obedience out of mutual submission to Christ to counter the scattered allegiances of modernity; they live the counsel of chastity to testify to the power of free, total, faithful, and fruitful love in a "culture of indifference and the temporary."[87]

CONCLUSION

Several lessons can be learned from our analysis of Wojtyła's preconciliar, conciliar, and postconciliar work, especially regarding marriage and the family. First, over a half century after the Council, there remains much work to be done in studying the origins of the conciliar texts, understanding key figures, and adequately assessing their role and influence on the modern Church. Many texts remain untranslated, understudied, and, therefore, underappreciated for the role they played in the Second Vatican Council. Since John Paul II's influence on contemporary Catholic moral theology is undeniable, from *Veritatis Splendor* to the countless magisterial documents on marriage and the family issued during his pontificate, it is crucial to understand and assess his thought accurately. One important way of providing such an appraisal is to show the development, continuity, and consistency of his thought from its early stages when he was a priest, to its mature form in the pontifical teachings. While much of his early work remains inaccessible to those in the English-speaking academy, it is an indispensable source from which to gain an accurate appreciation for his work. Indeed, an accurate assessment of his early career will help illuminate his papal corpus in new ways, on issues ranging from suffering, the role of the laity, the tasks of moral theology, and other areas about which he wrote and taught.

---

[87] See Pope Francis, "Meeting with Young People of Umbria," October 4, 2013, w2.vatican.va/content/francesco/en/speeches/2013/october/documents/papa-francesco_20131004_giovani-assisi.html; Pope Francis, "Overcome Indifference and Win Peace," January 1, 2016, w2.vatican.va/content/francesco/en/messages/peace/documents/papa-francesco_20151208_messaggio-xlix-giornata-mondiale-pace-2016.html#_ftn3.

Here, we have provided at least one area, marriage and the family, in which Wojtyła's early vision both shaped subsequent Church teaching through the debates and interventions at the Second Vatican Council, while itself being shaped by the lay people he encountered throughout his life. Wojtyła's pastoral experience with lay married persons, and those discerning the sacrament of marriage, led him to articulate an account of married love that takes into account both the doctrinal tradition of the Church as well as the lived experience of this doctrine by those who are called to the married vocation. Wojtyła always encouraged the exponents of the former to speak to the experience of the latter and the latter to conform their lives according to the rule of faith.

Secondly, much of contemporary moral theology of marriage and the family, even after the publication of Pope Francis' *Amoris Laetitia*, has focused on moral norms, particularly those governing the reception of the Eucharist by couples who find themselves in "irregular" situations and pastoral ministry to "difficult" situations.[88] Yet, much work remains to be done in moral theology in reflecting upon the sacramentality of marriage and the development of a specifically conjugal spirituality. Rather than focusing on moral norms, though important, it seems that Wojtyła's thought requires a deeper reflection upon the "shape" of the Christian married life. One of the important and key emphases in Wojtyła's early work (which later re-emerged in the "theology of the body") was that the vocation to sacramental marriage brought with it the task of working out a spirituality in keeping with the vocation. By this, Wojtyła did not mean that a spouse might join a "third order," such as the Secular Franciscans, Benedictine Oblates, or Dominican tertiaries. While certainly a spouse may follow this calling, this does not encompass the specifically married life, their common life as a couple, in which they signify in a real way the love of God, and who have been conformed to Christ's sacrificial love by their sacrament. Throughout his early work that led up to the Second Vatican Council and in his careful implementation of the Council, Wojtyła articulated a vision of marriage which took into account the deep riches of the human experiences of love and sought to relate these to the supernatural calling of Christians to participate in the intimate love of the Triune God. This vision trusts radically in the ability of sacramental grace to overcome human weakness. Shaped by the practice of the virtues, which are further specified by the counsels of poverty, chastity, and obedience, a couple is able to live their marriage as a gift and a task entrusted to them. A task requires certain rules, or modes of life,

---

[88] I am not downplaying the importance of the questions raised by chapter eight of this document. However, by focusing on the controversies surrounding this chapter, many have lost sight of the rest of the document's beautiful insights.

central to the very dynamic of the marital relationship itself, and conjugal maturity is particularly achieved through the practice of *ascesis*. Their joint ascetical endeavors, both individually and as a couple, conform them more perfectly to the cross of Christ and enable them to become witnesses to their family and community of the self-emptying love of God. Although such a vision of marriage is difficult, it is in fact possible when the couple "leans into" the grace of Christ and lives according to the truth about human love.[89]

Finally, a greater familiarity with the kind of "conjugal spirituality," especially an extensive reflection on the specific role of the evangelical counsels in marriage, which Wojtyła himself did not provide, can help illuminate and deepen one of Pope Francis's key insights in *Amoris Laetitia*. In chapter nine, Pope Francis proposes a "spirituality of marriage and the family," which is based on the fact that husband and wife, called individually as members of Christ's body but even more so as a couple, are invited into Trinitarian communion by virtue of their sacrament.[90] Theirs is a task of "daily sanctification and mystical growth" (*Amoris Laetitia*, no. 316). While these parallels between Francis's newest document on the family and Wojtyła's insights on marriage and the family from over sixty years ago should by now be clear, more work remains to be done in tracing the development and further developing the contours of a specifically conjugal spirituality which, while allowing for contingent social and cultural realities, remains a sure path by which spouses can, in their families and in their homes, go together rejoicing to the house of the Lord. **M**

---

[89] See Francis, *Amoris Laetitia*, no. 317: "Gradually, 'with the grace of the Holy Spirit, [the spouses] grow in holiness through married life, also by sharing in the mystery of Christ's cross, which transforms difficulties and sufferings into an offering of love.'" I am grateful to Marie Reimers for the image of "leaning into" the grace of Christ.
[90] See Francis, *Amoris Laetitia*, no. 314.

The Principle of Double Effect within Catholic Moral Theology: A Response to Two Criticisms of the Principle in Relation to Palliative Sedation

Gina Maria Noia

THE "PRINCIPLE," "RULE," OR "DOCTRINE" OF double effect evaluates the moral permissibility of an action having both good and bad effects according to four conditions, which concern: the action in itself, the actor's intention, the causal relations, and the proportionality of the good to the bad. I begin this paper by describing the current formulation of the principle in more detail. I then show how the Catholic Church relies upon double effect reasoning to draw a moral distinction between palliative sedation[1] and euthanasia. Next, I detail two criticisms by American bioethicists of the principle as it relates to palliative sedation. First, they contend that the principle problematically presupposes contentious positions, in particular, that death and intending death are bad. Second, they suggest that the principle lacks determinacy due to the "redescription problem," the problem that one can redescribe the object, intention, causal relations, and proportionality to match his or her intuition of the moral permissibility of the action.

Having traced the development of the principle and engaged its recent critics, I respond to these criticisms. The current formulation[2] of the principle of double effect is susceptible to some forms of these criticisms when it is considered as an isolated moral principle. However, I argue that the principle of double effect is not undermined by these criticisms when it is evaluated as a part of Catholic moral theology. I argue, first, that Catholic moral theology does not merely presuppose that death and intending death are bad. Rather, within Catholic moral theology, the principle is understood as an aid to discernment of the morality of an action, as one moral principle in the context of a broader moral system. Second, I argue that the principle

---

[1] Palliative sedation is also sometimes called "terminal sedation."
[2] I say "current formulation" because I do not preclude the possibility of a philosophical reworking of the principle that could make it more determinate both inside and outside of the Catholic moral tradition.

of double effect is still valuable within the Catholic tradition in at least four ways. The principle of double effect can: (1) be used as one way to articulate more fully why the Church teaches what it teaches, (2) aid individual discernment in particular situations, (3) assist theological debate, not despite, but because of the redescription problem, and (4) serve as a vehicle of case-based reasoning.

FOUR CONDITIONS OF THE PRINCIPLE OF DOUBLE EFFECT

The principle of double effect may be employed when considering the morality of an action that has both good and bad effects. The principle provides four conditions for such an act's being morally permissible.[3] Joseph T. Mangan's formulation of the principle is often cited by both theologians and philosophers:

> A person may licitly perform an action that he foresees will produce a good and a bad effect provided that four conditions are verified at one and the same time: [C1] that the action in itself from its very object be good or at least indifferent; [C2] that the good effect and not the evil effect be intended; [C3] that the good effect be not produced by means of the evil effect; [C4] that there be a proportionately grave reason for permitting the evil effect.[4]

Mangan seems to view the conditions as necessary conditions: an act with good and bad effects is morally permissible only if it meets all four conditions of the principle of double effect.[5] Mangan's phrase "provided that"[6] indicates the necessity of the conditions. Others view the conditions as sufficient conditions: an act with good and bad effects is morally permissible if it meets all four conditions.[7] Still

---

[3] Even proportionalists who reduce the principle of double effect to whether a good effect of an action is proportionate to the action's bad effect, still begin their treatments of the principle of double effect by recognizing four traditional conditions of the principle. See Bernard Hoose, *Proportionalism: The American Debate and Its European Roots.* (Washington, DC: Georgetown University Press, 1987), 101. I will not respond directly to proportionalists' objections regarding the principle of double effect.

[4] Joseph T. Mangan, "An Historical Analysis of the Principle of Double Effect," *Theological Studies* 10, no. 1 (1949): 43.

[5] Similarly, the *New Catholic Encyclopedia* states that, "Theologians commonly teach that four conditions must be verified in order that a person may legitimately perform such an act" (F. J. O'Connell, "Principle of Double Effect," in *New Catholic Encyclopedia* (New York: McGraw-Hill, 1967), 1021). "Must be" again seems to indicate the necessity of the conditions.

[6] Mangan, "An Historical Analysis of the Principle of Double Effect," 43

[7] See James F. Keenan, "The Function of the Principle of Double Effect," *Theological Studies* 54, no. 2 (1993): 300. Keenan seems to indicate this view as the traditional view: "Since the seventeenth century, the principle of double effect has been interpreted to mean that an act with two effects, one right and one wrong, can be

others view the conditions as necessary and sufficient conditions: an act with good and bad effects is morally permissible if and only if it meets all four conditions.[8] Further disagreement exists on the wording of the principle's four conditions and their application, which accounts for the differing moral conclusions based on the principle, especially regarding beginning-of-life issues.[9] However, the discrepant wording is not generally problematic in Catholic moral theology as it relates to palliative sedation.

PRINCIPLE OF DOUBLE EFFECT AND PALLIATIVE SEDATION IN CATHOLIC MORAL TEACHING

In this section, I explain the moral distinction, based on double effect reasoning, which the Catholic Church draws between euthanasia and palliative sedation. By "double effect reasoning," I mean reasoning which alludes to one or more of the principle's conditions to explain the moral permissibility of an act with both good and bad effects. I explain the Church's moral distinction between euthanasia and palliative sedation for four reasons. First, the principle of double effect originates within Catholic moral theology.[10] Second, the explanation of Church teaching[11] on palliative sedation will illustrate one commonly accepted application of the principle of double effect within Catholic moral theology. Third, the criticisms of the principle of double effect by American bioethicists that I examine concern end-of-life issues including palliative sedation. Fourth, I

---

performed when four conditions are met." Assuming Keenan uses the term "when" the way the term is commonly used in propositional logic, the term indicates the conditions as sufficient conditions. Note that on this view it is not necessarily the case that an action which fails to meet one or more conditions of the principle of double effect is morally wrong; it may be that another moral principle would be more helpful in this determination. Keenan's own position seems to be that the principle of double effect provides neither necessary nor sufficient conditions (see Keenan, "The Function of the Principle of Double Effect," 300), on which I comment in footnote 50.

[8] See, for instance, Tom L. Beauchamp and James F. Childress, *Principles of Biomedical Ethics*, 7th ed. (New York: Oxford University Press, 2013), 165: "Each is a necessary condition, and together they form sufficient conditions of morally permissible action."

[9] This difference is found much more in application of the principle of double effect to beginning-of-life cases than end-of-life cases. As such, demonstration of variation in wording corresponding to variation in application of the principle of double effect is outside the scope of this paper.

[10] See, for instance: Keenan, "The Function of the Principle of Double Effect," 294–315; Mangan, "An Historical Analysis of the Principle of Double Effect," 43–49; Alison McIntyre, "Doctrine of Double Effect," *Stanford Encyclopedia of Philosophy*, plato.stanford.edu/archives/win2014/entries/double-effect/.

[11] In this paper, I use "Church teaching" and other similar expressions to refer to the magisterial tradition of the Catholic Church.

ultimately defend the value of the principle within Catholic moral theology.

One of the Catholic Church's clearest applications of double effect reasoning is in its teaching on end-of-life issues. The Church uses double effect reasoning to draw a moral distinction between palliative sedation and euthanasia. Medical consensus today is that pain medication properly titrated would be highly unlikely to hasten a patient's death, so the moral distinction between palliative sedation and euthanasia has become more clear. Palliative sedation is not euthanasia as it does not cause or even hasten death. Nevertheless, I focus on the Church's moral distinction between euthanasia and palliative sedation—which was developed at a time when it was uncertain whether palliative sedation hastened death, and so might constitute euthanasia—since critics of the principle of double effect also focus on this distinction.

The Church teaches that euthanasia, "an act or omission which, of itself or by intention, causes death in order to eliminate suffering" (*Catechism*, no. 2277), is always morally wrong. However, the Church teaches that palliative sedation, the use of pain medication to ease the suffering of a dying patient, even if such use may shorten the person's life, can be morally permissible (*Catechism*, no. 2279). The Church's definition of euthanasia does not specify the actor (physician, caregiver, or patient), and thus encompasses both euthanasia and physician-assisted suicide as understood in American bioethics.[12]

The *Catechism of the Catholic Church* states, "The use of painkillers to alleviate the sufferings of the dying, even at the risk of shortening their days, can be morally in conformity with human dignity if death is not willed as either an end or a means, but only foreseen and tolerated as inevitable" (no. 2279). Here, the Church confirms that palliative sedation can be morally permissible, employing language from C2 and C3 of the principle of double effect. In employing this language, the Church arguably implies that palliative sedation can meet all four conditions of the principle of double effect: (C1) the use of painkillers to alleviate a patient's sufferings is morally good or at least neutral; (C2) it is plausible that in administering pain medication the actor may only intend to alleviate the patient's sufferings and merely foresee possibly shortening the patient's life; (C3) the shortening of the patient's life is not the means

---

[12] Physician-assisted suicide is defined as a patient's committing suicide using medical means provided by a physician. Euthanasia is defined as a physician's (or other person's) administering a lethal drug (or other treatment) to another person with the intention of causing death. See Charles Junkerman, Arthur Derse, and David Schiedermayer, *Practical Ethics for Students, Interns, and Residents: A Short Reference Manual*, 3rd ed. (Maryland: University Publishing Group, 2008), 72.

to the alleviation of the patient's sufferings; and (C4) the need to alleviate the dying patient's sufferings constitutes a proportionate reason to permit the possible shortening of the patient's life. Note that if the actor did intend to shorten the patient's life, this particular act of palliative sedation would fail to meet C2 and would not be justified by the principle of double effect. Rather, according to Catholic teaching, the act particular would constitute euthanasia.

The Congregation for the Doctrine of the Faith (CDF) likewise confirms that palliative sedation can be morally permissible and alludes to C2, C3, and C4 of the principle of double effect. The CDF's 1980 *Declaration on Euthanasia* recalls the teaching of Pope Pius XII: "'Is the suppression of pain and consciousness by the use of narcotics... permitted... (even at the approach of death and if one foresees that the use of narcotics will shorten life)?'... 'If no other means exist, and if, in the given circumstances, this does not prevent the carrying out of other religious and moral duties: Yes.'"[13] The CDF explains that in this case, "Death is in no way intended or sought, even if the risk of it is reasonably taken; the intention is simply to relieve pain effectively, using for this purpose painkillers available to medicine" (*Declaration on Euthanasia*, no. 3). The CDF assumes that the actor involved in palliative sedation has an intention for the good (C2), the CDF points to the painkillers, not death, as the means to the good effect of pain relief (C3), and the CDF requires that there is not another effective way of relieving the pain, suggesting the proportionality required by (C4). If there were another effective way to relieve pain, it would not be proportionate to risk the bad effect of death in achieving the good of pain relief.

The United States Conference of Catholic Bishops (USCCB) publishes a reiteration of Church teaching in the form of practicable directives for Catholic Health Care in the United States. These *Ethical and Religious Directives for Catholic Health Care Services* (ERDs) similarly employ language from C2, C3, and C4 of the principle of double effect when addressing the issue of palliative sedation.

> Patients should be kept as free of pain as possible so that they may die comfortably and with dignity. . . . Since a person has the right to prepare for his or her death while fully conscious, he or she should not be deprived of consciousness without a compelling reason. Medicines capable of alleviating or suppressing pain may be given to a dying person, even if this therapy may indirectly shorten the person's life so long as the intent is not to hasten death.[14]

---

[13] Pius XII, "Address to Those Taking Part in the IXth Congress of the Italian Anaesthesiological Society," February 24, 1957, AAS 49 (1957): 146.

[14] United States Conference of Catholic Bishops, *Ethical and Religious Directives for Catholic Health Care Services*, www.usccb.org/issues-and-action/human-life-and-

The ERDs require that the actor involved in palliative sedation does not intend the bad effect (C2); the ERDs note that painkillers "may indirectly shorten the person's life," indicating death is not the means to the alleviation of pain (C3); and the ERDs require a "compelling reason," suggesting a proportionate reason, for palliative sedation (C4).

AMERICAN BIOETHICISTS' CRITICISM

I now turn to American bioethicists' criticism of the principle of double effect as it relates to palliative sedation. I begin with Beauchamp and Childress's seminal work *Principles of Biomedical Ethics*, as it has been highly influential in both academic and popular American bioethics. Beauchamp and Childress identify what they see as two shortcomings of the principle of double effect, which lead them to discard the current formulation of the principle as unconstructive.

The first shortcoming involves what I call the "redescription problem." According to Beauchamp and Childress, proponents of the principle of double effect generally have no "practicable way to distinguish the intended from the merely foreseen"[15] and so can redescribe an act "to allow persons to foresee almost anything as a side effect rather than as an intended means."[16] Recall, for Catholic moral theology, that on the principle of double effect there is supposed to be a moral difference between cases of euthanasia, in which an actor necessarily *intends* the death of a patient, and morally permissible cases of palliative sedation, in which an actor *foresees* the death as an effect of his action, but does not intend the death. Beauchamp and Childress argue that a plausible analysis of intention, which is not subject to arbitrary redescription, implies that "any effect specifically willed in accordance with a plan, including tolerated as well as wanted effects"[17] is intended. The problem with this plausible analysis is that it delivers unwanted results for Catholic moral theology. On Beauchamp and Childress's analysis of intention, the relevant moral distinction between euthanasia and palliative sedation vanishes, as the actor intends the death of the patient in both types of cases. Bereft of a plausible analysis of intention, Catholic moral theology cannot determinately apply the principle of double effect because of the redescription problem. On what basis, or for what reason, can Catholic moral theology distinguish between unintended and intended foreseen

---

dignity/health-care/upload/Ethical-Religious-Directives-Catholic-Health-Care-Services-fifth-edition-2009.pdf.
[15] Beauchamp and Childress, *Principles of Biomedical Ethics*, 166.
[16] Beauchamp and Childress, *Principles of Biomedical Ethics*, 167.
[17] Beauchamp and Childress, *Principles of Biomedical Ethics*, 167.

effects? As Beauchamp and Childress write, "Much depends on the description of the terminal sedation in a particular set of circumstances, including the patient's overall condition, the proximity of death, the availability of alternative means to relieve pain and suffering, and so on, as well as the intention of the physician and other parties."[18]

The above suggests that, on account of the redescription problem, persons can redescribe not only intention but also the object of an act, causal relations, and proportionality to match their intuition of whether the action is morally permissible. In other words, persons may come to different conclusions regarding the object, intentionality, causality, and proportionality of an action, and thus will differ on whether a particular act in a particular circumstance is morally permissible. For instance, what is the object of the act of the physician who gives a lethal dose of morphine? Is the object of the act "administering morphine intravenously"? Is the object of the act "killing the patient"? Or, on the question of palliative sedation, what is the proportionality of risking death in order to relieve a patient's pain? Is it worth risking death in order to alleviate pain? Beauchamp and Childress are correct that much does depend on how the particulars are described.

The redescription problem seems to be a fatal flaw in a moral principle, since it seems that principles ought to yield determinate moral conclusions. Determinacy is one of the principal measures for evaluating moral theories.[19] One way in which principles may fail to yield determinate moral conclusions is if they "are excessively vague and so fail to imply, in a wide range of cases, any specific moral verdicts."[20] The redescription problem seems a problem for the principle of double effect precisely on this basis. The principle of double effect arguably is "excessively vague"[21] regarding what the object of an act is, when an effect is intended, what makes an effect a means, and when effects are proportionate "and so fails to imply, in a wide range of cases, any specific moral verdicts."[22] Consequently, as a decision procedure, the principle itself fails to arbitrate among different moral verdicts, though such arbitration is precisely what one expects from a moral principle.

---

[18] Beauchamp and Childress, *Principles of Biomedical Ethics*, 168.
[19] See Mark Timmons, *Moral Theory: An Introduction*, 2nd ed. (Plymouth, United Kingdom: Rowman & Littlefield, 2012), 13: "According to the *determinacy standard*, a moral theory should feature principles which, together with relevant factual information, yield determinate moral verdicts about the morality of actions, persons, and other objects of evaluation in a wide range of cases."
[20] Timmons, *Moral Theory*, 13.
[21] Timmons, *Moral Theory*, 13.
[22] Timmons, *Moral Theory*, 13.

As a second shortcoming of the principle of double effect, Beauchamp and Childress identify the principle's inability to determine "whether death is good or bad for a particular person."[23] They conclude with the criticism that the goodness or badness of death for a particular person, "must be determined and defended on independent grounds."[24] In making this criticism, Beauchamp and Childress seem to evaluate the principle of double effect as an isolated moral principle, and they are correct that the principle itself cannot decide or justify the goodness or badness of death for a particular person.

In a similar vein, Miller and Truog argue in *Death, Dying and Organ Transplantation* that the time has come to abandon the traditional norm that clinicians should not intentionally cause the deaths of their patients.[25] They reject the weight of the principle of double effect against their thesis for a few reasons: (1) It is difficult to distinguish between what one intends and what one merely foresees. (2) The principle of double effect, "begs the question of characterizing death as a bad or harmful effect in this context."[26] (3) In light of cases where living is apparently "a fate worse than death," it is "ethically dubious"[27] that clinicians should not intend the deaths of their patients. (4) Claims to the contrary notwithstanding, clinicians often intend the deaths of their patients (and this can be empirically shown). (5) The principle of double effect "obscures"[28] the fact that clinicians' intentions are "often multiple and ambiguous."[29]

In their objection (1), Miller and Truog, like Beauchamp and Childress, point to the redescription problem. Moreover, Miller and Truog's criticisms, like Beauchamp and Childress's, seem to evaluate the principle of double effect as an isolated moral principle. When the principle of double effect is considered as an isolated principle, some form of Miller and Truog's criticisms (2) and (3) may be appropriate.

Objection (4), that clinicians often intend the deaths of their patients, says nothing against the principle of double effect itself, though Miller and Truog claim that "this point tells against both the second and third condition of the doctrine of double effect."[30] In order for this point to challenge C2 and C3, however, C2 (regarding

---

[23] Beauchamp and Childress, *Principles of Biomedical Ethics*, 168.
[24] Beauchamp and Childress, *Principles of Biomedical Ethics*, 168.
[25] Franklin G. Miller and Robert D. Truog, *Death, Dying, and Organ Transplantation: Reconstructing Medical Ethics at the End of Life* (Oxford: Oxford University Press, 2012).
[26] Miller and Truog, *Death, Dying, and Organ Transplantation*, 16.
[27] Miller and Truog, *Death, Dying, and Organ Transplantation*, 16.
[28] Miller and Truog, *Death, Dying, and Organ Transplantation*, 18.
[29] Miller and Truog, *Death, Dying, and Organ Transplantation*, 18.
[30] Miller and Truog, *Death, Dying, and Organ Transplantation*, 17.

palliative sedation) must affirm that physicians do not intend the death of their patients when participating in palliative sedation[31] and C3 must affirm that death is not the means to the relief of suffering. However, contrary to Miller and Truog's suggestion, C2 does not necessarily affirm that physicians do not intend the death of their patients when participating in palliative sedation. Rather, C2 asks whether a physician intends the death of his or her patient. If the physician does intend the death, the particular act of palliative sedation would not be morally permissible. Likewise, C3 does not necessarily affirm that death is not the means to the relief of suffering. Rather, C3 asks whether death is the means to the relief of suffering. If death is the means to the relief of suffering, the act of palliative sedation would not be morally permissible. Thus, Miller and Truog's objection (4) does not challenge C2 and C3 of the principle of double effect as they claim. Rather, with objection (4), Miller and Truog seem to conflate the principle of double effect with one way in which the principle is often employed (to justify permissible cases of palliative sedation). In other words, this objection seems to appeal to sociological evidence in order to challenge the position often associated with the principle of double effect, that intending death is always morally wrong. Objection (3) already directly challenges this position.

Miller and Truog's claim in objection (5) that intentions are "often multiple and ambiguous"[32] rings true to experience. Even in less ethically significant matters, it seems true that intentions are "often multiple and ambiguous." Even when doing what one knows to be a good action, one may have difficulty sorting out one's motivations. Miller and Truog do not explain why they think the principle of double effect "obscures"[33] the multiplicity and ambiguity of intentions, but they cite an article by Timothy E. Quill.[34] Quill's concern is that the principle of double effect encourages "self-deception"[35] and "secrecy"[36] since it does not allow for an actor to have a "bad"[37] intention (even amidst many good intentions). Quill implies that rather than being honest about their intentions, which include "partial"[38] and

---

[31] Miller and Truog's discussion of the principle of double effect focuses on withdrawing life-sustaining treatment, rather than palliative sedation, but I apply their discussion to the closely related issue of palliative sedation in order to maintain this paper's focus on palliative sedation.
[32] Miller and Truog, *Death, Dying, and Organ Transplantation*, 18.
[33] Miller and Truog, *Death, Dying, and Organ Transplantation*, 18.
[34] Timothy E. Quill, "The Ambiguity of Clinical Intentions," *New England Journal of Medicine* 329, no. 14 (1993): 1039-1040.
[35] Quill, "The Ambiguity of Clinical Intentions," 1040.
[36] Quill, "The Ambiguity of Clinical Intentions," 1040.
[37] I put "bad" in quotes since Quill, like Miller and Truog, disputes that intending death is a bad intention.
[38] Quill, "The Ambiguity of Clinical Intentions," 1039.

"contradictory"[39] intentions, clinicians will give the impression that their intention is only to relieve the suffering of a patient so that their actions are justified by the principle of double effect. Like Miller and Truog's objection (4), this objection does not seem to be an objection against the principle of double effect itself but rather an objection against the influence of the principle of double effect and the closely associated positions that death and intending death is bad. Miller and Truog's objections (2) and (3) already directly challenge these positions. Quill concludes his article with a call for physicians to be honest about their intentions. Plausibly, then, Miller and Truog's objection (5) is also an objection against clinicians who do not admit that they intend the deaths of certain patients, insofar as this silence encourages the legal and ethical prohibition of physician-assisted suicide. Criticisms regarding the influence of the principle and clinicians' silence, however, are not challenges to the validity of the principle itself.

RESPONDING TO THE CRITICISMS

Although some of Miller and Truog's criticisms of the principle of double effect as it relates to end-of-life issues (objections (4) and (5)) are not applicable to the principle itself, other criticisms from Beauchamp, Childress, Miller, and Truog still stand. In particular, the principle problematically presupposes the contentious positions that death and intending death are bad. Additionally, the principle lacks determinacy due to the redescription problem. The principle of double effect indeed is susceptible to some forms of these criticisms when it is considered as an isolated moral principle. However, I argue that the current formulation of the principle of double effect is not undermined by these criticisms when it is evaluated as a part of Catholic moral theology. I argue, first, that Catholic moral theology does not merely presuppose that death and intending death are bad. Rather, within Catholic moral theology the principle of double effect is understood as an aid to discernment of the morality of an action, as one moral principle in the context of a broader moral system. This broader moral system does not presuppose but provides justification for the contentious positions. Second, I argue that although the principle does lack determinacy, this is not as problematic as the objection supposes. Moreover, the principle of double effect is still valuable within the Catholic tradition in at least four ways, and, according to one of these ways, the redescription problem can have a positive role in Catholic theology.

---

[39] Quill, "The Ambiguity of Clinical Intentions," 1039.

To contextualize the principle of double effect within Catholic moral theology, consider that the principle of double effect in Catholic moral theology is understood as an aid to discernment of the morality of an action. This consideration is both a historical point and a point regarding how the principle functions as a decision procedure. Historically, moral theologians originally adopted the principle as a general principle to aid priests in their role as confessors.[40] That is, the principle of double effect aided the priest in discernment of the rightness or wrongness of a penitent's action.

As a decision procedure which aids discernment, the principle of double effect serves as a reminder to consider the three traditional fonts of morality: the action (in itself and in its relation to the good and bad effects), the intention, and the circumstances (proportionality). In addition, the four conditions of the principle of double effect can also aid discernment in their interdependence. More precisely, insofar as it is a decision procedure, the principle of double effect can reveal to an actor, through his or her consideration of each condition, an honest description of each aspect of his or her act. For example, one's consideration of the relation of an action to the foreseen good and bad effects, as well as one's consideration of the proportionality of the good to the bad, can aid in discernment of one's true intention. One may be able to admit that, given the causal relations or the disproportionate ends, I "cannot not intend" the bad effect of this action. Imagine a physician who orders a dose of morphine sufficient to kill a patient, instead of ordering a low dose of morphine with instructions to titrate up as necessary. When the physician uses the principle of double effect as a decision procedure to judge whether his act is morally permissible, he may be forced to reflect on his using a lethal dose and thus the death of the patient as a means to relieve the patient's pain. Such reflection could lead to the realization that he or she intends the death of the patient.

On the other hand, the principle of double effect is merely an *aid* to discernment of the morality of an action because the principle of double effect is a principle and not a complete moral theory. Herein lies my response to Beauchamp, Childress, Miller, and Truog's criticism that the principle of double effect fails to justify and thus presupposes death as a "bad effect" and intending death as a "bad intention." The problem with these criticisms is that the authors seem to evaluate the principle not only as a principle pertaining to right action but as a principle pertaining to moral value as well. As a principle, the principle of double effect has limited scope. It is a principle that can help to evaluate the moral permissibility of acts (having both good and bad effects). It is a principle pertaining to right

---

[40] John Berkman, "How Important Is the Doctrine of Double Effect for Moral Theology? Contextualizing the Controversy," *Christian Bioethics* 3, no. 2 (2007): 91.

conduct. The principle of double effect cannot also help to evaluate the moral value of effects and intentions because the principle of double effect is not a principle pertaining to moral value. Thus, in criticizing the principle of double effect for failing to justify death and intending death as bad, Beauchamp, Childress, Miller, and Truog seem to expect the principle of double effect to function as a principle pertaining to moral value in addition to its functioning as a principle pertaining to right conduct. If this is their expectation, they misunderstand the scope of the principle.

Moreover, the principle does not presuppose the moral beliefs that death and intending death are bad. The principle of double effect makes no claims about the moral value of death or intending death. It would be consistent to uphold the principle and to believe that death and intending death are not morally bad. Consider the "values conflict case" in which someone is using the principle of double effect to determine if physician-assisted suicide is right for him or herself. This person does not view death and intending death as morally bad. This person would see the act of physician-assisted suicide as morally good or neutral (C1), but still might hold that the act has a good effect (e.g. relief of pain)[41] and a bad effect (e.g. separation from loved ones). The person might reflect that his or her intention is for the good effect (C2) and that the bad effect (separation from loved ones) is not the means to and does not cause the good effect (relief of pain) (C3). The person might decide that right now his or her level of pain is not proportionate to the bad effect of separation from loved ones and so determine that physician-assisted suicide is not morally permissible at this time. On the other hand, the person might decide that his or her level of pain is proportionate to the bad effect of separation from loved ones and so determine that physician-assisted suicide is morally permissible at this time.

Perhaps Beauchamp, Childress, Miller, and Truog intend to direct their criticisms, regarding the presupposing of contentious positions, to proponents of the principle of double effect, rather than the principle itself. If these criticisms are directed toward proponents of the principle, there is some truth to their claim: the principle of double effect is often invoked along with the moral values that death and intending death are bad. Nonetheless, if Beauchamp, Childress, Miller, and Truog intend to direct these criticisms to proponents of the principle of double effect, they cannot simply charge that proponents presuppose contentious positions since many proponents have good reasons for viewing death and intending death as bad. Rather, in

---

[41] I use relief of pain as the good effect in this example, even though studies show this is not the most common reason people request physician-assisted suicide.

fairness, they ought at least to acknowledge the broader moral theory or theories in which proponents employ the principle and contend with these theories if they disagree. If Beauchamp, Childress, Miller, and Truog wanted to direct their criticisms at the Catholic Church, for instance, they could not say that the Catholic Church merely presupposes death and intending death as bad. Rather, the broader Catholic moral system[42] includes a rich theology and philosophy of life and death matters, which includes justification for death and intending death as bad. Thus, the principle of double effect is not susceptible to the criticism that it problematically presupposes the contentious value positions. First, the principle does not presuppose any value positions, and second, the broader moral system in which the principle is commonly employed does not merely presuppose but rather provides argumentation for these positions.

This leaves Beauchamp, Childress, Miller, and Truog's criticism that the principle lacks determinacy due to the redescription problem. When the principle is evaluated as an isolated principle, there is an epistemic problem: how does one know when each of the four conditions is met? If persons cannot know when the four conditions of the principle of double effect are met, the principle fails to be determinate. Yet the principle's vulnerability to criticism regarding determinacy does not stop there. In the "values conflict case" above, a person could conclude via the principle of double effect that physician-assisted suicide could be morally permissible, but the Church teaches that physician-assisted suicide is never morally permissible. Thus, the principle seems to have at least two determinacy issues. First, as Beauchamp, Childress, Miller, and Truog indicate, the principle lacks determinacy due to the redescription problem: how does one know when object, intention, causal relations, and proportionality are correctly described? Second, the principle lacks determinacy regarding moral value as well: how does one know the moral value of effects and intentions? I address this second determinacy issue, which arose in my above response to Beauchamp, Childress, Miller, and Truog, before I respond to the first determinacy issue, since my response to the former also supports my response to the latter.

Again, the epistemic problem highlighted by the "values conflict case" is: how does one know the moral value of effects and intentions? The principle does not presuppose contentious value judgments, as Beauchamp, Childress, Miller, and Truog charge. On the contrary, the principle as an isolated principle fails to be determinate partially insofar as it does not provide a way to distinguish between morally

---

[42] I use "moral system" in a looser sense than "moral theory," which I take to refer to a particular, fully-developed moral theory. A moral system may include elements of multiple, non-contradictory moral theories, and it may not be fully developed.

good effects and intentions, and morally bad effects and intentions. I have argued that it is not within the scope of a principle of right action to make such value judgments. But it is within the scope of a moral theory to make such value judgments. Indeed, determinacy as a critical measure properly refers to a moral theory, together with its principles.[43] As I have alluded, when one employs (or evaluates) the principle within the context of the broader Catholic moral system however, the principle becomes more determinate regarding moral value.[44] This contextualized use of the principle of double effect has also been the historic use: in discernment of the rightness or wrongness of a penitent's action, priests drew from the broader Catholic moral system in order to inform their application of the principle of double effect.[45]

One way in which the principle becomes more determinate regarding moral value within the context of the broader Catholic moral system is in the Catholic Church's identification of certain acts, including euthanasia (defined as, "an act or omission which, of itself or by intention, causes death in order to eliminate suffering" [*Catechism*, no. 2277] as per se "intrinsically evil" (*Veritatis Splendor*, no. 79). It is always wrong to formally cooperate with or intend these acts, whether as means or ends. Thus, within Church teaching, there is clarification regarding the value of things whose moral value is contentious.

Moreover, in Catholic moral theology, the principle of double effect is part of more complicated teaching regarding discernment of moral value (and right action): the Church upholds the need for a conscience informed by Church teaching, the need for prayer, the virtues, especially prudence, and spiritual direction. It should not be denied that all four conditions of the principle of double effect can require very difficult work of discernment: there is a need to discern the moral value of the act in itself, effects, and intentions. There is also a need to discern the object of the act, actor's intention, causal relations, and proportionality between effects, which may involve the weighing of apparent incommensurables such as alleviation of pain

---

[43] Timmons, *Moral Theory*, 13.
[44] Note that to affirm that the principle becomes more determinate within a broader moral system does not contradict the view that the four conditions of the principle are sufficiency conditions. Sufficiency conditions are understood in propositional logic to refer to a logical relationship. In this case, if the conditions are satisfied then an act which has good and bad effects is morally permissible. Of course, this logical relationship does not tell one how to determine if the conditions are satisfied. In other words, the logical relationship indicates that the conditions are sufficient, but what satisfies the conditions may still require explanation.
[45] Berkman, "How Important Is the Doctrine of Double Effect for Moral Theology?" 91.

and risk of death. The theological helps (e.g., Church teaching, prayer, virtues, spiritual direction) that are part of the Church's broader moral system aid in this difficult discernment.

Applied to the "values conflict case" above, in which a person considers the moral permissibility of physician-assisted suicide, Church teaching that euthanasia is an intrinsic evil, together with a conscience informed by Church teaching, could guide the person's decision-making. Using the principle of double effect in the context of the Church's broader moral system, the person could now conclude that physician-assisted suicide is not morally permissible since the act fails to meet the first condition of the principle of double effect: the act in itself is not a morally good or neutral act since it meets the Church's definition of euthanasia. When employed in the context of Catholic moral theology, then, which includes value judgments and theological helps, the principle becomes more determinate.

However, as I have noted, even within Catholic moral theology, there is often substantial disagreement regarding application of the principle of double effect. Catholics do not always come to the same conclusion regarding the object, intentionality, causality, and proportionality of an action[46] and thus differ on whether a particular act in a particular circumstance is morally permissible. Regarding the "values conflict case," the person could question whether the act of physician-assisted suicide does morally constitute euthanasia on the basis that his or her description of the act in itself does not match the Church's description of the act of euthanasia. Indeed, often differences in application of the principle of double effect are due to the redescription problem, to which Beauchamp, Childress, Miller, and Truog rightly allude. Since employing the principle within Catholic moral theology does not solve the redescription problem, a defense against Beauchamp, Childress, Miller, and Truog's second criticism that the principle of double effect lacks determinacy due to the redescription problem is more difficult than a defense against their first criticism that the principle presupposes contentious value judgments. I acknowledge that the principle is still susceptible to the redescription problem even within Catholic moral theology's broader moral system, though the Catholic moral tradition does help to alleviate some of the principle's determinacy issues.

Arguably, the determinacy vulnerability of the principle of double effect highlighted by the redescription problem is due to differences in moral judgment. There is a growing philosophical consensus that the application of all moral principles involves moral judgment. There is no mechanistic procedure for applying an abstract principle to

---

[46] Disagreement persists, especially regarding beginning-of-life issues, despite appeals by Catholic academics to Thomistic theories of action and causality.

concrete cases.[47] The growing consensus is that persons have a capacity for moral judgment—something like what Aristotle called *phronesis* or like some, including the Catholic Church, call the virtue of prudence—the proper development and use of which helps them correctly to apply abstract moral principles to particular situations. As a result, moral theorists have become less concerned with a degree of indeterminacy. They recognize that insofar as all principles involve moral judgment, they will fail to be completely determinate. Catholic moral theology likewise presumes such a capacity for moral judgment, and, as I have already mentioned, proposes theological helps to the development and application of moral judgment. Thus, the redescription problem and the determinacy vulnerability of the principle of double effect is not necessarily a fatal flaw.

Perhaps these points attenuate the determinacy criticism of the principle of double effect but do not completely nullify the criticism. The more determinate a moral theory and its principles are, the stronger the moral theory.[48] The less determinate a moral theory and its principles are, the weaker the moral theory. Would the principle of double effect still have value if the redescription problem were insuperable? I argue that the principle of double effect is still valuable within Catholic moral theology in at least four ways.

First, the principle of double effect can be used as one way to articulate more fully why the Church teaches what it teaches (particularly since Church teaching already utilizes the language and conditions of the principle of double effect). The principle therefore has some explanatory power. More precisely, the principle of double effect goes some way toward *explaining* why certain act types are right and others are wrong.[49] Once one begins to apply the principle as a

---

[47] Maike Albertzart, "Principle-Based Moral Judgment," *Ethical Theory and Moral Practice* 16, no. 2 (2013): 339-354; John K. Davis, "Applying Principles to Cases and the Problem of Judgment," *Ethical Theory and Moral Practice* 15, no. 4 (2012): 563-577; Rosalind Hursthouse, *On Virtue Ethics* (Oxford: Oxford Univeristy Press, 1999).
[48] Timmons, *Moral Theory*, 258.
[49] Keenan seems to reject the notion that the principle of double effect has any explanatory power, and he would reject my implying throughout this paper that the principle has a justifying function. He argues that the principle of double effect "is a shorthand expression of the taxonomic relationship among a number of paradigm cases" (Keenan, "The Function of the Principle of Double Effect," 295). An action is not permissible because it meets the conditions of the principle of double effect; rather the "rightness of the solution is already internal to the case," as shown by its congruence with recognized paradigm cases. Keenan seems to argue that to use the principle in "geometric" fashion, as an explanatory or justifying moral principle, "vests the principle with unwarranted authority." As a result of using the principle geometrically, moralists attempt to resolve difficult moral issues in morally permissible ways (according to the principle of double effect), by proposing practical solutions that cause unnecessary harm. Keenan seems to grant that using the principle

decision procedure to a particular act, the principle becomes susceptible to the redescription problem; however, considered in the abstract, the principle's conditions can still accurately explain what makes certain actions right and others wrong. In other words, the principle of double effect indicates what it is about good/bad-effect-type actions that makes them right or wrong (object, intention, causal relations, and proportionality of the good to the bad), even if one cannot determine which features of a token act are referred to by the relevant terms. For instance, one knows that a bad intention makes an act impermissible, but one may not be able to determine if x is a bad intention.

Second, for moral questions that Church teaching addresses, the principle of double effect can also be used to guide application of Church teaching to a particular situation. For instance, knowing the Church's general teaching on euthanasia versus palliative sedation, the principle of double effect can help one discern whether he or she may consent to palliative sedation for a family member. The individual would have assurance that palliative sedation is not intrinsically evil and that the death of the family member would not be the means to relieve pain if the pain medication were properly titrated. Attending to the particulars of the situation, the individual would discern whether his or her own intent was for relief of pain and not for death, and he or she would also discern whether the severity of the pain the family member is experiencing is proportionate to the risk of death.

---

geometrically will result in some correct moral conclusions, though he does not think that geometric use of the principle will necessarily give correct moral conclusions. On the other hand, the principle may be used in "taxonomic" fashion, highlighting the congruency of new cases with paradigm cases, but, on this use, the principle is unnecessary, as one might directly appeal to paradigm cases. Keenan's paper deserves a full-length response, but let these following remarks suffice for now. I do not dispute Keenan's historical point that the principle developed in the context of casuistry. I also do not disagree with Keenan that epistemically, the principle of double effect is not necessary to prudentially discern the moral permissibility of an action. Nor do I necessarily disagree with Keenan that the principle of double effect may not be the best moral principle for evaluating all acts with both good and bad effects. However, none of these points exclude the possibility that in some, or even many cases, the principle of double effect explains why an act is morally permissible or impermissible, serving a justifying function. Keenan seems to argue that actions are permissible or impermissible due to their own "internal or prudential certitude" (Keenan, 309), but it is unclear what he means by this, so it is unclear why or how his position is incompatible with further explanation and thereby justification for an act. Moreover, I dispute an implication of Keenan's argument, that only taxonomic use of the principle of double effect reveals the misuse of the principle. Rather, in demonstrating the geometric use of the principle, Keenan entirely passes over the redescription problem. Even when the principle is used geometrically, attentiveness to the redescription problem can also highlight possible misuse of the principle. So, Keenan does not seem to successfully argue that the principle of double effect does not have explanatory or justificatory value or that geometric use of the principle is wrong.

Third, for open moral questions in the Catholic Church, the principle of double effect can assist theological debate, not despite, but because of the redescription problem. The redescription problem can be a sign of many diverse minds and hearts coming to the table. Such diversity can stimulate discussion, and so the redescription problem can in this way contribute (with the guidance of the Holy Spirit) to the development of Church teaching. When possible, academics can use the principle of double effect as a vehicle of case-based reasoning. They can think through an open question in Catholic morality using the description of object, intention, causal relations, and proportionality suggested by Church teaching on a relevantly similar issue.

Fourth, for open moral questions, or practically unclear issues, the principle of double effect can also aid individual discernment in particular situations. As I have mentioned earlier, the principle of double effect can serve as a reminder to consider the three traditional fonts of morality (act, intention, circumstance), and the principle's four conditions can aid discernment in their interdependence. Additionally, individuals can also use the principle of double effect as a vehicle of case-based reasoning, drawing on the description of object, intention, causal relations, and proportionality suggested by Church teaching on a relevantly similar issue.

In these four ways, the principle of double effect is still valuable within Catholic moral theology. Although it is important to point out (as Beauchamp, Childress, Miller, and Truog do) that the principle of double effect cannot always be determinate even within the Catholic moral tradition, and even less so outside of it, it should be clear that this does not render the principle useless within Catholic moral theology.

Conclusion

I have detailed two criticisms of the principle of double effect: that the principle presupposes contentious value judgments, such as the badness of death, and that the principle is unacceptably indeterminate due to the redescription problem. In response to these criticisms, I began by situating the principle in its historical and practical context: as an aid for Catholic priests to discern rightness and wrongness of the acts confessed by penitents. I argued that the broader Catholic moral system in which the principle is embedded does not presuppose the relevant contentious value judgments but contains an extensive account of values and disvalues. In addition, I argued that the indeterminateness of the principle is not clearly unacceptable, since all principles are indeterminate to an extent and since the teaching of the Church relating to value theory and moral discernment rendering the principle more determinate than it is when considered in isolation. Finally, I suggested that even if the indeterminacy remains problematic, the principle serves valuable functions within Catholic theology. According to one of these ways, the redescription problem can have a positive role by spurring discussion and development of Church teaching. ∎

Is Aquinas's Envy Pagan?

Sheryl Overmyer

ENVY IS BAD AND OBVIOUSLY SO. Evidence for this is enshrined through story upon story in Scripture. Envy first affected Adam and Eve, Gregory the Great tells us, through the serpent. They became persuaded by the serpent to "feel" what the serpent feels, to share the devil's heart. This first spark of envy set into motion the trajectory of salvation history, as the Book of Wisdom tells us: "By the envy [φθόνος] of the devil, death entered the world." (Wisdom 2:24). From this starting point come Cain and Abel, Jacob and Esau, Rachel and Leah, and Joseph and his brothers. This whole trajectory is only the action in the Book of Genesis.

Turning to the New Testament, envy leads the chief priests to hand over Christ, according to both Matthew, "because of envy they had handed Him over" (Matthew 27:18) and Mark, "the chief priests had handed Him over because of envy" (Mark 15:10). The contention and division that envy breeds in the young Christian community becomes a running preoccupation of Paul. The opening salvo of the Letter to the Romans proclaims that God's wrath is an appropriate response to habitual human sinfulness. God is justified in abandoning people to the consequences of their rebellion in "all unrighteousness, wickedness, greed, evil; full of envy, murder, strife, deceit, malice; [they are] gossips, slanderers, haters of God, insolent, arrogant, boastful, inventors of evil, disobedient to parents, without understanding, untrustworthy, unloving, unmerciful" (Romans 1:29–31). Likewise, Paul warns the Galatians: "Now the works of the flesh are evident, which are: immortality, impurity, sensuality, idolatry, sorcery, enmities, strife, jealousy, outbursts of anger, disputes, dissentions, factions, envyings, drunkenness, carousing, and things like these, of which I forewarn you, just as I have forewarned you, that those who practice such things will not inherit the kingdom of God," and then concludes, "Let us not be conceited, provoking another, envious of one another" (Galatians 5:19–21; 26). Paul is also troubled by the disparity between the content of the Gospel and the manner in which it is preached: "Some, to be sure, are preaching Christ even from envy and strife" (Philippians 1:15).

The Church Fathers took this clear cue from Scripture, warning Christians of envy's power to destroy charity's communal bonds. John

Chrysostom advises that the baptized person should train herself to respond to others' successes with humility and praise, rather than envy: "Would you like to see God glorified by you? Then rejoice in your brother's progress and you will immediately give glory to God. Because his servant could conquer envy by rejoicing in the merits of others, God will be praised."[1] Leo the Great rehearses the story of our salvation as he links Christ's redemption with the devil's envy (*invidia*) in a pattern of how God draws forth some greater good from an evil: "Christ's inexpressible grace gave us blessings better than those the demon's envy had taken away."[2] Augustine calls envy "the diabolical sin," for there is nothing more averse to love than envy.[3]

Gregory the Great is an exceptional source on envy's evil. The envious man is consumed by this affliction, one which he imposes upon himself, trapped while "his mind, pining away, is wounded by its own pain and is tormented by the happiness of another."[4] Those who are most near and like us become the target of our envy, "those whom we deem better than us in some respect."[5] Once we fall into envy, it is not just a sin. It is a sin that carries its own punishment: "When the rottenness of the sore [of envy] corrupts the vanquished heart, the exterior signs indicate how gravely the madness stirs up the mind. One's color is affected by the pallor, the eyes are weighted down, the mind is inflamed, the limbs freeze up, there is frenzy in the thoughts, the teeth are grating."[6] Envy also engenders other vices; in short, it is a deadly sin. Envy accompanies greed and pride: "The capital vices are conjoined by such a close connection that the one emerges from the other. For instance, the first offshoot of pride is vainglory, which, as it corrupts the oppressed mind, gives rise to envy; for as long as it craves the power of an empty name, it languishes with the fear that someone else will be able to acquire that power."[7] Gregory draws upon the wells of scriptural evidence to inform his understanding, ultimately providing an account that constitutes one of the tradition's richest resources on envy's vileness.

The scriptural witness and the work of Gregory the Great become Thomas Aquinas's Christian sources for his own most extended treatment of envy in his mature work, the *Summa Theologiae*. They are used in equal measure in the *Secunda Secundae*, Question 36—eleven and ten times, respectively. (Other Christian thinkers such as

---

[1] John Chrysostom, *Homiliae in Romanos* 71.5; PG 60, 448.
[2] Leo I, Sermon 73, 4; NPNF, Second Series, 12, 212.
[3] Augustine, *Instructing Beginners in Faith*, 4.8; PL 40, 315–316.
[4] Gregory the Great, *Morals on the Book of Job*, 5.46.85; PL 75, 728. Hereafter *Moralia*.
[5] *Moralia*, Sect 84; PL 75, 727.
[6] *Moralia*, Sect 85; PL 75, 728.
[7] *Moralia*, 31.45.88; PL 76; 621.

Damascene and Augustine receive two mentions; Jerome, Isidore, and Cassian receive one.) Indeed, everything discussed from Gregory's account thus far becomes useful to Thomas in building his account of envy. Thomas has ample resources for constructing a traditionally and conspicuously Christian account of envy, both as a mortal sin and a capital vice.

Yet, Thomas frustrates expectations. In Question 36, one is struck rather by Thomas's disproportionate use of Aristotle to formulate his account of envy. He relies heavily on Aristotle in a multitude of ways: to lay out envy's ontology, its moral significance, its inner dynamics, its relation to the other passions such as desire and hatred, and its devolution into outright vice. Thomas adopts this material more or less directly from Aristotle without alteration, turning Aristotle into *the* primary source for his account of envy. As he pieces together this account, Thomas features Aristotle more prominently than even Scripture or Gregory the Great, naming Aristotle as an authority fourteen times. Despite his periodic citation of Gregory, Thomas offers few Christian glosses of envy within the constructive and substantive portions of his account. This further underscores Aristotle's towering presence. In sum, Thomas's writing on envy in Question 36 yields what appears an entirely—what we will call, for lack of a better term—"Pagan Envy," shorn of theological content.

This account is puzzling. It runs against our intuitions about envy's importance for the Christian tradition. Envy is a capital vice, one of the seven deadly sins, an utmost offense against God, and, if one sticks to Question 36, the reader will search in vain for Thomas's appreciation of envy of the distinctly Christian kind. Rather, the reader must look to the larger framework of Thomas's writing on envy—its placement within the questions on charity (*ST* II-II qq. 23–46) as a vice opposed to spiritual joy. Only within this context does Thomas give his readers a framework for understanding envy as a theological vice. In these other questions, he affirms the critical threat that envy poses to the Christian life by describing its serial offenses against the greatest of virtues, charity. Thus, one must place Question 36 within the questions on charity as a whole to see decisively how envy threatens the edifice of the Christian life in a special way, captured by Gregory the Great's claim: "Even though the venom of our ancient enemy is infused into the human heart by every vice that is perpetrated, still, in the case of this particular type of wickedness the serpent stirs all his innards and spews forth the venom of engraving malice."[8] Ultimately, Thomas sides with the Christian insight that envy poisons our relationships with others, God, and even ourselves.

---

[8] *Moralia,* 5.46.85; PL 75, 728. Cited by Thomas, *ST* II-II q. 36, a. 4.

Thomas's questions on charity as a whole, including the single question on envy, transpose his concern from Aristotelian confines to a robustly "Christian Envy."

This essay first treats "pagan envy," then "Christian envy," and finally the relationship between the two, for an overall tri-partite structure. Taken in outline, it rehearses the way in which Aristotle's thought informs the key features of Thomas's account of envy. In so doing, it reveals Thomas's understanding of the interrelation between natural and supernatural wisdom on a microcosmic level. More than that, this essay tries to illuminate Thomas's contribution to the Christian intellectual tradition's suspicion of envy. Thomas assembles a structure that reveals the abundant ways that envy undoes the work Christ wrought in us, chewing up charity. It eats away at our relationships with others, indeed God, and even—if we can finally see it—ourselves. In this, Thomas echoes Cyprian of Carthage who wrote that,

> If any one closely look into this he will find that nothing should be more guarded against by the Christian, nothing more carefully watched, than being taken captive by envy and malice, that none, entangled in the blind snares of a deceitful enemy, in that the brother is turned by envy to hatred of his brother, should himself be unwittingly destroyed by his own sword.[9]

In all, Thomas describes how envy is adept in setting us at odds with everyone: ourselves, others, even God. Charity is set at odds with envy as charity is a share in the divine life that would rightly order all of our relationships through the singular superabundance of divine love.

PAGAN ENVY

The numbers bear out the claim that Aristotle is the primary source for Thomas's writing on envy. The *Summa* is not the only place that this is true. In Thomas's writing on envy in *De Malo*, for example, the *Nicomachean Ethics* is the single most cited text, and it exceeds citations of Scripture when taken as a whole.[10] In his constructive analyses ("sed contras," "responses," and "replies to objections"), Aristotle is the single most cited authority. In fact, the case for *De Malo* might be more complex than just this, since it is a disputation whose final form might incorporate counterarguments not present in the master's original. In that case, it is reasonable to conclude that Aristotle was as much, if not even more, present in Thomas's private disputations.[11]

---

[9] Cyprian, "The Treatises of Cyprian," 10.3; PL 13, 41.
[10] Aquinas, *De Malo*, Question 10, "Envy."
[11] Brian Davies, "Introduction" to *On Evil,* trans. Richard Regan (New York: Oxford University Press, 2003), 12.

This same pattern emerges in Thomas's most mature work, the *Summa*.[12] Thomas treats envy twice in the *Summa*. In his first installment, in the questions on the passions (*ST* I-II qq. 22–48), Thomas cites Augustine's *De Civitate Dei* the most, just one time more than the *Nicomachean Ethics*. And for the second time, when Thomas turns to envy at length in the questions on charity, once again he demonstrates his heavy reliance on Aristotle by citing Aristotle more times than Scripture. Every detail of Thomas's writing on envy—quantitative or substantive—confirms and supports this initial impression that Thomas is massively indebted to Aristotle on envy.[13]

Thomas relies first and foremost on Aristotle's anthropology to categorize envy. Thomas writes: "In *De Anima* 3 the Philosopher distinguishes two appetites, and he says that the higher appetite moves the lower appetite" (*ST* I q. 80, a. 2). Envy is both a passion and a vice of the will—both a movement of the sentient appetite and a principle of action of the intellectual appetite. Thomas uses Aristotle's differentiation of types to inform and structure his entire analysis of envy. In *De Malo*, Thomas writes about envy as a capital vice amongst others, and, in the *Summa*, he treats it twice: first in the *Prima Secunda* and then in the *Secunda Secundae*. Thomas's unflagging commitment to Aristotle's philosophical divisions informs his decision to treat envy twice, first as a passion and second as a habit.

Thomas also iterates Aristotle's understanding of the morality of the passions. Thomas's other potential sources are not as yielding on this point. His use of Aristotle, on the other hand, allows him to develop the interplay between passions, will, and reason. Aristotle writes in the *Nicomachean Ethics*, "It is not the one who becomes fearful or angry who is praised or blamed, rather, it is the one who becomes fearful or angry *in a certain way*."[14] Thomas understands Aristotle's claim as distinguish between (a) passions in their own right and (b) passions insofar as they are subject to the rule of reason and will.[15] Passions in their own right are morally neutral, isolated and

---

[12] *Summa Theologiae*, II-II q. 36; hereafter ST. For *ST* I, I use the English translation of the *Summa Theologiae* by the Fathers of the English Dominican Province (New York: Benzinger, 1948); for *ST* I-II, and if indicated, *ST* II-II, trans. Alfred Freddoso, www3.nd.edu/~afreddos/summa-translation/TOC.htm; and for *ST* II-II, Robert Miner, *Questions on Love and Charity: Summa Theologiae, Secunda Secundae, Questions 23-46* (Connecticut: Yale University Press, 2016).

[13] Since Thomas's earlier work on envy in *De Malo* has a comparatively nascent treatment of envy and does not offer a distinct contribution from the *Summa*, I streamline my considerations to follow by focusing solely on the latter.

[14] Aristotle, *Nicomachean Ethics* II.5, quoted in *ST* I-II q. 24, a. 1, ad. 3.

[15] *ST* I-II q. 24, a. 1, ad. 3. This acknowledges the distinction between passions (a) in their own right (*secundum se*) and (b) insofar as they are subject to the rule of reason

floating above human experience. Fear-as-such is neither good nor bad. Anger-as-such is neither good nor bad. This is the claim that (a) sets out: passions in their own right. Moving onto (b), passions insofar as they are subject to the rule of reason and will: we do not experience fear or anger as isolated and floating above human experience. Our fear and our anger are responses to the world in which we find ourselves. As *our* passions, we experience them as subject to the rule of reason and will. Although the passions are movements of a non-rational appetite, they bear moral significance because we are the kinds of beings that we are. We are tutored to expect that envy, merely as a passion that we experience moving through this world, shoulders serious moral weight.

Aristotle uses the metaphor of constitutional rule to characterize the dynamics between the passions and the intellectual soul. He writes in the *Politics*: "One finds in the animal both despotic rule (*despoticus principatus*) and constitutional rule (*politicus principatus*). For the soul rules the body with a despotic rule, whereas the intellect rules the appetite with a constitutional and royal rule."[16] The highest faculties of the human reign over the lower faculties. In turn, the lower either consent or rebel. Thomas adopts Aristotle's metaphor: "Political and royal rule is that by which someone rules free men, who, even if they are subject to the rule of the leader, nonetheless have something of their own by which they are able to resist the leader's command."[17] Thomas uses a curious phrase here, that of having "something of their own" (*habent aliquid proprium*), because he imagines the sentient appetite to have additional powers at its disposal—the power of imagining and power of our senses. For instance, we can heed the suggestions of imagination so closely that we choose to follow something pleasant that reason forbids or even resist something unpleasant that reason demands. Thus, the sentient appetite is a free subject that does not follow reason lockstep—compliant, docile, and tame. Rather, it maintains autonomy in the freedom to consent or rebel from reason's regal decrees. If the passions of the sentient appetite consent to reason's dictates, the whole kingdom of the self remains in good working order. If the passions rebel, disorder breaks out. The question arises: how does envy fit into this scheme? Is it possible for envy to obey reason, or is envy an inherent rebel, an unruly reaction of the sentient appetite?

For both Aristotle and Thomas, the basic ontology of the passions emphasizes their potential goodness. Yet they admit exceptions for passions that are good or bad in themselves. Aristotle reasons:

---

and will (*secundum quod subiacent imperio rationis et voluntatis*) in *ST* I-II q. 24, a. 1 co.

[16] Aristotle, *Politics*, I.2 cited in *ST* I q. 81, a. 3, ad. 2.

[17] Aristotle, *Politics*, I.2.

> Not every action nor every passion admits of a mean; for some have names that already imply badness, e.g. spite, shamelessness, envy, and in the case of actions, adultery, theft, murder; for all of these and suchlike things imply by their names that they are themselves bad, and not the excesses or deficiencies of them. It is not possible, then, ever to be right with regard to them; one must always be wrong. Nor does goodness or badness with regard to such things depend on committing adultery with the right woman, at the right time, and in the right way, but simply to do any of them is to go wrong.[18]

Thomas agrees. He explains that envy is always bad because it takes as its object something that is itself at variance with reason: sadness at the good of another (*tristitia de bono alterius*). Envy's fundamental movement is to withdraw from the genuine good of another. Were we to withdraw from a genuine evil, rather than from a genuine good, or to be drawn to a genuine good, rather than withdrawing, then these would be good passions. Envy is precisely the opposite. Sorry over the good of another is a withdrawal from a genuine good.

Returning to Aristotle and Thomas's shared structural metaphor of the passions as lowly subjects who may choose to consent or rebel from the regal decrees of reason, envy has no potential to be a loyal, dutiful subject as its object something at variance with reason—sorrow over the good of another. Envy is, thus, an anarchist outlaw. It cannot take its rightful place as a subject among other subjects who together seek to live in harmony for the greater good of the kingdom. Envy must be expelled from the kingdom altogether, a passion needing not so much moderation as eradication.

In usual fashion, Aristotle uses envy's near neighbors to clarify the notion of envy itself.[19] There are several other conditions that resemble envy that are not envy-as-such. For instance, what if someone has obtained a genuine good fortune that may bring harm to one's compatriots? In this case, one feels not so much sorrow over that good as fear that one's confreres may be harmed. This "ceases to

---

[18] Aristotle, *Nicomachean Ethics*, II.6, trans. Terence Irwin, 2nd ed. (Indiana: Hackett, 1999).

[19] Gabriele Taylor builds on Aristotle to distinguish between different types of envy itself: "object-envy" (or admiring envy) for which there are not exclusive goods, versus "state-envy" for which there are winners and losers; state-envy is more vicious. Sub-types of state-envy include its emulative and destructive types: "emulative-state-envy" by which we improve our standing with respect to another, versus "destructive-state-envy" by which we wish to spoil the other's elevation; destructive-state-envy is the worst, though emulative-state-envy with a particular (rather than general) object is as destructive. These types are not easily distinguished or distinguishable given the messiness of our interior lives. Here the point is to note how readily envy lends itself to destruction. Gabriele Taylor, "Envy and Jealousy: Emotions and Vices," *Midwest Studies in Philosophy* 13, no. 1 (1988): 233–49; here 234–8.

become envy," writes Aristotle, "and becomes fear."[20] Or for instance, what if one sorrows over the undeserved good fortune of another?[21] Aristotle calls this righteous indignation (*nemesis*) and holds it in high regard. He writes, "It is our duty both to feel sympathy and pity for unmerited distress, and to feel indignation at unmerited prosperity; for whatever is undeserved is unjust, and that is why we ascribe indignation even to the gods."[22]

Another example concerns jealousy (*zelus*). The case for jealousy is complex, in part because our everyday language conflates jealousy and envy. Admittedly, they are similar. Jealousy and envy both involve a person's relationship to something she regards as good—perhaps a material possession, a position of relative power, a particular relationship, or some personal characteristic. Yet, the terms differ. Jealousy involves an imagined or actual threat to something one holds dear or (hopes to) hold dear. In jealousy, one is concerned with losing something one loves or (hopes to) love. By contrast, envy involves one's feeling deprived in comparison to another. In envy, one is concerned to eliminate the discrepancy itself.[23] Aristotle sums these up as he writes that jealousy "is a good feeling felt by good persons, whereas envy is a bad feeling felt by bad persons. [Jealousy] makes us take steps to secure the good things in question, envy makes us take steps to stop our neighbor having them."[24] Thomas iterates each of Aristotle's conditions that resemble envy, adding only that with jealousy, Christians do well to distinguish between spiritual and temporal goods. Spiritual jealousy is great, and temporal jealousy is sometimes acceptable. This is a sliver within Thomas's actual writing on envy where he adds to Aristotle by introducing a Christian distinction. Yet the matter pertains to jealousy rather than envy.

Unlike jealousy, envy is unqualifiedly bad because it sets us against our neighbor's good. Envy involves comparison, and we envy only those people who we want to equal or surpass. Those are, according to Aristotle, "those who are near us in time, place, age, or reputation.... We do not compete with men who lived a hundred centuries ago, or those not yet born, or the dead, or those who dwell near the Pillars of Hercules, or those whom, in our opinion or that of others, we take to be far below or far above us."[25] Thomas renders Aristotle's social observations in an idiom that is updated for his contemporaries. He writes: "No one, unless he is insane, seeks to equal or surpass in glory

---

[20] Aristotle, *Rhetoric* II 9.22–3, trans. W. Rhys Roberts (New York: Dover Publications, 2004).
[21] Aristotle, *Nicomachean Ethics*, II.7.
[22] Aristotle, *Rhetoric* II 9.13–6.
[23] Gabriele Taylor, "Envy and Jealousy," 233–4. Cf. Luke Purshouse, "Jealousy in Relation to Envy," *Erkenntis* 60.2 (March 2004): 179–204.
[24] Aristotle, *Rhetoric*, II 11.34–6. Roberts translates *zelus* as "emulation."
[25] Aristotle, *Rhetoric* II. 10.6, 9–12.

those who are greater than him by much, for example, a common man vis-à-vis a king, or even a king vis-à-vis a common man, whom he surpasses by much. Hence a person does not envy those who are far removed from him by time or place or condition" (*ST* II-II q. 36, a. 1, ad. 2). In short, potters envy potters.

Envy, to Aristotle's mind, is fundamentally a social vice. It destroys right relationships with neighbors. Thomas, in an unexpected turn, elaborates this aspect of envy in terms of charity. He writes: "The object of each—of both charity and envy—is our neighbor's good, but according to contrary motions. For charity rejoices over our neighbor's good, whereas envy sorrows over the same good" (*ST* II-II q. 36, a. 3). Thomas cites 1 John 3:14 in his support: "We know that we have passed from death to life, because we love the brethren" (*ST* II-II q. 36, a. 3). This is precisely a moment when Thomas might offer a theological rendering of envy, or, at the very least, he might add a theological gloss, by alluding to how envy betrays the fuller Triune life in which we have been made participants by destroying our relationship with God.

Thomas disappoints on this score. He does not take a long-overdue theological turn. Instead, he takes the opportunity to remark on the inherent badness of envy itself. Then, he devotes his attention to an example that invokes people of varying moral excellence: the moral exemplar, very good people, and then ordinary folks. Their overall moral excellence is inversely proportional to their envy. Although this segue into examples does not pursue a theological line, it is still illustrative because it traces the dynamics of envy to help readers better understand how envy is destructive in more than one way (*ST* II-II q. 36, a. 4, ad. 3).

Thomas moves through his examples pedagogically. He starts with the moral exemplar. The exemplar's passions are completely in line with her reason. She does not feel a shade of adultery's concupiscence or a spark of homicide's anger. She does not feel a shred of envy. Indeed, she does not feel envy at all.[26] The point is that it matters not only whether we do or do not act on our envy but also whether we feel any envy at all. Envy is an excellent case to show that we are morally responsible not only for how we act on our passions but also for the very passions that we feel!

Second, we have those we might call very good people—people who are arguably better than most of us. Very good people are likely to have what Thomas calls an "incomplete" motion of envy. This is the case when such a person has the very first flash of envy that arises

---

[26] Perhaps the only example we have of a perfect human is Jesus Christ as man? He had the capacity for evil—and indeed felt many shades of sorrow—but never envy.

in us from our being naturally sensual beings but whose reason presently overrides this little start. (Thomas considers this kind of envy as morally culpable as the envy of little children who, as sensual beings, do not have the benefit of the use of reason.) Such would be the envy of the saints. Envy in very good people amounts to a venial sin, almost a natural consequence of having a sensitive appetite whatsoever.

Finally, envy for the majority of us is sinister, complex, and merits elaboration. Our envy has a natural, discernible trajectory as it completes a total arc from inception, to middle, to rest. Thomas calls this a "complete" motion of envy. Its first stage is underway when we set out to lessen the glory of another, "either in hiding, and so there is a whispering campaign, or clearly, and so there is detraction" (*ST* II-II q. 36, a. 4, ad. 3). Usually our efforts concentrate on spoiling our neighbor's possession of a good. Say, for example, that I envy a colleague's facility with ancient languages. My colleague is so fluent that she contests an expert's translation of an abstruse passage, and, in so doing, she may even help everyone else see that my skills in ancient languages are comparatively weak. Doubtless I wish that she were as bad (or worse) at ancient languages than me. Sometimes that may be enough. It may suffice in our envy to simply spoil another's possession of a good, with the demon on our shoulder consoling us, "As long as that jerk doesn't have it, I'm okay."[27]

Next the arc has a middle, and this depends on what happens to our neighbor and her good. If our neighbor has indeed experienced setback, we move from affliction over our neighbor's triumphs to triumph over our neighbor's affliction. Thomas regards this "joy at another's misfortune," what we call *schadenfreude*, as the daughter of envy (*ST* II-II q. 36, a. 4, ad. 3). Next there is the condition where we are unable to diminish our neighbor's glory, where our nasty efforts have had no effect. This middle stage means we go on envying, likely with increased intensity.

Then comes the terminus of the arc of envy as it turns into abiding and deep hatred. Here envy becomes self-defeating. It turns from our wanting not only for our neighbor to be deprived of the good, to our wanting the good itself to be harmed. Our desires so transform at this point that they become incomprehensible. We now belittle the goodness of the exact good we are after. Or we vitiate the goodness of everything else surrounding that good, thereby depreciating its value.

---

[27] Many a scholar has confessed to me that envy is an especially prevalent vice among academics. Envy has to do with external goods that are, by nature, scarce and limited. The competition for these goods might have been made even more acute by the economic downturn of 2008, which put the squeeze on desirable employment and the resources that make rigorous peer-reviewed (and university press) publishing possible.

Or we would rather the good be destroyed than another have it. At this final stage, we become ready to disregard, devalue, or destroy the goodness of the good we so desperately desire. This is the way in which envy spoils the good it covets. Gabriele Taylor adds: "If envy spoils the good it covets then the desires of the envious are doomed to failure; they can never achieve the position they hanker after. The situation of the envious would necessarily be a hopeless one. No wonder, then, that it should be thought of as a deadly sin, leading to the death of the soul."[28] Pause to consider that this claim is curious coming from an Aristotelian—to invoke the tradition of deadly sins without the resources to explain what they might mean within the framework she offers.

Does Thomas have anything more to add here, namely, everything from the tradition on envy's sinfulness? In short, no. At this point, we have a coherent précis of Thomas's writing on envy from the *Summa Theologiae, Secunda Secundae*, Question 36. Thus far, despite his occasional citation of Gregory the Great or Scripture, there is little in his actual constructive account of envy that either reflects or bears out his own Christian convictions. What we have so far is not simply a basic exposition of Thomas on envy, but an illustration that Thomas adumbrates the crucial fundamental features of envy drawing on Aristotle, primarily and, dare we say, exclusively at each and every step. We find no elemental concepts that fit ill with Aristotle's, no basic parts missing, no feature unaccounted for. Thomas and Aristotle are lockstep thus far, and, having encompassed envy's Aristotelian cast, it appears that this is all there is for envy.

CHRISTIAN ENVY

Thomas implies a single ancillary conclusion that is crucial for understanding the full trajectory of envy. It comes only at the very end of his treatment on envy—in the last reply in the last article in the last question. This is where he considers the whole impulse of envy, from beginning to end. He writes, "The terminus is in hatred itself, since just as a good that gives pleasure causes love, so does sorrow cause hatred" (*ST* II-II q. 36, a. 4, ad. 3). In this final moment, he sends his reader from Question 36 on envy back two questions to Question 34 on hatred.

In this earlier question, Question 34, Thomas devotes an article to the claim that hatred arises from envy. He iterates the point that envy causes hatred—that the good of our neighbor becomes sorrowful and consequently hateful. He goes further still in the question on hatred. He describes how our hatred turns from hatred of our neighbor's good,

---

[28] Taylor, "Envy and Jealousy," 241.

to hatred of the good of our neighbor, that is, to hatred of our neighbor herself. To wit, envy begins in sorrow by focusing on the good of our neighbor and ends in hatred by focusing on our neighbor herself. The passion of hatred is not skilled at differentiating its objects. Indeed, Thomas admits that reasoning about hatred is other than reasoning about other passions (*ST* II-II q. 34, a. 6, ad. 2).

There is more. Neither envy nor hatred stops at our neighbor. For hatred of neighbor is bound up in hatred of God. Thomas writes: "Because envy of our neighbor is the mother of the hatred that is directed toward him, it consequently becomes the cause of hatred that is directed toward God" (*ST* II-II q. 34, a. 6, ad. 2). This is the complete movement of envy. It stops not only at hatred of the envied good (in Question 36) but encompasses hatred of the envied neighbor and hatred of God (in Question 34).

Once one starts to read the questions on charity adjacent to the question on envy, it is hard to know when to stop, and so, despite relying on Aristotle as his primary source, Thomas gives us a distinctively Christian account of envy. His account encompasses the total range and consequences of envy by situating it within a theological frame of reference. Its all-encompassing scope, moreover, implies that accounts of envy that lack this frame remain incomplete. This frame of reference is so definitive for envy that one cannot find a remedy for envy outside of it. In so conceiving envy, it has no cure other than charity.

In effect, Thomas shifts the entire frame for envy from Aristotle to Christianity by including his question on envy (Question 36) in his questions on charity (Questions 23–46). Envy is a vice opposed to charity, which means that what was once an ordinary vice of character for Aristotle is now changed in kind and degree. Envy opposes, obstructs, and destroys our relationship with God as expressed in the inner dynamics of charity. Charity is the virtue by which God creates in us the capacity to love God and our neighbor and ourselves in God (*ST* II-II q. 25). These three aspects of the single virtue of charity are inverted in envy.

Our neighbor stands as the most obvious casualty of envy. It was said above that the object of each—of both envy and charity—is our neighbor's good but according to contrary motions since charity rejoices in our neighbor's good whereas envy sorrows over that same good (*ST* II-II q. 36, a. 3). Envy collapses in on itself in spiritual sorrow (*ST* II-II q. 28). Charity discovers in our neighbor's good the cause for the highest spiritual pleasure in joy. Envy seeks to spoil our neighbor's possession of the good and devolves into hatred of our neighbor's good altogether. Charity seeks to befriend all and is drawn into building up our neighbor's good. Envy is our impoverishment by our neighbor's good, because we are losers in a world of scarcity. Charity enriches us in the good of our neighbor, for our neighbor's good is a genuine intensification of our own abundant good. Envy gives us a specious good as our idol, asking us to honor deranged desire. Charity addresses our deepest longing with a joy that is completely full, even superabundant, and gives us more than suffices for our desire (*ST* II-II q. 28, a. 3). Envy is a hell on earth that we fashion, and, although we find it odious, we make ourselves at home. Charity points us heavenward as a foretaste of our ultimate blessedness, an increase in the joyful intensity of our participation in the Triune life. In all, depending on whether we are against or for our neighbor, comes sorrow or joy, destruction or edification, poverty or abundance, longing or fulfillment, hell or heaven.

Envy and charity are as much about us as about our neighbor. Our response to our neighbor's good says volumes about how we see ourselves.[29] When we give ourselves over to the convoluted logic of envy, we pin our problems on our neighbor. Our neighbor's good poses a threat to us only because we are lacking in some way ourselves. As envying selves, we see ourselves as limited and inferior, haunted by a sense of inadequacy and shortcomings. "The rational and straightforward response to this situation," writes Gabriele Taylor, "would be for [the envying self] to try to achieve that good, or, where this is not possible, come to terms with herself by finding other grounds for self-esteem. The envy-response runs counter to measures such as these by directing attention away from the supposed defect and focusing on the other's possession."[30] Envy is a misguided means of protecting ourselves. By shifting our critical gaze from the problem that lies in ourselves to an external threat, we further enact our own inadequacy. The self we protect in envy—the limited and inferior version of self, the self, marked by deficiencies and shortcomings—is not even worthy of that effort. Ironically, the envy-response moves us further away from what we truly desire, which is a self that is worthy of being loved unconditionally.[31]

From this vantage point, we are poised to appreciate Thomas's bold claim that envy's errant loves, desires, and pleasures are set aright by God. God is the one true unconditional lover. God, out of God's abundant love, gives us the capacity to love rightly. This is a process of transformation, and this transformation is radical. This is not a matter of taking our natural loves and pushing them further along their original path, nor is it taking our loves and then adding something more. Rather God's gift of charity so transforms our natural loves that it creates our very capacity to receive it (*ST* II-II q. 23, a. 2). Charity is our participation in a life not known to us before, the divine life,

---

[29] Taylor, "Envy and Jealousy," 243.
[30] Taylor, "Envy and Jealousy," 243.
[31] Taylor, "Envy and Jealousy," 244.

and, through this gift of participation, we can finally make good our relationships with our neighbors and ourselves.

Charity gives us even better names to call our neighbors: our brothers and sisters in God. The love of the Father and the Son is the same by which we love our brothers and sisters. This love is depicted by Thomas in a beautiful simile: "As the vision by which light is seen, and that by which color is seen are the same species … so too the act by which we love God and the act by which we love our neighbor are the same species" (*ST* II-II q. 25, a. 1). That is to say, there is a single habit of charity expressed in love of God and love of our brothers and sisters in God. Whereas envy sets us against the neighbor's good, indiscriminate self-giving love runs in the opposite direction. Such love blurs the lines between our brother and sister's good and our own good. Such love erases the boundaries of other and self that are foundational for envy to gain any traction. Thomas would affirm Gregory the Great's insight that "[i]f the soul be wholly ravished in love of the heavenly land, it is also thoroughly rooted in the love of our neighbor, and that without any mixture of envy."[32] So too, Thomas would echo John Chrysostom's advice that the baptized person should regard others' successes as their own: "Would you like to see God glorified by you? Then rejoice in your brother's progress and you will immediately give glory to God."[33] All good contributes to our single common good: God.

This single habit of charity—already encompassing love of God and love of our brothers and sisters in God—extends even unto us (*ST* II-II q. 25, aa. 1, 4). Thomas returns to the language of friendship that he uses to introduce charity to reflect on love of self (*ST* II-II q. 23; II-II q. 25, a. 4). Just as God befriends us in charity, and we love our friends in charity, we are to love ourselves as our friends. Whereas envy would have us see a fundamentally defective self, charity sees a self that is esteemed by and is worthy of God's love.

Overall, Thomas's work on envy under the umbrella of the questions on charity participates in and contributes to the Christian intellectual tradition. Through his systematic juxtaposition of this vice and this virtue, he clarifies the numerous ways that envy injures charity. Envy opposes the greatest of virtues and, in its opposition, destroys our greatest gift. Envy eats away at the bond of charity, turning love of our neighbor, ourselves, and God into hatred of our neighbor, ourselves, and God. Envy kills charity.[34]

---

[32] *Moralia*, 86; PL, 75, 729.
[33] John Chrysostom, *Homiliae in Romanos*, No. 71, 5; PG, 60, 448.
[34] *Moralia*, 5.46.85; PL, 75, 728: "By the bad quality of envy, even strong deeds of virtue go for nought before the eyes of God. Since the rotting of the bones from envy is the spoiling of strong things, even."

THE CURE FOR ENVY

Thomas's treatment of the cure for envy gives us a further and final glimpse into the movement and action of envy. More than this, it helps explain how Aristotle's account of envy relates to Thomas's theological account. In Thomas's thinking, the cure for envy lies in the perfection of charity within us.[35] Thomas calls this cure *spirituale gaudium*, "spiritual joy" (*ST* II-II q. 34 Preface).[36] Thomas portrays envy as a vice opposed to charity generally and *spirituale gaudium* specifically. Whereas charity is the virtue that perfects our will, spiritual joy is the affection that expresses this completion. Joy is categorized as a fruit of the Holy Spirit and an act (or effect) of charity (*ST* II-II q. 28, a. 1).

Much like the passions, the affection of joy is not inherently good or bad. Thus, its kinds include spiritual joy, natural joy, and even the joy that demons experience after a fashion (*ST* I q. 64, a. 3). The difference between these notions of joy is not one of degree but of kind. "Spiritual joy" takes as its object God. In the Christian understanding, God *is* Joy. God's joy is "full," (*impleatur*) and God alone enjoys God in a way in which it is worthy to rejoice. God's joy is infinite and worthy of the infinite goodness of God. God's joy is complete, absolutely speaking. God is the basis for all our joy. Without God, there is no joy whatsoever—natural or supernatural.[37] God's gift of charity makes us capable of joy. Thomas uses the language of "participation" to designate that our share of joy is a share in God. True joy measures the extent of our participation in God. As our joy becomes complete, it culminates all of our loves, sets to rest all our restless desires, and satisfies in true delight. This joy is the exaltation of our whole being in charity.

By using charity as a framework for envy, Thomas reminds us that we are embodied creatures whose destiny of friendship with God comes to fruition in a life suffused with joy. This speaks volumes for

---

[35] Thomas's work on this score sounds novel only because it sits at odds with cures presented in contemporary pastoral missives, neo-Aristotelian thinking, and other current interpretations of Thomas cited above. In fact, Thomas simply echoes the sum of Christian tradition on the cure being charity/joy: from the Church Fathers—including Cyprian of Carthage, John Chrysostom, Augustine, and Gregory the Great—through Thomas to later medieval thinkers—including Dante, Langland, Gower, and Chaucer.

[36] See Sheryl Overmyer, "Grace-Perfected Nature: The Interior Effect of Charity in Joy, Peace, and Mercy," *Questions on Love and Charity* (Connecticut: Yale University Press, 2016): 355–72.

[37] Without God, indeed, there would be nothing whatsoever. For discussion of this claim as it draws on Thomas's metaphysical ontology and use of analogical language, see Overmyer, "Three More Jigs in the Puzzle: The Unity of Analogy, Beatitude and Virtue in Thomas' *Summa Theologiae*," *International Journal of Systematic Theology* 15, no. 4 (2013): 374–93.

a particular vision of the Christian life—one of abounding, overflowing joy. Moreover, it speaks to a vision of the perfection of the *Imago Dei* in us. Thomas cites Psalm 85:3: "My heart and my flesh have rejoiced in the living God" (*ST* I-II q. 24, a. 3). His treatment of envy, both as opposed to the joy of charity and envy as a passion itself, reminds us that our passions are essential in our pursuit and enjoyment of God. We should not only be moved by our will but also by our sentient appetite, not only by charity but also by joy. We must feel rightly, in short.

With this distinctively Christian cure for the deadly sin of envy, one wonders if Thomas intends an analogue of this cure for Aristotle's envy. Does Thomas mean for something like natural joy to be a cure for pagan envy? Throughout the *Summa,* Thomas depends heavily upon analogical reasoning, which is especially conspicuous in its other parts: in the naming of God (*Prima Pars*) and in his treatment of happiness and the virtues (*Prima Secundae*).[38] Throughout these parts he is concerned with the conceptual complexity that connects our language and reality concerning God and us. He reflects that complexity through the immensely fruitful categories of imperfect/perfect, applied analogically. For example, whereas "perfect beatitude" designates God strictly speaking, "imperfect beatitude" refers to the way in which we know and love God. From this established primary meaning, this analogy can be extended to how our beatitude can be attained: whereas perfect eschatological beatitude cannot be had in this life, imperfect beatitude pertains to our flourishing as we are wayfarers. Whereas our supernatural end is attained in the infused virtues in perfect beatitude, our natural end is attained in the acquired virtues in imperfect beatitude.

It would be of little surprise to Thomas were we to extend this mode of reasoning to the cures of envy. We might say that our supernatural end is attained in spiritual joy as "perfect joy," while our natural end is attained in natural joy as "imperfect joy." Spiritual joy is for us the complete and total meaning of joy, whereas natural joy is an incomplete and partial meaning. Both kinds of envy find their respective cures in corresponding kinds of joy. Yet, analogical reasoning cannot proceed without a primary referent or reality, reminding us that the basis for all joys, including natural joy, is God.

The logic applies equally well, albeit differently to envy, because envy is not a perfection, rather it names the absence of one. This is where the threat of envy in all its forms becomes clearer. Perfect beatitude is threatened by Christian envy *and* what we have called pagan envy, conveying that the threat that envy poses for Christians to attaining their end is even more all-encompassing and greater than for non-Christians. This intensification of the stakes of envy echoes the

---

[38] Overmyer, "Three More Jigs in the Puzzle," 380–9.

abiding concern of Scripture and the Church Fathers. Recall that Cyprian of Carthage is concerned that envy turns to hatred of one's brother, as a man becomes "entangled in the blind snares of the deceitful enemy" whereby he "should himself be unwittingly destroyed by his own sword."[39] Leo the Great tells salvation history as an unfolding of Christ's work that finally defeats the devil's envy.[40] And Gregory the Great tells us how envy breaks the bonds of charity within the community, leading to other vices in its deadly undoing of divine love.[41] And Thomas? He situates his treatment of envy within a larger metaphysical-ontological structure that reveals the many ways in which envy is a grave threat to the love of Christ.

This full account of envy by Thomas reaches well beyond Question 36 alone. In fact, as Thomas presents envy, he does not separate out pagan envy and Christian envy. Rather Question 36 is taken up into the whole sweep of the questions on charity. Thomas gives an integrated and complete account of the scope of pagan envy as taken up into a theological framework. When Thomas writes of envy, even if seeming pagan through our myopic and selective reading habits, its true and absolute meaning refers to neighbor and God.

Thomas does not merely augment Aristotle's account of envy by "addition"—addition of God, of loving one's neighbor as oneself, of loving ourselves as God loves us, of a divine joy that is sheer gift, of our participation in the divine life. What happens in Thomas's writing on envy is not augmentation but transformation. As he integrates his understanding of pagan envy into Christian envy, he transforms it by permanently changing the stakes. Our envy never harms only our neighbor and ourselves but also and always harms our relationship to God. This means that Aristotle's fundamental human notion of what takes place in envy no longer suffices because all the human passions and habitual principles for action are in some way touched by the divine life. Perhaps then there is no real moment where Thomas's own meaning for envy is "pagan"? For Thomas, to write or speak of envy is to invoke the ways in which we frustrate true human flourishing—not merely in *eudaimonia*—but in charity and joy.[42]

---

[39] Cyprian of Carthage, "The Treatises of Cyprian," X.3; PL, 13, 41.
[40] Leo I, Sermon LXXIII, No. 4; NPNF 212.
[41] *Moralia*, Sect 85; PL, 75, 728.
[42] With thanks to the fellow participants of the *New Wine, New Wineskins* conference of 2015, and Sean Larsen. This project was assisted by a grant from the Faculty Research and Development Program, College of Liberal Arts and Sciences, DePaul University.

Resisting the Less Important:
Aquinas on Modesty

John-Mark Miravalle

IN OUR LIBIDINOUS AGE – and the corresponding umbrage it occasions – it is perhaps unsurprising that the virtue of modesty has been reduced to an almost exclusively sexual virtue. Popular books like Wendy Shalit's *A Return to Modesty*[1] or David and Diane Vaughan's *The Beauty of Modesty*[2] essentially view modesty as a woman's decision to avoid sexually provocative practices, particularly in matters of apparel. We find the same characterization with scholars. The second volume of Peschke's *Christian Ethics* presents modesty as a matter of sexual decency and decorum.[3] Nor is this a purely contemporary phenomenon. Tertullian's classic work *On Modesty* is concerned mostly with sins of the flesh.[4] Even in the *Catechism*, we find modesty relegated to the ninth commandment, where it is interpreted as an injunction against lust.

> Purity requires *modesty,* an integral part of temperance. Modesty protects the intimate center of the person. It means refusing to unveil what should remain hidden. It is ordered to chastity, to whose sensitivity it bears witness. It guides how one looks at others and behaves toward them in conformity with the dignity of persons and their solidarity... Modesty is decency. It inspires one's choice of clothing. It keeps silence or reserve where there is evident risk of unhealthy curiosity. It is discreet. (*Catechism of the Catholic Church*, nos. 2521-2522)

Happily, a little further the *Catechism* provides a more expansive portrayal of this virtue:

> There is a modesty of the feelings as well of the body. It protests, for example... the solicitations of certain media that go too far in the exhibition of intimate things. *Modesty inspires a way of life which*

---

[1] Wendy Shalit, *A Return to Modesty* (New York: Touchstone, 2000).
[2] David and Diane Vaughan, *The Beauty of Modesty* (Tennessee: Cumberland, 2005).
[3] Karl H. Peschke, S.V.D., *Christian Ethics: Moral Theology in the Light of Vatican II*, vol. 2 (Alcester, Ireland: C. Goodliffe Neale, 1993), 411-14.
[4] Tertullian, *On Modesty,* www.newadvent.org/fathers/0407.htm.

makes it possible to resist the allurements of fashion and the pressures of prevailing ideologies (no. 2523).

The last line clearly hints at the profoundly influential role modesty should play in the Christian life. A virtue that can offer sanctuary against the perpetual onslaught of trends and popular opinion doubtless consists in more than a sense of what to wear.

Thomas Aquinas follows this latter emphasis. When he discusses modesty, he devotes a significant number of questions to it, with only the last pertaining to matters of costume. The different modes of self-restraint which converge in constituting modesty yield a portrait of a person grounded in truth and defended from superficial influence. In this paper, I present Thomas's understanding of modesty as a holistic resistance to substitutes for genuine greatness. To assist in teasing out the distinctive properties of modesty, I propose further to contrast and compare modesty with Aquinas's discussions on vanity and magnanimity respectively. This may seem a strange medley of virtues and vices to consider concurrently, but all three are linked in delineating how to pursue depth and greatness, while avoiding shallowness. As I argue in the conclusion, in the current atmosphere of communications technology, Thomas's understanding of modesty – and its inseparability from magnanimity – takes on a special urgency.

MODESTY

Placing it at the tail end of the treatment on the virtues, Aquinas uses modesty as a kind of miscellaneous category under which to file the various forms of temperance not yet considered. Modesty comprises a set of "secondary virtues, those concerned with less difficult matters."[5] The result, at first glance, is a kind of hodgepodge of character traits that seem not to be easily relatable: *humility, studiousness, temperance in outward movements* and *temperance in apparel* (ST II.II, q. 160, a. 2). Putting these four elements together, however, ends up giving us a magnificently robust conception of what modesty should look like.

Humility, which the contemporary reader is likely to associate already with the term "modest," is a realistic recognition of one's proper limits. It restrains the impulse to make too much of oneself.[6] As Joseph Pieper elegantly puts it, "The ground of humility is man's

---

[5] Stephen J. Pope, "Overview of the Ethics of Aquinas" in *The Ethics of Aquinas*, ed. Stephen J. Pope (Washington, DC: Georgetown University Press, 2002), 45.

[6] Cf., Aquinas, *Summa,* II-II, q. 161, a. 2: "It belongs properly to humility that a man restrain himself from being borne towards that which is above him. For this purpose he must know his disproportion to that which surpasses his capacity."

estimation of himself according to truth. And that is almost all there is to it."[7] Humility prevents the vicious self-promotion which runs so counter to our picture of the modest person. Everyone recognizes, in principle at least, the ugliness of someone pretending to an excellence not possessed: someone talking authoritatively about a topic without knowing much about it, or a tone-deaf person insisting on being given a solo in the church choir. These and other ludicrous incongruities are mercifully precluded by a temperance born of accurate self-assessment.

And yet humility is also a far cry from the fawning, pathetic self-deprecators. One thinks of the Charles Dickens's character Uriah Heep, in *David Copperfield,* whose constantly describes himself as humble – or "Umble," – while his bogus humility is simply a camouflage for mean-spiritedness.[8] Quite the contrary, Aquinas is quick to point out that humility, like modesty as a whole, does not preclude the longing and hope for greatness – indeed, it makes greatness all the more attainable.[9]

Studiousness, the second component, seems further afield from modesty, but if truth is necessary for humility (modesty's primary ingredient) then the consequent necessity of studiousness becomes more intuitive. Studiousness is the virtue responsible for resisting curiosity, which is in turn the vice of inquiring about what one has no business inquiring about (ST II.II, q. 166, a.2, ad. 3; q. 167, a. 1). An easy illustration of intemperate inquisitiveness would be pursuing information which is demeaning, or unedifying, or directly contrary to the good of some relationship, like indulging one's morbid interest in certain torture procedures or seeking out gossip. When dealing with curiosity, Thomas seems less concerned with what the person *is* attending to and more concerned with what the person *is failing* to attend to, which is to say that the damage done is more related to the aspect of omission than of commission. Curiosity is deadly primarily as a distraction from one's obligations or from contemplating God or ultimately from doing or learning anything useful (ST II.II, q. 167, a. 1 and 2). It is the relative *triviality* of the intellectual content, not so much any spiritual toxicity which makes curiosity so malignant, and, by implication, studiousness becomes an important moral preventative.

With almost ubiquitous access to the internet, the virtue of focusing on what we should requires almost ceaseless vigilance. Everyone who sits down to a computer has to struggle, often minute-by-minute, against the lure of a limitless supply of unimportant but entertaining

---

[7] Josef Pieper, *The Four Cardinal Virtues* (Indiana: University of Notre Dame Press, 1966), 189.
[8] Charles Dickens, *David Copperfield* (New York: Penguin, 2004).
[9] Cf., Aquinas, *Summa,* II-II, q. 161, a. 1, c. and ad. 3.

discoveries on blogs, Google, YouTube, Facebook or Wikipedia. This has bearing not only on our various individual projects but on the common human call to true wisdom. As Pope Francis noted in *Laudato Si'*, "True wisdom, as the fruit of self-examination, dialogue and generous encounter between persons, is not acquired by a mere accumulation of data which eventually leads to overload and confusion, a sort of mental pollution" (no. 47).

In any case, the truth which is required for humility cannot be found through indulgent entertainment, nor will modesty be encouraged by squandering time on superficialities. Studiousness, the governance of where we direct our own attention, the mainstay against mental pollution, is vital for the depth of character to which modesty pertains. Appetition follows apprehension, and, if we fail to keep focused on the important things, the truths that matter, our passions and choices will be similarly disconnected from the ultimate goods on which our lives are meant to be centered.

Thirdly, modesty pertains to outward movements. If humility is inner modesty, then that modesty should be expressed externally; the body should express the person. Aquinas cites various authorities to corroborate this principle.

> Outward movements are signs of the inward disposition, according to Ecclesiastes 19:27, "The attire of the body, and the laughter of the teeth, and the gait of the man, show what he is," and Ambrose says that "the habit of mind is seen in the gesture of the body," and that "the body's movement is an index of the soul" (ST II.II, q. 168, a.1, ad. 1).

Probably we all know someone whose habits of manner or even whose style of walk seems calculated to draw attention. Interestingly, Aquinas devotes special attention to the examples of an excessively grave or excessively frivolous demeanor (ST II.II, q. 168, a.3 and a.4). One imagines the person who laughs and talks far too loudly at a party or who goes from one theatrical gesture to another. In any case, it is not enough to think or feel modestly about ourselves. We have to act modestly, have to temper the distinctive aspects of our personality that might be unpleasant or unedifying to others or makes us stand out disproportionately from others.

Naturally, a general norm about self-presentation will include precepts related to attire, since what we wear is perhaps the most vivid (although perhaps not the most profound) way human beings manage the way others view them. Thus, the fourth and final component of modesty is the habit of being balanced with respect to clothing. For Aquinas, modesty of clothing is neither directed exclusively to women nor predominantly against sexual provocation. While these issues emerge in the second article of the *Summa*'s question on modesty of apparel (ST II.II, q. 169, a. 2), in the first article Thomas is concerned with people generally (*homo* – not *vir* or *mulier*), and primarily people who simply care too much about their clothing, who are too attached to comfort in clothing, or who even think about their clothing too much. With a fine psychological touch, Aquinas criticizes specifically those who inordinately hope for the good opinion of others by dressing well, and those who inordinately hope for the good opinion of others by dressing badly (ST II.II, q. 169, a. 1). Regarding the former, he cites Gregory to the effect that men only buy overly expensive clothing out of vainglory. In other words, the cause of their immodesty is vanity, a disordered preoccupation with what other people think of them. This introduction of vanity at the conclusion of Thomas's treatment of modesty suggests the profitability of transitioning here to spend some time unpacking his insights on the moral disorder of vanity – which we would instinctively recognize as opposed to modesty since, while modesty resists disproportionate self-promotion, vanity revels in the spotlight.

VANITY AND MAGNANIMITY:
A CONTRASTAND COMPARISON WITH MODESTY

Vanity, like modesty, has undergone a historical reduction in connotation to the point that it now often refers merely to matters of physical appearance. A vain person is commonly regarded as someone who cares too much about how he or she looks. But traditionally the vice, like the virtue, enjoyed a much broader scope. Aquinas presents vanity (or vainglory) as being a disordered desire for the manifestation of one's own goodness. It occurs when one inordinately yearns for or delights in praise. This definition not only goes well beyond matters of physical appearance but also precludes any confusion between vanity and pride. Pride is the fundamental and universal sin, a disordered desire for some excellence, which Thomas says is essentially equivalent to disordered self-love (ST I.II, q. 84, a. 2, ad. 3). Vanity, like every sin, flows from pride, but vanity is specified by being directed to the praise or good estimation of others.

Granted, praise and the good estimation of others are not to be despised in themselves. What makes vanity sinful, what makes vainglory vain, is that the praise one desires is pointless: "The judgment of those thinking well of one so belongs to vainglory when one desires it without spiritual benefit to others or oneself" (*De Malo*, q.9, a. 1, ad. 8). Here we return to a theme already familiar from studiousness and modesty in apparel. Attention to what does not matter, like trivia, clothing, and what random people think of us, is a misdirection of our psychic energy. There is nothing inherently important in being noticed by others, and so we should not act like it is important: "It is requisite for man's perfection that he should know himself; but not that he should be known by others, wherefore it is not to be desired in itself" (ST II.II, q.132, a.1, ad. 3).

Simply because praise is not intrinsically valuable does not mean it is never valuable. Thomas enumerates three potential advantages of praise: first, when it gives greater glory to God; second, when it serves to edify one's neighbor; thirdly, when it encourages the recipient of the praise to continue in the good and strive to advance in virtue (ST II.II, q.132, a.1, ad. 3). Thus, we need not be indifferent to all compliments or contemptuous of all recognition. There is no need to brush aside every nice thing someone says about us. If being praised leads to any of these three goods, we can rejoice in it without guilt.

It is useless praise, notoriety that does no good, that we should guard against. This includes being praised for an excellence we do not possess—"glory in something false"—or being praised for something petty—"glory in a good that easily passes away" (*De Malo*, q. 9, a. 1). In the end, Aquinas is clear that being esteemed by others is, at best, only a means to some further good, and when desired for itself degenerates into a vice which leaves a trail of further vices in its wake.[10]

Perhaps the most interesting feature of Thomas's discussion of vainglory is the way he places vanity in stark contrast to magnanimity, the virtue whereby a person desires the greatness which may be expected of him, a greatness that is actually worthy of honor. Aquinas explains the contrariety between vainglory and magnanimity as follows:

> To think so much of little things as to glory in them is itself opposed to magnanimity. Wherefore it is said of the magnanimous man that honor is of little account to him. In like manner he thinks little of other things that are sought for honor's sake.... Again it is incompatible with magnanimity for a man to glory in the testimony of human praise, as though he deemed this something great; wherefore it is said of the magnanimous man that he cares not to be praised (ST II.II, q.132, a. 2, ad. 1).

Common sense tells us that recognition, when divorced, as it so often is, from genuine merit, is the quintessence of triviality and superficiality. A person who cares about what matters will not care much about being known, being noticed, being celebrated. A person who cares about what matters will not be vain.

The contrast between vanity and magnanimity, however, is not quite as simple as it may first appear. The vice of vanity, as we have seen, is a preoccupation with praise from others, but St. Thomas

---

[10] Aquinas lists the effects or 'daughters' of vainglory in *de Malo* q.9, a.3.

begins his description of magnanimity by saying that it is essentially "about honors." Whence, then, the contrast, if both magnanimity and vanity are about what other people say and think? One of these objections in fact appears in the first article on magnanimity, arguing that magnanimity, if it is really a virtue, cannot be about honors, since "the virtuous are not praised for desiring honors, but for shunning them" (ST II.II, q. 129, a. 1, obj. 3). Aquinas's response is to articulate more precisely in what sense the magnanimous person is concerned with honor:

> Those are worthy of praise who despise honors in such a way as to do nothing unbecoming in order to obtain them, nor have too great a desire for them. If, however, one were to despise honors so as not to care to do what is worthy of honor, this would be deserving of blame. Accordingly magnanimity is about honors in the sense that a man strives to do what is deserving of honor, yet not so as to think much of the honor accorded by man (ST II.II, q. 129, a. 1, ad. 3).

The great-souled individual, the person who yearns to be excellent, is perfectly justified in taking honor or praise as a normative principle as long as the praise in question is not the actual praise that society may or may not be pleased to grant, but the ideal praise proportionate to greatness. The virtuous evaluation of an act or a resolution does not involve asking, "Will I be admired for this?" but instead "Is this admirable?"[11]

It is not praise that matters, it is *being worthy of praise*, and praise and being worthy of praise are far from coextensive. This is the distinction which prompts Thomas to explore the relationship between magnanimity and humility (which is again, the chief component of modesty), both of which must ultimately be based on truth. With regard to oneself, magnanimity recognizes one's perfections and capacities; humility recognizes one's deficiencies and weaknesses. With regard to others, magnanimity recognizes that our neighbors are, like us, poor sinners whose judgment or character must not be mistaken as being absolute: thus "he does not think so much of others as to do anything wrong for their sake" (ST II.II, q. 129, a. 3, ad. 4). Humility, however, recognizes too that our neighbors have themselves

---

[11] Cf. Aquinas, *Summa*, I-II, q.2, a.3. Here, of course, God's estimation of our character is to be valued in a radically different way than the estimation of human beings, and that for two reasons. Firstly, because God's estimation of us is supremely accurate, whereas that of human beings is not. If God thinks we're excellent and happy, then we surely are; if men and women think we are excellent and happy, there is a good chance we are not – as the tragic personal histories of smiling celebrities so often illustrate. Secondly, for Thomas, God's knowledge is different from a human being's insofar as the way things are determines creaturely knowledge, while God's knowledge determines the way things are. In other words, God knowing that we are excellent and happy is what *makes* us excellent and happy.

been endowed by God, and, in that respect, we adopt towards them a deferential attitude.

Again, the criterion for the virtues is truth; "Hence it is clear that magnanimity is not opposed to humility: indeed, they concur in this, that each is according to right reason" (ST II.II, q. 161, a. 1, ad. 3). Where is human greatness to be found and where the deficiency? What is of great worth, and what is to be disdained? What matters, and what does not? Someone asking these questions, and living accordingly, will be automatically directed away from vanity, and towards modesty.

MODESTY TODAY

The practical directives of modesty along the lines indicated by Aquinas are fairly straightforward: resist disordered self-promotion; resist giving the mind over to irrelevancies; resist cultivating a style of self-deportment that attracts undue attention; avoid excessive anxiety regarding matters of wardrobe, or regarding what others think about something as relatively unimportant as clothing. Over and against these directives are the temptations of vanity, which prompt an overemphasis on superficialities, and in particular on what others think of us.

At the risk of sounding reactionary, it seems plain to me that the transformation of our own particular culture by communications technology has brought with it a radical challenge to the virtue of modesty, a challenge made not less comprehensive by being largely unconscious. If modesty is a holistic resistance to substitutions for genuine greatness, it appears the digital age is a time of unique inundation with temptations away from greatness and towards triviality.

We celebrate celebrities for being celebrities. Social networking platforms encourage us to share any thought or event, no matter how banal, with the world. Self-promoting references are affixed to what we used to think of as tools for contact with others. Advertisers or newsmakers sensationalize the patently insignificant simply through the raw force of repeated exposure, and we ourselves spend hours browsing through "friends" photos simply because we happened to be curious about their recent activities. We take and post pictures of ourselves wherever we go, at a restaurant or the Grand Canyon or a papal or presidential address. Also, the pictures which we post are almost uniformly flattering, and when anyone else posts more realistic pictures of us we remove them from our pages instantly. These are not cultural phenomena indicative of humility, studiousness, modesty of movement, or modesty of dress. They represent vanity blown to proportions that only mass media and digital reality could sustain.

And the strain tells. We worry that others will fail to appreciate our deeper value, and at the same time cheapen ourselves by posting shockingly intimate information (and sometimes images). We worry about peer pressure and do nothing to build up the defensive line of modesty against it, blaming peers instead of our sensitivity to pressure. Most of all, perhaps, we worry that our relationships are shallow, that friendships of real mutual understanding are growing rarer, as we say over and over, to an increasingly indiscriminate audience, "Look at me!"

Clearly, it is imperative to restore modesty to its rightful place and to stem the tide of vanity. As our discussion of Thomas suggests, magnanimity will play a fundamental role in that process. The virtue of magnanimity reminds us that greatness, excellence, the distinction between what people might think and what people should think are an indispensable aspect of this reform. Most crucially, magnanimity reminds us of the distinction between the important and the unimportant. God's estimation is important, and human attention is less important. The divine image in our neighbor is important, and how our neighbor looks or dresses is less important. Answering the big questions is important, and an entertaining two-minute video or 140-character status update is less important. Only when these relative value scales are recognized will love of what is praiseworthy yield a wholesome love of obscurity.[12] Only then may we expect the reappearance of modesty.

---

[12] Ronald Knox, in a magnificent homily entitled "The Charm of Our Obscurity," stated, "The point is that it is the instinct of the Catholic genius at its highest to court obscurity, to shun publicity, and, if it can do so without prejudice to the salvation of souls, to live and to die unknown." In *Pastoral and Occasional Sermons*, ed. Philip Caraman, S.J. (California: Ignatius Press, 2002), 223.

Agere Contra: An "Ignatian Option" for Engagement with American Society and Culture

Benjamin T. Peters

IN HIS REVIEW OF GEORGE WEIGEL'S *Evangelical Catholicism* for *Commonweal* in April 2013, William Portier declared:

> It is time to admit that the "Americanist" tradition…inherited from [John Courtney] Murray…is dead. If there was ever a harmonious fit between America and the Catholic natural–law tradition, there certainly isn't now. Catholics will not save America, as Murray dared to hope in 1960. Neither City on a Hill nor pagan cesspool, the United States is just our country.[1]

While there is much to Portier's statement, his claim that the "Americanist tradition" is dead stands out. For if he is correct, we are at an important historical moment in U.S. Catholicism: the end of an almost two-hundred year old argument (dating back at least to Orestes Brownson) that America is good for Catholicism and that Catholics are good for—and can even save—America. This is the bold assertion that has formed the way generations of Catholics have engaged with U.S. society and culture. And the demise of this belief has left many Catholics lost in a very real "moral wilderness"—to borrow a phrase from MacIntyre—searching for a new way to understand America.[2]

In order to address this new found predicament for American Catholics, I have broken my article into three parts. First, I look at some of the more recent discussions surrounding the idea that the Americanist proposition is no longer viable. Next, I suggest an alternative approach to social engagement that is rooted in Ignatian spirituality, one that is neither a wholesale withdrawal from nor blanket embrace of American life. Finally, I highlight some of figures

---

[1] William L. Portier, "More Mission, Less Maintenance," *Commonweal*, April 12, 2013, 29-31.
[2] See Alasdair MacIntyre, "Notes from the Moral Wilderness," in *The MacIntyre Reader*, ed. Kelvin Knight (Indiana: University of Notre Dame Press, 1998), 31-49.

who seem to embody this "Ignatian option," in particular Dorothy Day and Pope Francis.

THE VIABILITY OF THE AMERICAN PROPOSITION

Not long after Portier's review appeared in *Commonweal*, Patrick Deneen published a much talked about piece on *The American Conservative* website titled "A Catholic Showdown Worth Watching."[3] In it, Deneen, who teaches political science at Notre Dame, stated,

> The relationship of Catholicism to America, and America to Catholicism, began with rancor and hostility, but became a comfortable partnership forged in the cauldron of World War II and the Cold War. But was that period one of "ordinary time," or an aberration which is now passing, returning us to the inescapably hostile relationship? A growing body of evidence suggests that the latter possibility can't simply be dismissed out of hand: liberalism appears to be daily more hostile to Catholicism, not merely disagreeing with its stances, but demanding that they be changed in conformity to liberal views on self-sovereignty or, failing that, that the Church be defined out of the bounds of decent liberal society, an institution no more respectable than the Ku Klux Klan.[4]

Deneen then went on to distinguish three approaches to social engagement taken by U.S. Catholics. One, which he called "Liberal Catholicism," he dismissed outright as being doomed to oblivion— "fated to become liberalism *simpliciter* within a generation." But a second approach also exists, which he described as an "older American tradition of orthodox Catholicism" closely aligned with John Courtney Murray, SJ. According to Deneen, the basis of this approach has been that:

> Essentially, there is no fundamental contradiction between liberal democracy and Catholicism. Liberal democracy is, or at its best can be, a tolerant home for Catholics, one that acknowledges contributions of the Catholic tradition and is leavened by its moral commitments. While liberalism alone can be brittle and thin—its stated neutrality can leave it awash in relativism and indifferentism—it is deepened and rendered more sustainable by the Catholic presence. Murray went so far as to argue that America is in fact more Catholic than even its Protestant founders realized—that they availed themselves unknowingly of a longer and deeper tradition of natural law that undergirded the thinner liberal commitments of the American

---

[3] Patrick Deneen, "A Catholic Showdown Worth Watching," *The American Conservative*, February 6, 2014, www.theamericanconservative.com/2014/02/06/a-catholic- showdown-worth-watching/.
[4] Deneen, "A Catholic Showdown."

founding. The Founders "built better than they knew," and so it is Catholics like Orestes Brownson and Murray, and not liberal lions like John Locke or Thomas Jefferson, who have better articulated and today defend the American project.[5]

This is the Americanist tradition to which Portier was referring. A tradition that, as Michael Hanby has recently explained, has had a profound influence on U.S. Catholicism,

> Catholics generally find the argument for the compatibility of Catholicism with the principles of the American founding convincing because they believe that the argument has been vindicated by the growth and assimilation of the Church in the United States and by the apparent vitality of American Catholicism in comparison with Catholicism in Europe. Rarely do political or theological disagreements penetrate deeply enough to disturb this shared foundation.[6]

In short, Hanby concluded, "Liberal or conservative, postconciliar Catholicism is essentially Murrayite."[7]

But Deneen also distinguished a third approach, labeled "radical," that "rejects the view that Catholicism and liberal democracy are fundamentally compatible." This position is deeply critical of "contemporary arrangements of market capitalism, is deeply suspicious of America's imperial ambitions, and wary of the basic premises of liberal government."[8] Of course Deneen's argument here is not new. Richard Gaillardetz, for instance, has described three very similar approaches to what he called Catholic "cultural engagement": a "correlationist" approach, which he noted is advocated by theologians such as Charles Curran, J. Bryan Hehir, David Hollenbach, as well as Kenneth and Michael Himes; a "neo-conservative" approach advanced by George Weigel, Michael Novak, and the late Richard John Neuhaus; and a "radical" approach taken by Michael Baxter, William Cavanaugh, Michael Budde, David

---

[5] Deneen, "A Catholic Showdown."
[6] Michael Hanby, "The Civic Project of American Christianity: How the Public Significance of Christianity is Changing," *First Things*, February 2015, www.firstthings.com/article/2015/02/the-civic-project-of-american-christianity.
[7] Hanby, "The Civic Project."
[8] Deneen "A Catholic Showdown."

Schindler, and others associated with Dorothy Day and the Catholic Worker movement.[9]

Interestingly, while very different in there stances on particular issues, both Gaillardetz's "correlationist" and "neo-conservative" approaches ultimately seek to maintain Murray's notion of the relationship between America and the Church. For both Deneen and Gaillardetz, then, there seem to be really only two viable options for Catholics: either somehow revive Murray's project and embrace American society and culture or reject it. Or, as Deneen put it, U.S. Catholics must choose, "Whether the marriage between the Church and the State can be rescued, or whether a divorce is in the offing."[10] And the degree to which one views the American milieu as corrupt or hostile to Catholicism seems to determine the approach one would choose. For if it is sinful or lost, divorce should be inevitable, but, if it isn't, then the marriage can be saved. The underlying theological assertion here seems to be that it is primarily sin which must be resisted in Catholic social engagement.

Not surprisingly, this was also the theological assertion underlying Murray's account of "incarnational" and "eschatological humanism."[11] For Murray, Catholic withdrawal from U.S. political and economic institutions in the 1940s-50s was rooted in an "eschatological humanism" that he said regarded these institutions as completely corrupt, and so withdrawal from them was an "utter prophetic condemnation" of the United States—a "contempt for the world."[12] Murray contrasted this with an "incarnational humanism," which he clearly preferred, that took a more affirming approach to the structures and institutions in America as not sinful and therefore able to be embraced.

This paradigm continues to inform our discussions today and can be seen in Massimo Faggioli's critique of Baxter and Cavanaugh in *America* where Faggioli accused them of advancing an argument for "sectarian" withdrawal from corrupt American political and economic life.[13] It is also evident in the discussions over the so-called "Benedict Option" that began to appear in *First Things* in 2014. This option—influenced by MacIntyre's call for another St. Benedict—has been championed as of late by the likes of Rod Dreher and other self-described "crunchy-cons" as "a means of cultivating a new

---

[9] Richard Gaillardetz, "The Ecclesiological Foundations of Modern Catholic Social Teaching," in *Modern Catholic Social Teaching: Commentaries & Interpretations*, ed. Kenneth Himes, O.F.M. (Washington, DC: Georgetown University Press, 2005), 72- 98, 77-80.

[10] Deneen,"A Catholic Showdown."

[11] See John Courtney Murray, *We Hold These Truths*, (New York: Sheed & Ward, 1960), 184-193.

[12] Murray, *We Hold These Truths*, 185-189.

[13] Massimo Faggioli, "A View From Abroad" *America*, February 24, 2014, 20-23, 22.

counterculture that can resist the barbarian onslaught" through small communities of virtue, a renewed localism, and a return to the land.[14] As C.C. Pecknold noted, though—sticking to Murray's template—this option can be dismissed as "withdrawing" from a corrupt world.[15] In response, Pecknold has proposed a "Dominican Option," flowing out of St. Dominic's "missionary zeal," which could build a "'contrast society' that is still very much engaged with the world." But here too, criticism has emerged regarding the degree to which this option actually engages with society.[16] Along much the same lines, more recently a "Francis Option" has appeared, as well as a "Balthasar Option" which calls for Catholics to create "islands of humanity" within American life.[17]

IGNATIAN OPTION

It is in response to all this—and with an awareness that these discussions of "options" have become somewhat overblown—that I would like to suggest an "Ignatian Option" to social engagement, a form of engagement rooted in the very Ignatian notion that the Christian life entails something more than simply avoiding that which is sinful. At the heart of this Ignatian option is a spirituality rooted in the *Spiritual Exercises* of Ignatius of Loyola.[18] Ignatius introduced his *Exercises* by stating that their purpose was in "preparing and disposing our soul to rid itself of all its disordered affections and then, after their removal, of seeking and finding God's will in the ordering of our life for the salvation of our soul" (*Spiritual Exercises*, no. 1). Indeed, as John O'Malley, SJ, has noted, "the fundamental premise" of the

---

[14] Rod Dreher, "Benedict Option" *The American Conservative*, December 12, 2013, www.theamericanconservative.com/articles/benedict-option/. Dreher has recently published a book length version of this argument; see *The Benedict Option: A Strategy for Christians in a Post-Christian Nation* (New York: Penguin Random House, 2017).
[15] C.C. Pecknold, "The Domincan Option," *First Things*, October 6, 2014, www.firstthings.com/web-exclusives/2014/10/the-dominican-option.
[16] See C.C. Pecknold, "The Dominican Option and the Common Good," *Ethika Politika*, July 23, 2015, ethikapolitika.org/2015/07/23/the-dominican-option-and-the-common-good/.
[17] Tom Hoopes, "The 'Francis Option,'" *National Catholic Register*, July 8, 2015, www.ncregister.com/daily-news/the-francis-option. For Balthasar Option, see John Herreid, "Option, Option, Who's Got the Option?" *John Herreid*, July 23, 2015, herreid.org/blog/2015/07/23/option-option-whos-got-the-option/.
[18] According to John O'Malley, "conversion" is the underlying "dynamic" of the First Week of the *Exercises*—a turning toward a more devout life: "If the purpose of that Week was successfully achieved, individuals had found a new and happier orientation at the very core of their being and were thus set more firmly than before on the path of salvation." This "better ordering" of one's life is the essential concern of the *Exercises* as a whole. The other Weeks "were constructed with a view to confirming the First, while moving the person along to further issues." John O'Malley, *The First Jesuits* (Massachusetts: Harvard University Press, 1993), 40.

Exercises is the "immediate action of God on the individual" and "the continuous action of God in the whole process."[19]

In light of this purpose, the *Exercises* open with the "Principle and Foundation" (*Spiritual Exercises*, no. 23), which Ignatian scholars like George Ganss, SJ, have read as articulating the theological core of the *Exercises*.[20] For in these opening lines, Ignatius concisely described the essence of the Christian life when he stated, "Human beings are created to praise, reverence, and serve God our Lord, and by means of this to save their soul."[21] Here a particular theological anthropology emerges: human nature's ultimate destiny—"to save their soul"—is beyond our ability; and so too is the means by which this destiny can be attained—"to praise, reverence, and serve God." All of this suggests that Ignatius regarded desire for union with God as primary to the life of a Christian, a desire that calls each Christian to holiness.

Ignatius can be read as describing the practical implications of this call to holiness in the "Principle and Foundation" when he wrote:

> I must make myself indifferent to all created things, in regard to everything which is left to my freedom of will and is not forbidden. Consequently, on my own part I ought not seek health rather than sickness, wealth rather than poverty, honor rather than dishonor, a long life rather than a short one, and so on in all these matters. I ought to desire and elect only the thing which is most conducive for us to the end for which I am created. (*Spiritual Exercises*, no. 23)

For Ignatius, the Christian life entailed a great deal more than simply avoiding what is sinful. Indeed, it may often entail giving up even good things such as health, riches, honor, or a long life since over time desire for these things becomes an impediment to the holiness to which we are called. So for Ignatius, sin is not the primary reason for Christian detachment, rather it is a desire for union with God which often requires moving beyond or even going against—*agere contra*—our natural inclinations, much like the *"nada, nada, nada"* of John of

---

[19] O'Malley, *The First Jesuits*, 38, 43. O'Malley explained that this premise can be seen the two key features of the *Exercises*: its clear design aimed at carrying out a course of discernment and preparation for how to live in a new way in response to "an inner call for intimacy" with God, and its flexible and non-prescriptive character, which allows "the Creator to deal immediately with the creature and the creature with its Creator and Lord" (*Spiritual Exercises,* no. 15). John O'Malley, "Early Jesuit Spirituality: Spain and Italy," in *Christian Spirituality III*, eds. Louis Dupré and Don E. Saliers (New York: Crossroad, 1989), 5.

[20] George Ganss, SJ, *The Spiritual Exercises of Saint Ignatius: A Translation and Commentary* (Illinois: Loyola Press, 1992), 208-214.

[21] All quotes from Ignatius's *Spiritual Exercises* are taken from *Ignatius of Loyola: Spiritual Exercises and Selected Writings*, trans. George Ganss, S.J. (New York: Paulist Press, 1991), 120-214.

the Cross.²² It is worth noting that this view of human nature is also very much in concert with Thomas Aquinas's claim that our nature remains essentially unchanged after the Fall—it is not corrupted by original sin, but it does lose the gift of original justice that had ordered it.²³ While "fallen nature" remains unchanged and essentially good, for Thomas it is "left to itself" and insufficient.²⁴ Likewise, Ignatius's admonition that one be indifferent to created goods is not out of a belief that such things as health or a long life are sinful but rather because they are insufficient and cannot bring about our fulfillment. The *Exercises*, therefore, can be seen as a tool to help discern those things of the world that must be abandoned and those that can be perfected, all in light of the beatific vision.

But despite this orientation toward union with God, Ignatius seemed equally clear that he did not intend the *Exercises* to form members of a contemplative order. Rather, he wanted the *Exercises* to bring about an "election" or ordering of one's life "for the greater service and praise of God."²⁵ Service to the "active apostolate" thus became an essential component of Jesuit spirituality.²⁶ At the center of this spirituality is what the late Cardinal Avery Dulles described as the "practical mysticism" of Ignatius—sensitive to the "interior leading of the Holy Spirit" while at the same time dedicated "unswervingly to the service of the Church militant."²⁷

Not long after Ignatius's death in 1556, this "practical mysticism" began to fade within Jesuit spiritual writing. In fact, O'Malley has

---

²² See *Spiritual Exercises*, no. 13. Also, John of Cross, *The Ascent of Mount Carmel*, Book 1, Chapter 13.
²³ Thomas Aquinas, *Summa Theologica*, I-II, 82.
²⁴ See *ST* I.II, q. 17, a, 9. In summing all of this up, T.C. O'Brien, O.P.—an editor and translator of the Blackfriars' edition of the *Summa Theologiae*—noted that for Aquinas original sin does not deprive human nature of anything that is strictly proper to itself. Rather it is the gratuitous gift of original justice that is lost. Following the Fall, human nature is simply "left to itself" and it is in this sense that Thomas understood human nature as disordered—a disorder not caused by the corruption of sin, but by human nature's own "defectibility." For Aquinas, then, "fallen nature" is human nature "left to itself" without divine assistance—or as O'Brien put it, human nature "stays itself, but forlorn." See *St. Thomas Aquinas Summa Theologiae, vol.26, Original Sin (Ia2ae. 81-85)* trans. T.C. O'Brien, O.P. (New York: Blackfriars/McGraw-Hill Book Co., 1965), 151-158.
²⁵ O'Malley, "Early Jesuit Spirituality," 6.
²⁶ Joseph de Guibert, *The Jesuits: Their Spiritual Doctrine and Practice* (Illinios: Loyola University Press, 1964), 176-181.
²⁷Dulles noted that this synthesis had its roots squarely in the *Exercises*: "The rules laid down in the *Spiritual Exercises* on the discernment of spirits (*SE* 313-36) and on the choice of a state of life (*SE* 169-89) have given Jesuits a sense of the immediate presence of God, who calls each individual to union with Himself. The director of the *Exercises* is admonished to let 'the Creator and Lord in person communicate Himself to the devout soul' and 'permit the Creator to deal directly with the creature' (*SE* 15).

pointed out that already by the seventeenth-century two "strains" in Jesuit spirituality could be distinguished. One he described as "cautious and soberly ascetical, favorable almost exclusively to a methodical and even moralistic style of prayer."[28] Jesuits following this strain were "suspicious of contemplation and other higher forms of prayer as inimical to the active ministry" to which the Jesuits were committed.[29] While this strain would come to prevail within much of Jesuit spirituality, O'Malley noted that an alternative perspective also existed. This one was "more expansive" and "more syncretistic within the broad tradition of Christian spirituality" and was intent on developing "the implications of the affective and even mystical elements" in the life of Ignatius.[30] At the center of this second strain was Louis Lallemant (1587-1635), an often overlooked seventeenth-century French Jesuit, who was a prominent figure in what Pope Francis has recently described as the "mystical movement" in Jesuit history—a group which also included Jesuits like Jean Joseph Surin

---

But this personal mysticism was balanced in the case of Ignatius by intense devotion to the institutional Church. For him it was axiomatic that 'In Christ our Lord, the bridegroom, and in His spouse the Church, only one Spirit holds sway, which governs and rules for the salvation of souls' (*SE* 365). In the *Constitutions of the Society of Jesus* and in the 'Rules of Thinking with the Church' (*SE* 352-70) he stressed the need for unquestioning obedience to the hierarchy and especially to the pope as vicar of Christ on earth. In the *Spiritual Exercises* Ignatius wrote affectionately of the 'hierarchical Church' (*SE* 170, 353, 355) –a term which he apparently was the first to use." See, Avery Dulles, "Jesuits and Theology: Yesterday and Today" *Theological Studies* 52, no. 3 (Sept 1991): 524-538, 525.

[28] O'Malley pointed out that "the insistence on the practice of the virtues, the importance attached to sacramental confession of sins and the 'reform of life,' and the insistence in Ignatius's writings to his fellow Jesuits on the practice of obedience could easily lead, in less expansive minds, to moralism and a behavioralism that were far from the true intent of the saint." O'Malley, "Early Jesuit Spirituality," 14.

[29] O'Malley asserted that this strain "ran the danger of reducing Loyola to a small-minded master of hackneyed precepts." O'Malley, "Early Jesuit Spirituality," 17.

[30] Important here is also the fact that both these strains correspond with the two "tendencies" in Jesuit spirituality that Dulles stated were present by "the age of Vatican I." One favored a preference for the "Rules of Thinking with the Church" (*Spiritual Exercises*, nos. 352-370) found in the *Exercises* and certain passages from the *Constitutions* of the Society of Jesus which stressed obedience to the hierarchical Church—a tendency generally held by nineteenth-century neo-Thomist Jesuits who based their theology on "natural reason and on the authority of the papal and conciliar documents." Another tendency, always much less popular, emphasized "The Rules for the Discernment of Spirits" (*Spiritual Exercises*, nos. 313-336) and the "mysticism of Ignatius"—Jesuits working out of this tendency "sought to connect theology more intimately with prayer and the experience of the Holy Spirit." Dulles, "Jesuits and Theology," 531.

(1600-1665),[31] Jean Rigoleuc (1596-1658), as well as Jean-Pierre de Caussade (1675-1751).[32]

Unfortunately, Lallemant did not leave behind any published materials. What is known of his spirituality comes from the lecture notes of his former students at the Jesuit College in Rouen, such as Surin and Rigoleuc, which were eventually published as *La vie et la doctrine spirituelle de Père Louis Lallemant* in 1694.[33] Like the *Exercises*, a particular anthropology of human emptiness seeking the fullness of God emerges in this *doctrine spirituelle*:[34]

> There is a void in our heart which all creatures united would be unable to fill. God alone can fill it; for he is our beginning and our end. The possession of God fills up this void, and makes us happy. The privation of God leaves in us this void, and is the cause of our wretchedness.[35]

Starting from this view of the human person, Lallemant—following Ignatius—went on to teach a form of detachment from worldly things

---

[31] Surin's legacy largely surrounded his involvement, beginning in 1635, with a community of Ursuline nuns in Loudun and the demonic possession reportedly occurring in the convent. For twenty-five years, Surin suffered severe mental imbalances that he attributed to demonic possession. It was in this state that Surin wrote one of the great classics in spiritual writing, the *Spiritual Catechism* (1657). The *Catechism*, which gained the approval of Bossuet in 1661, carried the influence of both Surin and Lallemant into the eighteenth century where it helped shape the spirituality of Caussade and Jean Grou, S.J., in the nineteenth-century. Its influence even lasted into the twentieth-century where it had a "decisive effect" on Raissa and Jacques Maritain. Buckley, "Seventeenth-Century," 63. Surin's involvement at Loudun was memorialized in Aldous Huxley's *The Devils of Loudun* (New York: Harper & Brothers, 1953).

[32] See Francis's interview with Antonio Spadaro, S.J. "A Big Heart Open to God," *America*, September 30, 2013, 14-38, 20. Louis Cognet's list of seventeenth-century Jesuit "disciples" of Lallemant included: Rigoleuc, Surin, Champion, as well as Jean-Baptiste Saint-Jure (1588-1657), Jacques Nouet (1605-1680), Vincent Huby (1603-1693), Julien Maunoir (1606-1683), Francois Guillore (1615-1684), Jean Crasset (1618-1692), and Claude de la Colombiere (1641-1682), who was the spiritual director of St. Margaret Mary Alacoque (1647-1690). Louis Cognet, *Post-Reformation Spirituality*, trans. P. Hepburne Scott (New York: Hawthorn Books Publisher, 1959), 107.

[33] For an English translation, see, Alan McDougall, ed., *The Spiritual Doctrine of Father Louis Lallemant of the Society of Jesus, Preceded by an Account of his Life by Father Champion, S.J.* (Maryland: Newman Book Shop, 1946).

[34] As Michael Buckley observed, "The spirituality of Lallemant opens with an antithetical dynamic contrast. It is not that of contradiction but of privation and its fulfillment." Michael Buckley, S.J., "Seventeenth-Century French Spirituality: Three Figures," in *Christian Spirituality III*, ed. Louis Dupré and Don E. Saliers (New York: Crossroad Publishing Company, 1989), 28-68, at 56.

[35] McDougall, *The Spiritual*, 27. Huxley described Lallemant's spiritual life as: "The corollary of "Thy kingdom come' is 'our kingdom go." Huxley, *Devils*, 77.

in order to restore the emptiness that marks human nature and return it to "the perfect nudity of the soul" so that it could then be filled with the superabundance of grace.[36] This theology was even more clearly laid out in Rigoleuc's own writings where he presented a kind of three-tiered account of the Christian life which distinguished nature from both sin and the supernatural.[37] The Christian was called to not only reject "the way of passion and sin" but was also called to give up "the way of nature and the senses" in favor of something greater—what the French Jesuit described as "the way of grace and the spirit."[38]

For all this talk of the "perfect nudity of the soul" and "the way of grace and the spirit," it must be remembered that Lallemant's spirituality was at work in the formation of young Jesuits such as St. Isaac Jogues and the other North American martyrs. Michael Buckley, SJ, has noted that Lallemant helped form the lives of men given over in apostolic service "whose underlying determination [was] toward God as motive and in union with the Spirit as configuring guide."[39] In this way, Lallemant and this Jesuit mystical movement can be seen as trying to hold together Ignatius's "practical mysticism."

Despite its brief popularity, as Henri Bremond noted, by the eighteenth-century Lallemant and his "school" were largely forgotten or ignored within the Society of Jesus—with the exception of later Jesuits like Caussade and Nicholas Grou.[40] While something of this may have been due to internal opposition within the Society, it must also be remembered that Lallemant was part of an extraordinary group

---

[36] Buckley, "Seventeenth-Century," 57.
[37] See Pierre Champion, S.J., *La Vie du pere Jean Rigoleuc de la Compagne de Jesus. Avec ses traitez de devotion et ses lettres spirituelles* (Paris: chez Estienne Michallet, 1686), 305-311.
[38] For fuller description of this three-tiered account see, Peter Goddard, "Augustine and the Amerindian in Seventeenth-Century New France," *Church History* 67, no. 4 (Dec 1998): 662-684 at 669-671.
[39] Buckley, "Seventeenth-Century," 60. Buckley noted that the rapid expansion of Jesuit colleges in France at the time demanded so much active ministry that it threatened the interior life which Ignatius saw as necessary to sustain such work. He suggested that therefore one must presuppose "the dominant experience behind the *Doctrine spirituelle* to be that of apostolic call, and the rest of Lallemant falls easily into place" ("Seventeenth-Century," 62).
[40] Indeed, Bremond declared that "More integral, more original, twenty times more sublime and twenty times more austere, more demanding than Port-Royal, the school which we are going to study made little noise. Its contemporaries scarcely suspected that it existed; Saint-Beuve did not speak of it; and for the most part, the Catholic of today knows nothing about it except its name. Its founder, the Jesuit Louis Lallemant died in 1635 without having written anything. Among the disciples of that great man, only one, Father Surin, has achieved recognition [*glorie*], but a recognition that was contested, for a long time suspect, and one of infinite sorrow." Henri Bremond, *Histoire Littéraire du Sentiment Religieux en France depuis la Fin des Guerres de Religion jusqu'a Nos Jours, Vol. 5: La conquete mystique* (1923), trans. Buckley, "Seventeenth-Century," 60.

of spiritual writers—including Teresa of Avila, John of the Cross, Frances de Sales, and Cardinal Bérulle—who wrote from the period just after the Reformation until the end of the seventeenth-century.[41] Indeed, it was the Quietist controversy in the late seventeenth-century which brought about the abrupt end of this amazing flourish of spiritual writing. For almost immediately after Fénelon's submission to Pope Innocent XII in 1699, a very real anti-mystical attitude descended upon the Church and, as a result, spiritual writing of a more mystical nature largely disappeared from the public arena.[42]

This decline left a void that was quickly filled by a resurgent Jansenism which strongly promoted a rigorist asceticism coupled with the notion that only a few predestined souls would ever be able to attain mystical union with God.[43] In *The Mystic Fable*, Michel de Certeau pointed out that by the end of the seventeenth-century, the adjective "mystical" (*mystique*) had become the noun "mysticism" (*la mystique*).[44] Packaged as such, it was neatly marginalized and quarantined away as mystical prayer became understood as an extraordinary practice exclusively reserved for cloistered spiritual elites. As a result, any writing that emphasized the mystical or supernatural—the desire to go beyond one's nature—became suspect. Union with God and emphasis on the mystery of the supernatural in general quickly came to be seen as a phenomenon outside of the life of ordinary Christians, laity and secular clergy alike.[45]

The Quietist controversy, then, a relatively small affair mainly involving a limited number of French ecclesiastics, marks a significant turning point in the history of Catholicism. Indeed, Maurice Blondel identified "two Catholic mentalities" which emerged from the Quietist dispute and argued that they set the positions in all the major conflicts within nineteenth and early twentieth-century Catholicism.[46] And in

---

[41] O'Malley, "Early Jesuit," 21.

[42] C.J.T. Talar, "Prayer at Twilight: Henri Bremond's *Apologie pour Fénelon*," in *Modernists & Mystics,* ed. C.J.T. Talar (Washington, DC: CUA Press, 2009), 39-61at 39.

[43] For more on this period, see Robert McKeon's "Introduction" in Jean Pierre Caussade, *A Treatise on Prayer from the Heart: A Christian Mystical Tradition Recovered for All*, trans., ed. Robert McKeon (Missouri: Institute of Jesuit Sources, 1998), 28.

[44] Michel de Certeau, *The Mystic Fable, vol. 1, The Sixteenth and Seventeenth Centuries*, trans. Michael B. Smith (Illinios: University of Chicago Press, 1992), 16, 76-77, 107-113.

[45] William Portier and C.J.T. Talar, "Mystical Element of Modernist Crisis," in *Modernists & Mystics,* ed. C.J.T. Talar (Washington, DC: CUA Press, 2009), 1-22, 17.

[46] Alexander Dru, "Introduction" in Maurice Blondel, *The Letter on Apologetics and History of Dogma,* trans. Alexander Dru and Illtyd Trethowan (New York: Holt, Rinehart, and Winston, 1964), 25.

its aftermath, "a narrowing, suffocating, and hyper-intellectualization" of the tradition began which culminated in the form of neo-Thomism—what has been referred to "strict-observance Thomism"—that came to prevail in much of Catholic thought by the first half of the twentieth-century.[47] This was a form of Thomism marked by a two-storied account of nature and grace, with the supernatural building a kind of superstructure on a largely self-contained nature, that then informed a two-tiered notion of the Christian life with ordinary Christians called to simply avoid sin and follow the precepts of the natural law, while pursuit of holiness was reserved for the cloister.

And this theological dynamic endured well into the twentieth-century and was clearly operative in Murray's Americanist argument: Catholics could fit into the post-war "American consensus" by following the natural law and avoiding those aspects of American life that were sinful.[48] While Murray was certainly critical of some aspects of American life—such as the prohibition of the use of public tax dollars to support Catholic schools and the denial of the legal right to be a selective conscientious objector to war—that criticism was always in terms of natural law tenets.[49] A deeper critique of U.S. political or economic institutions was dismissed as the kind of "spiritual withdrawal" that marked "eschatological humanism."

It is this contrast between embrace or withdrawal that still seems to underpin discussions of Catholic social engagement today—and to which a more Ignatian option offers an alternative approach that is neither a wholesale withdrawal from American society and culture nor blanket embrace of it. Rather, it entails an ongoing discernment of how to live the Christian call to holiness within a particular historical and sociological context that is not always nurturing of that call. Therefore, it is an approach to social engagement that enables U.S. Catholics to assess what they encounter in their daily lives in light of their ultimate destiny and then chart how to negotiate the complexities of their lives in that light. In other words, an "Ignatian option" does not seek to save

---

[47]Portier and Talar, "Mystical Element," 9. For more on "strict-observance Thomism," see Helen James John, S.N.D., *The Thomist Spectrum* (New York: Fordham University Press, 1966); Aidan Nichols, O.P., *Reason with Piety: Garrigou-Lagrange in the Service of Catholic Thought* (Florida: Sapientia Press, 2008).

[48] Much has been written on Murray's efforts at post-war consensus building, for two excellent accounts, see John Murray Cuddihy, *No Offense: Civil Religion and Protestant Taste* (New York: Seabury Press, 1978), 49-100; Eugene McCarraher, *Christian Critics: Religion and Impasse in Modern American Social Thought* (New York: Cornell University Press, 2000), 89-119.

[49] In an address given at Western Maryland College on June 4, 1967, Murray presented his argument in support of selective conscientious objection, which was later published in "War and Conscience" in *A Conflict of Loyalties: The Case for Selective Conscientious Objection,* 19–30, ed. by James Finn, (New York: Pegasus, 1968). For his argument in favor of the use of tax dollars to support Catholic schools, see Murray, *We Hold These Truths,* 143-154.

the marriage between Catholicism and the United States nor to end it in divorce, but rather it seeks an annulment, an affirmation that the marriage never existed.[50] Again, as Portier put it, neither "City on the Hill nor a pagan cesspool, the United States is just our country."

DOROTHY DAY AND POPE FRANCIS

This kind of Ignatian approach can be seen in Dorothy Day's form of social engagement—a practice of selective non-participation in various American political and economic institutions such as not voting, opposing U.S. war-making, and resisting American consumerist culture. Unsurprisingly, this approach to engagement taken by Day and others associated with her has often been depicted by scholars—very much contemporary Murrayites like Dave O'Brien, George Weigel, and, more recently, Kristin Heyer—as a "perfectionist" or "sectarian" withdrawal from America.[51] However, Day's rejection of these institutions was not because she regarded them as necessarily sinful but rather that they presented obstacles to the holiness and union with God for which she longed. Indeed, this was the heart of Dorothy Day's spirituality, for, as she tells it in her most well-known work, *The Long Loneliness*, her spiritual journey was more than simply rejecting sin and embracing goodness, but rather it was one of giving up a life she described as "Natural Happiness" in order to pursue what she considered to be something greater, the supernatural happiness she found in the Catholic Worker.

In articulating this, Day divided her autobiography into three parts with Part I, "Searching," describing her life in the Old Left—a movement she called one of her "two great loves."[52] Her radical friends were presented as good, though very clearly lacking.[53] Day described her old comrades as dedicating their lives to heroically caring and fighting for people who were poor, unemployed, and disenfranchised. Writing decades after her conversion, she still remembered these radicals with admiration,

> The Marxists, the I.W.W.'s who looked upon religion as the opiate of the people, who thought they had only this one life to live and then oblivion—they were the ones who were eager to sacrifice themselves

---

[50] I would like to thank Michael Baxter for suggesting this annulment metaphor.
[51] See, David O'Brien, *Public Catholicism* (New York: MacMillan Publishing Co., 1989), 246; George Weigel, *Tranquilitatis Ordinis: The Present and Future Promise of American Catholic Thought on War and Peace* (New York: Oxford University Press, 1987), 150; Kristin Heyer, *Prophetic & Public: The Social Witness of U.S. Catholicism* (Washington, DC: Georgetown University Press, 2006), 76.
[52] Dorothy Day, *The Long Loneliness* (New York: Harper & Row, 1952), 149.
[53] At various points in her story, Day noted the suicides and depression within radical community, especially following the execution of Sacco and Vanzetti in 1927.

here and now, thus doing without now and for all eternity the good things of the world which they were fighting to obtain for their brothers. It was then, and still is, a paradox that confounds me. God love them![54]

Her portrayal of these radicals was clearly favorable, and she saw her life within the movement as having been, in many ways, a good thing—something she still very much admired and even wished her fellow Christians would imitate.[55] Yet it was this life that she left behind in favor of something she saw as much better.

This idea of leaving behind more than just what is sinful was illustrated even more vividly in "Natural Happiness," the second and pivotal section of Day's story. Presenting her life leading up to her conversion, Day recalled the happiness that she experienced with her other "great love," her common-law husband Forster Batterham. "Because I feel that this period of my life was so joyous and lovely," she recounted, "I want to write at length about it, giving the flavor, the atmosphere, the mood of those days."[56] Far from quickly noting a past of which she was ashamed, Day wrote a great deal about this period of her life, its simplicity and joy. She made it clear that she was very much in love with Forster: "I loved him in every way, as a wife, as a mother even. I loved him for all he knew and pitied him for all he didn't know.... I loved his lean cold body as he got into bed smelling of the sea, and I loved his integrity and stubborn pride."[57] That Day wrote these lines over twenty years after ending her marriage to Forster is evidence of the extent of her love for him. She presented her life with Forster as days filled with happiness.[58] When Day found herself praying in the midst of this life, particularly when she learned she was pregnant, she was explicit as to the reason: "I did not turn to God in unhappiness, in grief, in despair—to get consolation, to get something from Him.... I am praying because I am happy, not because I am unhappy."[59] Day wanted to make it clear, perhaps most especially to her old Marxist friends, that her life at the time of her conversion was not one of sadness.

She also wanted to make clear that this life of natural happiness was not enough. Indeed, it was this happiness which led her to seek something more, something better: "I was happy but my very happiness made me know that there was a greater happiness to be

---

[54] Day, *Long Loneliness*, 63.
[55] Day, *Long Loneliness*, 63.
[56] Day, *Long Loneliness*, 116.
[57] Day, *Long Loneliness*, 148.
[58] Day, *Long Loneliness*, 138.
[59] Day, *Long Loneliness*, 132.

obtained from life that any I had ever known."[60] Day knew that having Tamar and herself baptized would mean the loss of her life together with Forster.[61] As she described it,

> God always gives us a chance to show our preference for Him. With Abraham it was to sacrifice his only son. With me it was to give up my married life with Forster. You do these things blindly, not because it is your natural inclination—you are going against nature when you do them—but because you wish to live in conformity with the will of God.[62]

For Day, her conversion was a choosing of the better rather than the merely good, of going against—*agere contra*—her natural inclination in order to pursue the call to be a saint.[63]

In the third and final section of the book, "Love Is The Measure," Day described the supernatural life for which she longed. As Sandra Yocum has noted, Day portrayed life in the Catholic Worker in terms of renunciation and even mortification: mortification of "the body through exposure to vermin, cold and dirt; mortification of sight by 'bodily excretions, diseased limbs, eyes, noses, mouth;' mortification of the nose with 'smells of sewage, decay, and rotten flesh;' of the ears 'by harsh and screaming voices;' and of taste 'by insufficient food cooked in huge quantities.'"[64] The life of a saint is indeed a harsh and dreadful thing, often beyond any natural pleasure, merit, or happiness. It is a life that requires continual discernment of what leads to holiness and what does not. And such discernment was operative in Day's practice of pacifism, voluntary poverty, and Christian anarchy—practices that embody the non-state centered politics and non-market centered economics of the Catholic Worker.[65]

That Day would embrace such a spirituality is not surprising, for this was the spiritual vision given to her by Fr. Pacifique Roy and Fr.

---

[60] Day, *Long Loneliness*, 116. Day wrote (134), "I have always felt that it was life with him [Forster] that brought me natural happiness, that brought me to God."

[61] As Day explained, "To become a Catholic meant for me to give up a mate with whom I was much in love. It got to the point where it was a simple question of whether I chose God or man." Day, *Long Loneliness*, 145.

[62] Day, *Long Loneliness*, 256.

[63] Again, helpful here is Aquinas's discussion of fallen nature as essentially unchanged, but rather is "left to itself." *ST* I.II, q. 82. See fn. 25.

[64] Sandra Yocum Mize, "'We Are Still Pacifists': Dorothy Day's Pacifism During World War II," in *Dorothy Day and the Catholic Worker Movement: Centenary Essays,* eds. William Thorn, Phillip Runkel, Susan Mountin (Wisconsin: Marquette University Press, 2001), 472.

[65] Day wrote that she preferred the term "libertarian" as less offensive than "anarchist." Day, *The Long Loneliness*, 267.

John Hugo in the retreat that so profoundly shaped her.[66] As Day recalled,

> There was not much talk of sin in this retreat. Rather there was talk of the good and the better. The talk was of the choice we had to make and not that between good and evil. We have been given a share is the divine life; we have been raised to a supernatural level; we have been given power to become the sons of God.[67]

And this retreat was itself rooted in "practical mysticism" of Ignatius and Lallemant—a point emphasized by Hugo in his attempt to justify its theology in the face of criticism in the 1940s.[68] Indeed, Hugo employed a kind of Ignatian option in his defense of American Catholic conscientious objectors during World War II when he argued that their objection was not that the war was necessarily sinful—and in fact, it may very well have been justified by natural law thinking—but rather that participating in the war posed an obstacle to living a holy life.[69]

In a similar manner, I would propose this spirituality could be employed today to support U.S. Catholics who refrain from participation in electoral politics. For the argument could be made that partisan politics in the U.S. is so polarized and entrenched that participation in it has become corrosive to the unity of the Catholic Church in America. The mystical body has been divided along terms determined by the platform committees of the Republican and Democratic parties.[70] Sadly, the contrasting categories of "social justice Catholics" for whom global warming and *Citizens United* are among the most pressing concerns, and "right to life Catholics" who see *Roe vs. Wade* and same sex-marriage as overriding threats, have become as normal to U.S. Catholicism as the idea that are "liberal"

---

[66] Robert Ellsberg called Day's introduction to Hugo "among the most important encounters of her life." Robert Ellsberg, ed. *All The Way To Heaven: The Selected Letters of Dorothy Day* (Wisconsin: Marquette University Press, 2010), 134. Rosalie Riegle described the retreat as bringing about a "second conversion" in Day's life. Rosalie Riegle, *Dorothy Day: Portraits by Those Who Knew Her* (New York: Orbis Press, 2003), 83.
[67] Day, *The Long Loneliness*, 256.
[68] Hugo laid out the Ignatian roots of the retreat in *A Sign of Contradiction: As the Master, So the Disciple* (published by author, 1947).
[69] John Hugo, "Catholics Can Be Conscientious Objectors" *The Catholic Worker*, May 1943, 6-8, 10.
[70] The standard text on our current situation remains Robert Wuthnow, *The Restructuring of American Religion: Society and Faith Since World War II* (New Jersey: Princeton University Press, 1988); for another, more recent account, see Robert Putnam, David Campbell, *American Grace: How Religion Divides and Unites Us* (New York: Simon & Schuster, 2010).

and "conservative" parishes.[71] Refraining—or fasting—from participation in such divisive politics can be done out of the recognition that voting has become an obstacle to Christian unity and holiness, rather than as a condemnation of American political institutions as sinful or corrupt.

Finally, this Ignatian option can be clearly seen in the papacy of Francis, a Jesuit whom Austen Ivereigh labeled a "radical pope."[72] For in Francis, there emerges a particular emphasis on seeing holiness as fundamental to the Christian life, particularly for the folks he has referred to as the "holy middle class"—ordinary Christians, laity and secular clergy alike, who are called to a "common sanctity."[73] Such daily holiness or sanctity can be achieved, the Pope suggests, by "being able to do the little things of every day with a big heart open to God and to others."[74] That this echoes the emphasis of the Jesuit mystical movement—in particular, Caussade's notion of "the sacrament of the present moment"—is not surprising as Francis has acknowledged the deep influence these Jesuits have had on him.[75]

Following these early-modern Jesuits, Francis seems to recognize that such sanctity requires a process of continual discernment—always in light of the beatific vision—of what aspects of daily life offer a path to union with God and so can be embraced, and what must be rejected as obstacles to such holiness. Indeed in *Evangelii Gaudium,* he writes, "We need to distinguish clearly what might be a fruit of the kingdom from what runs counter to God's plan. This involves not only recognizing and discerning spirits, but also—and this is decisive—choosing movements of the spirit of good and rejecting those of the spirit of evil" (no. 51). But like Ignatius and Lallemant, the Pope makes clear that such discernment involves more than simply distinguishing that which is immoral. Indeed, when he decries contemporary consumerist "throw-away culture," the

---

[71] These categories are laid out in Public Religion Research Institute, "2012 American Values Survey," publicreligion.org/research/2012/10/american-values-survey-2012/#.VYGOyvlViko.

[72] Austen Ivereigh, *The Great Reformer: Francis and the Making of a Radical Pope* (New York: Henry Holt Co, 2014).

[73] Spadaro, "A Big Heart Open to God," 22.

[74] Spadaro quoted Francis as saying that he sees holiness "in the patience of the people of God: a woman who is raising children, a man who works to bring home the bread, the sick, the elderly priests who have so many wounds but have a smile on their faces because they served the Lord, the sisters who work hard and live a hidden sanctity. This is for me the common sanctity." Spadaro, "A Big Heart Open to God," 22.

[75] Spadaro, "A Big Heart Open to God," 20.

emphasis is not put on its sinfulness as much as on its emptiness and the hindrance it poses to a common sanctity:

> The great danger in today's world, pervaded as it is by consumerism, is the desolation and anguish born of a complacent yet covetous heart, the feverish pursuit of frivolous pleasures, and a blunted conscience. Whenever our interior life becomes caught up in its own interests and concerns, there is no longer room for others, no place for the poor. God's voice is no longer heard, the quiet joy of his love is no longer felt, and the desire to do good fades (*Evangelii Gaudium*, 2).

Francis explains that those who are caught up in such a life become "resentful, angry and listless" as they are no longer living the life for which they long (*Evangelii Gaudium*, 2).

This spirituality is expanded upon further in *Laudato Si'*, which, while portrayed by many as simply a statement on climate change or a condemnation of the "free-market," can be read as clear embodiment of Ignatius's "practical mysticism" which we have been discussing. In fact, at its heart, *Laudato Si'* is a call to a way of life that enables Catholics to resist a modern consumerism rooted in the "technocratic paradigm."[76] Such resistance would allow us to see "the deepest roots" (*radix*) of our contemporary social problems which, as the Pope notes, are beyond superficial political ideologies and instead have to do with things much more foundational: "the direction, goals, meaning and social implications of technological and economic growth" (*Laudato Si'*, no. 109). All of this entails a discerned renunciation of the things we encounter daily that keep us from being in proper relationship—what Francis calls an "integral ecology"—with our neighbor and the environment, and ultimately with God.[77] Many of the things that the Pope suggests could be given up—such as air-conditioning or social media or non-reusable shopping bags—are not presented as sinful *per se* but rather are seen as obstacles to this relational ecology (*Laudato Si'*, 47, 55, 211). It is in this sense that St. Francis of Assisi, *il poverello*, is held up by the Pope as a model of this type of discerned renunciation or selective non-engagement.[78]

It should not be surprising, then, that the Pope describes an authentic Christian—and likewise Ignatian—spirituality as one which

---

[76] Francis calls for "a distinctive way of looking at things, a way of thinking, policies, an educational programme, a lifestyle and a spirituality which together generate resistance to the assault of the technocratic paradigm." *Laudato Si'*, no. 111. For the Pope's definition of this paradigm, see *Laudato Si'*, no. 106.

[77] For a similar reading of the encyclical, see Jana Bennett "The Everyday Ascetic: Thoughts on *Laudato Si'*," *Catholic Moral Theology*, catholic moraltheology.com/the-everyday-ascetic-thoughts-on-laudato-si/.

[78] For an interesting connection between Francis of Assisi and Ignatian spirituality, see Ewert Cousins, "Franciscan Roots of Ignatian Meditation," in *Ignatian Spirituality*

calls for a growth marked by moderation and the capacity to be happy with little (*Laudato Si'*, no. 222). For Francis, it is "a return to the simplicity which allows us to stop and appreciate the small things…to be spiritually detached from what we possess, and not to succumb to sadness for what we lack" (*Laudato Si'*, no. 222). But while such a spirituality would appear "countercultural" in the context of our "throw-away culture," Francis does not regard it as some kind of a "withdrawal" in the sense of Murray's eschatological humanism, but rather he sees it as very much in accord with the "broader vision of reality"—a more accurate ecology.[79]

CONCLUSION

And so, by presenting an alternative to the options of either marriage or divorce when considering the relationship of Catholics to American society and culture, an Ignatian option—seen in Dorothy Day and Pope Francis—offers a form of social engagement that allows for the "need to distinguish clearly what might be a fruit of the kingdom from what runs counter to God's plan."[80] It is a process of continual discernment that will enable Catholics to selectively engage (or not) with society and culture while living out our call to holiness in this post-Americanist era.

---

in a Secular Age, ed. George Schner, S.J. (Ontario, Canada: Wilfrid Laurier University Press, 1984), 51-64.

[79] In a similar way, Francis noted in *Laudato Si'*, no. 98, that in depictions of Jesus found in the gospels, "His appearance was not that of an ascetic apart from the world, nor an enemy to the pleasant things of life."

[80] The fact that Francis highlighted Dorothy Day in his 2015 address to the U.S. Congress only confirmed this idea of their shared vision.

Human or Person? On the Burial of Aborted Children

Justin Menno

ON MARCH 24, 2016, INDIANA became the first U.S. State to enact legislation ensuring the dignified disposition of pre-born children killed through surgical abortion. In so doing, it helped to establish three key legal precedents in the context of burial law in the U.S. First, it explicitly recognized that the fetal remains of pre-born children killed through surgical abortion are indeed human remains. Second, it clarified that these remains belong in fact to the class of human remains and not pathological waste. Third, it ensured that these remains are accorded the same dignity and treatment as all other human remains.

A recent judicial order, however, has temporarily blocked the law in question, HEA 1337. On July 30, 2016, after hearing appeals from Planned Parenthood of Indiana and Kentucky, U.S. District Court Judge Tanya Walton Pratt issued a preliminary injunction against HEA 1337. In her order, Pratt not only blocked the law's provision on the dignified disposition of the remains of pre-born children killed through surgical abortion but indeed all three of its major provisions.[1] While the reasoning that Pratt employed in justifying her injunction against each provision of HEA 1337 is worthy of scrutiny and criticism in its own right, it is her use of person over human as the basis of her injunction that occupies the focus of this article.

To understand Pratt's argument, I outline four key points in HEA 1337's provision on the disposition of aborted children. Then, I summarize five of Pratt's major objections to this provision. Next, I critique Pratt's use of the category of personhood to exclude "fetal remains" from the class of "human remains" based on federal and state law on the handling of human tissue and the disposition of human remains. Finally, I provide a brief overview on the parsing of the categories of personhood and human being in Aquinas's commentary on the significance of Christ's burial. The result is a defense of using the term human, not person, to guide the disposition of the dead.

---

[1] *Planned Parenthood of Indiana and Kentucky, Inc., Dr. Marshall Levine, M.D., v. Commissioner, Indiana State Department of Health*, No. 1:16-cv-00763-TWP-DML (7th Circuit Jun. 30, 2016).

HEA 1337

The provision on the dignified disposition of aborted children in HEA 1337 contains several important parts, though here I draw out four. First, HEA 1337 defines "fetal tissue" for purposes of treating deceased pre-natal children.[2] Second, it clarifies that fetal remains, whether "aborted" or "miscarried," belong to the class of human remains.[3] Third, it further clarifies that these remains do *not* belong to the class of infectious and pathological waste.[4] Thus, they are not subject to laws governing the disposal of such waste. Fourth and finally, it ensures that these remains are accorded the same dignity and treatment as all other human remains.

In reference to the proper disposition of aborted children, HEA 1337 defines "fetal tissue" to include "tissue, organs, or any other part of an aborted fetus."[5] Thus, for purposes of burial law, it treats "fetal tissue" as functionally equivalent to fetal remains, but, in an important clarification, it then differentiates the treatment of fetal tissue in the context of burial law from the treatment of fetal tissue in the context of medical law. In this regard, HEA 1337 clarifies that tissue samples taken in the course of fetal surgery are not subject to burial law on the disposition of aborted children.[6] Rather, they are subject to medical law on the "disposal" of pathological waste.[7] In this light, HEA 1337 clearly distinguishes "fetal tissue" as fetal remains in the context of burial law from fetal tissue in the context of medical law. The first is subject to the act of *disposition* in the care of the dead, and the second is subject to the act of *disposal* in the care of the living.

Second, in reference to the proper categorization of the remains of aborted children, HEA 1337 clarifies that these remains indeed belong to the class of human remains. In an indirect way, it affirms this point in ensuring that "aborted" and "miscarried" children receive a "final disposition," an act that applies only to the care of human remains.[8] It further reinforces this point in requiring a "burial transit permit" to the place of final disposition, a requirement that again applies only to the care of human remains.[9] In a more direct way, HEA 1337 then categorizes the remains of aborted children as human remains in applying statutory code on the "cremation" of "human remains" to the particular cremation of "aborted" or "miscarried" children.[10]

---

[2] 410 Indiana Administrative Code, § 35-2-1 (a).
[3] Indiana Code, § 16-34-3-4 (a).
[4] Indiana Code, § 16-41-16-4 (d).
[5] Indiana Code, § 35-46-5-1.5 (b).
[6] Indiana Code, § 35-46-5-1.5 (c).
[7] Indiana Code, § 35-46-5-1.5 (c).
[8] Indiana Code, § 16-34-3-2 (a) and IC § 16-41-16-7.6 (b).
[9] Indiana Code, § 16-34-3-4 (a).
[10] Indiana Code, § 16-21-11-6 and IC § 16-34-3-4.

Third, building on this categorization, HEA 1337 further clarifies that the remains of aborted children do *not* belong either to the class of "infectious waste"[11] or that of "pathological waste."[12] In light of defining "infectious waste," it then specifies that this term includes items like "biological cultures," "contaminated sharps," "blood products," and "animal carcasses."[13] It makes clear that the term "does not include an aborted fetus or a miscarried fetus."[14] Moreover, in light of defining "pathological waste,"[15] HEA 1337 specifies that the term includes "tissues," "organs," "body parts" or "body fluids" that are "removed" in the course of a "surgery, biopsy, or autopsy."[16] Like before, it makes clear that this term "does not include an aborted fetus or a miscarried fetus."[17]

Finally, in reference to the proper treatment of the remains of aborted children, HEA 1337 ensures that these remains are treated like all other human remains. In this regard, it requires that the remains of "aborted" or "miscarried" children either be "cremated" or "interred."[18] Thus, it makes clear that these remains are subject to methods like cremation and interment specific to the disposition of human remains.

OBJECTIONS TO INDIANA'S DIGNIFIED TREATMENT OF ABORTED CHILDREN

In her argument against HEA 1337's provision on the dignified disposition of aborted children, Judge Tanya Walton Pratt relies on a combination of at least five distinct and interlocking objections. First, Pratt disagrees that burial law is the controlling province of state law. That is, Pratt assumes that federal law is not only applicable to state law on the disposition of human remains but ultimately measures it. She assumes this is so despite the fact that there is no uniform federal law on the disposition of human remains. Nonetheless, Pratt maintains that HEA 1337's provision on the disposition of aborted children is subject to federal consideration. Specifically, in agreement with the plaintiffs, she maintains that this provision is subject to substantive due process considerations in constitutional law.[19] Thus, she claims that this provision must be evaluated in terms of whether it is

---

[11] Indiana Code, § 16-41-16-4.
[12] Indiana Code, § 16-41-16-5.
[13] Indiana Code, § 16-41-16-1 (a).
[14] Indiana Code, § 16-41-16-1 (d).
[15] Indiana Code, § 16-41-16-5.
[16] Indiana Code, § 16-41-16-5.
[17] Indiana Code, § 16-41-16-5.
[18] Indiana Code, § 16-21-11-6 (b).
[19] *Planned Parenthood of Indiana*, 16-17.

"rationally related to a legitimate government interest" or not.[20] In light of this claim, Pratt makes clear that substantive due process tests are not very exacting on the part of defendants. In fact, she notes that the State of Indiana only has to show that HEA 1337's provision on the disposition of aborted children has a "conceivable state of facts that supports" it.[21] In other words, the State of Indiana "only" has to show that this provision is not "patently arbitrary,"[22] a low standard indeed.

Pratt then applies constitutional law to state burial laws. In particular, she states that constitutional law *on the question of personhood* applies to HEA 1337's provision on the disposition of aborted children. In this effort, she first turns to Indiana's stated interest "to treat fetal remains with the same dignity as other human remains."[23] And in light of this, she then turns to the plaintiff's argument against this interest. Thus, she considers the argument that Indiana's interest "stems from the legally indefensible assumption that embryonic and fetal tissue at any stage in the first trimester is a human being."[24] Moreover, she considers the further argument that Indiana's interest contravenes the Supreme Court's apparent refusal "to decide that human life begins at conception and that a fetus is a human being."[25]

In light of these considerations, Pratt then rejects the legitimacy of Indiana's stated interest in the disposition of aborted children. She defends her rejection based on the Supreme Court's holding that a "fetus is not a 'person'" in its interpretation of the Fourth Amendment.[26] In support, she sets out her rejection in the form of a conditional legal principle, "If the law does not recognize the fetus as person, there can be no legitimate state interest in treating an aborted fetus the *same* as a deceased human."[27]

Second, based on the abovementioned principle, it seems apparent that Pratt maintains that the category of personhood controls the category of human or human being and, even more to point, that the category of personhood determines what is human and what is not. However, in making this determination, Pratt does not rely on what

---

[20] *Planned Parenthood of Indiana*, 17, quoting *Charleston v. Bd. Of Trustees of Univ. of Ill. at Chi.*, 741 F.3d 774 (7th Cir. 2013).
[21] *Planned Parenthood of Indiana*, 17, quoting *Hayden ex rel. A.H. v. Greensburg Community Sch. Corp.*, 743 F.3d 576 (7th Cir. 2014).
[22] *Planned Parenthood of Indiana*, 17.
[23] *Planned Parenthood of Indiana*, 18, quoting Filing No. 54 at 35.
[24] *Planned Parenthood of Indiana*, 18, quoting Filing No. 57 at 11-12.
[25] *Planned Parenthood of Indiana*, 18.
[26] *Planned Parenthood of Indiana*, 18, quoting *Coe. V. County of Cook*, 162 F.3d 491, 495 (7th Cir. 1998), citing *Roe*, 410 U.S. at 158, and *Casey* 505 U.S. at 912.
[27] *Planned Parenthood of Indiana*, 18.

the Supreme Court has said about this issue. In abortion-related cases like *Roe*, the Supreme Court has never categorically stated that someone can only be considered legally human if they are first legally recognized as a person. Rather, Pratt sides with the plaintiffs' understanding of what the Supreme Court has inferred about this topic in abortion-related cases like *Roe*.

Third, in according privileged status to the category of personhood in making determinations about the dead, Pratt maintains that the category of personhood can be predicated of the living and the dead *in the same way*. Pratt attributes controlling status to the category of personhood in making determinations about the dead based on her appeal to the Supreme Court's holding that a "fetus is not legally a person."[28] In this regard, she grounds determinations about the rights and interests of the dead based on the rights and interests of the living and, even more importantly, the application of the category of personhood to the dead based on the attribution of this category to the living. It is certainly true that the Supreme Court has attributed a certain functionalist content to the category of personhood in making determinations about the rights and interests of the living, especially in abortion-related cases like *Roe*.[29] It is not clear, however, that the Supreme Court has done the same in making determinations about the rights and interests of the dead. Despite this ambiguity, Pratt posits that the fetal remains of aborted children do not belong to the class of human remains. She reiterates the principle that someone can be considered legally human if and only if they are first legally recognized as a person, draws on the Supreme Court's position in *Casey* that a "fetus is not legally a person" for purposes of the Fourteenth Amendment, and, based on these two premises, concludes that fetal remains are not human remains.

Fourth, despite this determination, Pratt denies that the category of personhood is sufficient to determine whether the remains of aborted children belong to the class of human remains. That is, she concedes that the disposition of human remains is not *absolutely* measured according to the category of personhood. In considering Indiana's stated interest in "promoting respect for human life" by "ensuring that fetal remains" are "treated" in a "humane" manner,[30] Pratt adds a potentiality test. She agrees with the defendants that the Supreme Court has recognized an "interest in promoting respect for human life in all stages in pregnancy."[31] She further agrees that the Supreme Court has recognized "a substantial state interest in potential life

---

[28] *Planned Parenthood of Indiana*, 18, quoting *Coe. V. County of Cook*, 162 F.3d 491, 495 (7th Cir. 1998), citing *Roe*, 410 U.S. at 158, and *Casey* 505 U.S. at 912.
[29] See Kaczor, "Lessons of History," 68-70.
[30] *Planned Parenthood of Indiana*, 18, quoting Filing No. 54 at 38.
[31] *Planned Parenthood of Indiana*, 19, quoting *Gonzales*, 550 U.S. at 157.

throughout pregnancy."[32] In applying the Supreme Court's holding on legitimate state interests in "the life within the woman," she tests Indiana's interest in promoting respect for "human life" by focusing on the modifier "potential" rather than the modifier "human." Building on this point, she asserts that the state has a legitimate interest in pre-viable children only in the case of their "life" or "potential life."[33] Stated negatively, she asserts that "any legitimate interest the State has in a potential life during a pregnancy is no longer present once the pre-viability pregnancy is terminated."[34] Combining her personhood and potentiality tests, she concludes that Indiana "does not have a legitimate state interest in treating fetal tissue similarly to human remains."[35]

Fifth and finally, Pratt concludes that "whether or not an individual views fetal tissue as essentially the same as human remains is each person's own personal and moral decision."[36] She gestures toward *Roe*'s assertion that no scientific or legal consensus exists on the question of when human life begins.[37] Specifically, she cites Roe's assertion that the Supreme Court is incompetent to "speculate" on this very question,[38] and she indicates that this assertion is applicable to the question of whether fetal remains are human remains. Thus, she concludes that federal courts are incompetent to speculate on whether fetal remains are human remains. In effect, just as *Roe* excluded pre-viable children from the protection of law on the basis of an asserted incompetency, so too does Pratt exclude aborted children from the protection of law on the basis of the same.

DISTINGUISHING PERSON AND HUMAN

Pratt's argument turns on the idea that personhood controls the category of human and so determines what is and is not human. For her, this principle implies that aborted fetuses are not human remains because fetuses are not persons. This poses problems for evaluating HEA 1337 as her position presumes a certain continuity and even identity between the content of personhood in treating the living and the dead. In other words, she presumes that the category of personhood applies in burial law the same way that it does in other types of law, especially abortion law.

---

[32] *Planned Parenthood of Indiana*, 19, quoting *Casey*, 505 U.S. at 846, 876.
[33] *Planned Parenthood of Indiana*, 19.
[34] *Planned Parenthood of Indiana*, 21.
[35] *Planned Parenthood of Indiana*, 21.
[36] *Planned Parenthood of Indiana*, 21.
[37] On this point, see Clark D. Forsythe, *Abuse of Discretion: The Inside Story of Roe v. Wade* (New York: Encounter Books, 2013), 114.
[38] *Planned Parenthood of Indiana*, 21, quoting *Roe* 410 U.S. at 159.

Burial law, however, has long used the category of the human, and not that of personhood, to determine what is human and what is not.[39] It makes an explicit distinction between "human remains" and "personal effects."[40] The category of personhood designates what the deceased *had*, and it uses the category of human to designate what the deceased *is*. Thus, inasmuch as laws on disposition apply to the body of the deceased and not to the possessions of the deceased, the category of the human, and not that of personhood, guides the care and treatment of the dead.

While some states use the category of personhood to talk about the dead,[41] they do not use the category of personhood to determine whether human remains are recognized as human remains. Like most states, Indiana defines "human remains" without any reference to the category of personhood. Specifically, it defines "human remains" as "any part of the body of a human being in any stage of decomposition or state of preservation."[42] Moreover, federal code on the identification of "human remains" discusses the term without any reference to the category of personhood or to a personhood test.[43] In fact, the one and only test that federal code employs is a DNA test. While this test can evaluate whether particular remains are human, it cannot demonstrate personhood.

Pratt's preference for person over human in dealing with the dead leads to problems distinguishing between "fetal remains" and "fetal tissue." Throughout her injunction, she treats these two categories as interchangeable. In federal code, the respective definitions of "fetal tissue" and "human organ" help to clarify what fetal tissue is and what it is not. In reference to the first, federal code defines "human fetal tissue" as "tissue or cells obtained from a dead human embryo or fetus after a spontaneous or induced abortion, or after a stillbirth."[44] In so doing, it makes clear that the relevant modifying category is "human" and not personhood, and it likewise makes clear that the relevant subject matter is human "tissue or cells."

While human organs and even the human body as a whole can be reduced to tissue and cells, federal code does not permit such a reduction. In defining what "human organ" is, it specifies that the term means "the human (including fetal) kidney, liver, heart, lung, pancreas, bone marrow, cornea, eye, bone, and skin or any subpart

---

[39] See Tanya D. Marsh, *Disposition of Human Remains: A Legal Research Guide* (New York: William S. Hein & Co. Inc., 2015), 3-7.
[40] For a representative example, see California Health and Safety Code, § 8-3-2-5-8344.5(b).
[41] See, for example, Delaware Code Title 12, § 260 et seq.—Disposition of a Person's Last Remains.
[42] 410 Indiana Administrative Code, § 22.5-1-5.
[43] 10 U.S. Code, § 1565a.
[44] 42 U.S. Code, § 289g-1 (g).

thereof."⁴⁵ In so doing, federal code makes clear that the category of human "fetal" organ is legally distinct from that of "human fetal tissue." Thus, in no way does it permit the conflation of human "fetal" organs with human fetal tissue. By implication, it does not permit the conflation of deceased human fetal bodies with human fetal tissue.

What federal code implies about the non-reducibility of fetal remains to fetal tissue, HEA 1337 makes explicit in its twofold definition of "fetal tissue." As noted earlier, HEA 1337 defines "fetal tissue" in the context of burial law and in the context of medical law. And the difference between these two definitions marks an important material difference. For purposes of medical law, HEA 1337 treats "fetal tissue" as any tissue or cells of a fetal human. But for purposes of burial law, it treats "fetal tissue" as functionally equivalent to the remains of a deceased fetal human, whether aborted or miscarried. That is, it clearly defines "fetal tissue" as "tissue, organs, or any part of an aborted fetus" or "a miscarried fetus." Thus, it defines the *whole* of a deceased fetal human by reference to a *part*. In the end, it is apparent that, by "fetal tissue," HEA 1337 means human fetal remains in the context of burial law.

ON THE BURIAL OF CHRIST

In addition to these legal distinctions between person and human, Christian understanding of Christ and his burial provide additional reasons for distinguishing between person and human, especially as it pertains to the dispositions of bodies.⁴⁶ The personhood of Christ is *unique*. Unlike us, Christ is a divine person. Thus, the proper subject of the hypostatic union, the union of human nature and divine nature in Christ, is the eternal Son of God, the second person of the Trinity. In virtue of this union, there is no *independent* human person in Christ. In this regard, it is important to note that, in Christ, the respective attributes of human nature and divine nature are predicated of one and the same Son of God, the second person of the Trinity. In this light, it follows that if there was an independent human person in Christ, then the divine attributes could not be ascribed to him, for they can only be predicated of a divine person. Despite the lack of an independent human person in Christ, he became *fully human* in the incarnate Son. In virtue of the incarnation, Christ truly became man, but his human nature had its existence not in itself, but properly in the existence of

---

⁴⁵ 42 U.S. Code, § 274e-(c)(1).
⁴⁶ For more on each of the following points, see the discussion of the term "hypostasis," and even more specifically, the discussion of the distinction between anhypostasis and enhypostasis, in Edward T. Oakes, S.J., *Infinity Dwindled to Infancy: A Catholic and Evangelical Christology* (Michigan: Eerdmans, 2011), 448-450.

God. Finally, though the personhood of Christ is certainly not without capacities, it is *not* reducible to them, either in whole or in part. In this regard, the personhood of Christ, doctrinally understood, is not set in functionalist or capacities-based terms. Rather, it is set in substantial or ontological terms.

Despite the uniqueness of Christ's personhood, the subject of his burial nonetheless helps to inform the question of the proper ordering and assignment of categories like personhood and humanity in the treatment of the dead. Aquinas takes up the question of Christ's burial in the supplement to the third part of the *Summa* (*ST,* Suppl. III q. 51). Aquinas first asks whether it was fitting for Christ to be buried (*ST,* Suppl. III q. 51, a. 1). In reply, he notes that some argue that it was not at all fitting either because it seems to lack salvific significance or because it seems unbecoming to God. Nonetheless, Aquinas answers in the affirmative and supplies at least three reasons for doing so. His first reason is most relevant to the primary concern of this section. In affirming the fittingness of Christ's burial, he claims that it serves to confirm the truth of Christ's death. Furthermore, he indicates that it serves to reinforce the truth of Christ's full humanity, for it is in virtue of his humanity that his body is subject to corruption and death.

Aquinas does not understand Christ's burial as contingent on the abiding union of Christ's deceased body with the unique subject of his body, the eternal Son of God. Rather, he understands it as contingent on Christ's full humanity (*ST* Suppl. III q. 51, a. 1). In regard to the question of whether the fittingness of Christ's burial belongs to Christ in virtue of his personhood or in virtue of his humanity, it seems clear that Aquinas affirms the latter. He is not alone in this affirmation. In fact, in rendering this judgment, Aquinas stands in basic agreement with Patristic theologians like Augustine.[47] In sum, inasmuch as Christ's burial is significant in its own regard, it further demonstrates for Christians that the category of humanity, and not that of personhood, is the proper guide to the treatment of the dead.

Conclusion

The current injunction on Indiana's statute on the dignified disposition of aborted children raises a number of important challenges. On a legal level, this injunction urges more critical reflection on the proper ordering and assignment of the categories of personhood and human being in law. Even more significantly, it urges more critical reflection on the uses and abuses of these categories to make certain areas of law like burial law subject to others like abortion law. Inasmuch as Pratt suggests that human being is contingent on

---

[47] See Augustine, "On the Care to Be Taken for the Dead," in *The Fathers of the Church: St. Augustine, The Retractions* (Washington, D.C.: The Catholic University of America Press, 1998), 265-266.

personhood, she concludes that, in the absence of personhood, there is not only an absence of human existence but even the absence of a material human remainder. Thus, she concludes that remains of aborted children are not human remains. I have laid out two responses to Pratt, one legal, another theological. First, burial law, for its part, has long used the category of human or human being, and not personhood, to guide the care and treatment of the dead. Second, reflection on the burial of Christ has done much the same in commenting on the care and treatment of Christ's crucified body. In considering each of these subjects, moral theologians have important resources to press the case for the priority of the category of human, and not that of personhood, in the legal treatment of the living and the dead. M

Jesus is the Jubilee: A Theological Reflection on the Pontifical Council for Justice and Peace's *Toward a Better Distribution of Land*

Matthew Philipp Whelan[1]

> The story of Naboth is an old one, but it is repeated every day.
> —St. Ambrose of Milan, *On Naboth*

> Do we realize that something is wrong in a world where there are so many farmworkers without land, so many families without a home, so many laborers without rights, so many persons whose dignity is not respected?
> —Pope Francis, *Address at the World Meeting of Popular Movements*

IN ANTICIPATION OF THE GREAT Jubilee of the year 2000, during which the Church prepared to celebrate the mercy of God and the forgiveness of sins,[2] the Pontifical Council for Justice and Peace issued a document entitled, *Toward a Better Distribution of Land* (hereafter *TBDL*).[3] The document states in its opening section, "Presentation," that its purpose is "to address and quicken awareness of the dramatic human, social and ethical problems caused by the phenomenon of the concentration and misappropriation of land,"[4]

---

[1] Many thanks especially to Natalie Carnes, Nathan Eubank, Pete Jordan, John Kiess, T.J. Lang, Sheryl Overmyer, Jonathan Tran, Bharat Ranganathan, and William Whelan for helpful comments on earlier drafts of this essay.

[2] Preparation for the Great Jubilee began with Pope Saint John Paul II's 1994 Apostolic Letter *Tertio Millennio Adveniente*, and it was formally convoked with the 1998 papal bull *Incarnationis Mysterium*.

[3] Pontifical Council for Justice and Peace, "Toward a Better Distribution of Land: The Challenge of Agrarian Reform," November 23, 1998, www.vatican.va/roman_curia/pontifical_councils/justpeace/documents/rc_pc_justpeace_doc_12011998_distribuzione-terra_en.html.

[4] Block and Yeats raise important questions about whether land concentration in all cases amounts to misappropriation. See Walter Block and Guillermo Yates, "The Economics and Ethics of Land Reform: A Critique of the Pontifical Council for Justice and Peace's 'Toward a Better Distribution of Land: The Challenge of Agrarian Reform,'" *Journal of Natural Resources & Environmental Law* 15, no. 1 (1999): 37-69. For one response to these concerns, see Mark E. Graham, *Sustainable Agriculture:*

problems that "affect the dignity of millions of persons and deprive the world of the possibility of peace." These problems are both systemic and widespread. They result from the accumulation of "countless unacceptable injustices," which have led to "scandalous situations of property and land use, present on almost all continents."

TBDL gathers a decades-long ecclesial conversation about agrarian reform, which participates in an even deeper tradition of moral reflection on the problem of the concentration of land and property. During Pope Pius XII's pontificate after World War II, this conversation develops into an explicit call for agrarian reform as one way to pursue a better distribution of land.[5] The conversation has continued ever since, among other places, in *Gaudium et Spes* (no. 71), in *Populorum Progressio* (nos. 23-24), in the many documents of the Catholic bishops of Latin America and the rest the world,[6] in *Caritas in Veritate* (no. 27), and most recently, in Pope Francis's *Laudato Si'* (nos. 6, 52, 67, 71, 93-95, 134), as well as his address at the Second World Meeting of Popular Movements in 2015 in Bolivia, from which one of the epigraphs is taken.[7]

A Christian Ethic of Gratitude (Oregon: Wipf & Stock Publisher, 2009), 146, see 142–146.

[5] See Pius XII, "The Question of Agricultural Reform," *Papal Letter Transmitted by J.B. Montini to the 22nd Social Week at Naples,* September 15, 1947; Pius XII, "Problems in the World of Agriculture," Address Before the First International Congress for the Problems of Agriculture, July 2, 1951; Pius XII, "The Vocational Tasks and the Cultural Mission of the Farmer," *Address to the Italian Farmers' Association,* April 16, 1958. For more context, see Matthew Philipp Whelan, *The Land of the Savior: Óscar Romero and the Reform of Agriculture* (Ph.D. Dissertation, Duke University, 2016), chapter 3.

[6] In addition to the documents of the General Conferences of Latin American Bishops held in Rio de Janeiro (1955), Medellin (1968), Puebla (1979) and Santo Domingo (1992), TBDL mentions Episcopal Conference of Paraguay, *La tierra, don de Dios para todos* (Asunción, June 12, 1983); South Andean Bishops, *La tierra, don de Dios* (March 30, 1986); Episcopal Conference of Guatemala, *El clamor por la tierra* (Guatemala de la Asunción, February 29, 1988); Apostolic Vicariate of Darien, Panama, *Tierra de todos, tierra de paz* (Darien, December 8, 1988); Episcopal Conference of Costa Rica, *Madre Tierra: Carta pastoral sobre la situación de los campesinos y indígenas* (San José, August 2, 1994); Episcopal Conference of Honduras, *Mensaje sobre algunos temas de interés nacional* (Tegucigalpa, August 28, 1995). The National Episcopal Conference of Brazil, and particularly the Pastoral Commission for Land, have spoken out several times on the subject of agrarian reform: *Manifesto pela terra e pela vita a CPT e a reforma agrária hoje* (Goiânia, August 1, 1995); *Pro-memória da Presidência e Comissão Episcopal de Pastoral da CNBB sobre as consequências do Decreto n. 1775 de 8 de Janeiro de 1996* (Brasília, February 29, 1996); *Exigências Cristãs para a paz social* (Itaici, April 24, 1996).

[7] Apostolic Journey of His Holiness Pope Francis to Ecuador, Bolivia, and Paraguay, *Address at the Second World Meeting of Popular Movements*, Expo Feria Exhibition Centre, Santa Cruz de la Sierra, Bolivia, July 9, 2015.

What follows is an extended reflection upon the central theological claims of *TBDL*: that creation is a gift God gives to humankind in common; that dominion names the practice of care for it; and that God's covenant with Israel and the gathering of those who are grafted into it in Christ preserve these understandings of creation and dominion. The Jubilee year as described in Leviticus 25 is the thread that ties these claims together. As I reflect upon these intertwined claims, my engagement with *TBDL* is at times critical. Although the document does not always make all the connections clear or elaborate adequately upon them, at its heart is the idea that God's gift of creation for the sustenance of all creatures expresses God's dominion, which God invites humans to imitate. My concern is not with this idea but with how it gets obscured because *TBDL* does not attend adequately to sin, the damage it does to creation, and God's work to repair that damage in Israel and in Christ and to restore the world to its created form. The inattention to sin is evident especially in the document's failure to maintain crucial distinctions between pre- and postlapsarian dominion, which it tends to conflate. One of the primary purposes of this essay, then, is to clarify the shape of God's dominion and its creaturely imitation, as well as to show how this yields a distinctive construal of property and what it means to possess it. From this theological vantage, care for the common gift of creation is dominion's true form, which must be distinguished from dominion as domination. This view presumes the ontological priority of prelapsarian dominion and God's ongoing work in Israel and in Christ to restore it, despite the damage sin does to it.

This inattention to sin is also evident in *TBDL*'s treatment of the Jubilee, which the document presents as a model from which to draw inspiration for social and economic transformation. In so presenting the Jubilee, *TBDL* ends up isolating it from the unfolding story of God's merciful response to sin, which culminates in Christ. In contrast, I argue the Jubilee reveals how the right understanding of dominion begins with the right understanding of creation and its preservation in Israel's covenantal life, as well as to how creation and covenant ultimately point to Christ. It is in relation to Christ that true dominion comes most clearly into focus, along with the risks of its practice in a fallen world. Underlying my concerns is therefore a constructive purpose. I contend that a fuller, christological understanding of the Jubilee deepens the story the document wants to tell about the struggle for a better distribution of land in our world.

CREATION AND DOMINION

TBDL responds to what it calls the concentration and misappropriation of land by offering a theological reflection upon

God's creation as a common gift.[8] "The underlying nature of creation," the document states, is "a gift of God, a gift for all, and God wants it to remain so. God's first command [to have dominion, see Gen 1:28] is therefore to preserve the earth in its nature as gift and blessing, not to transform it into an instrument of power or motive for division" (no. 23). According to this passage, the right understanding of dominion flows from the right understanding of creation as a gift God gives to humankind to use in common. On this view, dominion names the preservation of creation as a gift God gives to human creatures in common. In this section, I examine this conception of dominion and suggest why maintaining the distinction between pre- and postlapsarian dominion is crucial for its intelligibility.

In order to approach *TBDL*'s consideration of creation and dominion, we must begin with God's creation of heaven and earth—and all that is seen and unseen—from nothing. Without God's creative and conserving presence, creation would return to nothing. In the words of Psalm 104, "[W]hen you take away their breath, they die and return to their dust. When you send forth your spirit, they are created; and you renew the face of the ground." Creation is therefore a gift in a unique sense because it is a gift that makes all other gifts possible, a gift upon which all other gifts depend. This conviction animates St. Paul's questions to the Church in Corinth: "What do you have that you did not receive? And if you received it, why do you boast as if it were not a gift?" (1 Corinthians 4:7) The use of created things is always the use of what has first been given.[9]

Along these same lines, the gift of creation is additionally unique because those who use what has been given are themselves gifts, whose existence and agency are given to them, among other reasons, to help preserve the earth in its nature as gift and blessing. The

---

[8] *TBDL* is divided into three main parts. The first describes the processes by which ownership of land has become concentrated throughout the world. The second, which is my focus in this essay, turns to principles drawn from scripture and the Church's social doctrine in order to articulate a theological response to the concentration of land. The third and final section discusses the implementation of agrarian reform in order to promote a more just distribution of land. As the organization of the parts suggests, the document follows the traditional see-judge-act method. Among the first references to this method in the Church's social doctrine is in Pope Saint John XXIII's 1961 encyclical *Mater et Magistra* (see no. 236), though the method itself predates John's usage of it and was popularized by Cardinal Joseph Cardijn in Europe in the 1920s in his work with the Young Christian Workers movement. See Rodney Stinson, *See, Judge, Act: Caroline Chisholm's Lay Apostolate* (Sydney: Yorkcross Pty Ltd, 2009). See Pope Francis's comments about see-judge-act method in his *Address to the Leadership of the Episcopal Conferences of Latin America during the General Coordination Meetings*, Rio de Janeiro, July 28, 2013.
[9] For more on this point, see Kenneth L. Schmitz, *The Gift: Creation* (Wisconsin: Marquette University Press, 1982).

command to exercise dominion signals how humans are meant to participate in God's giving of the gift of creation in common. This is why for *TBDL*, and for theological reflection on these matters more generally, when we speak of creation, we must keep in view not only the earth and its fruits but also the work of human hands.

I draw attention to dominion, not only because it is central to the document, but also because it has a vexed history, especially in terms of legitimating the damage humans have done to what God has made—a history well beyond the bounds of the present essay to explore.[10] In recent years, scholars like Peter Harrison have examined that history, differentiating, for instance, between modern and premodern construals of dominion. Patristic and medieval exegesis, Harrison shows, tends to interpret the exercise of dominion in terms of mastery over the passions internal to the person rather than a person's mastery over an externalized nature. The disordering of the soul as a consequence of sin is the primary issue. Of course, because human creatures are a microcosm of creation, this internal disordering has important repercussions for humankind's relation to the rest of creation. But that is secondary to the mastery of the passions.[11]

On Harrison's telling, this understanding of dominion changes in the early modern period. For various reasons—including the decline of the idea of the human creature as a microcosm of creation, as well as transformations in scriptural hermeneutics, which led to an exclusively literal reading of Genesis—early modern thinkers increasingly understand dominion as the exercise of human control over an externalized nature.[12] Figures like Francis Bacon, Thomas Sprat, Joseph Ganvill, and others speak of a restored dominion over nature, which they associate with modern science. According to Ganvill, for instance, the new science gives to its practitioners "ways of *captivating Nature*, and making her *subserve* our *purposes* and

---

[10] For instance, Daniel Hillel refers to dominion as articulated in Genesis 1 as "arrogant and narcissistic," in contrast to Genesis 2, whose account of humankind's vocation in the created order he deems "more responsible." Daniel Hillel, *The Natural History of the Bible: An Environmental Exploration of the Hebrew Scriptures* (New York: Columbia University Press, 2007), 245. In Lynn White's estimation, because of the injunction that humankind exercise dominion, the Judeo-Christian tradition "bears a huge burden of guilt for environmental deterioration." Lynn White, "The Historical Roots of Our Ecologic Crisis," *Science* 155, no. 3767 (1967): 1203–7.

[11] Peter Harrison, *The Territories of Science and Religion* (Illinois: University Of Chicago Press, 2015), 136–138. See also Peter Harrison, "Reading the Passions: The Fall, the Passions, and the Dominion over Nature," in *The Soft Underbelly of Reason: The Passions in the Seventeenth Century* (London: Routledge, 1998), 49–78.

[12] Harrison, *The Territories of Science and Religion*, 138–141; Peter Harrison, "Subduing the Earth: Genesis 1, Early Modern Science, and the Exploitation of Nature," *Journal of Religion* 79 (1999): 86–109; Peter Harrison, *The Bible, Protestantism, and the Rise of Natural Science* (New York: Cambridge University Press, 2001), 49, 55–56, 204–209, 229–251.

designments," restoring "the *Empire* of *Man* over *Nature*." The implications of the new science for agriculture are not lost on Ganvill: "*Lands* may be *advanced* to scarce credible degrees of *improvement*, and innumerable other *advantages* may be obtained by an *industry* directed by *Philosophy* and *Mechanicks*."[13]

I reference Harrison's work to indicate how the meaning of dominion is not univocal. It has a long and complex history, which is germane to our present concerns because *TBDL* is clearly at pains to differentiate rival conceptions of dominion. Ultimately, the document commends a view at odds with the typical usage of the term.

Returning to the exposition of *TBDL*, what is crucial to see at this juncture is how dominion is bound to humankind's imaging of God (see Genesis 1:28). The document insists that conformity to the image enables the proper exercise of dominion (nos. 22-23).

Although *TBDL* does not say so explicitly, an important point follows. As Ellen Davis observes, the notion *imago Dei*—to which we can also add the notion of dominion—is "inherently both powerful and open-ended."[14] After its invocation in Genesis 1, it largely disappears until St. Paul uses it to describe Jesus Christ (2 Corinthians 4:4; Colossians 1:15, 3:10).[15] According to Davis, the meaning of *imago Dei* therefore "cannot be fully grasped within the first chapter of the Bible, even by the most thorough exegete. Rather, one must keep reading, and living in biblical faith, in order to know what our creation in the image of God yet might mean."[16] This is a significant observation, for it suggests that for Christians both *imago Dei* and dominion must be read in relation to Christ.

Although *TBDL* also does not do so explicitly, it is helpful to distinguish between pre- and postlapsarian forms of dominion. Dominion as first described in Genesis 1 concerns the former. It is entrusted to humankind prior to the fall and the subsequent banishment of Adam and Eve from Eden. In other words, it is entrusted to humankind prior to the long and still ongoing story of the damage sin has done to creation, including, crucially, to the task of dominion itself.[17] For this reason, dominion as it initially appears in the bible must be distinguished from its postlapsarian forms.

Dominion originally centers upon and participates in God's provisioning of food for the sustenance of all creatures. Note the rhythmic repetition and celebration of seed-bearing plants in their

---

[13] Harrison, *The Territories of Science and Religion*, 139, see 136–141.

[14] Davis, *Scripture, Culture, and Agriculture*, 56.

[15] References to humankind being made in the image and likeness of God can be found in Genesis 5:1-3, 9:6; Wisdom 2:23; Sirach 17:3.

[16] Davis, *Scripture, Culture, and Agriculture*, 56.

[17] Pope Francis emphasizes this point in *Laudato Si'*, nos. 66-88.

variety and fecundity in Genesis 1:11-13. The purpose of seeds and plants, as the closing bracket states, is for the sustenance of what God has made. Plants and trees are for humans, and green plants are for other creatures. As Davis writes, "The juxtaposition of the divine image in humans and the detailing of divine food provision would seem to suggest that recognizing and perpetuating the sufficiency God has provided is an important element of how we humans are to live out our unique resemblance to God and exercise [dominion] among the creatures."[18] Absent, of course, is any association of dominion with violence, bloodshed, or the consumption of flesh.[19]

While *TBDL* fails to distinguish between pre- and postlapsarian forms of dominion, it does employ a distinctive notion of dominion, which it associates with "care for creation" (no. 22). Here dominion names a manner of possession and use of land and created goods that enables them "to remain at the disposition of all, not just a few" (no. 22). These and other passages suggest the document's understanding of dominion has an important, though unspecified, relation to dominion's original form, which retains a kind of ontological priority. *TBDL* seems to understand dominion as a responsibility human creatures exercise as members of created order that is first and foremost a gift God gives for humans and other creatures to use in common.

TBDL regards dominion, then, not as a subset of human activity, such as work or labor.[20] Rather, dominion is a much more comprehensive arena of human agency, which encompasses the manifold ways humans acknowledge and preserve creation as a common gift. Moreover, according to the document, this is not the task of the few but rather is incumbent of all human creatures. It "belongs to the human person as such and, hence, to all. Indeed, it is humanity in its entirety which must shoulder responsibility for creation" (no. 23).

The document's understanding of dominion differs profoundly from dominion in its more familiar sense, what *TBDL* refers to as the "despotic and unbridled" use of created things, which takes "no care of the earth and its fruit, but despoils it for personal advantage" (no. 22). Once again, although the document does not say so explicitly, this more familiar sense registers the damage sin does to dominion. We might call these two rival conceptions dominion-as-care and

---

[18] Davis, *Scripture, Culture, and Agriculture*, 58; for an elaboration of these themes, see 48–53, 57–59.

[19] The consumption of creaturely flesh is a concession that occurs with the Noachian covenant (Genesis 9:1-4).

[20] Such a view is characteristic of transformations in early modernity, when thinkers begin to associate dominion with the masculine exercise of control or mastery over the natural world, epitomized by the new science. See Harrison, *The Territories of Science and Religion*, 124–141.

dominion-as-domination. For the latter, what epitomizes dominion is exclusive control of access, use, and disposal over created goods. The jurist William Blackstone approximates its ideal type when he defines property as "that sole and despotic dominion which one man claims and exercises over the external things of the world, in total exclusion of the right of any other individual in the universe."[21]

Blackstone's understanding of property is by no means restricted to a particular time or place, but it clearly acquires a new kind of power and pervasiveness in modernity. Legal scholar Jedediah Purdy observes that it increasingly came to function as the "centerpiece" of economic and social life, the "keystone institution" of a whole "social vision," whose "paramount feature…was the power to exclude."[22] If Purdy is right, this understanding of property is in profound tension with the one advanced by *TBDL*, which insists, "we cannot do whatever we want with the goods that God has given to all" (no. 25). On the document's terms, dominion is properly understood as care for creation, and it is epitomized, not by the enclosure of what is common for the exclusive use of some, but by a way of using what is common that preserves it as common.[23]

THE JUBILEE

After the foregoing account of creation and dominion, *TBDL* turns to covenant—to God's calling of a people, the life of this people with

---

[21] William Blackstone, *Commentaries on the Laws of England [1765]*, vol. II (Illinois: University of Chicago Press, 1979), 3.

[22] Jedediah Purdy, *The Meaning of Property: Freedom, Community, and the Legal Imagination* (Connecticut: Yale University Press, 2011), 5, 16.

[23] *TBDL*'s understanding of dominion can also be helpfully contrasted with John Locke's. At first glance, Locke's view in *Two Treatises on Government* appears to accord with the one we have been examining, for Locke insists that the earth is a gift God originally gives to humankind in common. But as Locke continues, his position diverges subtly but importantly from that of *TBDL*, especially in terms of how he understands labor and its relationship to the gift: "Whatsoever…[a person] removes out of the state that nature hath provided and left it in, he hath mixed his labour with it, and joined it to something that is his own, and thereby makes it his property. It being by him removed from the common state nature placed it in, it hath by this labour something annexed to it that excludes the common right of other men." On Locke's terms, then, a person's labor is his own property, upon which no one can have a claim but the laborer himself. In this way, the fruits of labor belong to the laborer alone, and the activity of labor marks for Locke the *removal* of goods from the commons and the *exclusion* of the claims of others upon those goods. To be fair, Locke does provide this caveat: the exclusion of others holds "at least where there is enough, and as good, left in common for others." John Locke, *Second Treatise of Government*, ed. C. B. Macpherson (Indiana: Hackett Publishing Co, Inc., 1980), §§26–27. Creation for Locke therefore still remains in some sense a common gift, even as labor delimits an exclusive sphere of private property. On this point, see Block and Yates, "The Economics and Ethics of Land Reform," 43–44.

God under the law, and the preservation of dominion as care for creation as common gift within it. Clearly, the document points out, the exercise of dominion characterizes Israel's life. It can be seen in the commandments against stealing and coveting[24] and in the centrality of God's gift of land to the people as an inheritance (no. 24). With regard to the latter, *TBDL* is alluding to the apportioning of the land of Canaan to Israel and its distribution by lot to the various tribes upon entry into it (Numbers 26:52-56, 33:53-54 and Joshua 13-19), to be held by them on the condition of covenantal obedience.[25] Allotments are distributed according to need: large landholdings are apportioned to large groups and small landholdings to smaller ones (Numbers 26:54). Though the land is given by God to be the possession of Israel as a whole (Numbers 33:53), particular landholdings belong to those upon whom the lot falls (Numbers 33:54). Throughout the Old Testament, land as an inheritance is variously described as the possession of Israel (Deuteronomy 4:21; 15:4), of its tribes (Joshua 11:23; 17:6), and of particular houses (Joshua 24:28; Judges 2:6; 1 Kings 21:3). In these and other passages, both collective and personal forms of ownership are in view.

Here we begin to see that, despite the damage that sin does to creation and to the task of dominion, God is at work in the world and especially in Israel to repair the damage. Among other places, we see this in the way Israel's dominion relates to God's claim that the land is God's. The allotments are themselves an institutional expression this. They are to be distributed among all of Israel, a distribution whose inclusiveness imitates God's own dominion (no. 24). As *TBDL* points out, Israel's life is meant to be different from that of other

---

[24] *TBDL* cites Deuteronomy 5:21, but see also Exodus 20:15, 17, as well as the legislation of the so-called Book of the Covenant in Exodus 21:28-22:15.

[25] For the purposes of this essay, I leave to the side the issue of the so-called conquest narratives of Israel's entry into the land and the divine authorization of war. See Exodus 17:8-16; Deuteronomy 7:1-5; Joshua 6:1-5. For an extremely insightful presentation of these narratives and the problem of war in the Old Testament more generally, see Stephen B. Chapman, "Martial Memory, Peaceable Vision," in *Holy War in the Bible: Christian Morality and an Old Testament Problem* (Michigan: William B. Eerdmans Publishing Co., 2013). After a careful and detailed engagement with scripture and an extensive evaluation of recent scholarship, Chapman concludes that "in Israel's distinctive use of various ancient near Eastern traditions regarding warfare, and in Israel's consistent effort to limit justifiable warfare primarily to the context of its entry into the land, and in Israel's location of its true security in God's faithfulness rather than in human might, the canonical Old Testament presents war as a time-conditioned, concessive practice at odds with God's ultimate will for humankind. ...From this perspective, Christians can view God's willingness to enter even into the morally contested and compromised arena of Israelite warfare as pointing ahead to the incarnation of Christ." See Chapman, "Martial Memory, Peaceable Vision," 62–63.

peoples, which is evident in God's will that the entirety of Israel participate in possession of the land (no. 24).[26]

The outworking of the claim that the land is God's can likewise be seen in how Israel deals with the reality of dispossession in its midst. The document describes the proper response as the introduction of "numerous limitations to the right of ownership," naming as instances the following prohibitions: reaping to the edges of the field, gathering up fallen fruits and grains, and stripping vineyards and olive groves bare (no. 25; Leviticus 19:9-10, 23:22; Deuteronomy 24:19-22). These stipulations are meant to ensure that the dispossessed are not deprived access to the land. I will have more to say about these passages below and whether they are best characterized as limitations upon ownership, but for the moment, it is sufficient to observe how the overarching theological claim that the land is God's takes institutional expression in Israel's life in terms of enabling the poorest and most vulnerable to share in the use of it.

As *TBDL* observes, bound up with God's will for the participation of Israel in the possession of land is a specific claim of justice that orders Israel's life, upon which the prophets base their critique of the abuse of poor and vulnerable landholders (nos. 24-25). This is vividly seen in the account of Naboth's vineyard, in which Naboth refuses to relinquish his ancestral inheritance in response to King Ahab's desire for it. Consequently, Ahab has Naboth killed, leading Elijah to pronounce God's sentence upon Ahab and his heirs for his actions (1 Kings 21). The prophet Micah articulates the injustice in view when he condemns those who "covet fields, and seize them; houses, and take them away; they oppress household and house, people and their inheritance" (2:2).

Episodes like this show the damage sin has done to dominion and how some in Israel exercise it as domination. But they also show that this is not God's will and that God is also at work in and through Israel to repair dominion. God insistently and unceasingly calls this people to order its dominion in relation to God's—a call that is constitutive of Israel's identity and life on the land. God's words in the midst of the Jubilee provisions of Leviticus are at the center of this call: "The land shall not be sold in perpetuity, for the land is mine; with me you are but aliens and tenants" (25:23). The Jubilee is among the clearest instantiations of the claim that the land is God's and its implications for dominion. The Jubilee, like the Sabbath, is the ultimate measure of time, marking God's ongoing and graceful work in the world through the people of Israel. The Jubilee legislation requires Israel to order the

---

[26] With the exception, of course, of the Levites, who are instead to receive tithes and other offerings (Numbers 18:20-24; Deuteronomy 10:8-9; 12:12; 14:27-29; 18:1-2).

entirety of its economy—its labor, its land, its buying and selling, and so on—to the time of Jubilee, so that Israel's life together can be illumined and transformed by it. In this manner of measuring time and transforming space, we encounter God's work to restore creation, including the practice of dominion.[27]

The Sabbath is the day upon which Israel rests, a rest that includes laborers, livestock, and even strangers. It is a day determined primarily by God's act of creation, recalling God's rest on the seventh day (Genesis 2:1-3; Exodus 20:8-11; 31:16-17). It grants Israel a glimpse of the world in its original form as God's creation. At the same time, the Sabbath is also determined by God's liberation of Israel from the sin that damages creation. It recalls God's freeing Israel from bondage in Egypt for the worship of God (Deuteronomy 5:12-15; Exodus 3:16-18; 5:1; 7:16; 8:1, 20, 27). The Sabbath therefore celebrates God's work both in creating the world and in restoring it.

Of course, the Sabbath is not simply a day. Every septennial, it is a whole year, a time when Israel is to include land in its rest. During the Sabbath year, there is to be no sowing, pruning, reaping, or gathering in order for land to lie fallow (Exodus 23:10-13; Leviticus 25:1-7). God assures the people that if they are faithful, they will not lack food because God will bless the crop of the sixth year (Leviticus 25:18-42) in the same way God rains bread from heaven upon Israel (Exodus 16).

Once again, we see how the Sabbath orders Israel's practice of dominion toward the restoration of creation. As Margaret Baker puts it, "In the Sabbath year, all Israel returned to the original state of creation, sharing equally with the animals whatever grew of itself from the earth."[28] All households, livestock, and wild animals are to rely exclusively on what land yields of its own accord. In other words, all are to become gleaners, a practice that, it is important to note, recalls God's original provisioning of food for all creatures and humankind's unique participation in it. Recalling the first chapters of Genesis, where God gives humans dominion (Genesis 1:28-29, 2:15) and where God graciously and abundantly provides plants and trees for the sustenance of all creatures (Genesis 1:29, 2:16), dominion's original form is a kind of gleaning or gathering, which not only preserves what

---

[27] For more on Jubilee as the return of Israel and its use of created things to their source in God, as the restoration of God's purpose for them, see Samson Raphael Hirsch, *The Pentateuch Translated and Explained*, trans. Isaac Levy, vol. 3 (New York: Judaica, 1989), 2.739.

[28] Margaret Baker, "The Time is Fulfilled: Jesus and Jubilee," *Scottish Journal of Theology* 53, no. 1 (2000): 24.

God has made but also leaves sufficient sustenance for others. Eden, after all, means 'abundance,' 'plenty,' 'fullness.'[29]

East of Eden, the practice of gleaning acquires additional resonances, For instance, it recalls Israel's forebears who gathered manna in the wilderness. During this crucial period of moral formation, those who gathered more manna than they needed in this mysterious field of God had nothing left over and those who gathered too little lacked nothing (Exodus 16:18).[30] Again, the ordering of Israel's dominion is toward taking only what people need so that there is sufficient sustenance for others. At the same time, the gleaning associated with the Sabbath also puts all of Israel in the position of the most vulnerable among them—the stranger, the orphan, the widow, and all those forced to gather what remains after the fields are harvested. In this way, gleaning is meant to help Israelites remember that they are "strangers and sojourners" on God's land and that their dominion ultimately amounts to a kind of tenancy (Leviticus 25:23).

The Jubilee year extends and deepens the renewal of God's creative and salvific work celebrated on the Sabbath. The Jubilee follows a Sabbath of Sabbaths, which means it falls approximately every fifty years (Leviticus 25:9).[31] On this year, the trumpet sounds in a proclamation of *deror*, meaning 'liberty' or 'release' (Leviticus 25:10).[32]

The biblical practice of Jubilee and its ongoing significance for agrarian reform is the theological heart of *TBDL* (see nos. 26, 60-61). The document's interest in Jubilee relates primarily to its being the institutional exemplification of God's will that the people of Israel as a whole share in the possession of land. Jubilee, in the document's words, "translates God's lordship directly onto the social and economic planes" (no. 26). How does it do this? *TBDL* mentions the defense of three expressions of liberty: the return of land to its original owners, the return of people to their families and property, and rest for the land (no. 26). Some comments upon these expressions of liberty and their significance in light of the foregoing are in order.

---

[29] See David Toshio Tsumara, *The Earth and its Waters in Genesis 1 and 2: A Linguistic Investigation* (Scheffield: JSOT Press, 1989), 136-137; Richard S. Hess, "Eden—a Well-Watered Place," *Bible Review* 7, no. 6 (1991): 28–33.

[30] For reading of this episode, which emphasizes Israel's training into an alternative moral economy of eating from the one Israel knew in Egypt, see Davis, *Scripture, Culture, and Agriculture*, 66-79.

[31] There is disagreement whether the Jubilee is the seventh Sabbath year itself or the following year, that is, every forty-ninth or every fiftieth year. See Margaret Baker, "The Time is Fulfilled: Jesus and Jubilee," 23.

[32] Jacob Milgrom defines *deror* as 'release,' 'flow,' or 'freedom.' See Jacob Milgrom, *Leviticus 23-27* (Connecticut: Yale University Press, 2001), 2167.

As we have already seen, the commandment of Sabbath rest, like the allotment of land to the families of Israel, is deeply woven into God's covenant with Israel. While rest for land during the Jubilee continued the normal septennial Sabbath rest, the restoration of property and people is unique to the Jubilee year. The rationale for restoration comes at the center of Leviticus 25 in a verse already cited above: "This land shall not be sold in perpetuity, for the land is mine; with me you are but aliens and tenants. Throughout the land that you hold, you shall provide for the redemption of the land" (Leviticus 25:23-24; see *TBDL* no. 26).

What this rationale indicates is that among the primary purposes of the Jubilee is to preserve the original familial allotments of land, which is why un-allotted land falls outside the bounds of the legislation (Leviticus 25: 29-34). The legislation envisions the ties of kinship as the primary way of preventing original owners from losing control of their land, with relatives stepping in to redeem land once it has been sold (Leviticus 25: 25-26). However, if land has been sold, and if neither the original owners nor their kin can pay the price of redemption, land can change hands, but only until the time of Jubilee, when all land is to be released and returned to its original owners (Leviticus 25: 26-29).

Just as for land, so, too, for people. Much of Leviticus 25 concerns not only the release of land but also laborers as well. The latter part of the chapter presumes that people, like land, might also fall into the hands of others. When economic disaster comes upon a household, people might hand over not only their land but also their lives because they have no other way to survive. Relatives who fall into such difficulties are to receive hospitality and support from their kin (Leviticus 25: 35-37). When relatives sell themselves, their kin should intervene. Debtors who cannot repay what they owe and have no one to redeem them are to be welcomed into the household of their creditors, not as slaves but as laborers (Leviticus 25: 47-55). The rule throughout is that need and hardship should never be an occasion for further exploitation.

The Jubilee likewise renders these arrangements impermanent. On the Jubilee, all people are to be released from their debts in order to return to their families and their land (Leviticus 25: 39-43, 54-55).[33] In the intervening period, redemption payments for land and people are assessed according to the proximity of the Jubilee year (Leviticus 25: 15-17, 50-52). In other words, the closer the time to Jubilee and its release, the less the market value for land and labor. In short, according to Leviticus 25, Jubilee functions as the fundamental

---

[33] Because the legislation is bound to Israel's covenantal life with God and the original allotment of land, the legislation does not apply to those outside of Israel (Leviticus 25:44-46).

reference point for Israel's economy, continually ordering and reordering Israel's land, labor, and dominion toward a more determinative reality, the God who is their beginning and end.

The Jubilee preserves the original allotments of land according to need and the participation of all of Israel in the possession of land on that basis. The participation of all in possession—and the ongoing work to preserve the participation of all—is how Israel acknowledges that land belongs to the God who gives it to all, and how Israel's dominion imitates God's. Amassing great wealth that could be passed down from generation to generation is among the gravest threats to the participation of all in possession, hence the recurrent return of land to its owners and families to their inheritance. The Jubilee therefore serves as an ongoing reminder of how God gives land to Israel in common to build up Israel's common life, so that Israel can be blessing for all the families of the earth (Genesis 12:3). Crucial to the Jubilee legislation is the preservation of the original allotments, and the bond between people and land that persists despite the obstacles that come between them. What are impermanent are the obstacles, not the originary bond.

The inability to alienate land in perpetuity not only preserves the participation of Israel as a whole in its possession. It also transforms the character of Israel's dominion, loosening the grip of possessors upon land and the lives of others, reminding them that they ultimately control neither. By means of this pedagogy of grace, Israel's dominion becomes non-proprietary.[34] To return to the language of *TBDL*, Israel's dominion is not meant to be despotic and unbridled domination. Emmanuel Lévinas puts the point well in his *Nine Talmudic Readings*, "If Moses brought us out of Egypt, split the sea, and fed us manna, do you think, then, that under his leadership we are going to conquer a country the way one conquers a colony? ... Do you think that we will appropriate a plot of land for ourselves so that we can use and abuse it? We are going...toward this land in order to experience celestial life."[35] The Jubilee is the instantiation of celestial life on earth.

---

[34] I borrow the phrase "non-proprietary possession" from Joan Lockwood O'Donovan, who uses it in a different context, but which is likewise applicable to this one. See Joan Lockwood O'Donovan, "Christian Platonism and Non-Proprietary Community," in *Bonds of Imperfection: Christian Politics, Past and Present* (Michigan: Wm. B. Eerdmans Publishing Company, 2003).

[35] Emmanuel Lévinas, "Promised Land or Permitted Land: From the Tractate Sotah, Pp. 34b-35a," in *Nine Talmudic Readings*, trans. Annette Aronowicz (Indiana: Indiana University Press, 1990), 65–66.

SIN

As I have been trying to suggest, one of *TBDL*'s central theological claims is that God's dominion is epitomized by the gift of creation for the sustenance of all, and it is this dominion that God calls Israel to imitate. St. Athanasius makes a similar point in his *Resurrection Letters* when he describes Israel's being "purified in the wilderness," "trained to forget the customs of Egypt."[36] The gift of land to Israel, along with the various stipulations upon its use that we find in Leviticus 25 and elsewhere, is part and parcel of this purification and training as Israel learns to imitate the shape of God's own dominion. Here we encounter how, over the course of the biblical narrative, the meaning of dominion, like the notion of *imago Dei* from which it derives, is increasingly clarified as God shares God's life of communion more fully with creation. Throughout, the original form of dominion and its restoration retains ontological priority.

TBDL's treatment of Jubilee, however, leaves important questions unresolved. Perhaps foremost among them: what transpired after the gift of original dominion that made the Jubilee necessary? In other words, what about sin? We have been wrestling with this problem all along in discussing the distinction between pre- and postlapsarian dominion. As we have already seen, *TBDL* is certainly aware of certain problematic resonances of dominion. The document mentions sin on a handful of occasions, and it frames the discussion of agrarian reform and the "climate of terror" in which it often takes place in relation to sin (see nos.12, 33, 60-61). However, *TBDL* fails to reflect in any sustained way upon sin and its consequences for the topic at hand.

One place this failure becomes particularly apparent is in the document's description of how Israel's law introduces "limitations to the right of ownership" (no. 25), which I touched upon above.[37] *TBDL* cites as instances of such limitations the passages against reaping to the edges of the field, gathering up fallen fruits and grains, and stripping vineyards and olive groves bare. Until this point, the document has been attempting to differentiate dominion-as-care from dominion-as-domination. Yet here we are being told that the law must place limitations upon a dominion that seems to have gone awry, which has lost a sense of its vocation as care. In other words, dominion-as-domination seems suddenly to have acquired primacy and has become constitutive of dominion as such.

---

[36] Philip Schaff and Henry Wace, eds., *St. Athanasius: Select Works and Letters* (New York: Christian Literature Company, 1892), Letter VI, no. 12.

[37] Similar language is reproduced in the commentaries on *TBDL*. See, for instance, "Land Policies Unjust," *Catholic New Times*, February 8, 1998, 2, which describes how "religious principles and social responsibility place conditions on the right to private property and give owners precise obligations."

If my characterization is correct, what is perplexing is that the scriptural passages under consideration are not informed by a conception of dominion-as-domination, which is exercised by an owner in total exclusion of all others. Rather, what is at stake in these passages is the more basic issue of what dominion is, what its true practice entails, and how God is working in Israel to restore it. As these passages indicate, among the defining features of dominion is not exclusion of others but their inclusion. Those deprived of land—paradigmatically the poor, the widow, the stranger, and the orphan—are permitted access to others' land in order to make ends meet. They are included as sharers in Israel's land and its fruits.

Those who have land are simply told not to strip their fields bare but to leave the edges and the gleanings for others. The rationale is the same as that of Leviticus 25: "I am the LORD your God" (Leviticus 19:9-10; 23:22; Deuteronomy 24:19-20). In other words, the practice of leaving sustenance for others is meant to remind those with land of the one to whom their land belongs, the one who gives it to them for the good of all. That the edges and the gleanings do not fall within the ambit of their control is an institutional expression of this truth. God's will is for others, especially those in need, to have access to the edges and the gleanings. This access, moreover, does not belong to those in need incidentally, as a result of the goodwill of landowners. It belongs to them as a matter of justice; it is theirs. Leaving the edges and the gleanings serves to remind landowners that they are like aliens and tenants on God's land, which God gives them in order to learn to practice God's dominion upon it.

An important implication of these considerations is that for Israel to accumulate land, in the words of the prophet Isaiah, by joining "house to house" and adding "field to field" (5:8), or for Israel to harvest to the edges and strip them bare, is not to fail to place adequate limitations upon ownership. It is to fail to own at all. It is best described as stealing because it takes from the poor, the widow, the stranger, and the orphan what belongs to them. Perhaps this is why in Leviticus the subsequent verses move immediately into the topic of stealing and false dealing (Leviticus 19:11-13).

The commonality of the gift of land is not an extrinsic imposition upon dominion, which is understood above all as private and exclusive possession. Rather, commonality has to do with what land most fundamentally is, which conditions how Israel is meant to hold it. On this view, the concentration and misappropriation of land, to use *TBDL*'s language, is problematic because it so blatantly contradicts God's dominion over creation, which Israel's vocation is to imitate. This contradiction darkens God's life of communion as it is imaged among humankind, which is why for Isaiah, such concentration and misappropriation tends toward solitude. Those who join house to house and add field to field, the prophet tells us, "dwell alone in the midst of the land" (Isaiah 5:8).

CATHOLIC SOCIAL DOCTRINE

In addition to the scriptural passages we have been considering, *TBDL* exposits dominion in relation to the Church's social doctrine, which "continu[es] the path indicated by Sacred Scripture" (no. 27). Here the document assumes that that the Church's doctrine is part of, in Walker Percy's words, "the career in time of that unique Thing, the Jewish-People-Jesus-Christ-Catholic-Church…God's entry into history through His covenant with the Jews, through His own incarnation, and through His institution of the Catholic Church as the means of man's salvation."[38] In other words, the Church has not left Israel's world, but still finds herself situated within it.[39]

We should therefore not be surprised that *TBDL*'s concerns about the concentration of land continue to find expression in the Church's life. As the document states, "In the social teaching of the Church, the process of concentration of landholdings is judged a scandal because it clearly goes against God's will and salvific plan, inasmuch as it deprives a large part of humanity of the benefit of the fruits of the earth." Moreover, it is "the cause of conflicts that undermine the very life of society, leading to the break-up of the social fabric and the degradation of the natural environment" (no. 27).

On *TBDL*'s exposition, the central, pertinent feature of Church teaching is what the document refers to as the "common destination of earthly goods," a principle based upon "the biblical view of the earth as God's gift to all human beings" (no. 28, 29-31). The phrase common or universal destination of created goods comes from *Gaudium et Spes* (nos. 69-71). In *Laborem Exercens*, Pope Saint John Paul II calls it "the first principle of the whole ethical and social order" (no. 19), and, in *Sollicitudo Rei Socialis*, he refers to it as "the characteristic principle of Christian social doctrine" (no. 42). This principle merits further examination because it yields a distinctive construal of property and dominion upon which the Church bases her critique of land concentration, and her call for agrarian reform.

Expounding the principle, however, raises similar complexities to those we have been examining throughout this essay, specifically in

---

[38] Walker Percy, *The Message in the Bottle: How Queer Man Is, How Queer Language Is, and What One Has to Do with the Other* (New York: Open Road Media, 2011), 140.

[39] This is a paraphrase of Willie Jennings's poignant question: "when did we [Christians] leave Israel's world?" He reminds them: "The worlds of Christian language are inside Israel's house." Willie James Jennings, *The Christian Imagination: Theology and the Origins of Race* (Connecticut: Yale University Press, 2011), 160.

terms of how to understand *Gaudium et Spes*'s claim that people should regard the goods that they "legitimately possess" not only as their "own" but as "common" (no. 69). In explaining what *Gaudium et Spes* means, *TBDL* again introduces the language of limits, which only generates confusion. The "right to private property," the document states, "is not...unconditional." It therefore must be "circumscribed within the limits of the fundamental social function of property" (no. 30). Later we read that the right of all to use the goods of creation "sets a limit on the right of private property" (no. 31).

To be fair, *TBDL* is not always consistent in its language. Elsewhere, it employs strikingly different formulations.[40] However, the language of limiting and circumscribing gives the impression of distinct goods in competition with one another—the right to private property and the social function of property—that must be adjudicated and balanced. More precisely still, it suggests that the right to private property must be limited or circumscribed in order for property's social function to be fulfilled, as if the social function were an addendum upon it.

The problem is that this leaves the conventional picture of dominion-as-domination firmly in place. On this picture, the decisive issue becomes whether or not there should be limitations upon dominion. However, both positions—that there should and should not be limitations—mistakenly assume that limitations are external or alien impositions upon dominion-as-domination, operating upon it as if from the outside. In other words, the difference between these positions is not how they imagine dominion, but whether or not the limitations upon dominion are warranted. Both fail to question adequately the picture of dominion as sole, despotic, and exclusive.

This conventional picture profoundly misleads insofar as the decisive issue for Church teaching is what property is and what it means to possess it properly. Like the scriptural passages we have been examining, the Church contests certain widespread assumptions about the meaning of dominion. She holds that the concentration of land in *latifundia*—the modern iteration of joining house to house and adding field to field or reaping to the edges of the field and stripping them bare—is not best described as a failure of placing adequate limitations upon dominion. Rather, it is really a failure of dominion

---

[40] *TBDL*, for instance, speaks of "perverse inequalities in the distribution of common goods" (no. 27), "the fundamental social function of property" (no. 30), and "the social function directly and naturally inherent in goods and their destination" (no. 31). But the issue that remains unaddressed is the relationship between what *TBDL* calls "the natural and primary right" to the use of earthly goods, which has a "universal application" (no. 28, see no. 29), and the need to "circumscribe" the right to private property "within the limits of the fundamental social function of property" (no. 30).

and therefore a form of thievery. For this reason, Wilhelm Emmanuel von Ketteler, the Bishop of Mainz who had an important influence on Pope Leo XIII and the writing of *Rerum Novarum*, referred to the conventional picture of dominion as a "crude doctrine" that effectively "sanctions the right to steal, since...stealing means not only to take what belongs to others, but also to hold back what rightfully ought to belong to others."[41]

With this in mind, let us return once again to *Gaudium et Spes*'s claim that people should regard the goods that they "legitimately possess" not only as their "own" but as "common" (no. 69). The Pastoral Constitution is drawing upon St. Thomas Aquinas's *Summa Theologiae*. In describing the second of humankind's twofold competence with regard to the use of created things—the competence as to their use (*usus ipsarum*)—Thomas writes, "Now with regard to this, no man is entitled to manage things merely for himself, but as common (*ut proprias, sed ut communes*), so that he is ready to share them easily (*de facili*) with others in the case of necessity" (*ST* II–II q. 66, a. 2).

The claim being made here is that the goods themselves—indeed, everything a person possesses—is a common gift. The common character of the goods—that they in some sense belong not only to their possessors but to others as well—is essential for understanding what they are. Commonality is not an extrinsic imposition upon these goods, which would leave intact the picture of property as essentially private, with the social function operating as a limit from the outside. Rather, the claim is that commonality is intrinsic to what property is. As *Gaudium et Spes* goes on to say, property *"by its very nature...*has a social quality" (no. 71, emphasis added).

The common character of property also has important implications for dominion or what Church teaching tends to describe in terms of right use. People are to manage what they have for themselves as well as for others, drawing these others into the orbit of concern as they use and manage what they have. According to Thomas, the fundamental measure of right use is the readiness to use possessions to care for those in need, the willingness to share them *de facili*—easily, readily, without difficulty. Thomas quotes 1 Timothy 6:17-18 to bolster the point: "As for the rich of the world, charge them to give easily (*facile*), to communicate to others, etc."

Gaudium et Spes observes that none of this implies that it is illegitimate for people to take what they or their dependents need, all of whom are also included in the community of common use (no. 69). The Pastoral Constitution does, though, enjoin people "to come to the

---

[41] Wilhelm Emmanuel von Ketteler, "The Six Sermons," in *The Social Teachings of Wilhem Emmanuel von Ketteler* (Washington, D.C: University Press of America, 1981), 16.

relief of the poor and to do so not merely out of their superfluous goods" (no. 69). This obligation implicates the use and management of all created goods because God gives them to humankind as a whole for common use. Therefore, according to this view, those who have the world's goods must learn to see themselves as facilitators of common use or, in the words of *TBDL*, "instrument[s] to implement the principle of the universal destination of material goods" (no. 30).

The commonality of the goods in question leads *Gaudium et Spes* to invoke the so-called *ius necessitatis* or law of necessity to elaborate the point. According to this law, those in extreme destitution can take what they need to survive from others' surfeit (no. 69). In discussing this passage, *TBDL* again invokes the imperative to place limitations upon the right of private property (no. 31). In contrast, when Thomas takes it up in the *Summa Theologiae*, he points to an altogether different account of dominion. He does not suggest, as the document does, that thievery by those in extreme need is a proper limitation upon property. Rather, Thomas insists that the description thievery is inaccurate. The goods such people take belong to them because of their need. In other words, those in need do not (legitimately) take what belongs to others; they take what is theirs, what their "need has made common" (*ST* II-II q. 66, a.7 sed contra; ad. 2). We can add that, in doing so, they bear witness to the truth that creation is a common gift, even if the laws of a polity fail to reflect it.

On this basis, *Gaudium et Spes* condemns situations in which "there are large or even extensive rural estates which are only slightly cultivated or lie completely idle for the sake of profit, while the majority of the people either are without land or have only very small fields" (no. 71). The Pastoral Constitution goes on to call for the "distribution" of these "insufficiently cultivated estates" (no. 71)—a call that continues to resound in Church teaching.

As should now be evident, the understanding of dominion we have been examining has profound implications for moral description, which John Paul II makes explicit in a 1979 meeting in Cuilapan in Oaxaca, Mexico. In a speech, he addresses the "leaders of the peoples" and the "powerful classes," and then proceeds to tell them that they keep unproductive "lands that hide the bread that so many families lack."[42] In keeping more land than they can possibly use, they keep what in fact belongs to those in need. These leaders and powerful people are therefore like thieves, John Paul's language suggests, whose robbery is written into the very landscape they inhabit. Blessed Óscar Romero speaks in similar terms to the oligarchy in the midst of

---

[42] Pope John Paul II, *Apostolic Journey to the Dominican Republic, Mexico, and the Bahamas*, Cuilapan, Mexico, January 29, 1979.

the agrarian conflicts of 1970s El Salvador. "They possess for themselves," Romero says in his penultimate Sunday homily, "the land that belongs to all Salvadorans."[43] Romero's point is not that those in possession of the land in question lack legal titles to it. Rather, he is giving voice to a law that is more basic and fundamental than positive law, to which positive law is ultimately accountable. In light of this law, Romero refers to a dominion so disordered by sin that it is best described as thievery.[44]

In his book on the Landless Workers' Movement in Brazil (in Portuguese: *Movimento dos Trabalhadores Sem Terra*),[45] Mario Losano examines the Landless Workers' Movement as a contemporary application of the law of necessity. Among the questions Losano poses is this: what are these landless workers doing when they start farming and living on land that is titled to another but is either not being used or is being used as an opportunity for speculation? Are these workers, as they themselves say, *occupying land* on the basis of a law of need that is superior to positive law? Or, as their opponents charge, are they *lawless invaders, usurping others' property?*[46] The difference between these descriptions and the moral landscapes they evoke is not negligible. Because landless workers and their supporters are often accused of communism and of advocating the abolition of property, Losano reminds us that they aspire to become smallholders themselves.[47] What they protest is not property but one particular understanding of it under whose banner some keep the land that hides the bread of the many, the land that belongs to all.[48]

---

[43] Óscar Arnulfo Romero, *Homilías (VI)*, ed. Miguel Cavada Diez (San Salvador: UCA Editores, 2005), 420.

[44] In this connection, it is noteworthy that the *Catechism of the Catholic Church*'s treatment of the commandment against thievery begins, not with a defense of property rights as enshrined in positive law, but with the common destination of created goods, from which the entirety of the teaching on property and possession derives; see *Catechism of the Catholic Church*, nos. 2401–2425. See also Pope Francis, *Evangelii Gaudium,* no. 57, and Papa Francesco, *Udienza Generale*, Piazza San Pietro, June 5, 2013.

[45] For more on the controversy of the reception of *TBDL* in Brazil and the role of the Brazilian bishops' conference in its writing, see Leslie Wirpsa, "Officials Hail Vatican Paper on Land Use," *National Catholic Reporter*, April 3, 1998, natcath.org/NCR_Online/archives/040398/040398a.htm.

[46] Along these lines, Gerald Schlabach writes of how *campesinos* in Honduras speak of *recuperaciones* or recoveries of land, implying the return of what belongs to them. Gerald Schlabach, "The Nonviolence of Desperation: Peasant Land Action in Honduras," in *Relentless Persistence: Nonviolent Action in Latin America* (Pennsylvania: New Society Publishers, 1991), 64–77.

[47] Mario Losano, *La Función Social de la Propiedad y Latifundios Ocupados: Los Sin Tierra de Brasil* (Madrid: Editorial DYKINSON, 2006), 137-138.

[48] In relation to popular movements like the MST, see Pope Francis, *Address at the World Meeting of Popular Movements*, Santa Cruz de la Sierra, July 9, 2015.

JESUS IS THE JUBILEE

Jubilee is the theological heart of *TBDL*. The document states that its call for agrarian reform arises out of "the jubilee tradition in the Bible." "The spirit of the Jubilee," it continues, "urges us to cry 'Enough'!" to injustice and exclusion (nos. 60-61). Note how the Jubilee functions here as a blueprint of sorts for social and economic transformation.[49] The somber note upon which the document ends only intensifies this impression. Widespread "acquiescence to evil," we are told, has produced "a disturbing cultural and political void." Not only is there little possibility of "change and renewal," but "justice and solidarity remain absent and invisible" (no. 61). This bleak assessment indicates that the Jubilee as *TBDL* understands it is utopian; it is literally *ou-topos* or 'no-place,' a social and economic program yet to be enacted. Cardinal Etchegaray, then president of the Pontifical Council for Justice and Peace, confirms this when he describes agrarian reform as "a utopia," but a "feasible" one.[50]

One problem with this understanding of the Jubilee is the failure to grapple with sin and the conditions that led to the Jubilee in the first place. Why, in other words, the periodic need for restoration if not for the damage sin has done and continues to do to what God has made? Moreover, apart from the sin to which the Jubilee is itself a response, there is the additional matter of Israel's own resistance to its implementation. It is unclear, for instance, whether the Jubilee was ever actually practiced by Israel.[51] Scriptural passages like Leviticus 26:34-35 and 2 Chronicle 36:20-21 suggest that only with exile will the land make up for the Sabbaths it lost while the people of Israel lived upon it and neglected their covenantal obligations. Among the clearest reference to the Jubilee elsewhere in scripture comes in Jeremiah 34:8-22, where the prophet speaks of Israel's failure to implement it.

This problem is in fact so deeply embedded in Israel's life that Isaiah addresses its resolution in an eschatological register. Isaiah envisions God's new creation to include—not only the absence of all weeping, premature death, and infant mortality, and not only long and blessed lives for God's people, and wolves and lambs feeding peacefully together—but the final and decisive overcoming of the

---

[49] For a similar use of the Jubilee, see Andrea Schultze, "The Challenge of Jubilee to the Situation of Church Land in South Africa Today: Some Reflections after the Eighth Assembly of World Council of Churches," *International Review of Mission* 88, no. 350 (1999): 254-266; Graham, *Sustainable Agriculture*, 36–37.

[50] Quoted in "Land Policies Unjust."

[51] Robert Gnuse, *You Shall Not Steal: Community and Property in the Biblical Tradition* (New York: Orbis Books, 1985), 40–45; Craig L. Blomberg, *Neither Poverty nor Riches: A Biblical Theology of Material Possessions* (Michigan: William B. Eerdmans Publishing Co., 1999), 44–45.

obstacles between people and land: "They shall build houses and inhabit them; they shall plant vineyards and eat their fruit. They shall not build and another inhabit; they shall not plant and another eat" (Isaiah 21-22). Isaiah's vision is of creation's final restoration—including the gift of land to all of Israel—which has yet to be fully enacted in Israel's life.[52]

My point is that much more remains to be said about the theological significance of the Jubilee for agrarian reform and for Christian life more generally, which can only be intimated here. Specifically, much more remains to be said about why and how Christians believe Isaiah's vision of restoration is fulfilled by Christ, whose coming makes creation new (see 2 Corinthians 5:17; Galatians 6:5; Ephesians 2:15; 2 Peter 3:13; Revelation 21:1-5). Jesus is the Jubilee of God. This christological understanding of Jubilee, I want to suggest, illumines the story *TBDL* wants to tell about agrarian reform, because it illumines how creation and covenant find fulfillment in Christ.

Traditionally, Christians have read Jesus's inauguration of his ministry in Luke 4:16-21 in terms of the Jubilee year.[53] On this view, Isaiah's words about "the acceptable year of the Lord"—the proclamation of good news to the poor, release to the captives and to the oppressed, and recovery of sight to the blind—find their term in the person and work of Jesus Christ. "Today this scripture has been fulfilled in your hearing," Jesus says to his listeners (Luke 4:21). He is the acceptable time of the Lord become flesh and blood. But this fulfillment does not amount to a straightforward blueprint for social and economic transformation, a clear program to be put into practice. Rather, it points to a reality much more complex and mysterious, which is bound to the person of Christ, the ἄφεσις ('release,' 'liberty,' 'forgiveness') associated with him (Mark 1:4, 3:29; Luke 1:77, 3:3; Acts 2:38, 10:43), and the cross he bore for the redemption of humankind (Ephesians 1:7; Col 1:14).

The fulfillment of which Jesus speaks in Luke 4 therefore has everything to do with the story of Israel's failure and God's merciful response to it in him. For the crucial though neglected context of the Jubilee in *TBDL* is sin and the damage sin has done to what God has made. Canonically speaking, the Jubilee comes after Israel's grumbling in the wilderness (Exodus 14:10-12; 15:24-24), the failure to heed God's instructions not to gather manna on the Sabbath

---

[52] See Bruno's comments on Isaiah 61 as pointing to the eschatological restoration of Israel in Christopher R. Bruno, "'Jesus Is Our Jubilee'...But How? The OT Background and Lukan Fulfillment of the Ethics of Jubilee," *JETS* 53, no. 1 (March 2010): 94.
[53] Bruno, "'Jesus Is Our Jubilee'" 95–99.

(Exodus 16:27-29), and the fashioning of the Golden Calf (Exodus 32). It comes in the midst of and in response to Israel's sin.

As Ephraim Radner observes, the Jubilee concerns the restoration of the created communion between God and what God has made. It reflects God's work of "mercifully reordering" the devastation sin unleashes in the world.[54] The Jubilee is offered for Israel's transformation, given so that Israel can fulfill its vocation as a blessing to the nations. In the Jubilee, we can therefore discern God patiently and mercifully at work, "pull[ing] the world, in the reflected experience of Israel, back into its created form."[55] Like the gift of God's glory filling the tabernacle at the end of Exodus (40:34-38), in the Jubilee we see God's response to sin is not to withdraw God's life but to give it more fully.

For this reason, in commenting upon these verses from Luke 4 about the acceptable year of the Lord, figures like St. Cyril of Alexandria understand them as addressing the mystery of the incarnation. Cyril writes out of the conviction that God's definitive response to sin is Christ, the gift of God's own life. As Cyril asks in his *Commentary on Luke*, what does the proclamation of the Lord's favor mean? "It signifies the joyful tidings of His own advent, that the time of the Lord…had arrived."[56] Jesus is himself the acceptable year of the Lord, and the Jubilee is sharing in the life he offers. The time of which Cyril writes does not measure or mark Jesus's arrival as an ordinary occurrence in time. Christ's advent is time's very "fullness" (Galatians 4:4), the coming of the one in whom "all things hold together" (Colossians 1:17). It is time's final measure.

Understood christologically, the social and economic order envisioned by the Jubilee is, in Radner's words, "one of mercy and finally forgiveness—which does not order life in a utopian manner, but rather gathers history…in the direction of God's own coming to it and suffering for it."[57] In this regard, it is important to observe that the way of mercy—the way of the love that willingly enters into and bears the misery of others—must always run the risk of suffering and rejection. In his *Commentary on Luke*, Cyril reminds us of the cost of God's merciful work in Christ: "For that was the acceptable year of [the Lord] in which Christ was crucified on our behalf."[58] Humankind crucified its Jubilee. But as Cyril continues, Christ's crucifixion is the

---

[54] Ephraim Radner, *Leviticus* (Michigan: Brazos Press, 2008), 268.
[55] Radner, *Leviticus*, 267.
[56] Cyril of Alexandria, *Commentary on Luke: Sermons 12-25* (Oxford: Oxford University Press, 1859), Homily 12. See also Thomas Aquinas, *Catena Aurea*, vol. 3, St. Luke (Southampton, United Kingdom: The Saint Austin Press, 1997), 153–158.
[57] Radner, *Leviticus*, 273.
[58] Cyril of Alexandria, *Commentary on Luke: Sermons 12-25*, Homily 12.

first fruits of a coming harvest, for it "trampled upon the power of death,"[59] making possible new paths of mercy among his followers. In other words, the fulfillment of the Jubilee in Christ implies participation in his ecclesial body, whose members are being trained by God's grace into the mercy of their Lord.

None of this is to dismiss or even to downplay the challenge posed by the Jubilee to social and economic forms, the organization of land and labor, the meaning of dominion, and so on—all of which *TBDL* rightly perceives. The point is simply that the Jubilee concerns more than the implementation of policy, as crucial as good policy is.[60] For the Jubilee illumines why the struggle for a better distribution of land often occurs within a climate of terror. Such a struggle participates in the long and ongoing story of humankind's refusal to acknowledge the truth that creation is a common gift and to live into the vocation of dominion-as-care.[61] Because of this, Radner observes that the reordering of social and economic ties called for by Leviticus 25 "is a struggle whose full resolution comes only in the form of martyrdom."[62]

We should therefore not be surprised that, as Óscar Romero observes in his December 16, 1979, homily, "many who have tried to identify with the archdiocese's thinking on agrarian reform, which is the Church's thinking on agrarian reform, have suffered and will continue to suffer."[63] In another homily, from several months earlier, Romero speaks of the "testimony of the blood," which has become "an ordinary voice," and also how, from his chair as archbishop, he has been trying to "interpret the language of so much blood being poured out."[64] In March the following year, as the second Revolutionary Governing Junta rolled out its agrarian reform legislation in the midst of massive social upheaval, the blood of which Romero spoke would include his own. As Romero and so many others like him witness, those who work to give others the land due them in justice often risk laying down their own lives in charity.

While the focus of *TBDL* is agrarian reform, the document's significance far exceeds this issue alone. Among other things, *TBDL* helps us to reflect upon the extent to which commonplace conceptions of dominion are deeply and complexly implicated in sin. The document likewise points to the extensive healing humankind needs— a healing that, in Thomas's language, helps people learn to do the good

---

[59] Cyril of Alexandria, *Commentary on Luke: Sermons 12-25*, Homily 12.
[60] Radner, *Leviticus*, 270, 269.
[61] Radner, *Leviticus*, 273.
[62] Radner, *Leviticus* 273. I would not say *only* in the form of martyrdom, as Radner does, but *often*.
[63] Romero, *Homilías (VI)*, 72.
[64] Óscar Arnulfo Romero, *Homilías (V)*, ed. Miguel Cavada Diez (San Salvador: UCA Editores, 2005), 25.

that is proportional to their nature, so as to care for what is common in ways that preserve it as common (*ST* I-II, q. 109, a. 7, ad. 3). St. Ambrose begins his treatise *On Naboth* with these words, which are cited in the epigraph: "The story of Naboth is an old one, but it is repeated every day" (no. 1.1). The repetition to which Ambrose refers is not only the repetition of those who unjustly take the lands of others, which is still a frequent occurrence in our world. Above all, it is the ordinary enclosure of "what was given in common for the use of all," the countless ways people continue to keep and use for themselves what God wishes to "grow for the many" through them.[65] 𝕸

---

[65] "On Naboth," in *Ambrose*, ed. Boniface Ramsey (New York: Routledge, 1997), nos. 1.2, 2.4, 7.37, 12.53.

Laudato Si' on Non-Human Animals

Anatoly Angelo R. Aseneta

Francis's *Laudato Si'* has turned our attention to the ecological crisis and gave rise to lively discussions about ecological issues and our responsibilities to our common home. In addition, the encyclical also shows a particular concern towards non-human animals and provides directions on how we should treat them who are our fellow inhabitants. This essay looks at what *Laudato Si'* teaches about the treatment of non-human animals, especially its strengths and weaknesses in light of the existing Catholic tradition. I hope to show that, despite the way Francis extends Catholic teaching on concern for non-human animals, there is still room for improvement, specifically by directly addressing ways in which humans use non-human animals.

To fully appreciate what Francis has written, the first part of this essay provides a brief overview of the Catholic tradition and teaching on the treatment of non-human animals prior to *Laudato Si'*. I limit myself to two important sources. The first one is Thomas Aquinas whose theses on non-human animals have significantly influenced how the Catholic moral tradition approached questions on the ethical status of non-human animals.[1] The second is the *Catechism of the Catholic Church*, being the most significant post-Vatican II magisterial document on non-human animals.[2] Several works have done significant analysis of these sources. Therefore, rather than a comprehensive and thorough review, these will be dealt with in broad strokes, identifying their central problems to situate and assess *Laudato Si'*.

The second part evaluates the contributions of *Laudato Si'* on the treatment of non-human animals in light of these central problems, pinpointing where it does well and falls short. The encyclical letter's

---

[1] James Gaffney, "The Relevance of Animal Experimentation to Roman Catholic Ethical Methodology," in *Animal Sacrfices: Religious Perspectives on the Use of Animals in Science*, ed. Tom Regan (Pennsylvania: Temple University Press, 1986), 153.

[2] John Berkman, "From Theological Speciesism to a Theological Ethology: Where Catholic Moral Theology Needs to Go," *Journal of Moral Theology* 3, no. 2 (June 2014): 12.

treatment of this topic is quite progressive while at the same time remaining balanced and rooted in tradition and previous teaching. Nonetheless, it lacks a direct treatment of certain ways in which non-human animals are used. Treating such issues at the level of an encyclical letter concerned with our common home would have been opportune and could have substantially add to the Church's teaching on the treatment of non-human animals.

The third and final part identifies sources from which the Church can draw from in order to further extend its teaching on the treatment of non-human animals, specifically in addressing the ways humans use them. These sources suggest valuing encounters with non-human animals, recognizing their God-given *telos*, refusing to view concern for non-human animals as taking away concern for humans, and finally building upon the *Catechism of the Catholic Church*'s language of justice in our treatment of non-human animals.

PART I: THE PLACE OF NON-HUMAN ANIMALS IN THE CATHOLIC TRADITION
A. Thomas Aquinas

Influenced by Aristotle and other classical thinkers as well as by the rigid hierarchy of defined ecclesiastical and civil roles of his time, Aquinas developed a hierarchical view of creation both in terms of complexity and value. In this hierarchy, humans—being the most spiritual and rational and thus the most sublime—are at the top followed by non-human animals, and finally plants. Beings less sublime than humans are considered "less perfect" and serve the needs of the "more perfect" (*ST* I q. 47, a. 2). Humans are thus free to use less perfect beings for their benefit. Because of his understanding of creation in these terms, Aquinas is criticized as being anthropocentric.[3]

However, it would be unfair to simply dismiss Aquinas as anthropocentric without any qualifications. His hierarchical understanding of creation must be seen in the context of his sacramental view of creation and his perceived *telos* of non-human creation. Aquinas affirmed the godliness of all creation and the inherent goodness of all creatures as unique manifestations of the Triune God (*ST* I q. 47, a. 1). If this is the case then this hierarchy does not give humans a right to use less perfect creatures in an abusive manner.[4] Furthermore, for Aquinas, the entire physical universe

---
[3] Anne M. Clifford, "Foundations for a Catholic Ecological Theology of God," in *"And God Saw That It Was Good:" Catholic Theology and the Environment*, eds. Drew Christiansen and Walter Grazer (Washington, DC: United States Catholic Conference, 1996), 40.
[4] Clifford, "Foundations for a Catholic Ecological Theology of God," 40.

(which includes plants, non-human animals, and humans) is ordered towards "ultimate perfection" which, in turn, is destined to God. The perfection of the physical universe gives glory to God's goodness (*ST* I q. 47, a. 2). Thus, while hierarchical, creation is by no means anthropocentric.[5]

For Aquinas, non-human animals, or in his own terms, "irrational creatures," are not to be "loved out of charity." Influenced by Aristotle, Aquinas interprets love philosophically as friendship. He is thus stating that one cannot extend friendship to non-human animals. Precisely because of their irrationality, they cannot be direct objects of human friendship or of Christian charity (except metaphorically) which contains the whole of Christian morality. Only God and humans are the proper objects of such kind of love. They can, however, be indirect objects of love. One may love them out of charity if we see them as the good things that we desire for others to give honor to God and to provide for human use. Thus, it is not really for their own sake that they are loved or moral concern is shown to them, but for the sake of God and humans (*ST* II-II q. 25, a. 3).[6]

The situation becomes more problematic when we read the core argument of Aquinas against animal cruelty. For Aquinas, cruelty against animals is wrong because it corrupts the virtue and character of the abuser. This in turn makes animal abusers more likely to display the same behavior towards humans. Furthermore, he also writes that injuring an animal is wrong because it might lead to a material loss for someone (*SCG* III-II 112, 13). Thus, it is not the harm caused to animals *per se* which makes animal cruelty wrong. In this sense, non-human animals are not accorded any value for their own sake.[7] Despite the beautiful things Aquinas has to say about the inherent goodness of each creature, his explicit ethical treatment of non-human animals is wanting.

B. The Catechism of the Catholic Church

Aquinas's perspective has influenced the Catholic tradition on the treatment of animals. This becomes more apparent in how the *Catechism* treats the same subject. The *Catechism* spends four paragraphs concerning non-human animals. These sections read as follows:

---

[5] John Berkman, "Towards a Thomistic Theology of Animality," in *Creaturely Theology: On God, Humans and Other Animals*, eds. Celia Deane-Drummond and David Clough (London: SCM Press, 2009), 24.

[6] See also Gaffney, "The Relevance of Animal Experimentation," 152–53.

[7] Robert N. Wennberg, *God, Humans, and Animals: An Invitation to Enlarge our Moral Universe* (Michigan: William B. Eerdmans Publishing Company, 2003), 120–2.

2415 The seventh commandment enjoins respect for the integrity of creation. Animals, like plants and inanimate beings, are by nature destined for the common good of past, present, and future humanity. (Cf. Gen. 1:28–31). Use of the mineral, vegetable, and animal resources of the universe cannot be divorced from respect for moral imperatives. Man's dominion over inanimate and other living beings granted by the Creator is not absolute; it is limited by concern for the quality of life of his neighbor, including generations to come; it requires a religious respect for the integrity of creation. (Cf. CA 37–38)

2416 Animals are God's creatures. He surrounds them with his providential care. By their mere existence they bless him and give him glory. (Cf. Mt. 6:2; Dan. 3:79–81) Thus men owe them kindness. We should recall the gentleness with which saints like St. Francis of Assisi or St. Philip Neri treated animals.

2417 God entrusted animals to the stewardship of those whom he created in his own image. (Cf. Gen. 2:19–20; 9:1–4) Hence it is legitimate to use animals for food and clothing. They may be domesticated to help man in his work and leisure. Medical and scientific experimentation on animals is a morally acceptable practice, if it remains within reasonable limits and contributes to caring for or saving human lives.

2418 It is contrary to human dignity to cause animals to suffer or die needlessly. It is likewise unworthy to spend money on them that should as a priority go to the relief of human misery. One can love animals; one should not direct to them the affection due only to persons.

In "From Theological Speciesism to a Theological Ethology," John Berkman carefully reads through the *Catechism*'s treatment of non-human animals and concludes that it is ambiguous yet still offers resources for the development of Catholic teaching on concern for non-human animals. The first thing he notes is that the *Catechism*'s discussion on the morality of treating non-human animals follows the method of old moral manuals which treats such issues under the seventh commandment ("You shall not steal") which protects human property.[8] This presupposes that the environment in general and non-human animals in particular are the "properties" of humans.

Furthermore, Berkman points out, the *Catechism* does not have a single view about the morality of treating non-human animals. Instead, it contains a multiplicity of views which are at best in tension and at worst incompatible with one another. On the one hand, section 2416

---

[8] Berkman, "From Theological Speciesism to a Theological Ethology," 24–25.

of the *Catechism* states that non-human animals are God's creatures and He surrounds them with His providential care. They give glory to God by their mere existence. Here, we can see that the *Catechism* accords non-human animals value in themselves, something which Aquinas also acknowledges by affirming the inherent goodness of all creatures as divine manifestations of the Trinity. Because of this, humans *owe* them kindness and gentleness. In *For Love of Animals*, Charles Camosy strengthens this point noting that, by using the word "owe," the *Catechism* employs a very strong language: the language of justice. Moreover, we are even exhorted to follow the examples of saints who treated non-human animals with kindness.[9]

On the other hand, section 2418 treats non-human animals in a different way by providing instrumental reasons against animal cruelty, namely, that it is "contrary to human dignity." This is clearly reflective of the treatment of non-human animals by Aquinas which does not accord them intrinsic value. Furthermore, the same section also gives an unclear moral guidance by asserting that they should not be made to suffer or die "needlessly." This moral guidance maybe read in two ways, according to Berkman. First, if this is read in light of section 2415—non-human animals are destined for the common good of humanity—then almost any reason can be acceptable to make them suffer and die as long as it is considered a need for the good of humanity. If this same passage is read in light of section 2416—God surrounds non-human animals with His providential care and we owe them kindness—then one needs to have very strong reasons for causing them to suffer and die.[10]

In section 2417, the *Catechism* tells us that God entrusted non-human animals to the stewardship of humans which makes it legitimate for humans to use them to provide for their needs. The same section specifies ways humans may use them: for food, clothing, and domestication to help humans in work or for leisure. Medical and scientific experimentation are also considered morally acceptable so long as it "remains within reasonable limits" and "contributes to caring for or saving human lives."

What, however, does constitute "reasonable limits" and who should identify these limits? Furthermore, while the "caring for or saving human lives" criteria would certainly make cosmetic testing on animals unacceptable (unless it really contributes to caring for or saving human lives), what of other biomedical research? Almost any experiment would appear to be permissible, if it is justified as an effort to care for or save human lives. Lastly, if we really need to use animals for human necessity, does this mean that we can make them suffer and

---

[9] Charles Camosy, *For Love of Animals: Christian Ethics, Consistent Action* (Ohio: Franciscan Media, 2013), 73.
[10] Berkman, "From Theological Speciesism to a Theological Ethology," 25–26.

terms. While affirming that humans possess a "particular dignity above other creatures" (no. 119) and that there can be no ecology without an "adequate anthropology," thereby rejecting "biocentrism" (no. 118), Francis condemns a "tyrannical anthropocentrism unconcerned for other creatures" (no. 68). He stresses that "we must forcefully reject the notion that our being created in God's image and given dominion over the earth justifies absolute domination over other creatures" (no. 67). The ultimate purpose of creation is not to be found in us but in God (no. 83). The Pope thus finds total technical dominion over creation to be unacceptable (nos. 115–16).

With regards to the relationship between humans and non-human animals in general, *Laudato Si'* still upholds the uniqueness of humans which distinguishes us from the rest of creation. This includes the capacity for reason, to have abstract thoughts, to invent, and create art among others (nos. 81 and 90). At first glance, this might be interpreted in a way which furthers the distinction between humans and non-human animals to the extent of blurring the kinship between them. However, a closer reading of the encyclical tells us otherwise. *Laudato Si'* calls our attention to a universal communion which excludes nothing and no one. In fact, throughout the encyclical, Francis stresses the interconnection of all things (nos. 85, 120, and 137–8). As Francis writes:

> Everything is related, and we human beings are united as brothers and sisters on a wonderful pilgrimage, woven together by the love God has for each of his creatures and which also unites us in fond affection with brother sun, sister moon, brother river and mother earth. (no. 92)

Despite this call for a universal communion, Francis still prioritizes the relationship between and concern for humans. A universal communion cannot be authentic if one is concerned with non-human animals while being indifferent to the problems faced by humans. Disapproval is also shown when more zeal is present in protecting species rather than defending the dignity of human beings (nos. 81–92). While we should be concerned when other beings are treated irresponsibly, we are called to be "particularly indignant" at the gaping inequalities present in society (no. 90). Given that Francis upholds the uniqueness and special place of humans in creation, this should hardly be surprising. Though not citing the *Catechism*, the encyclical appears to affirm the former's injunction of giving priority to human misery.

Keeping these general perspectives in mind, we turn to the encyclical's specific treatment of non-human animals. In several instances of *Laudato Si'*, Francis discusses the status and treatment of non-human animals. The lengthiest of these is the third section of chapter one which dedicates ten paragraphs (nos. 32–42) to the issue of the loss of biodiversity. Francis writes that climate change and other environmental problems result in the extinction of different species which are "extremely important resources" as food and medicine. While he clearly refers to the "instrumental value" of non-human animals, the pope adds that they also possess "value in themselves" regardless of their usefulness to humans or to the ecosystem (nos. 25 and 32–33). That being so, he condemns the loss of species in especially strong terms.

> Each year sees the disappearance of thousands of plant and animal species which we will never know, which our children will never see, because they have been lost for ever. The great majority become extinct for reasons related to human activity. Because of us, thousands of species will no longer give glory to God by their very existence, nor convey their message to us. We have no such right. (no. 33)

The loss of diverse animal species is often caused by short term economic, commercial, and production plans. More often than not, projects are assessed only in light of their impact on air, land, and water but not on the loss of species. Even endeavors considered necessary for development, such as the building of highways, new plantations, and the damming of water sources, did not escape criticism. Whatever benefits come from these projects can be outweighed by the adverse effects. As Francis writes, "Where certain species are destroyed or seriously harmed, the values involved are incalculable" (no. 36).

Whereas John Paul II (e.g., *Sollicitudo Rei Socialis*, nos. 26 and 29) and Benedict XVI (*Caritas in Veritate*, no. 48) have pushed for the inclusion of environmental factors in planning development projects,[20] Francis goes further by explicitly including the protection and preservation of animal species in planning these projects. This is clearly a demanding view which places concern for non-human animals at a high level. We are called to find alternatives to lessen the impacts of developmental projects not only to the environment in general but also to animal species in particular and so exercise far-sightedness in planning (*Laudato Si'*, nos. 35–36).

Given that Francis and Catholic tradition recognize the unique value and place of humans in creation, it is not surprising that the loss of human culture is more serious than the loss of plant or animal species.

> The disappearance of a culture can be just as serious, or even more serious, than the disappearance of a species of plant or animal. The

---

[20] For a greater discussion of these, see Celia Deane-Drummond, "Joining in the Dance: Catholic Social Teaching and Ecology," *New Blackfriars* 93, no. 1004 (March 2012): 198–204.

> imposition of a dominant lifestyle linked to a single form of production can be just as harmful as the altering of ecosystems. (*Laudato Si'*, no. 145)

Even so, Francis shows concern for the loss of animal species. By saying that the disappearance of the latter "can be just as serious" as the disappearance of the former, Francis actually raises concern for the loss of animal species while recognizing the unique value and place of humans.

Apart from showing concern for the loss of biodiversity, *Laudato Si'* also reiterates the teaching of the *Catechism*. While human intervention on plants and non-human animals is permitted when it concerns the necessities of human life, it is only morally acceptable "if it remains within reasonable limits [and] contributes to caring for or saving human lives" (no. 130). He stresses that the *Catechism* firmly teaches that human powers have limitations and "it is contrary to human dignity to cause animals to suffer or die needlessly" (no. 130).

In his call to a universal communion and fraternity which excludes nothing and no one, Francis warns that our indifference and cruelty towards any creature would sooner or later also show itself in our treatment of human beings.

> We have only one heart, and the same wretchedness which leads us to mistreat an animal will not be long in showing itself in our relationships with other people. Every act of cruelty towards any creature is 'contrary to human dignity.' (no. 92)

This resonates with Aquinas's view that animal cruelty is wrong not really because it causes non-human animals suffering but because it might lead to the mistreatment of humans. The concern that animal cruelty can lead to human violence is not in itself wrong. We only need to reflect on how workers, particularly undocumented ones, are treated inside "factory farms"[21] and the numerous studies which confirm the link between animal cruelty and human violence.[22] The problem would be if this is the *only way* Francis thinks about animal cruelty. It is not. The pope affirms the *intrinsic* value of *each* creature, which "must be cherished with love and respect" (nos. 33 and 42).

---

[21] Camosy, *For Love of Animals*, 95.
[22] See, for instance, the studies cited in "Animal Cruelty and Human Violence," *The Humane Society of the United States*, www.humanesociety.org/issues/abuse_neglect/qa/cruelty_violence_connection_faq.html; "Animal Abuse and Human Abuse: Partners in Crime," *People for the Ethical Treatment of Animals*, www.peta.org/issues/companion-animal-issues/companion-animals-factsheets/animal-abuse-human-abuse-partners-crime/.

> Every creature is thus the object of the Father's tenderness, who gives it its place in the world. Even the fleeting life of the least of beings is the object of his love, and in its few seconds of existence, God enfolds it with his affection. (no. 76)

Moreover, his claim that the Blessed Mother *grieves* for creatures destroyed by humans is striking. As *Laudato Si'* poignantly states:

> Mary, the Mother who cared for Jesus, now cares with maternal affection and pain for this wounded world. Just as her pierced heart mourned the death of Jesus, so now she grieves for the sufferings of the crucified poor and for the creatures of this world laid waste by human power. (no. 241)

These statements are strong indicators that *each* non-human animal has intrinsic value. Cruelty to non-human animals is therefore wrong not only because of the risk of mistreating humans but also because it harms creatures who have a value of their own and are cared for by God. It is not only a perversion of the caring relationship between humans and non-human creation but also an offense against God as it goes against the proper use of God's gifts.[23]

While Francis clearly and forcefully confirms the intrinsic value of each non-human creature and condemns cruel acts done to them, *Laudato Si'* remains within Catholic tradition. The encyclical openly affirms the intrinsic value of non-human animals and, at the same time, recognizes the unique value and special place of humans in creation. What would help advance this "chastened anthropocentrism"[24] is a direct treatment of the uses of non-human animals in order to limit the rather broad margin given by the *Catechism*. The encyclical touches directly on actions people can take that address many of the specific issues affecting our common home, keenly grasping the extent and complexity of the ecological crisis.[25] For non-human animals, the pope could have tackled whether their use for clothing, their processing in "factory farming" (which not only harms non-human animals but also the ecosystem)[26] and their roles in biomedical research are within the bounds of the "necessities of

---

[23] Thomas Ryan, "Ecology" in *The New Dictionary of Catholic Social Thought*, eds. Judith A. Dwyer and Elizabeth L. Montgomery (Minnesota: The Liturgical Press, 1994), 309.
[24] Bernard Häring, *Free and Faithful in Christ: Moral Theology for Priests and Laity*, vol. 3, *Light to the World, Salt of the Earth* (New York: Crossroads, 1981), 180–81.
[25] Anthony Annett, "The Next Step: How *Laudato Si'* Extends Catholic Social Teaching," *Commonweal*, August 14, 2015, https://www.commonweal-magazine.org/next-step.
[26] Camosy gives a detailed description of this practice. For more details see Camosy, *For Love of Animals*, 83–96.

human life" and "caring for or saving human lives." Does genetic manipulation where scientists are able to produce animals that will be born with or develop diseases such as diabetes and breast cancer fall within these bounds?[27] Even if we grant that need to use non-human animals, are such practices consequently permissible?

PART III: EXTENDING THE CHURCH'S TEACHINGS ON THE TREATMENT OF NON-HUMAN ANIMALS

For all the wonderful things Francis teaches about non-human animals, one thing that is wanting is directly questioning or touching on the ways humans use (or rather, *misuse*) non-human animals. This could, in turn, fail to limit the rather broad permissiveness given by the *Catechism* for the use of non-human animals. However, the Church has a rich tradition from which it can draw to attend to this issue. First, treating such issues would be in continuity with papal concern for non-human animals. Francis's predecessors have addressed the treatment of non-human animals, albeit outside an encyclical letter or official Church teaching. For instance, in *Love and Responsibility*, John Paul II wrote,

> Intelligent human beings are not only required not to squander or destroy ...natural resources, but to use them with restraint .... In his treatment of animals in particular, since they are *beings endowed with feeling and sensitive to pain*, man is required to ensure that the use of these creatures is *never attended by suffering or physical torture*.[28]

In responding to journalist Peter Seewald's question "are we allowed to make use of animals, and even to eat them?" Benedict XVI replied,

> That is a *very serious question*. At any rate, we can see that they are given into our care, that we cannot just do whatever we want with them. Animals, too, are God's creatures.... Certainly, a sort of industrial use of creatures, so that geese are fed in such a way as to produce as large a liver as possible, or hens live so packed together that they become just caricatures of birds, *this degrading of living*

---

[27] Susan Kopp and Charles C. Camosy, "Animals 2.0: A Veterinarian and a Theologian Survey a Brave New World of Biotechnology," *America*, May 13, 2015, www.americamagazine.org/issue/animals-20; Charles Camosy and Susan Kopp, "The Use of Non-Human Animals in Biomedical Research: Can Moral Theology Fill the Gap?" *Journal of Moral Theology* 3, no. 2 (June 2014): 60–62. The latter article especially provides details regarding these kinds of biomedical research.
[28] Karol Wojtyla, *Love and Responsibility*, trans. H.T. Willetts (California: Ignatius Press, 1993), 25. Emphases added.

creatures to a commodity seems to me in fact to contradict the relationship of mutuality that comes across in the Bible.[29]

Second is human experience, an indispensable source of moral theology which has led to the development of moral doctrine.[30] While difficult to quantify or qualify, human experience is still necessary for, without it, a moral system will become a mere abstraction separated from reality.[31] In his 1990 World Day of Peace Message, John Paul II spoke of our contact with nature which has a "deep restorative power" which in turn leads us to care for it.[32] In the same manner, our experience of meaningful encounter with animals can also have a "restorative power" in the sense of restoring the proper relationship which should exist between humans and non-human animals. We should be reminded that humans and non-human animals were created on the same day, which implies a special kind of kinship between them and that, originally, God intended non-human animals to be human companions.[33]

Third, this encounter with non-human animals should not be selfish but with the gaze of Jesus who sees the Father's love in each and every creature and their importance in God's eyes (*Laudato Si'*, no. 96). Our eyes should be open to recognize each creature's God-given *telos*. In the sixth day of the first creation story (Genesis 1: 24–31), particularly on the creation of non-human animals, God created and pronounced them to be good without referring to humans (*Laudato Si'*, no. 46). This serves as a theological basis for a metaphysical teleology of non-human animals. In the words of Camosy and Kopp, "Animals were created 'good' by God independent of any instrumental value they may have for us …. God created animals 'good,' *period*, to flourish in their own right as the good kinds of things they are."[34]

Each individual creature, therefore, has its own nature and *telos* which God wills for them to achieve in its fullness.[35] Humans cannot

---

[29] "Pope Benedict XVI Continues Tradition of Papal Concern for Animals," *People for the Ethical Treatment of Animals*, www.peta.org/features/pope-benedict-xvi/. Emphases added.
[30] James T. Bretzke, *Handbook of Roman Catholic Moral Terms* (Washington, DC: Georgetown University Press, 2013), 111; See John T. Noonan, Jr., "Experience and the Development of Moral Doctrine," *CTSA Proceedings* 54 (1999): 43–56.
[31] Bretzke, *Handbook of Roman Catholic Moral Terms*, 111.
[32] John Paul II, "XXIII World Day for Peace 1990 Message: Peace with God the Creator, Peace with All of Creation," 8 December 1989, w2.vatican.va/content/john-paul-ii/en/messages/peace/documents/hf_jp-ii_mes_19891208_xxiii-world-day-for-peace.html.
[33] Camosy, *For Love of Animals*, 46–47.
[34] Camosy and Kopp, "The Use of Non-Human Animals in Biomedical Research," 65. Emphasis on the original.
[35] Camosy and Kopp, "The Use of Non-Human Animals in Biomedical Research," 65.

just dispose of them arbitrarily. It is noteworthy that Jean Porter argues in *Nature as Reason* that the recognition of the *telos* of non-human animals does not require theism or empirical data. Rather one can discern from intuition what it means for a creature to be healthy and flourishing.[36] Again, this points to human experience as a valuable font of moral norms. The recognition of the *telos* of non-human animals means people have to consider and respect the overall flourishing of each animal as the kind of creature it is[37] and the fact that they are each loved by the Father as the creatures they are.

Fourth, we should not think that giving attention to non-human animals would mean taking attention away from humans. We should not fall into what Wennberg calls the "logic of the line approach." This approach sees a long line of concerns starting with human needs and with animal welfare towards the end of the line. Human needs should be met first before turning to non-human animals. However, if one were to follow this reasoning, non-human animals will never be given attention due to the sheer magnitude of human needs. Instead of having this flawed perspective, one must have a "moral and spiritual wholeness" which embraces concern for humans, non-human animals, and the environment.[38] People who follow the logic of the line mistakenly take love as a "rare fluid to be economized" rather than a "capacity which grows by use."[39] Caring for non-human animals does not necessarily (and should never) mean lessening attention to humans nor placing animals above or at equal footing with humans. The challenge is overcoming moral narrowness, expanding sympathies, and learning priorities.[40] We should be reminded of St. Francis of Assisi, who "is the example par excellence of care for the vulnerable and of an integral ecology lived out joyfully and authentically" (*Laudato Si'*, no. 11). His love for the poor did not prevent him from caring for God's creatures nor did his care for creation take away attention to the poor.

Finally, we could build more upon the *Catechism*'s teaching that humans "owe animals kindness" since they are God's creatures and He surrounds them with His providential care. In light of this, Camosy extends the virtue of *justice* into non-human animals. According to him:

---

[36] Jean Porter, *Nature as Reason: A Thomistic Theory of the Natural Law* (Michigan: William B. Eerdmans Publishing Company, 2005), 100–2.
[37] Camosy and Kopp, "The Use of Non-Human Animals in Biomedical Research," 69.
[38] Wennberg, *God, Humans, and Animals*, 13.
[39] Mary Midgley, *Animals and Why They Matter* (Georgia: University of Georgia Press, 1983), 119.
[40] Wennberg, *God, Humans, and Animals*, 13–14 and 201–3.

> A serious kind of injustice takes place when we refuse to recognize certain individuals or groups as the kinds of beings to which we owe moral behavior .... Christian justice means consistently and actively working to see that individuals and groups—especially vulnerable population on the margins—are given what they are owed.[41]

If God loves each creature, if they have their intrinsic value, and if we owe them kindness, does not injustice take place whenever they are treated the way they are in factory farms?

If one were to utilize these aspects of the Church's tradition—papal writings, human experiences with non-human animals, seeing animals as creatures God loves, not pitting human needs against animal needs, and expanding a sense of justice toward animals—the church could clarify what really constitutes legitimate human use of non-human animals and limit how humans use them. For instance, the *Catechism*'s allowance of the use of non-human animals for clothing and food could be further qualified. With the advances in clothing technology and the availability of alternative materials such as synthetic or faux leather and fur, can one still consider the use of non-human animals for clothing to be within the bounds of human necessity?

Regarding the use of non-human animals as food, needed nutrients found therein can also be found in non-human animal sources. Yet, it must also be recognized that not everyone is capable of totally giving up meat, so, perhaps the best thing that can be done is to avoid meat as much as possible. If there is a *real* need to eat meat, reasonable efforts should be made to source meat from ethical sources rather than from "factory farms."[42]

Finally, while the use of non-human animals for blood sports and violent entertainment would be clearly ruled out, we should also turn our attention to the use of non-human animals for circuses and other entertainment purposes. Not only would such activities appear not to recognize their God-given *telos*, but it is also doubtful whether using non-human animals for such purposes constitutes legitimate human necessity.

Of course, it can be argued that it can fall within legitimate human need if it provides employment. However, we cannot simply dismiss

---

[41] Camosy, *For Love of Animals*, 3 and 7.
[42] Julie Hanlon Rubio provides an excellent discussion of this topic in her article "Animals, Evil, and Family Meals" in *Journal of Moral Theology* 3, no. 2 (2014): 35–53. A related article is John Berkman's "Are We Addicted to the Suffering of Animals? Animal Cruelty and the Catholic Moral Tradition," in *A Faith Embracing All Creatures: Addressing Commonly Asked Questions about Animals*, ed. Tripp York and Andy Alexis-Baker (Oregon: Cascade Books, 2012), which discusses how eating meat, especially that coming from "factory farms," is a form of material cooperation in evil.

the kindness that we owe to non-human animals as creatures that God loves in meeting such valid human necessities. Both needs would have to be taken into account rather than be pitted against each other. This principle also applies, I believe, to the *Catechism*'s approval of the use of non-human animals for helping humans in their work such as in the case of animals used in ploughing and work unrelated to entertainment. As much as possible, sufficient efforts should be made to find alternatives to the use of non-human animals for work, but, if a real need exists for them to help humans, their welfare should be looked after and their use should never be degrading and attended by torture and suffering. In so doing, we live an integral ecology which unites concern for non-human animals and humans.

These are just some of the ways in which the Church's teachings on the treatment of non-human animals can be extended or clarified. These topics are quite intricate in themselves already and can, hopefully, give rise to further discussions on how to limit the use of non-human animals. One thing is for certain though: these aspects of the Catholic tradition and *Laudato Si'* should make us more discerning on the ways we use and treat non-human animals and how our activities affect them. We should make *reasonable efforts* to avoid using them and to find ways to treat them with the respect that is their due whenever they are used out of *real* necessities and not just out of convenience and pleasure under the guise of necessity. Doing so will help us give the kindness that we owe to non-human animals who are also our brothers and sisters. M

Contributors

Anatoly Angelo R. Aseneta formerly taught theology courses at the University of Santo Tomas in Manila City, Philippines. He is completing his doctoral studies at the Loyola School of Theology of the Ateneo de Manila University in Quezon City, Philippines. He received his M.A. in Theological Studies with a Specialization in Moral Theology from the same institution. His research interests include Catholic social teaching, Joseph Cardinal Bernardin's *Consistent Ethic of Life*, Church teachings on the environment especially *Laudato Si'*, and animal welfare.

Joshua Evans is Assistant Professor of Health Care Ethics at Regis University in Denver, Colorado. He holds a Ph.D. in moral theology/ethics from The Catholic University of America, and he writes on issues at the intersection of patristic thought and fundamental moral theology.

Conor Hill received his Ph.D. in Theology from the Pontifical John Paul II Institute for Studies on Marriage and Family in Washington, DC. He has been a board member of the New Wine, New Wineskins: Young Catholic Moral Theologians since 2014. He has taught at the University of St. Francis in Joliet, Illinois, and at DePaul University. Currently, he is the headmaster at Chesterton Academy of the Holy Family, a classical high school in the west suburbs of Chicago.

Kent Lasnoski is an Assistant Professor of Theology and Philosophy at Wyoming Catholic College. He is author of the award-winning monograph *Vocation to Virtue: Christian Marriage as a Consecrated Life*. His work in marriage, sexual ethics and bioethics appears in *Nova et Vetera*, *Josephinum*, and *NCBQ*. He is an associate editor of *Dappled Things* and Editor of the CTSA Proceedings. He, his wife, and their family of seven children live in Lander, WY, amidst the beautiful Wind River mountains.

Justin Menno is a doctoral candidate in theology at the University of Dayton. His research interests include the intersection of theology and sociology in the 1930s, and how the treatment of the dead informs the treatment of the living. He currently teaches at Catholic Central High School in Grand Rapids, Michigan.

John-Mark Miravalle received his S.T.D. from the Regina Apostolorum in Rome. He is the author of *The Drug, the Soul, and God: A Catholic Moral Perspective on Antidepressants* (University of

Scranton, 2010) and *Why God? Why Jesus? Why the Catholic Church?* (School of Faith, 2014) and for the last three years has held the post of Assistant Professor of systematic and moral theology at Mount St. Mary's Seminary.

Gina Maria Noia is a doctoral candidate in Theology and Health Care Ethics at Saint Louis University. Gina is also the Ethics Consultant for St. Alexius Hospital in St. Louis, MO, and a teacher for Paul VI Pontifical Institute. Her research interests include the Catholic moral tradition, faith and reason, sexual and reproductive ethics, and clinical ethics. She is currently completing her doctoral dissertation on Catholic methods in bioethics, with a focus on the topic of assisted reproductive technologies.

Sheryl Overmyer is Associate Professor in the Department of Catholic Studies at DePaul University. Most recently, she is the author of *Two Guides for the Journey: The Summa Theologiae and Piers Plowman on the Virtues* (Cascade, 2016). She is currently working on a project on the education of the emotions.

Benjamin T. Peters is an Associate Professor of Theology and Director of the Honors Program at the University of Saint Joseph. He teaches and writes on moral theology, particularly within the context of U.S. Catholicism. He is the author of *Called to be Saints: John Hugo, the Catholic Worker, and a Theology of Radical Christianity* (Marquette).

Alessandro Rovati earned his Ph.D. in Philosophy at the Università Cattolica del Sacro Cuore di Milano, Italy, in 2015. During his graduate work, he studied at Duke Divinity School to combine his extensive philosophical training with theological reflections on the current life of the church amidst contemporary society. Now working in the Department of Theology and Political Philosophy at Belmont Abbey College in North Carolina, Dr. Rovati's scholarship focuses on Christian Ethics, Moral and Political Philosophy, Catholic Social Teaching, and Political Theology. He has contributed the chapter "War Is America's Altar" in the forthcoming edited volume *Cultural Violence and Peace* (Brill), travelled across dioceses to teach ministers, educators, and lay faithful, and his articles have appeared in *Quaestiones Disputatae* and various online publications. Dr. Rovati is now working on two books, *Putting Hauerwas in His Place* and *Learning the Gaze of Christ: A Theological Engagement with Pope Francis*.

Kevin Schemenauer is an Assistant Professor of Moral Theology at Saint Meinrad Seminary and School of Theology. He wrote his dissertation on Dietrich von Hildebrand's treatment of procreation, which was published as *Conjugal Love and Procreation: Dietrich von Hildebrand's Superabundant Integration* with Lexington Books in 2011. His current research focuses on the social character of the family. Kevin and his wife Frances have three young boys.

Matthew Sherman teaches moral theology at Marian University, Indianapolis, where his classes include introductory theology, fundamental morals, social ethics, bioethics, and marriage. His research is largely in the area of historical morals and family life. His current projects include Augustine's understanding of the goodness of creation in the *Confessions*, the moral worldview of Benedictine philosopher and liturgical reformer Virgil Michel, and the role of the Eucharist in family ethics. He received his Ph.D. in theological ethics from Boston College.

John Sikorski serves as the Assistant Director of the Office of Family Life for the Diocese of Fort Wayne-South Bend and as an adjunct instructor at the University of Notre Dame and St. Meinrad Seminary and School of Theology. He is a doctoral candidate in moral theology at the University of Notre Dame, where his research focuses on bioethics, marriage and family life studies, liturgical theology, and Catholic social teaching.

Medi Ann Volpe is a Research Fellow in Catholic Theology at Durham University, St. John's College. She did her graduate work at Duke University with Stanley Hauerwas. Her research focuses on identity and formation for Christian practice, and she is currently completing a book that examines accounts of Christian identity in the work of Rowan Williams, Kathryn Tanner, and John Milbank, and bringing them into conversation with Gregory of Nyssa.

Matthew Philipp Whelan is a St. Andrews Fellow in Theology & Science, hosted by Baylor University. He holds degrees from the University of Virginia (B.A.), Centro Agronómico Tropical de Investigación y Enseñanza (M.Sc.), and Duke University (M.T.S., Ph.D.), and his articles have appeared in *Nova et Vetera*; *CrossCurrents*; *Biodiversity and Conservation*; and *Agriculture, Forestry, and Fisheries*. Currently, he resides in Waco, Texas, with his wife, Natalie, along with their three daughters, Chora, Edith, and Simone.

Articles available to view
or download at:

www.msmary.edu/jmt

> The
>
> *Journal of Moral Theology*
>
> is proudly sponsored by the
>
> Fr. James M. Forker Professorship
> of Catholic Social Teaching
>
> *and the*
>
> College of Liberal Arts
>
> *at*
>
> Mount St. Mary's University

die in any way to satisfy necessity? It is one thing to say that we need a non-human animal for this human necessity and quite another on how non-human animals are to be treated to fulfill this necessity. In not sufficiently providing concrete limitations, the *Catechism* thus seems to give a broad margin for humans to decide when and how to use non-human animals.

Finally, section 2418 directs that, while it is acceptable to love non-human animals, they should not be given affection that should be given to humans alone. A correlated injunction is giving priority to human misery. While not citing the *Summa*, it echoes Aquinas's thought that non-human animals are not to be loved out of charity or with the kind of love that should be directed to God and humans. Berkman reads this as a rebuke for "poor souls" who prefer the company of non-human animals or who devote their lives to their companion animals.[11]

For all its difficulties, the *Catechism*, like Aquinas's writings, should not be easily dismissed. Despite its ambiguous and even conflicting views, this magisterial document still affirms the legitimacy of love for non-human animals by highlighting God's providential concern for them and the lives of saints who have shown them love and compassion.[12] Furthermore, by delineating the ways in which humans may use non-human animals, the *Catechism* implicitly rejects practices such as the use of non-human animals for blood sports and their torturing and killing for entertainment purposes. Finally, as Camosy notes, the *Catechism* even uses the language of justice to describe our relationship with non-human animals and demands of us not to cause them needless suffering and death.[13]

C. A Reappraisal of the Place of Non-Human Animals in the Catholic Tradition

The most common charge against the Catholic tradition's treatment of non-human animals is that it is anthropocentric. It prioritizes human interests over the interests of non-human animals, consistently placing humans at the center of creation and making judgments according to what will benefit humans.[14] This tendency can be seen in the "give priority to human misery" injunction of the *Catechism* and in

---

[11] Berkman, "From Theological Speciesism to a Theological Ethology," 25–26.
[12] Berkman, "From Theological Speciesism to a Theological Ethology," 26.
[13] Camosy, *For Love of Animals*, 73.
[14] Reynaldo D. Raluto, *Poverty and Ecology at the Crossroads: Towards an Ecological Theology of Liberation in the Philippine Context* (Quezon City, Philippines: Ateneo de Manila University Press, 2015), 40 and 107; Donal Dorr, *Option for the Poor and for the Earth: Catholic Social Teaching* (Quezon City, Philippines: Claretian Publications, 2013), 429–32.

Aquinas's justification for using less perfect beings by more perfect beings as well as prohibiting harm of non-human animals because it might lead to temporal loss for humans.

Part of the cause of this anthropocentricism is that the Catholic tradition emphasizes human dignity more than the integrity of non-human animals. This overemphasis obscures the connection which should exist between them.[15] For Frear, the likely cause is neither because of biblical texts about humanity being God's image and likeness nor about human dominion over creation. Rather, it is the traditional dualistic understanding of human nature with its sharp distinction and division between material body and rational soul wherein only in the bodily realm do humans have similarity with creation and non-human animals.[16]

While it is evident that the Church prioritizes humans over non-human creatures, the dominion that humans have over creation and, thus, non-human creation is not limitless. In *Sollicitudo Rei Socialis*, John Paul II teaches that this dominion is not "an absolute power, nor can one speak of a freedom to 'use and misuse,' or to dispose of things as one pleases" (no. 34). Likewise, in *Caritas in Veritate*, Benedict XVI points out that nature contains a "grammar" put by God "which sets forth ends and criteria for its wise use, not its reckless exploitation" (no. 48). Thus, the Church's anthropocentric outlook is nuanced and qualified. It markedly differs from the commonly understood anthropocentrism which sees that there is no limit to the human exploitation of creation. On the contrary, the Church's anthropocentric outlook is balanced and strictly limited by the teaching that creation has its own God-given integrity and order which humans must respect.[17] In this perspective, humans *do* have priority, but this does not deny the value of non-human animals and the attendant responsibilities towards them. In fact, the emphasis on human dignity can be a powerful source of commitment if it implies a unique moral responsibility of humans for other creatures and the rest of creation.[18] Human dignity should be interpreted in light of this relationship with the rest of creation.[19]

PART II: *LAUDATO SI'* ON NON-HUMAN ANIMALS

While the Church rejects an anthropocentrism which removes concern for non-human creation, *Laudato Si'* does so in much stronger

---

[15] Raluto, *Poverty and Ecology at the Crossroads*, 107–8.
[16] George L. Frear, Jr., "Animals, Rights of," in *The New Dictionary of Catholic Social Thought*, eds. Judith A. Dwyer and Elizabeth L. Montgomery (Minnesota: The Liturgical Press, 1994), 43.
[17] Dorr, *Option for the Poor and for the Earth*, 430.
[18] Wennberg, *God, Humans, and Animals*, 200.
[19] Denis Edwards, *Ecology at the Heart of Faith* (New York: Orbis Books, 2008), 16, 20, and 22.